Jenifer Neels
1973

The Greek Dark Ages

The
Greek Dark
Ages

V. R. d'A. DESBOROUGH

LONDON/ERNEST BENN LIMITED

First published 1972 by Ernest Benn Limited
Bouverie House, Fleet Street, London EC4A 2DL

Distributed in Canada by
The General Publishing Company Limited, Toronto
© *V. R. d'A. Desborough 1972*

Book designed by Kenneth Day
Drawings and maps by Pamela Mara

Printed in Great Britain

ISBN *0 510–03261–3*

Preface

Of the tasks that face an author at the completion of a book that of writing a preface is the most congenial, since it affords him the opportunity to render due thanks for all the help he has received.

First and foremost I pay tribute to my family, who must often have wondered when an end would be made. Their patience, their encouragement on the many occasions of frustration and depression, and their assistance both active and passive, have been invaluable.

My way has been aided and smoothed by two grants from the Meyerstein Fund, and I am much indebted to the administrators of this Fund.

I have received generous and unstinted assistance from many official bodies. Above all, my debt to the Managing Committee and Officers of the British School at Athens, that most admirable centre of research, is incalculable. My warmest thanks are also due to Professor Marinatos, Inspector-General of the Greek Service of Antiquities, to all the officials of this Service, and to the Directors of the foreign Schools of Archaeology in Greece.

As well as this, I have received unlimited kindness and help from individuals. My indebtedness to Dr A. M. Snodgrass will be clear from the Introduction and elsewhere in the book: engaged in research along similar lines to mine, he has allowed me to make full use of his ideas, and has rescued me from occasional misapprehension and error. Many others have given freely of their time, knowledge, and advice, and of these I would like to make particular mention of Miss O. Alexandris, Professor P. Amandry, Professor M. Andronikos, Mr J. N. Coldstream, Professor P. Courbin, Mr R. A. Higgins, Dr V. Karageorghis, Professor L. Morricone, Mr R. V. Nicholls, Professor M. R. Popham, Mr L. H. Sackett, Mrs Seiradhakis, Professor Evelyn Smithson, Lord William Taylour, Mr P. G. Themelis, and Mr J. Travlos.

The typing of the manuscript has been a laborious business, and I would like to record my admiration and gratitude to Mrs Young and to Mrs Mead, Fellows' Secretary at New College.

Finally, my appreciation goes to the publishers, for their forbearance in the face of long delays on my part, and to Mr S. Rossiter, who suggested the work, for his confidence in its value.

V. R. D'A. D.

New College,
Oxford

Contents

Maps and Plans

Acknowledgements

The author wishes to record his deep gratitude to many institutions and scholars in providing material for this work.

He has benefited greatly by being permitted to mention, describe, and often to illustrate hitherto unpublished material. In this respect warm thanks are recorded to the following: the Visitors of the Ashmolean Museum for a bottle-shaped vase; the Managing Committee of the British School at Athens, Professor M. R. Popham, Mr L. H. Sackett, and Mr P. G. Themelis (for objects from Lefkandi); Professor L. Morricone for information and photographs of his excavations in Kos; Lord William Taylour for photographs of vases from Mycenae and information concerning the tholos tomb at Kokevi; and Mr J. Travlos for allowing the use of his latest, and at that time unpublished, plan of Athens as a basis for the plan in this book.

Due and grateful acknowledgement is also made to the following for permission to reproduce published photographs:

The Managing Committee of the British School at Athens: material from the School's Annual, from *Fortetsa*, and from *Excavations at Lefkandi 1964–66*.

The Director of the École Française d'Athènes, Professor Amandry: material from Delphi and Argos.

The Director of the Deutsches Archäologisches Institut at Athens, Professor Jantzen: material from *AM, JdI*, and *Kerameikos* I and IV.

The Director of the Scuola Italiana at Athens, Professor Levi: vases from Petrokephali.

The Director of the Service of Antiquities in Cyprus, Dr Karageorghis: material from Kouklia, Idalion, and the Cyprus Museum.

The Editor-in-Chief of the American Journal of Archaeology, Professor Stilwell: material from Kourion, Erganos, and Dirmil.

The Visitors of the Ashmolean Museum: a spearhead.

The Trustees of the British Museum: objects of bronze and gold.

Professors E. Akurgal and J. M. Cook (Old Smyrna); Miss O. Alexandris (Athens); Dr Alexiou (Karphi goddesses); Professor Andronikos (Vergina); Mr G. Bass (Dirmil); Miss S. Benton (Ithaca); Mr J. Boardman (Knossos); the late Mr Brock (Knossos); Professor J. L. Caskey (Ayia Irini); Mr A. Choremis (Nichoria); Mr J. N. Coldstream (Derveni and Ithaca); Professor Courbin (Argos); Professor Dakaris (weapons from Epirus); Mr Higgins (jewellery and the anthropoid figure from Kos); Mr Hood (Knossos); Professor Sp. Marinatos (Kephallenia); Mr Mastrokostas (Teichos Dymaion); Professor Popham and Mr L. H. Sackett (Lefkandi); Mrs Seiradhakis (Karphi); Professor Evelyn Smithson and Mr Tombazis (Nea Ionia); Lord William Taylour (Mycenae); Mr and Mrs Theocharis (Hexalophos and Iolkos); Professor Emily Vermeule (Achaea); Dr Yalouris (Ancient Elis).

The author is, finally, much indebted to Dr H. W. Catling for a drawing of a sword of Naue II type.

Note on the line drawings

With the exception of Figures 26a, 27, and 35, all the illustrations are based on actual objects or constructions; the references in the captions are to the original drawings or photographs.

Introduction

The period covered by this book is perhaps slightly over two hundred years, from about 1125 B.C. to about 900 B.C. This may sound a little vague, but any claim to greater precision would be dishonest. All that can be said is that, in the light of present knowledge, these are the most likely dates.

It could be argued that Greece remained in a state of darkness until at least the middle of the eighth century, in other words until the probable time that the Greeks recovered the art of writing, until the first occasion of a more or less accurate record of certain events. This may indeed be more correct, but there is strong and increasing evidence that at least for the Aegean the period after 900 B.C. was one of increasing progress, wealth, and expansion, suggesting that our ignorance is not due to their obscurity.

The analysis of this period is based almost wholly on the archaeological material. The likelihood that the Dark Age Greeks were literate is, in my opinion, exceedingly remote; even supposing, however, that some small fraction of the population was able to write, it is clear that later Greeks had no access to any written material. All depended on the vagaries of the oral tradition, which was in any case singularly reticent about the events of these centuries. This does not mean that its evidence is entirely to be disregarded, but it cannot provide an adequate or reliable basis. I have devoted a brief section only to it; there seems no satisfactory middle way between a very lengthy account and a very short one, and I have chosen the latter. There are, of course, many works dealing with the oral tradition, of which Forsdyke's *Greece before Homer* (1956) is an admirable introduction to what is an extremely complex problem.

There has so far been no survey of this period as such, though as it happens two very recent works of greater scope cover it in depth. The one is J. Bouzek's *Homerisches Griechenland* (1969), which appeared too late for me to make use of it – it is of particular interest in stressing the connexions with Central Europe. The other is A. M. Snodgrass's *The Dark Age of Greece* (down to the eighth century), which will have appeared shortly before this volume and to whose author, through his great kindness in sending me some of the galley proofs, and in many other matters, I owe much: his work and mine should be considered as complementary to each other.

The fact that no full account should as yet have appeared is due to our lack of knowledge. Had such an account come out ten years ago, it would have been totally inadequate; even now it may be rather premature, for one thing that is reasonably certain is that it will be out of date ten years hence – but that is the fate of most works based on archaeology.

From the point of view of material culture, the Greek Dark Ages have little to offer or excite. There are indeed achievements, considerable in relation to the times themselves, but not to be compared with those of the Mycenaeans before or of the Archaic and Classical Greeks later. The main interest lies elsewhere. The Dark Ages, by their nature, exercise a fascination and present a challenge. What really was happening? How far, by the use of all the available evidence, and always paying due regard to the dangers inherent in an incomplete and shadowy picture, can we recover the course of events or even in a small degree understand the atmosphere of the age? However slight and tentative the conclusions may be, any advance is an addition to knowledge. Such an addition to knowledge, furthermore, has a wider significance: the more we know about the Dark Ages, the better we shall be able to see how and why the preceding civilisation failed and the succeeding one arose. I have therefore endeavoured to set out the evidence and the problems arising out of it. Occasionally, I have suggested an answer to a question; no doubt these answers will in course of time be found to be wrong, or misguided, but it is my hope that they will lead others to deeper research.

I

The Background
to the Dark Ages

1 The Mycenaean World

It is impossible to understand the Dark Ages of Greece without a knowledge of the prosperity and consequent decline of the Mycenaean Age which came before it. This chapter is therefore devoted to the Mycenaeans, a horizontal account of their greatness, and a vertical account of their decadence. The evidence used is chiefly that of archaeology, of the inscribed tablets found in excavations, and of the Homeric epic; and this evidence dates mainly from the thirteenth and twelfth centuries B.C.

The greater emphasis is laid on the situation during the thirteenth century, as during this time Mycenaean civilisation was still in full flower and its institutions intact. The period of decline of the twelfth century is treated much more summarily, since later chapters also cover it to some extent – it may then seem that it is not necessary to discuss it at all at this stage, but during the later analysis the evidence is dealt with on a regional basis, with the preceding background forming a necessary introduction to the start of the Dark Ages in each particular district, and thus no complete picture is available such as this chapter provides, however briefly. Some discussion of the twelfth century is in any case desirable at this point, since Mycenaean civilisation, though severely shaken at the end of the thirteenth century, persisted deep into the twelfth.

The archaeological picture of any period is mostly based on the achievements of its craftsmen and artists in durable materials. Of these materials, there would seem in Mycenaean times to have been plenty. The builder was well supplied with stone and wood, and the potter was in no lack of clay; the metalsmith, on the other hand, was obliged to import his metals, for the most part, from outside. The working of iron was as yet a process known only to a few – and to none in the Aegean area; but copper for the many bronze works came in quantity from Cyprus. Silver was relatively scarce, but gold was evidently easily accessible from the East; and so also was ivory. As well as this, there was a fair supply of semi-precious stones, such as rock crystal, agate, onyx, and chalcedony, used for gems and for necklaces, though beads of glass were often considered adequate for the latter.

The Mycenaeans were highly skilled in the use of all these materials. The painted pottery was unrivalled in its world; the objects in metal display no less skill and technique, and the ivories were sculpted by masters of their craft. Painters produced lively and brilliantly coloured frescoes, whether of stylised patterns, humans, animals natural and fabulous, or creatures of the sea. Of the woodworker's art we know less, for this material is perishable; even so, the discovery of little models of columns gives a fair indication of the elaboration and artistry of the full-size ones, which we know to have been of wood. Above all, however, the architects and stonemasons arouse one's admiration, whether by virtue of the splendid ashlar masonry of the latest beehive tombs, where the technique is seen at its best (Fig. 26), or in the similar masonry of the foundations and walls of the most important palatial buildings, or in the massive construction, stone-faced with interior rubble filling, of the fortifications, or indeed in the monumental sculpture, as still visible in the Lion Gate superstructure at Mycenae.

Such artistry and craft were not to be seen again in Greece for at least four hundred years. But it was a perfection of technique rather than of the spirit, and the reason for this is that it seems to have been encouraged for only one purpose, the magnificence of the ruling class. The Homeric epic tells us that each district had its own king, and this is amply confirmed by the material remains: on the mainland of Greece from Messenia to Thessaly there are several palaces of the period, and there can be little doubt that more will be found. Herein were the splendid throne-rooms with their central hearths flanked by columns, and their frescoes, where the king gave audience, seated on his throne, sceptre in hand (thus Homer, and a sceptre has in fact survived, found in Cyprus but very possibly of this period and from Greece), and dispensed his religious duties. What Homer does not tell us, however, is that the palaces were also the centres, under the king, of a complex bureaucratic administration, wherein all classes had their strictly allotted roles, and wherein all manufactured and raw materials and all bodies, whether human or animal, were meticulously scrutinised and recorded. For this knowledge we are indebted to the inscribed tablets which destruction by fire has preserved for us at Pylos and at Mycenae, at Knossos and at Thebes – thereby, incidentally, establishing the existence (unknown to Homer) of writing, though this knowledge was probably the preserve of a small minority.

Even if there were no other evidence, the great royal citadels and tombs would suggest the existence of a fair-sized population, for their construction would have involved many thousands of men. So also must the roads, traces of which have been found in Messenia, the Argolid and Boeotia, for they are no mere paths, but highways capable of taking wheeled traffic. There is in any case a great deal more evidence, for the tally of inhabited sites, whether known by excavation or by survey, whether identifiable by settlement or by cemetery, now exceeds five hundred over the whole of Greece and the Aegean, excluding Crete – and the vast majority of these are on the mainland, this and not the sea being the focus of Mycenaean civilisation until the twelfth century, in spite of the extensive overseas trade.

These statistics introduce us to those of lower standing than the kings and nobles; in a sense, we know rather less about them, but even so the material they provide is of great interest. We know, for example, that their houses were often well built, with at least the foundation of stone. But it is their family graves that are the most illuminating (Fig. 27). They were cut in the soft rock, usually had a rectangular chamber (hence the name chamber tombs), and were provided with a passage way or *dromos*. They may be only poor copies of the beehive tholos tombs, but they are never-theless well constructed, there are hundreds of them, and they have the advantage over their grandiose relatives that they were not so likely to attract the attention of the tomb robbers – nor, when discovered, were their contents found to be so desirable. It is from the objects placed in these chamber tombs that we know most about the prized lifetime possessions of their occupants – the vases, almost always of good quality, the necklaces and other ornaments, of rather varying excellence, the weapons (which were rare), and perhaps an indication, though impossible to interpret, of religious beliefs from the little female terracotta figurines.

No picture of Mycenaean Greece would be complete without some knowledge of its flora and fauna. As one travelled from town to village, or from district to district, what sort of conditions would one find?

The very numerous settlements imply that the land of the plains was reasonably extensively cultivated. There is in fact evidence for wheat and barley and rye, for beans and peas and other vegetables; there were vine-yards and olive groves, as today. The domestic animals were also mostly those of modern times: the sheep and the goat, the pig and the cow, contributed to the food supply, and so did the hen; there were oxen for ploughing, horses and donkeys for transport, and curly-tailed dogs for hunting; only the cat had, it appears, no place yet by the fireside.

But the plains are relatively small pockets set in a predominantly wild and mountainous country, and may have been more thickly covered with woods and forests than they are now. There is evidence for pine and oak, sycamore and palm, but we cannot tell in what density. Did the roads within the inhabited districts form a link between one district and another? Homer's heroes travelled overland, and this may be a correct tradition. Away from the plains, there will have been room and shelter for deer, and for the boar, the hunting of which constituted one of the main sports of the nobles, and whose tusks were coveted as the outer coverings for helmets. Were there perhaps even lions? They are represented on hunting scenes, and presumably on the Lion Gate,[1] but we cannot be sure.

On the whole the physical and climatic conditions could have been very similar to those of modern Greece, verging on the subtropical (the probability that houses had flat roofs would also suggest this), reasonably fertile, and capable of supporting a not inconsiderable population. Indeed, all the evidence indicates that the population was large and fairly pros-perous, an orderly community controlled by the kings and their all-pervasive bureaucracy.

But were the various mainland and Aegean areas knit into a single whole? The material culture, in its many aspects, is so uniform that one must at the very least conclude that links between one small kingdom and another were of the closest. Besides this, it must be pointed out that the

[1] Unfortunately the heads are missing.

land or
people ?

Hittites knew of a land called Ahhiyawa, uncertainly located but very probably in the Aegean area, of an importance suitable for a combined power, but less suitable for any of the lesser districts when taken separately; and Homer's Agamemnon would appear to have the role of a High King – though of course this may have been only for the purposes of the expedition against Troy. There is no solid proof that Greece and the Aegean formed a union of kingdoms under one overlord, but I think that the balance of probability is that such was the case. And if there was a High King, he would have had his seat at Mycenae.

The centre of Mycenaean civilisation lay on the mainland, strongest in the Peloponnese (excepting its north-western area) and in Attica and Boeotia, less strong in Thessaly apart from the district round coastal Iolkos, the modern Volos. It also, however, spread its tentacles over the central and southern Aegean, especially the Dodecanese, and there was even a precarious hold on the west coast of Asia Minor, at Miletus. Although this was primarily a land power, sea trade not only within the Aegean but outside it – for example, to Sicily and south Italy and to the east Mediterranean – seems to have been regular and frequent.

On the whole, the Mycenaeans (especially their rulers) must have made their world a pleasant place to live in. And so it continued until the latter part of the thirteenth century, that is to say within about three generations of the beginning of the Dark Ages which form the central theme of this book. During these generations the changes that came about are little short of fantastic. The craftsmen and artists seem to vanish almost without trace: there is very little new stone construction of any sort, far less any massive edifices; the metal-worker's technique reverts to the primitive, and the potter, except in the early stages, loses his purpose and inspiration; and the art of writing is forgotten. But the outstanding feature is that by the end of the twelfth century the population appears to have dwindled to about one-tenth of what it had been little over a century before. This is no normal decline, and the circumstances and events obviously have a considerable bearing on the nature of the subsequent Dark Ages, and must be in part at least a cause of its existence. The following account will give both a statement of the archaeological facts, and an analysis of the possible historical interpretations of these facts, when taken as a whole.

It is indeed possible to recognise the signs of impending trouble within the very conditions of seeming prosperity outlined above. Among the builder's achievements mention was made of massive fortification walls, and it is a fact that such constructions usually belong either entirely or in their extension to the thirteenth century. There is not much evidence for the south Peloponnese, though even here nearly a dozen of the settlements were surrounded by walls whose date of construction is not certain. On the north-west coast of the Peloponnese, however, at Teichos Dymaion in Achaea, there is a citadel of considerable size and strength, probably fortified in the thirteenth century. In the Argolid, the centre of the Mycenaean world, this century produces extensive fortification works at Mycenae and Tiryns, and those of Midea are hardly less impressive; Argos, too, was fortified. As one leaves the Peloponnese, at the Isthmus, there are stretches of a wall with projecting towers at intervals, unconnected with any settlement, built in the thirteenth century, its precise purpose unknown, but evidently defensive in character. A similar picture is found in central Greece: the defences of the Acropolis at Athens were strengthened, most probably between 1250 and 1200; the walls of the great fortress of Gla in Boeotia belong to the thirteenth century, and so possibly may those of Krisa, below Delphi. In Thessaly, however, the northernmost part of Mycenaean mainland penetration, the situation is less clear (and in any case it is likely that this district was normally reached by sea rather than overland); the site of Petra, a few miles inland from the coastal Iolkos, has extensive walls, but one cannot be sure that they are even Mycenaean; and Iolkos itself does not seem to have been fortified.

Such is the chief evidence on the mainland – and there are numerous fortified settlements of smaller size, whose walls cannot usually be precisely dated. In and across the Aegean, there is very little fortification work of this period at all, with the exception of Miletus, where the walls were built in the thirteenth century, but quite possibly by Hittites rather than by Mycenaeans.

The conclusion must, I think, be that the Mycenaeans on the mainland did not feel too secure, for all their prosperity. These fortifications cannot be explained simply as grandiose enhancements to the power and prestige of the kings; it is far more likely that their purpose was defensive. This seems to be confirmed by the fact that on three of the major sites, Athens, Mycenae, and Tiryns, considerable skill and engineering ability were devoted to providing a source of water within the citadel – in the case of Athens this was carried out not long before 1200.

There was, then, an atmosphere of foreboding, of imminent danger. The nature and source of the danger may be left for the moment; it will be better first to consider the manifestations of the various calamities that overcame the Mycenaeans. Very briefly, this is what happened.

The really serious disasters were those which overwhelmed the Greek mainland just before 1200 B.C. A number of settlements were destroyed or severely damaged. There are not many, but it was their prominence that mattered, as they include some of the royal centres. Mycenae and Tiryns were involved in two successive disasters, probably fairly close in time to each other, the second, it appears, being the more calamitous. At the time of these second destructions, rather than of the first, Nestor's palace at Pylos was totally burnt, and there were other disasters at Gla in Boeotia, Krisa near Delphi, Teichos Dymaion in Achaea, and a large settlement near Sparta.

Equally important, when placed alongside the destructions, is the evidence for the abandonment of a very great number of settlements in those districts which had suffered disaster or where, as in Attica, disaster had seemed imminent. The figures, as most recently assembled, are as follows. In the south-west Peloponnese (chiefly Messenia and Triphylia) the number of known sites falls from about 150 in the thirteenth century to 14 in the twelfth, in Laconia from 30 to 7, in the Argolid and Corinthia from 44 to 14, in Attica from 24 to 12, in Boeotia from 27 to 3, and in Phocis and Locris from 19 to 5. Three additional points may be noted: a few of the sites which continued to be inhabited into the twelfth century were abandoned soon after its beginning; a few sites were occupied in the twelfth century only; and all the twelfth-century sites still exhibit the characteristic Mycenaean culture. Some caution is necessary in accepting the above figures as for the most part they depend on surface survey only, and certain regions need further exploration, but even so the repetition of similar situations from district to district is cumulative and convincing. There must have been a phenomenal decrease in the population in the districts concerned.

It will be noted that no figures have been given for one district where disaster struck, that is to say Achaea. In this area the number of twelfth-century sites not only did not decrease as opposed to those of the thirteenth century, but actually increased. There was, however, a good reason for this paradox, and it brings us to an analysis of what should naturally be a complementary feature to disaster and abandonment, flight to other areas. Obviously a substantial number of people will have perished, but there will also have been a great dispersal to other areas. One such area was Achaea, a mountainous district in the north-west of the Peloponnese – and it should be noted that it was within the shelter of the mountains that they settled, whereas the damaged fortress of Teichos Dymaion, in fact soon reoccupied, was on the coast and a long way from any natural protection. There were also other parts of the mainland to which people fled, mostly to rather out-of-the-way sites on the Aegean-facing coast: Epidaurus Limera in eastern Laconia may be one, but the evidence is not sufficient for proof; Asine in the Argolid is probably another, and the extensive cemetery at Perati in east Attica, of early twelfth-century origin and whose period of use belonged almost entirely to this century, is a definite third; mention may also be made of Lefkandi in Euboea, so close to the mainland that it almost qualifies as part of it, where a flourishing (though, as we shall see, not untroubled) twelfth-century settlement can be contrasted to only slight traces of thirteenth-century habitation. These movements, however, account for only a small proportion of the exodus: large numbers went overseas. Some made their way westwards, to the island of Kephallenia, and presumably to Ithaca as well. Most took the eastward sea route. Within the central Aegean, a new settlement was founded at Emborio on Chios, very much on the fringes of the Mycenaean world; and such evidence as we have from Naxos may perhaps suggest an increase in population, but that is somewhat tendentious. In Crete, on the other hand, there is clear evidence that a group of Mycenaean refugees arrived c. 1200 B.C. The most substantial body, however, journeyed to Cyprus where, even if it was not responsible for the destructions that took place on that island at this time, it certainly had a profound influence on Cypriot culture, and may have for a while been dominant – it was an ill-fated choice, as further disasters soon overcame those who settled, but that is another matter. And finally we may note the presence of a rather isolated and not very prosperous twelfth-century Mycenaean community at Tarsus in Cilicia, previously under Hittite control (the Hittite empire had also recently been overwhelmed, in the general turmoil of the times).

It is now time to probe the possible causes of the catastrophic period which led to the decimation of many of the central regions and to many attendant losses, involving the general political cohesion, the whole system of rule and bureaucracy, the disappearance of the knowledge of writing, and the lessening of many skills and arts.

The various known factors, the destructions – especially of certain important citadels – the wholesale desertion of great tracts of mainland Greece, the consequent flight by land to remote and isolated districts or sites on the mainland, and by sea both westwards and eastwards (above all to Cyprus), all these suggest that there was an invasion, or a series of invasions, affecting the central and southern mainland only (Thessaly may have been relatively unaffected, the islands of the central Aegean certainly were), and that these brought about a situation so desperate that there was a mass exodus of the survivors from their age-old towns and villages, an exodus involving rich and poor, powerful and weak, alike.

If, however, there was an invasion, one would naturally expect the invaders to take over the country they had overrun. Of this there is no sign whatever. It may be argued that their culture was so primitive that they left no material trace of their occupation, but even so one would surely expect some change in or addition to the culture and customs, especially the burial customs, of the Mycenaeans. But this does not happen: in spite of the losses discussed above, what remains is, so far as one can tell, purely Mycenaean. Even in Messenia, where depopulation seems to have been almost total, there is simply a gap, and a fairly long one, in occupation of any sort, exception being made of barely a dozen Mycenaean communities. It is possible that we have overlooked the kind of site that intruders would use to settle in, but it does not seem likely. One would then have to assume that the invaders went on elsewhere, or retreated. This is by no means impossible, but before accepting the theory of invasion from outside one must consider two alternative theories.

The one alternative is that the upheaval was caused by local risings either of a previously subjected element, or of one kingdom against another. Such a possible cause cannot be ruled out, though account must be taken of the earlier disquiet that led to the strengthening of fortifications, and to massive new ones, even to the extent of attempting to build a wall at the Isthmus of Corinth, even to the construction of elaborate water-supplies for the citadels in case of siege. Growing local unrest on the part of the less prosperous or enslaved might result in such precautions, but it seems doubtful, and one would expect different measures. Fear of neighbouring kingdoms, or even fear of the more powerful within one's own kingdom, would be more plausible, but even here the assurance of a water-supply for the beleaguered is difficult to explain in the light of a local rising, whether of serfs or nobles, for in the Argolid at least the water came from outside the citadels, and these engineering feats must have been common knowledge. But the main objections seem to me to be the remarkably widespread nature of the destructions, the fact that the most powerful kingdoms were the worst affected, and the very high degree of consequent depopulation. I would be prepared to accept local risings of whatever sort as subsidiary and consequent phenomena, but hardly as the main cause.

The second alternative arises partly from the difficulty of understanding how any invasion or series of invasions can have had so drastic an effect, whether the invaders settled or not, and seeks to show that the catastrophe was due to natural causes. The theory has been advanced by Professor Rhys Carpenter that there was no invasion, but a sharp climatic change. Instead of north-easterly winds bringing storm and rain during the winter, there came a steady wind across the Mediterranean from the west, which would not collect much rain, and would shed this rain only on passing over a mountain, leaving the areas beyond that mountain unwatered. The summers were rainless anyway; now the winters would be relatively dry, with a consequent and increasingly serious effect on vegetation of all kinds, and hence on the supply of food – and indeed there would also be insufficient water in many parts. This would inevitably lead to famine and disease, and the only remedy would be departure to some land where conditions were different. The mass exodus could be accounted for in this way, and the destructions of the major centres could be attributed to fierce fires (always a hazard when wood was extensively used) caused by the excessive dryness.

In support of his theory, Professor Carpenter can show that such a phenomenon is perfectly possible climatically, and he can produce some evidence from the ancient sources – though not bearing directly on the mainland of Greece.[2] Furthermore, he envisages this period of drought as persisting for some three hundred years, even though not continuously in its most severe form. If it were true, it would mean the physical alteration of much of the face of Greece precisely during the Dark Ages, it would be the main cause of their coming into being, and would of course affect our whole conception of the economy of the period.

It is, however, a theory that has weaknesses, as Professor Carpenter realises. It fails to account for the earlier nervous state of mind which led to the building of fortifications, and the ensuring of a water-supply within citadels; the known areas of desertion and survival do not, I believe, agree with what one would expect, if his explanation is correct; and there is as yet no proof that such climatic conditions did hold, at least in this area. Fortunately, it may before long be possible to prove or disprove this theory by the process of pollen analysis; until then, one can do no more than bear in mind the conception of a severe drought, whether short-lived or extending over centuries, as a possibility. Nor does it in any case rule out the possibility of an invasion.

On the whole, it seems that the idea of an invasion, or more than one, in spite of its disadvantages, is the most likely to be correct. And it will have

---

[2] It may be added that recent evidence has come to light showing that in the east Mediterranean at this time there were drought and famine, and earthquakes as well.

been an invasion in which the invaders withdrew, even though they were ✳
probably a continuing potential and actual menace throughout most of
the twelfth century. This retreat is a point of some importance. The oral
tradition of the Greeks preserved a story of a series of movements into
Greece at very much this time (two generations after the Trojan War,
which should probably be assigned to the middle of the thirteenth century),
originating in the north-western districts which lay outside the Mycenaean
world, properly speaking. The chief of these movements was that of the
Dorians, led by kings of Mycenaean descent, and the main target was the
Peloponnese, where these invaders warred against local Mycenaean rulers
and emerged victorious. So far, the tradition is acceptable, but it goes on to
tell us that the invading groups immediately settled in many areas of the
mainland; and for this, as we have seen, there is no archaeological evidence
at all. If the tradition is true, and the invaders did settle, then they would
surely have had some influence over the whole way of life, and one ought
perhaps to suppose that the Dark Age started c. 1200 B.C. But if they did
not settle, as the archaeological picture suggests, then the tradition is either
partially wrong, or incorrectly dated. I prefer the explanation based on the
present archaeological material, that of a land whose few inhabitants were
descendants of those who had held it for centuries.

Assuming then that, after invasion, the Mycenaean part of the mainland
of Greece was still inhabited by Mycenaeans, what effect did the catastrophe have on their whole way of life? The answer must be interpreted in
the light of the various factors already mentioned, the failure to return and
reoccupy so many towns and villages, the loss of writing, the deterioration
in craftsmanship and in building technique, the fragmentation of pottery
styles. It seems fair to conclude that any central political power, that of a
High King, if it existed earlier, now disappeared. For if there was an
overlord, his residence was Mycenae, and even though it seems that an
attempt was made for a while to retain Mycenae as a stronghold, and even
though the potters of the Argolid produced in the early or mid-twelfth
century a highly sophisticated style, known as the Close Style, it is inconceivable that any king who still reigned at Mycenae could have pretended
any longer to rule the whole of Mycenaean territory. Furthermore, the
losses, together of course with the depopulation, signify that the whole
elaborate bureaucratic system must have broken down; which may have
been no bad thing.

The evidence from Cyprus, indeed, where the immigrant Mycenaean
groups of c. 1200 B.C. were probably responsible for fine stone constructions, and metal and ivory artefacts in the best previous tradition, suggests
that it was the upper classes who, making use of their no doubt excellent
ships, had made their way here from the mainland of Greece. And the fact
that the only royal sceptre of almost certain Mycenaean workmanship that
we have was found in a tomb in Cyprus supports this suggestion. It is
probable that many of the rulers, if they were not killed, fled overseas,
though one or two will have stayed either where they were, as for example
at Iolkos in Thessaly, or moved to somewhere else on the mainland, as for

Wall across Isthmus (Hesperia 35 - 1966, 346 f.)

example to Achaea in north-west Peloponnese, and perhaps even to Perati in east Attica and to Lefkandi in Euboea. In the unaffected central Aegean, however, such local rulers as there were presumably retained their power, and such evidence as we have of a common culture suggests that there may have been something like a maritime league of little Mycenaean states.

The greatest effect of all, however, must have been a psychological one, primarily on the inhabitants of the mainland. They had seen their whole way of life destroyed or seriously endangered, and at least the generation that witnessed the catastrophe must have lived under the shadow of a constant fear. This will certainly have been true of those who stayed, but those who fled will have taken the same atmosphere with them.

It is possible that, given time and peaceful conditions, there might have been a recovery. And indeed there may have been a partial one, to judge from the appearance of at least three highly individual and spirited styles of pottery towards the middle of the twelfth century, in the Argolid, in the central Aegean (derived from Crete) and in Euboea at Lefkandi (Pl. 1). This, however, was not political recovery; it reflected a temporary lull combined with the potter's delight at finding himself free of the previous conventions.

close style

But there was no real or abiding peace. Lefkandi suffered a disaster, probably in the early twelfth century, and there was another one later; the citadel of Iolkos in Thessaly was destroyed, perhaps about 1150 B.C.; Mycenae itself was once again sacked at some time between 1150 and 1100; Emborio on Chios was wiped out, and so was Miletus, both probably before 1100 B.C. – so there was no security in the Aegean, either; and Teichos Dymaion in Achaea once again fell to violence, towards the end of the century or even later, this time to be abandoned for good. Some at least of these events had as their consequence the flight of yet more Mycenaeans in the second half of the twelfth century: some probably went to Crete, and a fair number certainly made their way to Cyprus, where they had as profound an effect on the island as their predecessors.

Were these disasters also the result of invasion? In the case of Emborio and Miletus it seems very likely, but at Mycenae the firing of the Granary could have been the result of local trouble. At Iolkos and Lefkandi it is impossible to tell – and indeed still really impossible in every case. Whatever happened, however, there must have been a considerable further weakening and decline, and it is noticeable that, except in Achaea and Kephallenia, even the standard of vase-making deteriorated; the effect was probably most markedly felt in the central Aegean group.

Can one in any sort of way picture the conditions that existed in the second half of the twelfth century? On the basis of the existing archaeological material – and it must be stressed that we have as yet nowhere near the complete evidence, and that as often as not new discoveries tend to upset or modify our preconceived ideas – the following tentative statements may be made.

Certain areas still retained a relative compactness, the communities who inhabited Achaea, and those of Kephallenia and, most probably, Ithaca (though mixed with a non-Mycenaean element). Certain areas were almost deserted, the south-west Peloponnese and very possibly Laconia. Apart from this, one gets the impression of small communities, by no means isolated from each other, but making no attempt to combine for mutual protection, with few stonemasons or craftsmen left, and in any case with insufficient manpower either to fortify their settlements or to resist any intrusion. A few of these communities may have had a reasonable number of inhabitants – Perati, Iolkos, Naxos, perhaps those of Kos and Rhodes. But I think that for the most part they were tiny little groups distributed over the landscape, living as at Mycenae in the ruins of the former great towns, in the shadow of the departed greatness. Each community no doubt had its chief, a sort of petty king, but in most cases the earlier ruling families had been slain or had fled.

In general there must have been a tendency towards greater isolation of community from community. With an extremely small population, large tracts of cultivated land will have become overgrown, and the roads will soon have fallen into disrepair. The principal means of communication will have been by sea, but it would appear that the Aegean also became increasingly unsafe during the twelfth century – one cannot prove that there was piracy, but very likely it existed.

It would be wrong to say that the survivors had been reduced to poverty, but there had been a progressive loss of political cohesion, and hence progressive weakness; there was as well, no doubt, a fundamental and permanent feeling of insecurity. There was also a poverty in the sense of material facilities and achievements – little or no building, no writing, poor metalwork. Even so, this does not constitute a Dark Age; the lowering of standards does not prevent us from recognising that what remained was predominantly Mycenaean in character.

II

The Early Dark Ages

2 Three Styles of Pottery

When one speaks of a Dark Age, the first problem is one of definition, both geographically and chronologically. In Greece, I am considering this age partly in relation to the preceding Mycenaean age, over its whole area as already defined, and partly in relation to the future history of Greece and the Aegean. I have shown how a series of catastrophes at about the end of the thirteenth century effectively destroyed the unity of the Mycenaean world, but for some long time afterwards there was survival – even in parts a surprising revival – which cannot be called a Dark Age. The Dark Ages begin, I would think, when the main characteristics of the preceding age are irremediably and finally lost. This was unlikely to happen at one and the same time over the whole of the extensive Mycenaean area, and I do not believe that it did.[1]

I commence with one major assumption – that, for reasons which will emerge only after I have reviewed the evidence, the area where the Dark Ages started was that of central Greece – Boeotia, west Attica, the Argolid, Corinthia, and probably Elis. I do not say that other areas may not in time be added, when more has been found and published: there is still so much that is unknown and unclear. As things stand, however, the Dark Ages seem first to be visible in the area mentioned, and the new culture which pervades it is known as Sub-Mycenaean.

Given this assumption, it is then necessary to define and describe the culture, and to give an approximate date for its first appearance and duration, absolutely so far as is possible, and in any case in relation to that of other districts. The Sub-Mycenaean culture will be found to have a number of characteristic features, of which the most distinctive, and the essential one for chronology, is the type of pottery – the one feature which, paradoxically, reveals not an irrevocable break with the preceding civilisation, but a clear continuity.

What I intend to do is first to analyse the origins, background, and nature of this Sub-Mycenaean pottery (including that of Lefkandi in Euboea which belongs to its later phase), without any consideration of other features or discussion of individual sites. In its early stages, this pottery seems to be rather isolated, but towards the end, especially in Athens, and also to some extent at Lefkandi, ceramic influence from Cyprus made itself felt. This will lead on to a brief analysis of the Cypriot

---

[1] This is of course a subjective judgment, and I cannot stress too greatly that the interpretation of the evidence is purely my own. I shall try to set out the evidence as fully as possible, but the manner of its setting out, the way I shall discuss it, will be tendentious – it would be almost impossible for it not to be so.

pottery known as Late Cypriot III B (L.C. III B), and of the general situation in that island, and from this I shall be able to demonstrate, since the Cypriot series is reasonably securely dated, that the end of Sub-Mycenaean, at least in Athens, came about the middle of the eleventh century. The discussion of Cypriot pottery will show that its style had earlier been greatly influenced not only by Mycenaean features, but that there were also some elements indicating links with Crete. So I shall proceed to a discussion of the contemporaneous Cretan style, which is called Sub-Minoan. In this way, three major styles of the first period of the Dark Ages will be dealt with, and at the same time some preliminary idea will emerge both of the earlier troubled background and of the atmosphere of the times in each of the areas concerned.

From here I shall return to the central Sub-Mycenaean area, and deal with it in greater detail, site by site, and discuss the material other than pottery. I shall then attempt to give an account, based on the whole evidence, of the conditions prevailing in the area.

I shall continue by considering the areas, so far not mentioned, surrounding the Sub-Mycenaean area of central mainland Greece, both with regard to their earlier history and the situation throughout the time when Sub-Mycenaean culture was current. There will be sections on the central Aegean, on the central and south Peloponnese, and on what I have termed the Northern Crescent – north-west Peloponnese, the Ionian islands, north-west Greece, Thessaly (with a side glance at Macedonia), and the districts between Thessaly and Boeotia.

Having thus completed the circle I shall discuss, again on the basis of the whole evidence, the vital question of the origin of the Sub-Mycenaean culture, whether it was a spontaneous local growth, or was partly introduced by new arrivals – and if the latter, from where.

The whole section will be completed by a discussion of the situation in Crete.

Sub-Mycenaean Pottery

The name given to the culture is in fact that originally given to its pottery, and in this sense entirely correctly, for the pottery is almost wholly Mycenaean in tradition. On the other hand, the context in which this pottery is nearly always found, that is to say, in cist tombs or earth-cut tombs used for one or two burials only, as opposed to the preceding multiple-burial chamber tombs, or in settlements which as a rule, where identifiable, are differently situated from their predecessors, clearly denotes a change from the Mycenaean way of life – and this is confirmed by a new pattern of grave offerings.

Even in the pottery, though purely Mycenaean in character, there is a profound difference in spirit from what had been current at the time of the great catastrophes of the end of the thirteenth century, possibly less than a

A

B

C

PLATE I LATE HELLADIC III C POTTERY

A) Argive Close Style. Stirrup jar; ·28 m. Fürtwängler and Löschcke, *Mykenische Vasen*, pl. 38, 393.

B) Central Aegean Style. Stirrup jar; ·22 m. *Ann.* 27–8 (N.S.), 189, fig. 196 *b*.

c) Lefkandian Style. Pyxis; ·181 m. *Excavations at Lefkandi 1964–66*, 18, fig. 35.

hundred years before. What had happened, and how had it come about?

The Late Helladic III C (L.H. III C) pottery which at about the turn of the century succeeded Late Helladic III B (L.H. III B) exhibits two main features. First, there is far less uniformity than had existed previously; a number of districts produced highly individual styles, and of these I shall for the time being set aside the developments in Kephallenia, Ithaca, and Achaea, as they have little relevance for Sub-Mycenaean (see pp. 88–94). Secondly, there was a gradual change in the manner of decoration. The previous pottery was already to some extent stylised, and the general system of decoration was an open one. At the beginning of the twelfth century the surviving open style was augmented and eventually superseded by a much closer one, in which the tendency was to cover more areas with paint, and further to conventionalise and elaborate the decorated areas. This latter tendency manifested itself in three separate styles (Pl. 1). There is the Close Style of the Argolid, the Octopus Style of the central Aegean (almost invariably confined to stirrup jars), and the curiously fantastic style of Lefkandi in Euboea, which emerged after a destruction subsequent to the end of L.H. III B. Of the three developments, both the Close Style and the Octopus Style can be described as a sort of incredibly intricate symmetrical doodling; but not so the style of Lefkandi, with its human and animal representations.

These innovations catch the eye, but they are to be found on a small proportion only of the pottery, the remainder being very simply decorated as a rule, in an increasingly geometrical manner, rectilinear or curvilinear. This is a factor which must be borne in mind, as well as the fact that, throughout Greece and the Aegean, in spite of local individualities, there were many common features, both in shape and in decoration.

The elaborations were important, for they indicate a renaissance of the Mycenaean potter's free imagination and inventiveness. But they did not last very long. The Lefkandi style disappeared completely, giving way to an extreme simplicity, in which the decoration, when found, consisted largely of wavy or zigzag lines. The Close and Octopus styles suffered a progressive deterioration, and the eventual outcome seems to have been either a very confused attempt to reproduce the closeness of decoration, in which all symmetry and order were abandoned, and resulting in complete chaos, or in a realisation that, much as at Lefkandi, nothing but the simplest kind of motive lay within the potter's scope, with triangles and concentric semicircles and wavy lines as the main stock in trade – or a decision to abandon decoration altogether. And this was more or less the situation when Sub-Mycenaean pottery first made its appearance. At the same time, the quality of fabric and technique had deteriorated as well. The downhill course, only momentarily relieved by a brilliant recovery, then punctuated by further trouble and destruction (including a final disaster at Mycenae), had been precipitate.

So then to the Sub-Mycenaean pottery which, as I have said, I shall deal with as a ceramic phenomenon recognisable only in certain areas, during the course of which the later stages of L.H. III C may, I believe, have persisted elsewhere. Originally, Sub-Mycenaean was defined as the characteristic ware of the cist-tomb cemeteries in Salamis and in the Athenian Kerameikos. Since then, however, the publication of material from the Argolid, Ancient Elis, Corinthia, Thebes in Boeotia, and Lefkandi in Euboea has shown that variations of this pottery were current in these districts and sites as well.

There are nine main types of vase, with occasional subdivisions, as shown in Figs. 1–10.[2] In discussing each, I shall indicate such regional and chronological distinctions as are valid or possible. Two initial points deserve emphasis. This analysis is based entirely on vases found in tombs, and so the picture is incomplete, for in certain cases vase types were either unsuitable for placing in tombs, or else just not favoured for such use. Secondly, the profiles illustrated are deceptive, for there may be considerable variation, as also in the decoration.

First, there is the *neck-handled amphora*, of Mycenaean origin. This was a jar for storage or for carrying liquids, one to two feet in height. The general shape is as shown, but it may be noted that there was a rare variant with handles from shoulder to lip. The body profile, rather as in related types of closed vases, tended to become more ovoid in the later phase; and the base is usually flat, or flattish, underneath. The usual system of decoration was one of bands, over the lip, at the bottom of the neck, below shoulder and belly and over the base, with extensive unpainted areas, except for the shoulder, which might have a simple motive of Mycenaean type (spiral, tassel), and the belly, which could have wavy lines reaching from one handle base to the other. On the whole, there are very few of these vases, for the simple reason that they were too large to put into a cist tomb. Ancient Elis is an exception to this – as also in the amphorae from here being mostly covered with paint. Athens is also an exception in the later stages, but in this case it heralds the growing popularity of cremation, the ashes being deposited in this type of vase, which was then placed in a specially prepared pit.

The neck-handled type has a companion, the *belly-handled amphora*. There are three varieties, each with a Mycenaean pedigree. The one, with a low straight collar neck, is not illustrated; the second has a short flaring neck, and the third a rather taller neck and a sharply out-turned lip.[3] The base, as in the neck-handled amphora, tends to be flat underneath, but the body is somewhat more globular. Rather the same system of banding was used, but while the Athenian amphorae were otherwise mainly left free of paint, the reverse is the case for the three from Argos and Ancient Elis. Detailed decoration is again simple, languettes or vertical wiggly lines or cross-hatched triangles on the shoulder, wavy lines or zigzags on the belly. This type of vase was as rare as its companion, and for the same reason.

The third vase type, the *amphoriskos*, looks like a sort of miniature

[2] In each figure I incorporate the Cretan and Cypriot shapes for purposes of comparison, and also the late Dark Age (Protogeometric) developments in the case of Athens and central Crete.

[3] Note a vase of this type from the L.H. III C cemetery at Perati (no. 590).

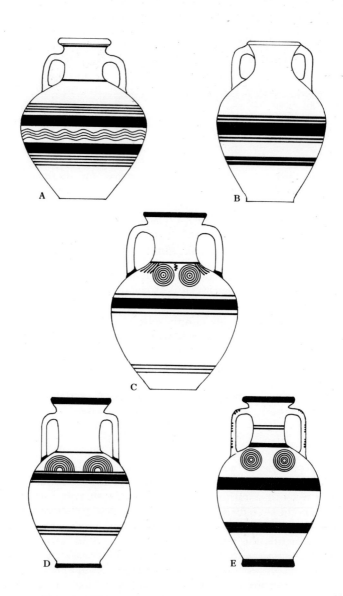

FIG. 1 NECK-HANDLED AMPHORAE
A) Athens, Sub-Myc.; ·34 m. *Ker*. I, pl. 26, no. 421.
B) Knossos, Sub-Min.; ·38 m. *BSA* 53–4, p. 242, fig. 28, no. VI A4.
C) Athens, PG; ·385 m. *Ker*. I, pl. 29, no. 522.
D) Athens, PG; ·435 m. *Ker*. I, pl. 57, no. 572.
E) Knossos, PG; ·355 m. *Fortetsa*, pl. 16, no. 226.

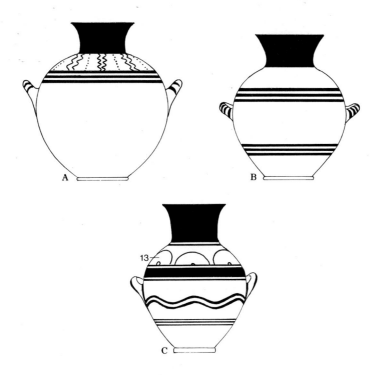

FIG. 2 BELLY-HANDLED AMPHORAE WITH SHORT FLARING NECK
A) Athens, Sub-Myc.; ·382 m. *Ker.* I, pl. 54, no. 562.
B) Athens, PG; ·295 m. *Ker.* I, pl. 54, no. 563.
c) Athens, PG; ·383 m. *Ker.* IV, pl. 11, no. 904.

amphora, and has very clear Mycenaean antecedents. The handles were almost always set on the belly, but there was also a type with vertical shoulder handles, so far known only at Lefkandi. The width of neck and mouth may vary considerably, and so may the body profile; the vase usually had a ring base. As to decoration, it was customary to paint the neck and to have the rest of the vase banded. The almost invariable decorative motive was a single or double wavy line between the handles, though just occasionally a simple motive, such as vertical bars, could appear on the shoulder. I would not like to venture on any distinction of a chronological nature, but regionally there was a startling difference in popularity: while in Athens and on Salamis this type of vase was more popular than any other (there are over fifty), only two are known from the Argolid, and none from Ancient Elis.

The next shape, the *stirrup jar,* is perhaps the most distinctive

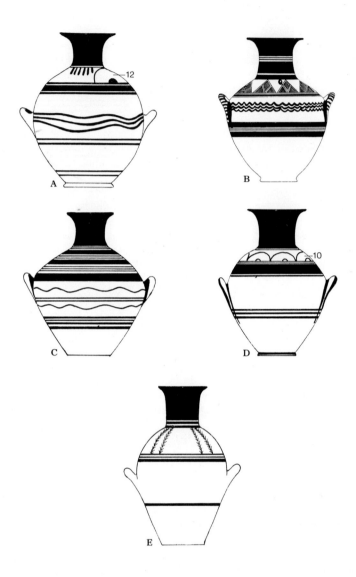

FIG. 3 BELLY-HANDLED AMPHORAE WITH STRAIGHT NECK AND EVERTED LIP
A) Athens, Sub-Myc.; ·66 m. *Ker*. I, pl. 54, no. 549.
B) Kouklia, L.C. III; ·475 m. *RDAC* 1967, p. 10, fig. 5, no. 22.
C) Knossos, Sub-Min.; ·44 m. *BSA* 63, pl. 53*a*.
D) Athens, PG; ·40 m. *Ker*. IV, pl. 10, no. 1073.
E) Knossos, PG; ·555 m. *Fortetsa*, pl. 10, no. 165.

Mycenaean vase of all that survived into this period. By the time Sub-Mycenaean started, however, there had been some deterioration. In the general shape of the body, it may well be that the earliest stirrup jars had an outline where the greatest diameter was set rather high, but thereafter there seems to have been no logical development – in some cases the craftsmanship is extremely poor and clumsy. Two minor features had been taken over from the immediately preceding late III C vases (when they first appeared), a rather high knob on the disk of the stirrup, and an airhole on the shoulder; these features are to be found on most (but not all) of the vases of the Sub-Mycenaean series. The system of decoration below the shoulder is one of thin and thick bands, with the whole occasionally painted over (the stirrup jars of the Argolid have noticeably wider unpainted zones than those of Athens). On the shoulder itself one gets vertical wiggly lines, or multiple hand-drawn semicircles, often with the central arc painted in (half-moon filling); just occasionally there could be a supporting zone of decoration, a zigzag or triangles. Regional differences are hard to establish, but chronologically there was a clear decline in the popularity of this shape as time went on, the lekythos – the next vase type to be discussed – gradually taking its place. The process is particularly clear in Athens, and the two miserable examples from the Lefkandi cemetery are one of the indications that the tombs from this site fall relatively late within the period. At Ancient Elis, however, where not one was found, I would not be quite so sure that this absence is a necessary criterion of lateness.

The *lekythos*, as has been said, eventually took the place of the stirrup jar. A few lekythoi had already appeared in L.H. III C, so the type is once again Mycenaean. In construction, the body is as variable in profile as that of the stirrup jar, and there is usually an airhole on the shoulder. The lip is a little crude in the early stages, but by the end has acquired a rather pleasing flat funnel shape. As a general rule, the handle comes up vertically to just below the lip, but at Ancient Elis it joins the lip itself, and the later lekythoi of the Argolid have the same feature. The base is usually of the ring type, but may have a low conical shape. As to decoration, the neck is banded or painted over, and the area below the shoulder is normally banded. The same motives as on the stirrup jar are to be found on the shoulder, vertical wiggly lines, concentric semicircles (with or without half-moon filling), and cross-hatched or concentric triangles; of these the semicircles have not yet been found in the Argolid and this could be a genuine point of difference between this series, and that of Athens, Salamis, and Lefkandi. Unusual motives are a row of dots on a late lekythos from Mycenae, and the fringed triangles of one of the lekythoi of Ancient Elis, which reflect a similar motive on Ithacan pottery.

The chief difference between the lekythos and the *jug* is that the latter has a wide mouth – a dumpy little round sort of vase, with good Mycenaean antecedents. The neck is always painted over, and so may the rest of the body be, but the shoulder can be left free for a cross-hatched triangle, and there may be reserved bands below the shoulder. There are only a few of these jugs, but they tend to turn up on all sites, and at Lefkandi are the

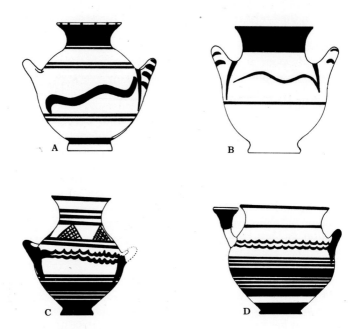

FIG. 4 AMPHORISKOI
A) Athens, Sub-Myc.; ·08 m. *Ker*. I, pl. 16, no. 440.
B) Athens, Sub-Myc.; ·108 m. *Ker*. I, pl. 17, no. 432.
C) Kouklia, L.C. III; ·157 m. *RDAC* 1967, p. 11, fig. 6, no. 27.
D) Kouklia, L.C. III; ·18 m. *RDAC* 1967, p. 11, fig. 6, no. 5.

ancestors of a type that continued well into later times.

Next comes the *trefoil-lipped oinochoe*, its mouth much better adapted for pouring than that of the jug. As usual, the shape is to be found in L.H. III C – there is a splendid Close Style one from Mycenae – but it was not common. In Sub-Mycenaean times (when it was not particularly common, either) the mouth and trefoil tended to be rather cumbersome, and the body had the heaviness found in other shapes. The handle usually comes up to the lip, but there is a variant, a small type of oinochoe whose handle rises above the lip. There was no favoured system of decoration, and only in three cases was there a subsidiary motive, sets of languettes pendent from the neck. The distribution is very uneven – none at Ancient Elis, just one small one with high handle from the Argolid, one at Lefkandi, but from Salamis and Athens fourteen. There may be a regional distinction here, but it is not so clear as for the amphoriskoi.

The last two types are open vases, the bowl and the cup.[4]

---

[4] There must have existed the very large bowl, or *krater*, but this was plainly unsuitable for use in cist tombs, nor was it used in this area as a container for ashes.

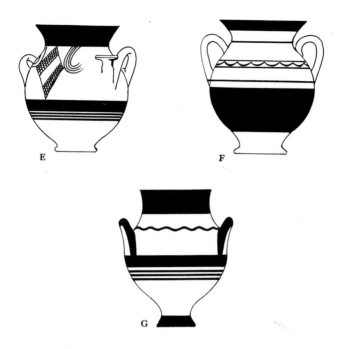

E) Knossos, Sub-Min.; ·20 m. *Fortetsa*, pl. 3, no. 3.
F) Lefkandi, Sub-Myc.; ·116 m. Skoubris tomb 16.
G) Knossos, PG; ·16 m. *Fortetsa*, pl. 6, no. 49.

The *bowl*, as will be seen in the illustration, has two horizontal handles, a slightly flaring lip, and a distinctive foot which (perhaps only in the later stages) could be low conical in form. These vases were always painted inside – at times with a reserved circle at the bottom and a reserved band below the lip – and more often than not wholly painted outside as well, though one occasionally finds a reserved zone between the handles, and a wavy or zigzag line encased within it, as is first to be seen in the Granary class of L.H. III C. Another feature sometimes to be observed, of similar latish III C origin, and in certain districts favoured on other shapes and continuing beyond Sub-Mycenaean, is the practice of leaving the lower body and the foot free of paint. Bowls are to be found everywhere except at Ancient Elis.

The *cup* is as shown, small and one-handled. Painted inside, it might have a simple wavy line and a supporting band on the outside, or be monochrome, or painted over except either for a reserved band on the lower body or the foot unpainted. Absent, like the bowl, from Ancient Elis, there

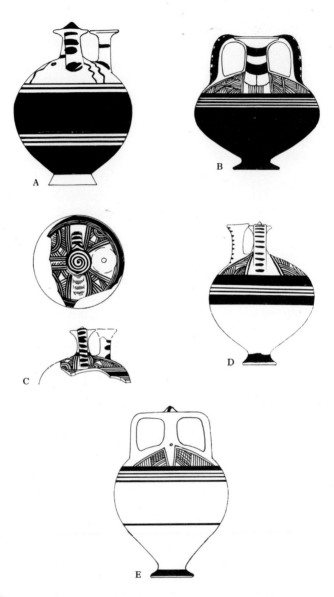

FIG. 5 STIRRUP JARS
A) Athens, Sub-Myc.; ·153 m. *Ker.* I, pl. 10, no. 508.
B) Kouklia, L.C. III; ·135 m. *RDAC* 1967, p. 13, fig. 8, no. 14.
C) Knossos, Sub-Min.; fragmentary, *BSA* 53–4, p. 242, fig. 28, no. VI A2.
D) Knossos, Sub-Min.; ·15 m. *BSA* 53–4, p. 242, fig. 28, no. VI A1.
E) Knossos, PG; ·165 m. *Fortetsa*, pl. 15, no. 218.

were only one in the Argolid, three in the Kerameikos cemetery, and five
from Salamis; at Lefkandi it was the most common shape of all.

These then are the main types of vase. All are wheel-made – indeed, the
almost complete absence of hand-made pottery is remarkable.[5] It will be
clear how appropriate the term Sub-Mycenaean is: every shape, without
exception, can be shown to be descended, whether directly or indirectly,
from the preceding Mycenaean pottery. Standards had, however, deteriorated sharply; this applies not only to the making of the vase, but also to
the quality of the paint and to the decoration, which is of the simplest.
Horizontal wavy lines, vertical wiggly ones, variations of triangular complexes, hand-drawn semicircles, languettes – this is about all, until the
latest stage. It was a virtual bankruptcy; and it is not only that the decorations were simple, they were often carelessly applied. So often, especially
on the smaller vases, the potter took the easy way out, and covered most of
the vase with paint. In sum, it is very much a Dark Age style – even the
word 'style' is hardly appropriate.

It is difficult to make regional distinctions, because of the very small
number of vases involved – under forty from the whole of the Argolid,
fewer than twenty at Ancient Elis; Lefkandi is well represented with
nearly a hundred, but the tombs here belong to the latest stage of Sub-
Mycenaean; only in Athens and on Salamis (the two being closely related)
is there a substantial and continuous series. The clearest difference is, as
has been seen, in the distribution of amphoriskoi; there are other variations in popularity of shape and decorative motives, but until much more
evidence is available I would hesitate to commit myself to any specific
conclusions.

On the chronological side it is also difficult to recognise development or
progressive variation, as the style is bad, and the workmanship slovenly. It
has, however, been argued that the earliest Sub-Mycenaean of the Argolid
precedes that of Athens; and it is certainly true that in the former region
the connexion with the preceding L.H. III C is clearly visible, whereas in
the latter it is not. Apart from this it is evident, both from internal evidence
and from the succeeding Protogeometric style, that the stirrup jar was
gradually ousted by the lekythos.

So far, it must appear that the Sub-Mycenaean style of pottery was dull,
drab, and degenerate, defying clear analysis. Fortunately, this is not quite
all, for in Athens the ultimate stage of the Sub-Mycenaean style is somewhat apart, quite distinctive, and we can see improvements and fresh ideas
leading up to the introduction of the Protogeometric style. Improvement
was partly tectonic: the closed vases in particular start to assume a more
pleasing and proportioned ovoid shape, and it has been conjectured that a
faster-running potter's wheel was used from now on. In decoration, a
number of new motives appeared, such as the chequer design and the
solidly painted triangles and diamonds; motives were more copiously
used, series of panels of decoration are found, and more than one zone,
with careful and satisfying juxtaposition – and above all there was the new

---

[5] There are hand-made pyxides (small containers with a lid and fastening attachments) from
Athens; see p. 144.

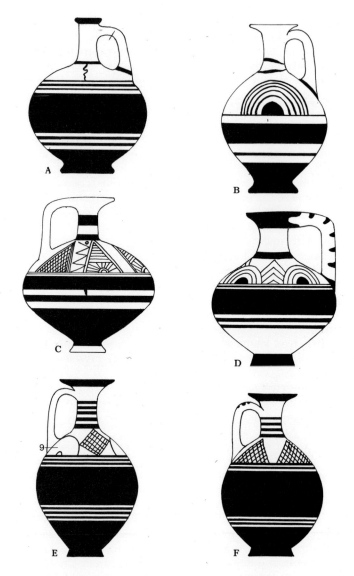

FIG. 6 LEKYTHOI
A) Athens, Sub-Myc.; ·14 m. *Ker.* I, pl. 12, no. 459.
B) Athens, Sub-Myc.; ·11 m. *Ker.* I, pl. 13, no. 494.
C) Kouklia, L.C. III; ·11 m. *RDAC* 1967, p. 13, fig. 8, no. 9.
D) Idalion, L.C. III; ·092 m. Karageorghis, *Nouveaux Documents,*
     p. 191, fig. 47, no. 13.
E) Athens, PG; ·17 m. *Ker.* IV, pl. 18, no. 2022.
F) Athens, PG; ·19 m. *Ker.* IV, pl. 19, no. 2086.

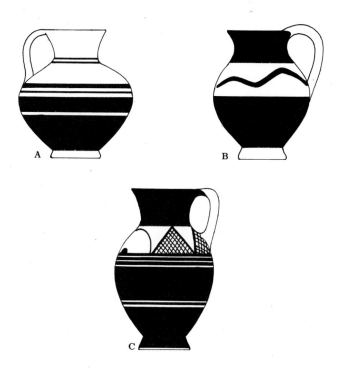

FIG. 7 JUGS
A) Athens, Sub-Myc.; ·06 m. *Ker.* I, pl. 25, no. 496.
B) Lefkandi, Sub-Myc.; ·07 m. Skoubris tomb 40.
C) Eleusis, PG; height unknown. *Ker.* I, pl. 48, no. 1085.

Athenian invention, the multiple brush fitted to one arm of a pair of com-
passes, whereby sets of circles and semicircles could be rendered with
geometrical exactness, and which is one of the most characteristic
features of the Protogeometric style, but appears for a while in context
with vases which are still Sub-Mycenaean. Finally, there was a surprising
number of vase types that were altogether new, most of which belong only
to this final phase. Thus one gets a small jar with almost vertical sides, best
described as a bottle, tripod vases, vases shaped like birds (duck vases),
boxes on four struts, a pyxis with high handles, a kantharos (a bowl with
vertical handles from body to lip), a ring vase, and a pilgrim flask. The
number of known shapes is just about doubled (see Pls. 2–4 and 6).
    At Lefkandi (see Pls. 39–40) a similar phenomenon is observable,
though here the vital spark which led the Athenian potter to experiment
with his decoration, and eventually to create a new style altogether, is
missing. But, as in Athens, one gets a number of vase types which supple-

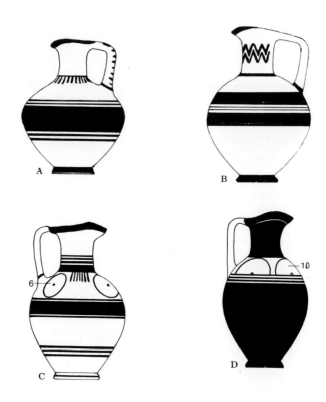

FIG. 8 TREFOIL-LIPPED OINOCHOAI
A) Athens, Sub-Myc.; ·20 m. *Ker.* I, pl. 24, no. 438.
B) Kourion, L.C. III; ·23 m. *AJA* 41, pl. IV, no. 69.
C) Athens, PG; ·27 m. *Ker.* I, pl. 68, no. 545.
D) Athens, PG; ·19 m. *Ker.* IV, pl. 15, no. 2072.

ment the basic nine already discussed. Here also there is a bottle-like vase,
and two duck vases. Several triple vases have been found, and three small
hydriai (with two belly handles and one vertical handle from shoulder to
lip); a large four-handled bowl is unique, and a three-handled high-
footed shallow bowl introduces a type which recurs later. In particular, the
low conical feet, and the ovoid shape of some closed vases, should be noted
for future reference. On the basis of this relatively large number of unusual shapes, from the fact that there were only two stirrup jars (and those
of poor workmanship), and from the appearance of dress pins of iron (see
p. 68), it is reasonable to conclude that these tombs were first used during
the concluding stages of Sub-Mycenaean.

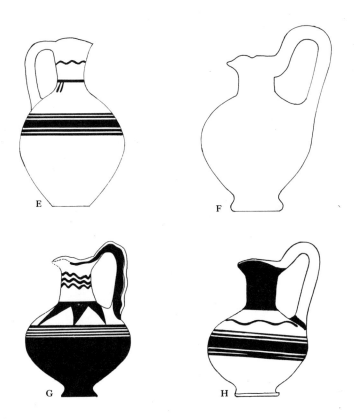

E) Knossos, PG; ·205 m. *BSA* 55, pl. 35, no. V8.
F) Athens, Sub-Myc.; ·09 m. *Ker* I, pl. 25, no. 511.
G) Kouklia, L.C. III; ·16 m. *RDAC* 1967, p. 13, fig. 8, no. 10.
H) Knossos, Sub-Min.; ·118 m. *BSA* 53–4, p. 241, fig. 27, no. VII 9.

    This evidence from Athens, and to a lesser extent from Lefkandi, is of particular importance because it constitutes the first breakthrough of the Dark Ages. What had happened? There is no doubt that the native genius of the Athenian potter had been awakened, but it was not spontaneous. There are a number of signs, both in vase types and in decoration system, that the awakening was due to contact with the pottery of Cyprus just at this time. To understand it, one must consider the earlier background of the situation in Cyprus, and discuss the style of pottery (L.C. III B) contemporary with Sub-Mycenaean.

FIG. 9 BOWLS AND SKYPHOI

A) Athens, Sub-Myc.; ·078 m. *Ker.* I, pl. 22, no. 434.
B) Athens, Sub-Myc.; ·088 m. *Ker.* I, pl. 23, no. 464.
C) Cyprus, unknown provenience, L.C. III; ·09 m. *CVA* Cyprus 2, pl. 24, no. 7.
D) Karphi, Sub-Min.; ·10 m. *BSA* 55, p. 21, fig. 14, no. 1.
E) Knossos, Sub-Min.; ·105 m. *Fortetsa*, pl. 3, no. 11.
F) Athens, PG; ·125 m. *Ker.* I, pl. 30, no. 525.
G) Athens, PG; ·16 m. *Ker.* IV, pl. 23, no. 2032.
H) Athens, PG; ·155 m. *Ker.* IV, pl. 22, no. 1091.

FIG. 10 CUPS

A) Athens, Sub-Myc.; ·082 m. *Ker*. I, pl. 23, no. 437.
B) Kourion, Cypro-Geometric I A; ·088 m. *LMTS*, pl. 15 *d*.
C) Karphi, Sub-Min.; ·07 m. *BSA* 55, p. 21, fig. 14, Cup 1.
D) Knossos, Sub-Min.; ·062 m. *Fortetsa*, pl. 3, no. 10.
E) Athens, PG; ·09 m. *Ker*. IV, pl. 24, no. 1082.
F) Athens, PG; ·127 m. *Ker*. IV, pl. 24, no. 1104.
G) Knossos, PG; ·133 m. *Fortetsa*, pl. 6, no. 57.

PLATE 2 BOTTLE-SHAPED VASES
A), B) Athens; ·097 m., ·121 m. *Ker*. I, pls. 27 and 37.
c) Cyprus; ·132 m. (Ashmolean Museum.)

PLATE 3 PILGRIM FLASKS
A) Athens; ·17 m. *Ker*. I, pl. 62.
B) Cyprus (Kouklia); ·18 m. *RDAC* 1967, pl. II, 16.

Late Cypriot III B Pottery

Briefly, the situation in Cyprus had been as follows. At about the same time as, or soon after, the catastrophes of the end of the thirteenth century on the mainland of Greece, Cyprus as well was visited by destructions. Whether Mycenaean migrants were responsible one cannot say, but it is clear that they arrived, and profited from the disaster: the characteristic pottery of some of the major sites on reoccupation was early Mycenaean III C, and the development of the bronze industry at this time can also probably be attributed to these new arrivals, suggesting that this was a migration of considerable importance, a further indication of which may be the fine and massive ashlar constructions which now appeared. This did not mean that native Cypriot features were overwhelmed and expelled, for the local pottery persisted. It may be that there was a fusion between the Mycenaeans and the surviving inhabitants. Also, there was no continuing influence from the Aegean (though the respective areas probably remained in touch): there is little or no trace in Cyprus of any of the elaborate Aegean styles of the twelfth century.

Any thought of peaceful progress was, in any case, rudely interrupted

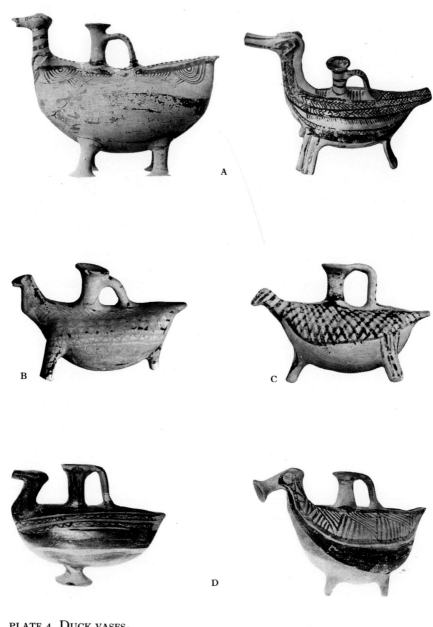

PLATE 4 DUCK VASES
A) Achaea; ·199 m., ·221 m. *AJA* 64, pl. 4, 45 and 46.
B), C) Athens; ·107 m., ·14 m. *AM* 78, Beil. 54; *AD* 23, ii, pl. 31 *c*.
D) Lefkandi; ·101 m., ·122 m. *Athens Annals* II, 101, fig. 8.

by a further wave of destructions, which seems to have occurred before the middle of the twelfth century, and ceramically it looks as though the Mycenaean inspiration virtually disappeared, as the local features of the pottery became much more prominent. Then, however, somewhere within the second half of the century, the same thing happened as before, a further arrival of migrants (very possibly in more than one wave) from the Mycenaean world, perhaps as a result of the events that led up to the final destruction of Mycenae. A new type of pottery, its main characteristic a fondness for wavy lines, especially on bowls, began to oust the previous mixture of local Cypriot, Late Cypriot III A (L.C. III A), and the few ceramic survivals of the earlier Mycenaean settlers, and in the end, towards the end of the century, it almost completely took over. But this was not quite all, for at about the turn of the century another group of newcomers made their way to Cyprus, and these came from Crete; the main evidence for their arrival seems to be the appearance of the terracotta figurines of goddesses with upraised arms, but the newcomers also brought their pottery with them and one or two features of this, as I shall explain later (pp. 57 ff.), were assimilated into the new style, L.C. III B, and lasted from perhaps shortly before 1100 to c. 1050 B.C., the latter date being calculated on the basis of connexions with Syria and Palestine. And it is in the latest phase of this style, originally mainly Aegean in inspiration, that we find our links with the latest Sub-Mycenaean.

In the analysis which follows I shall concentrate rather on the later phase. The earlier pottery displayed a preference for decoration in bulk, a sort of Close Style, and inclined to the curvilinear motive; later, motives were more sparingly applied, and it became a rather more open style, with rectilinear motives much more prominent, always with the exception of the by now traditional wavy line.

To start with, one may consider the nine vase shapes normally typical of Sub-Mycenaean central mainland Greece (see Figs. 1–10 where relevant). All are to be found in Cyprus, witnesses simply to the extent of the influence of Mycenaean pottery on the island – though that itself is an important fact.

The *neck-handled amphora* is very rare – only two examples known – and may be disregarded. The *belly-handled amphora* was, however, reasonably common, and the tendency was towards a straight neck and sharply everted lip. As to decoration, the belly always has the characteristic wavy-line motive, while the shoulder has a considerable variety of curvilinear and triangular motives. This particular shape could conceivably have provided the immediate inspiration for a similar one found in the latest stages of Sub-Mycenaean in Athens.

The *amphoriskos* was extremely popular, but the profile is usually sharper and better proportioned than in central Greece: as there, wavy lines adorn the belly, but in Cyprus the shoulder is also decorated. The *stirrup jar* was fairly common; the profile is also much sharper than in the Sub-Mycenaean series, and the shoulder decoration is susceptible of considerable complexity, and often includes a triangular motive enclosing a

FIG. 11 DUCK VASES
A) Kouklia. *RDAC* 1967, p. 15, fig. 10, no. 39.
B) Kouklia. *RDAC* 1967, p. 15, fig. 10, no. 40.
c) Idalion. Karageorghis, *Nouveaux Documents*, p. 189, fig. 46, no. 18.
D) Karphi. *BSA* 55, p. 27, fig. 20.
E) Vrokastro. *Vrokastro*, p. 152, fig. 92, 1.

semicircular one, the origin of which appears to be Minoan (see p. 57), and which was unknown to the Sub-Mycenaean potter. The *lekythos* is not quite so common, though prominent in a tomb at Idalion – whether in Cyprus it was thought of as an alternative to the stirrup jar I am not sure. The shoulder decoration, triangles and semicircles, is very similar to that of the Sub-Mycenaean style (much cleaner looking, though), but the air-hole is not so often found, and the handle invariably comes up to the lip, not to the neck.

There are a number of *jugs*, usually plain, of a rather different type from the Sub-Mycenaean ones. There are also several *trefoil-lipped oinochoai*, divisible into two types, one with handle to the lip, and wavy lines on the neck (a common feature on certain other shapes), and one with a handle up which a snake climbs, rising above the level of the lip, wavy lines on the

PLATE 5 KALATHOI
A) Cyprus (Kouklia); ·15 m. *RDAC* 1967, pl. I.
B) Knossos; ·125 m. *Fortetsa*, pl. 3, 1.

neck, and cross-hatched triangles or filled pendent triangles on the shoulder – altogether more elaborate than in central Greece. *Bowls* are common. They have high conical or flaring feet (conceivably this also was an idea adopted by the Athenian potter), and the body tends to be rather angular. Bands are the only decoration, as a rule – the wavy line is almost totally absent from the tomb groups (mainly late L.C. III B) that we have: and this is curious, since the wavy line was extremely common on bowls in the earlier settlement material and is indeed, as I have said, one of the main indications of a new migratory descent from the Aegean in the latter part of the twelfth century. The answer must be that this motive had gone out

PLATE 6
A) Tripod bowl, Athens. *Ker.* I, pl. 64, no. 555.
B) Duck vase, Cyprus (Kouklia). *RDAC* 1967, pl. III, no. 41.

of fashion for bowls (only ?) by late L.C. III B. *Cups*, finally, are high footed
– and always have the wavy line.

So far, then, there is some concordance between the Cypriot shapes and
those of Sub-Mycenaean. There are, however, other shapes as well. Of
these, the *kantharos*, which does not make its way to Greece at all at this
time (unless there is a possible link with a not unsimilar late Sub-
Mycenaean vase), is common; *kalathoi* can be exotically decorated
(Pl. 5), but are few in number, as are the *kylikes*, both remnants of the
Mycenaean tradition, which also have no place in Sub-Mycenaean
Greece. Nor do the *shallow bowls*, which seem to belong to the native
tradition. But then there are four shapes which are characteristic of the
Cypriot style, the *bottles* and *duck vases* (with or without bird head),
found surprisingly frequently; and *ring vases* and *pilgrim flasks*, rather
more rare. The first two in particular are typical of the later stage of
L.C. III B and of the transition to Cypro-Geometric: and these are the
four which appear in Athens or at Lefkandi just at the time of transition
from Sub-Mycenaean to Protogeometric (see Pls. 2–4 and Fig. 11). So it
seems extremely likely from these shapes that there was a connexion between Cyprus and at least Athens at this time, and that the influence was
from Cyprus. We have already seen that the particular shape of the
L.C. III B belly-handled amphora may have been transmitted, and perhaps even the conical foot for bowls and cups. As well as this, there is some
evidence for borrowing in decoration, not in any particular motive, perhaps, but in the conception of the system. It is worth while, in this context,
comparing the decorative system of a duck vase from Cyprus with that of
two tripod bowls from Athens – and it will be noted that in each case a

circular vertical handle has been incorporated into the making of the vase (Pl. 6). These various features, taken as a whole, very strongly suggest an impressive influence of Cypriot over Athenian pottery at a time when, on the one hand, L.C. III B pottery was nearing its end and moving toward Cypro-Geometric I, and when, on the other hand, Sub-Mycenaean was ready for transformation into Protogeometric in Athens. And since the date in Cyprus is reasonably fixed somewhere near 1050 B.C., a similar date must be applicable for the end of Sub-Mycenaean in Athens.

Why the influence of Cypriot pottery should have been felt in Athens at this particular time, and no other, is a question to which I suggest an answer later (pp. 82 f.). Why it should have happened at all is, I think, fairly clear. It is true that in shape and decorative elements the two styles show many similarities, but while in the Sub-Mycenaean area the potter's inspiration was dead or moribund, in Cyprus one gets the impression of a living style. The technique and quality are better, the profiles sharper; decoration was applied with a sense of proportion, and there were many variations and juxtapositions which show the (limited) inventiveness of the potter – nor was he afraid to introduce human and animal figures. On the whole, the Cypriots appreciated a nicely decorated vase. The essential difference is between the purposeful and the purposeless, and it is therefore only natural that those in the Sub-Mycenaean area, when they encountered the Cypriot style, should borrow from it.

Epilogue on Cyprus

The Cretan links with Cyprus, briefly mentioned above, open the door for a return to the Aegean, and a survey both of the general background and of the pottery style of Crete at this time. Before going on to this, however, it is worth while asking whether the reasonable quality and liveliness of the Cypriot L.C. III B pottery style meant that Cyprus was in a flourishing state in the first half of the eleventh century.

On the surface, one would expect a period of depression such as apparently, to judge from its pottery, existed in the Sub-Mycenaean area. There had been two waves of destruction in the preceding hundred years or so, and at the beginning of the eleventh century there was the supplementary visitation of an earthquake. And on at least three occasions the island had been descended upon by newcomers from the Aegean. But the first destruction had not been altogether a disaster; the infusion of Mycenaean stock acted as a spur, especially in the bronze and ivory industries and perhaps also in architectural skills. Then, however, there was the second destruction. This was certainly of some magnitude, but it does not appear to have led to a complete loss of culture, even though it resulted in further depopulation. During the twelfth century, for example, we find that the island was in fairly continuous contact with other lands of the east Mediterranean, and it was at this time that the knowledge how to work in iron was introduced, although it was not, so far as we know, much used.

PLATE 7 PYXIDES
A) Cyprus; ·134 m. *CVA* Cyprus 2, pl. 33, 1.
B) Karphi; ·17 m., ·16 m. *BSA* 55, pl. 7, K22, K115.

During the first half of the eleventh century we get the following rather hazy picture. Our knowledge of the period is based on six sites only (and little enough material from these): Enkomi and its successor Salamis, Kition, Idalion, Kourion, Kouklia (Old Paphos), and Lapithos on the north coast. In view of the thoroughness of survey in Cyprus, this may represent the true state of affairs reasonably accurately, and it therefore looks as though the total population was very small, in spite of the new influxes. The various skills, whether Aegean or Cypriot, were not lost. The excavations at Kition have revealed that building and rebuilding in stone went on, even after the earthquake. There is evidence for bronze and ivory-working, though not so impressive nor so plentiful as in the twelfth century. And there are a few objects of iron – indeed, as we shall see, it was almost certainly from Cyprus that the knowledge how to work this metal was introduced to Athens and Lefkandi, from the iron objects there found, at precisely the same time as we get the influence of Cypriot pottery.

What one gets, then, is a picture of very mediocre prosperity, but one of peace, in which the arts and crafts were still appreciated — it is perhaps symptomatic of settled conditions that the inhabitants of Kition decided not to rebuild their town wall after the earthquake. In relation to Sub-Mycenaean central Greece, Cyprus can be called almost flourishing, and one can hardly speak of a Dark Age here.

We can now come back to the analysis of styles, and proceed to discuss the situation in Crete. The following ceramic elements were common to this island and Cyprus in the first half of the eleventh century: for vase types, the feeding-bottle (a spouted jug), the duck vase, the bottle, the kantharos, the amphoriskos with false spout by one handle, and the pyxis with high handles; for decoration, the triangle enclosing a semicircle, the wild goat, and possibly the birds (see Pl. 7 and Figs. 4 and 11). All these, it has been claimed — with the exception of the amphoriskos — could have come from Crete to Cyprus, about 1100 B.C. or shortly afterwards. In fact, one can be reasonably certain about the direction of transmission only for the pyxis, the wild goat (the characteristic Cretan *agrimi*), and the triangle enclosing the semicircle — and even for this latter decorative motive I am not entirely certain.

It is in any case desirable that the Cretan pottery should be discussed, and this requires, as for Cyprus and for Sub-Mycenaean, a brief introduction. Unfortunately, matters are not quite so clear-cut as in the other two areas.

The Sub-Minoan Pottery of Crete

The Minoan ceramic tradition was as persistent as the Mycenaean; and the difference between Late Minoan III B (thirteenth century) and Sub-Minoan (roughly the first half of the eleventh century) was just as great as between L.H. III B and Sub-Mycenaean. The interval between was in Crete, as on the Greek mainland, a time of stress, reflected not so much in actual destruction as in traces of the arrival of newcomers, including Mycenaeans, in the desertion of old sites and the occupation of new ones, and particularly in the foundation of new settlements which were naturally fortified and sometimes remote and inaccessible.

About 1200 B.C., the abandonment of a number of sites (settlements and cemeteries) and the creation of new ones, in central and east Crete, was accompanied by the appearance, alongside Minoan ware, of pottery clearly displaying the influence of early L.H. III C. There follows a blend of an open style with an elaborate one, very much as happened in Greece and the central Aegean. The open style combined the Minoan and Mycenaean strains; the elaborate style, known as the Fringed Style, was something new, but based on earlier developments in Crete itself. One of its principal manifestations was the octopus motive as applied to stirrup jars, and here the influence on the parallel style current in the central Aegean is undeniable, and it must be in part contemporary with it. In Crete, however, the idea of elaboration was not confined to stirrup jars (nor were octopods the sole decoration for this type of vase): the elaborate style is to be found on most vases where a good area of relatively level surface allowed it – bowls and kraters, tankards and pyxides (see Pls. 7 and 20). It was a very flamboyant style, full of curves, and often with the distinctive fringes that have given rise to its name (Fig. 12); and animals and birds also had their part to play in it. It is of interest that much of our evidence comes from Karphi, a most remote and inhospitable settlement on a north-western spur of the Dictaean range, founded during this period; the pottery at least suggests, not a rather depressed community, as one might expect, but an atmosphere of lively inventiveness, and it is clear that touch was not lost with the rest of the island – nor with regions beyond (see pp. 120 ff.). So far as concerns the pottery, in fact, we can deal with the central and eastern parts of Crete as a fairly homogeneous whole – as to western Crete the situation is not yet clear, though it is known that there was settlement there during the twelfth century.

When we come to Sub-Minoan we find that the Fringed Style has been much diluted and constricted, and for the most part discarded; and we also find that most of the decorative motives of the open style have been forgotten. Instead, we encounter something very like the simplification and geometricisation that is so characteristic of Sub-Mycenaean; as with Sub-Mycenaean, and indeed as with L.C. III B, the rectilinear tends in time to supplant the curvilinear; and there is a similar tendency either not to apply decoration at all or to cover large areas of the vase with paint.

What produced this change or deterioration is not clear, but there may well have been some unrest. Certain new ceramic elements seem to have been introduced by the latter-day Mycenaeans, and the emigration of a number of Cretans to Cyprus c. 1100 is a factor that suggests some trouble on the island. This I shall come back to later (p. 114); for the moment it is the relationship of Sub-Minoan to Sub-Mycenaean and L.C. III B that is the subject of discussion.

A brief analysis of the shapes current in Sub-Minoan will serve to illustrate the similarities and differences. There is, however, one important preliminary difference in the nature of the material, in that whereas in Sub-Mycenaean central Greece and in Cyprus I have concentrated almost entirely on vases deposited as offerings in tombs, in Crete the major role played by the settlement of Karphi during this period means that one cannot fairly discuss the Sub-Minoan style without taking its pottery into account. The pottery also from the settlement of Kastri (in the east of the island), though it may not continue into the Sub-Minoan period, has some relevance.

First the nine vase types which were defined as basic to Sub-Mycenaean (see Figs. 1–10 where relevant).

The *neck-handled amphora* was a rarity in tombs – there is only one,

FIG. 12 SHERDS OF CRETAN FRINGED STYLE FROM KARPHI
Karphi. *BSA* 55, p. 33, fig. 23 *c*; p. 35, fig. 25 *g*.

from the Gypsades cemetery near Knossos: its handles come up to the lip, the body is oval, sliced off by a flat base (a feature common to Cretan pottery now and later), and the only decoration is thin bands enclosing a thick one below the shoulder, two bands of medium size below the belly, and a simple curvilinear motive on the shoulder. A non-Minoan shape, it could have been introduced from the Mycenaean area not long before the start of Sub-Minoan, as other similar amphorae have been found at Kastri, thought to have been deserted before this time, as well as at Karphi.

The *belly-handled amphora* was perhaps introduced later than the neck-handled variety, since the shape is not known either at Kastri or at Karphi. The only two so far found come from the Knossos area, the one from Gypsades, the other from Ayios Ioannis. The necks are of medium height, painted, and the lips flare sharply outwards; the two bodies differ somewhat in profile, but neither is well proportioned, and both end in a flat base. The decoration is one of sets of thin and thick encircling bands, with simple motives in between, wavy lines on the belly in both cases and, for the Gypsades amphora, languettes, vertical lines, and cross-hatching on the shoulder. The type could have been introduced from Cyprus, even as perhaps it was into Sub-Mycenaean.

Closely related to these are two vases from Phaestos, the only main difference in shape being the addition of two small handles on the shoulder. As to decoration, the one resembles those from the Knossos area, but the other, with its dark-ground effect, is much more elaborate; the reserved bands round the neck recall the Cypriot practice, but it would be rash to conclude that there was any influence.

Amphoriskoi with belly handles are almost as rare as amphorae – one in the Spring Chamber sanctuary at Knossos, one and possibly a few more

from Karphi, and one at Kavousi in east Crete. Their origin was presumably Mycenaean, but the neck is rather wider than in L.H. III C. Necks
and handles are painted, but little of the body except for a band round the
belly and vertical strokes or zigzags above it. There is also one example,
from the Teke area (tomb Π), of a variant type, with false spout beside one
of the handles, and decoration of rather late schematised Fringed Style;
the point of interest is that not unsimilar ones have been found in tombs
of latish L.C. III B date in Cyprus.

As opposed to the amphoriskoi, *stirrup jars* were common, nor do they,
as happened in Sub-Mycenaean, lose popularity during this period –
indeed, they are still to be found well into the succeeding Protogeometric
style. There is a considerable variation in size and profile; the custom of
inserting an airhole had made its way to Crete, but was by no means always
used, and the disks of the 'stirrup' are usually either flat or with only a
slight knob. The system of decoration was quite different from that of
Sub-Mycenaean; apart from the rare and debilitated survivals of the
octopus decoration, the usual shoulder motives are triangles with rectilinear or curvilinear fillings – there seems to have been a sort of horror of
simplicity – or a triangle enclosing a semicircle, again with the interstices
filled, a feature frequently found in Cyprus in L.C. III B (pp. 51 f.), and
forming one of the main ceramic links between the two islands. Indeed,
Cyprus and Crete share very much the same spirit of decoration in general
for their stirrup jars.

With the stirrup jar retaining its popularity it is not surprising to find
that *lekythoi* are poorly represented; I know of only one, from the Kephala
tomb near Knossos, and this is closer to L.H. III C than to Sub-Mycenaean.

There is little that need be said about the *one-handled jugs*, as this is a
type of vase that may be found anywhere. There are only a few of them,
very simply decorated. *Trefoil-lipped oinochoai* were also scarce – one at
Vrokastro in east Crete, one from the Gypsades cemetery, and one from a
tomb at Liliana near Phaestos. The only noteworthy feature is the thick
wavy line round the neck of the oinochoe from Vrokastro, which may just
possibly reflect Cypriot practice.

Bowls were common. There are two main types, of which the earlier is
shallow, and has relatively vertical walls to the belly, then turning sharply
inwards to the foot. There were two of these in the reoccupation level of
the Kephala tomb, and a fair number at Karphi; they tend to have fairly
elaborate and varied decoration, and some could well belong to Late
Minoan III C rather than to Sub-Minoan. On the other hand, three from
a tomb at Phaestos have the straight-sided and angular look, but are
deeper and painted all over, and these must be Sub-Minoan. They may
represent a half-way house to the second type, which is relatively deep, has
a gently curving profile, and seems clearly to have its roots in Late Mycenaean III C of the Granary class. They may be painted all over, one bowl
has a rough zigzag in a panel between the handles, and several display the
very late Mycenaean practice of leaving the lower body and foot unpainted
– it was presumably from this type, perhaps in combination with the

amphoriskos, that there eventually developed the extremely distinctive and widespread vase known as the miniature bell-krater, characteristic rather of the ninth century, but whose early evolution belongs to Sub-Minoan.

Cups, nothing like so common as bowls, may also be divided into the two varieties, shallow with straight sides – as at Karphi where there is often the curious feature of blobs of paint dabbed on the sides – and with a curved profile, of which a few have been found at Knossos (but not elsewhere), usually clay ground with zigzag or vertical-stroke motives – no wavy lines – just one being painted all over except for the lower body.

So far, it is reasonable to conclude that these vase types of the Sub-Minoan period show some influence from some stage of L.H. III C, and that there are one or two points of contact with Cyprus; but they have little in common with Sub-Mycenaean except through the earlier Mycenaean influence. One would be hard put to it to find links with the Minoan pottery of the thirteenth century, and there are few traces left even of the twelfth-century Fringed Style.

This is, however, only half the story, as there were at least ten other shapes current in Sub-Minoan. Some of these need only a passing mention: Karphi produced a couple of small broad-bellied *jars* (*pithoi*), and also a fair number of *two-handled jugs* (a kind of miniature neck-handled amphora), of which latter type only one other is known, from the Kephala tomb. One of the Karphiot tombs (for it had a cemetery as well as a settlement) contained the only example of a *bottle-shaped vase*, perhaps to be connected with those from Cyprus. There are just two *kantharoi* – again, maybe, a link with Cyprus – one from Karphi and one from the Liliana cemetery. About a dozen *feeding-bottles* (spouted jugs with basket handle) were found at Karphi, but elsewhere only one, from the Liliana cemetery.[6] Vases of this type have been found both on the Greek mainland and in Cyprus.

The appearance of a few *kylikes* in eastern Crete (Karphi, Vrokastro, Dreros) is of interest. Unknown in the Sub-Mycenaean area, this vase type persisted to a late stage elsewhere – Kephallenia, Ithaca, north-west Greece, west Thessaly (see pp. 88 ff.), at Lefkandi (the late L.H. III C settlement), and in Cyprus. Characteristics of this late stage are a conical body shape, and swollen or ribbed stems, and these are known in Crete (though not the ribbed stems). It was not really a Minoan shape (there was a one-handled version which survived into the twelfth century at Kastri), but it is by no means obvious where this particular variant came from. The Vrokastro and Karphi kylikes might in any case belong to Late Minoan III C rather than to Sub-Minoan.

Then there is the *bird vase* (Fig. 11). There are more than ten of these, of Sub-Minoan date, and they are to be found in all parts of Crete from which our material comes. There are two main classes: both have a spout at the front, and a carrying handle on the back, and linear decoration, but the one has a single ring base or a highish foot, while the other has three

[6] In the Knossos district, the shape appeared in the Protogeometric period, so it may be accidental that none has yet turned up in a Sub-Minoan context.

little stumpy legs. Properly speaking, in fact, the name 'bird vase' is not really applicable. As we have seen, such vases appear both in the Sub-Mycenaean area and in Cyprus. In Sub-Mycenaean there are bird heads and no spouts: in Cyprus both varieties are known, so this island could be the common source (as I believe), or else the spouted type was transmitted from Crete to Cyprus, transformed into the bird-headed type, and then passed on to Athens and Lefkandi. The problem is, however, slightly complicated by the fact that three of these, fully-fledged and bird-headed, have been found in the latest chamber tombs of a site in Achaea, with L.H. III C pottery: these, and the conclusions they lead to, I shall discuss later (p. 93).[7]

As opposed to the kylix and the bird vase, the *pyxis* (Pl. 7) is a characteristically Cretan shape. It may be straight-sided, with concave neck and two vertical handles from just below the neck to the rim, but this version is only found once, in the Teke cemetery. The usual type is also straight-sided, but had vertical handles along all or part of the sides to above the rim. It was particularly popular at Karphi, where it was often vividly decorated, and it has also been found at Kavousi and in the Gypsades cemetery – and is known to continue into the Protogeometric period in both north and south central Crete. The type provides a further example of communication between Crete and Cyprus, for a recently published pyxis of this type from Cyprus, with remarkable decoration (Pl. 7) and datable to L.C. III B, certainly got its inspiration from Crete. Oddly enough, there is a vase from Lefkandi, of Late Sub-Mycenaean or Early Protogeometric date, which is by no means unsimilar in shape to the Cretan pyxides – but its decoration is so dull and simple that it is difficult to imagine that there was any direct contact between Lefkandi and Crete. And yet its appearance requires some explanation.

Another shape, characteristic of Sub-Minoan, was the *kalathos*, the wide, shallow bowl, which had no place in the Sub-Mycenaean series. There is a handleless variant, and a two-handled one. The former is a well-known Minoan type, usually plain, probably used for religious offerings. The latter is further divisible in accordance with the type of handle: those with vertical handles to the rim or on the rim belong to the Minoan tradition, but those with two horizontal handles below the rim, usually banded, and with the occasional horizontal wavy line between the handles, are of late Mycenaean parentage, and have been found only in the Knossos district and in the plain of the Mesara.

Finally there is the *krater*. Here we have a shape whose origin is probably traceable to the early L.H. III C ceramic influence, but was enthusiastically accepted by the Minoan potters, and which in the course of Late Minoan III C was one of the chief recipients of the Fringed Style. The only known pieces that presumably belong to Sub-Minoan are the three fragments from the Spring Chamber sanctuary, whose decoration exhibits the dying phase of the Fringed Style. Outside the island there is, unfortunately, little comparable material, chiefly due to the lack of settlement evidence,

---

[7] There are also two from L.H. III C chamber tombs on Naxos.

but one krater sherd from Kition in Cyprus could even have been imported from Crete.

The review of these additional vase types serves if anything further to emphasise the differences between Sub-Minoan Crete and Sub-Mycenaean mainland central Greece, on the one hand, and on the other hand to confirm the links between Crete and Cyprus (not that there was a complete absence of communication between Crete and central Greece, as will be seen, p. 119). One also gets the impression that Crete's links with its own Minoan past, though there, had become appreciably weaker.

It is possible to point to differences in use of vase types as between one region and another, for example between north and south central Crete, and between these and eastern Crete, but the meagreness of the material robs such differences of much of their significance. The conclusion is that there was a distinctive (though not always too easily distinguishable) style current in Crete, called Sub-Minoan – not altogether happily, for it was not of a single origin. It may further be concluded that this style was at least partly contemporary both with L.C. III B in Cyprus and with Sub-Mycenaean, since the latter phase of L.C. III B coincided with the period of transition from Sub-Mycenaean to Protogeometric, and since there are clear links between Cyprus and Sub-Minoan Crete during most if not the whole of L.C. III B. Doubts and difficulties remain – for example, the direction of certain ceramic influences between the two islands could affect the relative chronology, and there is always the problem of localised survival. It would in any case seem very likely that Sub-Minoan pottery was in use in Crete throughout the eleventh century.

3 Sub-Mycenaean Central Greece

Having reviewed the three early Dark Age ceramic styles of central Greece, Crete, and Cyprus, given a brief account of their respective twelfth-century backgrounds, and established that they were more or less contemporary and covered at least the first half of the eleventh century, it is now possible to return to the crucial Sub-Mycenaean area, and consider it in greater depth and detail.

Since *Athens* affords the fullest known evidence, and since the chronological sequence is clearest, especially at the time just before, and of, the first appearance of Protogeometric pottery, it will be best to start there (see the plan, p. 136).

Whereas there had been Mycenaean settlement on the north slope of the Acropolis, and even on the Acropolis itself for a while during the twelfth century, what we know of the Sub-Mycenaean period indicates that the then inhabitants occupied the relatively unprotected ground of the Agora, where there had been no previous Mycenaean buildings. This conclusion is based on the number of pits and wells containing Sub-Mycenaean (and later, Protogeometric) pottery in that area; no house foundations have been uncovered, but this is hardly surprising in a district continuously built over ever since then until modern times.

The bulk of our material comes, however, not from these pits and wells, but from the cemeteries, and it is most impressive. The main cemetery of some hundred and twenty tombs is that of the Kerameikos, about a mile north-west of the Acropolis; but there were other smaller groups, between the Kerameikos and the Acropolis, on the Acropolis itself (astonishingly, as it was at no other time used for burials), and to the south and east of it. Recent excavations are widening the circle, and the ever-growing total of graves shows that there must have been a sizeable population at this time, certainly much greater than in the recent (or even perhaps the distant) past; it is my impression – but no more than that – that as the Sub-Mycenaean period, the early Dark Ages, progressed, the inhabited area gradually increased, and continued to do so in the later Dark Ages.

Most of the burials were within cist tombs, in other words individual graves lined and covered with slabs (see Fig. 28, p. 269): these were the earliest, and continued throughout the period. A number of earth-cut graves, not among the earliest, were also found, these being similar to the cist tombs but lacking the lining of slabs. The dead were usually laid out in an extended position, with arms folded; these, then, were all inhumations, and this practice persisted till the end of Sub-Mycenaean; at some time during the period, however, cremation started to be used, and towards the end became much more common until, at a time roughly contemporaneous with the start of the Protogeometric style, it was adopted as the universal practice for adults.

As to the offerings within the graves, I have already discussed the pottery, and will only stress again one or two points: first, the gradual take-over by the lekythos from the stirrup jar; and second, the whole situation at the end of the period, when there was a brief phase of experiment and re-thinking of ideas, started by contact with Cyprus and its pottery, culminating in the local genius who set the Protogeometric style on its way.

The chief objects other than pottery were those of personal adornment (see Chapter 20), finger rings, fibulae (brooches), and long dress pins.

Rings were the most numerous: women's graves often contained several, while men are not known to have had more than one.[1] There were over seventy of them, almost all of bronze; at least eight, however, were of iron, in all except one case belonging to the end of Sub-Mycenaean – the importance of this metal needs emphasis, as it was precisely during the early Dark Ages that it started to be worked in Greece and the Aegean. The iron rings and most of the bronze ones are plain, the bands sometimes thin, sometimes massive, at times a complete circle, at other times with the ends overlapping. Three unusual types, all of bronze, deserve mention: five tombs contained rings made by twisting wire into a double or triple spiral; eight tombs had in all nine rings with a shield-like bezel of Mycenaean type, two of them however having an impressed dotted decoration unfamiliar to the Mycenaean world; and there is one ring, from a fairly late context, of a northern type, with double-spiral terminals (see Pl. 60, p. 303).

Fibulae were also numerous, chiefly due to the thirteen found in Kerameikos tomb 108 (Pl. 8). All are of bronze, and have been found in male as well as in female burials. As with the rings, they disappear completely from the latest tombs of this period, and only reappear in Late Protogeometric – I think this may be accidental. As to the shapes, there were only two of the violin-bow type (Fig. 34), and the rest were arched fibulae or some variant of this type (Fig. 34). The two violin-bow fibulae were both found in the latish tomb 108 (in company with eleven arched fibulae and twenty rings, see Pl. 8), and they are of the kind with leaf-shaped bow, with incised decoration on it. Of the arched fibulae there were over thirty (this is, indeed, the characteristic early Dark Age type); the arches are sometimes plain, sometimes of twisted wire; occasionally, instead of a regular arch, they are stilted, and the arches gradually develop two strengthening nodules, a feature that became more or less standard in the subsequent period in Athens. It is not clear exactly how these fibulae were placed on the dress, but recent research has suggested that they were shawl attachments (see pp. 295 f.).

---

[1] It is a curious fact that during the last stage of the Sub-Mycenaean period, and throughout Protogeometric, rings were only very rarely found – there might be some connexion with the rite of cremation, but the persistence as offerings of pins argues against this.

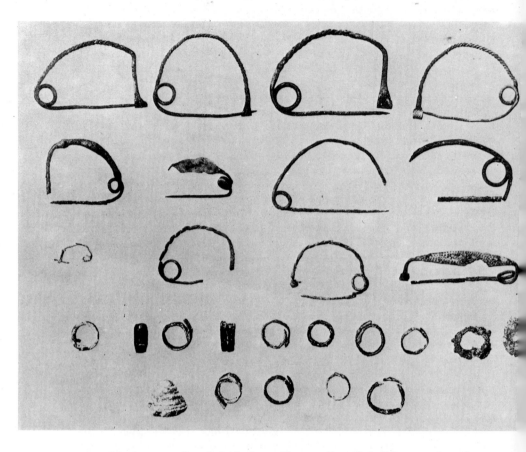

PLATE 8 ATHENS. Small finds from Kerameikos Sub-Myc. tomb 108. *Ker.* I, pl. 28.

The long dress pins – an adjunct to the dress which had no place whatever in the Mycenaean world – are hardly less numerous than the fibulae. Principally to be found in female burials, they are nevertheless not entirely unknown for men, and are usually to be found in pairs, one on each shoulder, thus indicating their position on the dress. Their length is prodigious, varying between twenty-five and fifty centimetres.

There are two main types (Fig. 33, p. 296). Type A has a globular bulb near the top, and a curved or nail-like head; type B has no bulb, but an elongated swelling where the bulb would be in type A and, often, shallow incised rings above and below this swelling; the head may just be plain or have a slight protuberance. It is difficult to establish which type was the first to appear, but by the Protogeometric period type A had completely taken over. There is also one dress pin of unusual type, with a thick rectangular shaft forming its upper part – it appears to be related to type B. Finally, there are two much shorter pins, with roll-top heads, associated with the later burials (Fig. 32 for both types).

The metal was usually bronze, but there were five pins of iron, one of which had a spherical ivory head, and all from the latest tombs.

One would have expected to find numerous weapons, but these seem to be confined to the very end of the Sub-Mycenaean period and to two tombs (Figs. 38, 39A): one contained an iron sword, the other an iron dagger (with bronze rivets) and a bronze spearhead.[2] All were of types known to the previous Mycenaean world, but the sword was of a particular sub-type best known in Cyprus, so there may be yet another instance of Cypriot influence (see pp. 141 f.).

As well as these, there were fragments of iron, ivory, and wood, whose purpose is not clear, and a bronze bracelet. And finally, there were just a few spiraliform rings for the hair, and these were the only objects of gold; what is notable is that two of them were made of doubled wire (Pl. 60), a technique unknown to the Mycenaean world, and of northern origin.

A fair amount of space has been devoted to describing the material from Athens, but, as the various features recur elsewhere in the Sub-Mycenaean area, other sites can be dealt with more briefly. So far as cemeteries are concerned, Athens provides the following pattern. Cist tombs and earth-cut graves were the custom. Until nearly the end of the period, the objects deposited were vases of uniform lifelessness, rings, fibulae, and dress pins, all of bronze except for one iron ring, one or two hair spirals of gold, a few other miscellaneous objects, but no weapons. At the end of Sub-Mycenaean the picture is different: an increasing number of cremations, a renaissance in the pottery, no fibulae, very few finger rings but including iron ones, pins both of bronze and iron, gold hair spirals, and a very few weapons.

The natural site to follow Athens is the hundred-tomb cemetery on the nearby island of *Salamis*. All burials, except for two (perhaps three) cases of cremation, were inhumations in cist tombs, but here there was a difference from Athens in that the dead were buried in a contracted position. The pottery is entirely similar to that of Athens, but has been considered, on grounds of style, to have started a little earlier; at the other end, there is no trace of the transitional period which culminated in the Proto-geometric style. The other types of object are also the same. The rings included fragments of the shield-bezel type, and there was one iron ring. The fibulae were all of the simple arched variety, and the pins, like the fibulae all of bronze, were of type A, except for one roll-top one. Apart from this there were three hair rings of gold wire, a shallow bronze bowl, two beads of glass, a bead of faience, and the steatite head of a pin.

From Salamis it is best to turn to the easternmost site, that of *Lefkandi*,[3] on the south-west coast of Euboea, where in some respects the same pattern

---

[2] A bronze shield-boss (Pl. 25) was the only item of armour – used to cover the mouth of a cremation urn, as later.

[3] For a discussion of the history of this site as a whole, see pp. 188 ff.

is found as at Athens in the latest phase of Sub-Mycenaean. Here there had been a fairly flourishing settlement, inhabited throughout L.H. III C times, with the final phase exhibiting a sharp decline in the quality of the pottery. After this there was a break, as the next identifiable settlement material is no earlier than the last quarter of the tenth century. No tombs of the Mycenaean period have yet been found, but a few hundred yards from the settlement a cemetery (called the Skoubris cemetery, to distinguish it from the other cemeteries nearby, see pp. 188 f.) has so far produced over sixty tombs, associated with pyres, and containing material that partially covers the gap in occupation mentioned above: most of the tombs can be dated to Late Sub-Mycenaean or to Early Protogeometric, just four being appreciably later, Early Geometric of the ninth century.[4]

So far as concerns the Sub-Mycenaean period, the manner of burial shows a variation on the Athenian pattern, in that the tombs contained only the offerings to the dead, while the dead themselves were cremated in the nearby pyres. As to the offerings (Pls. 39–40), the pottery seems to show only the latest stage of Sub-Mycenaean, as has been seen. The other objects do not contradict this judgment, and in certain instances confirm it; and they are of very much the same type as in Athens. Finger rings were reasonably common, with nothing unusual about their shape, except for fragments of what is almost certainly another of the kind with double-spiral terminals. Fibulae were most numerous (eleven in one tomb); there were three with leaf-shaped bow, but most were of the arched type (some of twisted wire) or stilted. There were not so many dress pins, but both types A and B were found. These are the three regular and generally recurring types of dress accessory, and two significant points may be noted. First, the fibulae and finger rings are present in much greater quantity than in Athens at this time; and second, iron as well as bronze was used – not for rings, only rarely for the fibulae, but so far for the majority of the dress pins.[5] Apart from these, there were hair rings and an earring, all of gold except for one of bronze – it is a curious fact that the only known gold objects of this period were hair accessories – a number of sea shells, a necklace made up of tiny faience beads, and an iron dagger,[6] of much the same type as that found at Tiryns.

It will be clear that this is a site of considerable importance, in certain ways the equal of Athens. Whether it can be taken as representative of Euboea as a whole is very doubtful, though the very slight evidence from *Chalcis* suggests the same situation, the arrival of the Sub-Mycenaean culture during its final phase. The significance of this I shall discuss later (pp. 78 f.).

---

[4] It is very possible that the Mycenaean settlement may have persisted during much of the early phase of the Dark Ages. The presence of one lekythos, of latest L.H. III C type, said to have been found in a tomb, now destroyed, of this cemetery, suggests an almost complete chronological continuity.

[5] Certainly contemporaneous: as fibulae and dress pins both in bronze and in iron were found in the same tombs.

[6] This might be Early Protogeometric in date rather than Sub-Mycenaean (Pl. 41).

Back on the mainland, Boeotia can surely be included in the area covered by the new culture, but so far only on the basis of a small cemetery of eleven cist tombs at *Thebes*, which has produced vases ranging from Sub-Mycenaean to Protogeometric. These tombs, it is worth noting, either overlay or cut into an earlier Mycenaean settlement.

Whether Phocis, north of Boeotia, also belongs to the Sub-Mycenaean sphere I am not sure, and so shall discuss its evidence at a later period, when dealing with what I have termed the Northern Crescent (p. 105). We can then turn to the north-east Peloponnese.

The evidence from Corinthia is slight, but sufficient to show that it belongs within the central Sub-Mycenaean area. At *Isthmia*, a single sherd only of this period has been recovered – unconnected with any Mycenaean pottery. At *Corinth*, however, as well as a handful of sherds, traces have been discovered of a rather poor house; all we have is a hearth and five vases – witness perhaps to the low standard of life at this time. And most recently, valuable confirmation of occupation during the period has been revealed, in the shape of two pit graves, with child inhumations, very contracted. The one, with two burials, contained a lekythos, an arched fibula, and a fragmentary bronze pin (in other words, the usual pattern); the other had an arched fibula, an oval bezel of bronze with attachment for a ring, and the ring to which it may have been attached – but of iron.

The Argolid is of much greater importance. It was earlier the probable centre of Mycenaean civilisation, and here one might expect some continuity. There are three sites which are known to have been inhabited in Sub-Mycenaean times: Mycenae, Argos, and Tiryns. To these may be added a fourth site, Asine, though it is rather marginal.

At *Mycenae* the evidence for a Sub-Mycenaean settlement is not entirely satisfactory, although a certain amount of pottery has now been identified. Nor is the cemetery material particularly impressive, as so far only two tombs, of the cist variety, have been found – though a number of stray complete vases must have come from tombs. The one tomb contained a couple of vases only, but the other (Pls. 9, 10) had a number of bronze objects, a ring with double-spiral terminals, three arched fibulae, and two long dress pins of type B, with small nail-like head and incised rings above and below the shaft swelling. The vases, I would think, are late in the period, and include a stirrup jar with decoration similar to that of the experimental transitional phase in Athens. The tomb itself, finally, was built within the ruins of earlier Mycenaean houses – as at Thebes.

The cemetery at *Tiryns* also overlay the Mycenaean settlement, and in it five tombs can be assigned to Sub-Mycenaean – three were earth-cut, one was a cist tomb, and the fifth was apparently too destroyed for one to be certain. Of objects other than pottery there were no pins, but two of the tombs produced an arched fibula of twisted bronze wire and five rings of the same metal. The most important tomb, a double burial – male and female – was that from which came not only two bronze rings, but a splendid array of weapons and armour – two daggers, a spearhead, a shield-boss, and a helmet: and the daggers are of iron.[7] Influence from the north

---

[7] There was also a stirrup jar. See Fig. 13 and Pls. 11 and 12.

PLATE 9 MYCENAE. Vases from late Sub-Myc. tomb.

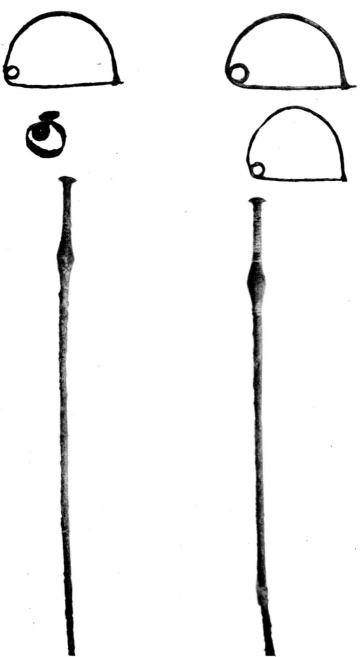

PLATE 10 MYCENAE. Bronze objects from late Sub-Myc. tomb. *PPS* for 1965, pl. XXIII *d* and *e*.

FIG. 13 TIRYNS TOMB XXVIII
Shield-boss (diameter ·105 m.) and dagger (length ·31 m.). *AM* 78,
p. 13, figs. 6 and 8.

is represented in the helmet, from the earlier Mycenaean culture in the
spearhead, and perhaps links with Cyprus in the daggers – and possibly
the shield-boss. The tomb should be contemporary with the period of
transition in Athens to Protogeometric. As opposed to this useful material,
no trace of a settlement has yet been uncovered.

Fortunately, the scarcity of settlement material at Mycenae and Tiryns
has been to some extent remedied by the excavations at *Argos*. Not that
there were any house foundations, only habitation deposits, containing
little but pottery. As at Athens – and more clearly – there appears to be a
break with the preceding Mycenaean: the areas where, respectively,
Mycenaean III C and Sub-Mycenaean pottery was found in no case
coincided. Apart from this there is not much to say, as the sherds have not
yet been published in detail; but there is one feature of special interest and
value – the presence of a furnace probably for the extraction of silver from
lead (Pl. 31), all the more remarkable since practically no objects of silver
are known to us throughout the Dark Ages. It seems to have been in use
from probably the end of Sub-Mycenaean times to the early phases of
Protogeometric (see pp. 162, 165).

The break evident in the pattern of settlement is not, surprisingly,
reflected in the burials. Several cist tombs and earth-cut graves have
indeed been found (the contents are not yet fully published, but they
include two dress pins), but as well as this six or seven chamber tombs (two
of them, admittedly, re-used) have been discovered to contain burials with
pottery and other objects assignable to this period, thus providing a
solitary exception to the pattern of burial custom known elsewhere in the
Sub-Mycenaean region, namely that if one finds, not so much the pottery,
but certain types of object, as already noted, one does not find them in
chamber tombs, except very rarely, and then in association with ornaments
and other objects of conventional Mycenaean type. At Argos they are
found on their own – there were four rings (not that these are exceptional),
an arched fibula of twisted wire, and six long dress pins (see Fig. 33).

PLATE 11 TIRYNS. Helmet from tomb XXVIII. *AM* 78, pl. 6.

All of these are of bronze. The pins are divided, as those in Athens, into two types: type A, with bulb and nail-head (found with the fibula), and type B, with elongated swelling on the shaft – but in this case with strongly moulded ridges, or a series of consecutive bulbs, above and below the swelling, as opposed to the incised rings found at Mycenae and Athens. There is also one pin of unusual type, with a long flattened and incised top to its shaft, which recalls the one from Athens with rectangular head.

So these Sub-Mycenaean chamber tombs are atypical. It is not so much a matter for surprise that chamber tombs should continue to be used in Sub-Mycenaean times, for some of the original inhabitants must have stayed on, in order to provide the ceramic continuity. It is just that it does not seem to have happened anywhere else in this area. And at the same time, there seems clearly to have been a break in the settlement.

These are the three main sites, but it is also worth mentioning a fourth, *Asine*, as it is known that the Mycenaean settlement survived far down into the twelfth century, but when it came to an end there was nothing to follow it – a piece of negative evidence which corresponds to that of some other sites. There is a cist-tomb cemetery, but it contained nothing earlier than Protogeometric.[8]

To sum up on the Argolid, it seems to follow the pattern already set, but with one major exception, the association of Sub-Mycenaean objects

[8] It has been claimed that three vases (one from the latest Mycenaean settlement, two from the 'Geometric' settlement) belong to this period, but the attribution is, to my mind, not entirely convincing.

PLATE 12 TIRYNS. Stirrup jar and spearhead from tomb XXVIII. *AM*
78, pl. 4,7; 5,1.

with chamber-tomb burials. Once again, it may be noted that the deposit
of weapons is so far confined to the latest stage.

Finally, we come to the westernmost site, *Ancient Elis*, isolated from the
rest of the main area, but in culture characteristically Sub-Mycenaean.
It is, as so often, a matter of a cemetery. There were fourteen earth-cut
graves, covered with stone slabs; each tomb contained from one to three
inhumed bodies, but due to later disturbance it was impossible to tell their
original position. The pottery is even more poor and undistinguished than
elsewhere, chiefly remarkable for the large number of amphorae (comprising seven out of the seventeen vases), and for the absence of stirrup
jars, but there seems no doubt that it is stylistically Sub-Mycenaean. Once
again, the familiar pattern of small finds is repeated: six rings, four arched
fibulae and six long dress pins, both main types being represented; all are
of bronze. As well as these, there were two bronze swords (Pl. 13A), one long
and one short. The long one reflects a type current earlier in the Mycenaean
world, but with a particular shape to its hilt that has its closest parallel on
a sword said to have come from Ithaca. The short sword has earlier
parallels in north-west Greece, at Perati in east Attica during the twelfth
century, and on Kos in the Dodecanese back into the thirteenth. So here
we have survival from earlier times, as well as the new pattern. Finally,
two beads of amber prove contact with the north or west (see p. 90).

There is no evidence of Mycenaean occupation on this site, nor any
successor to the cemetery. The tombs and their contents are entirely
different in character from those of the late Mycenaean Achaean cemeteries
not far to the north (see pp. 91 f.), and it is of the greatest interest to have
this material in this particular area, by no means easy of access either from

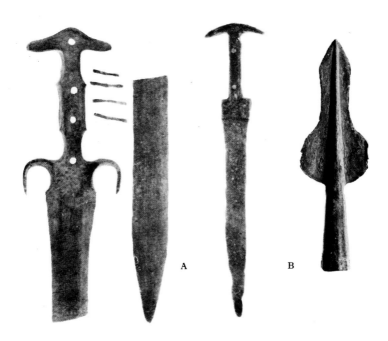

PLATE 13
A) Swords from Ancient Elis. *Ergon* for 1963, figs. 124 and 127.
B) Spearhead from near Thebes. *LMTS*, pl. 22 *d*.

Corinthia or from the Argolid. The one point that is unclear, unfortunately, is whether these burials belonged to early or to late Sub-Mycenaean.

It is now possible to give some sort of a general survey of the situation in those parts of central Greece where the Sub-Mycenaean culture established itself, and I shall attempt to do this, partly on a chronological basis, the early and late phase of the period, lasting from *c.* 1125 to *c.* 1050 B.C. This is a rather uncertain proceeding at times, for we cannot always be sure to which phase the evidence of a particular site may belong: for example, it seems reasonable to include Lefkandi only under the later phase, but in which category should one place the material from Corinth or from Thebes, or even perhaps from Ancient Elis? For some aspects also, it will be apparent that the conclusions may apply equally to the whole period.

First of all, the culture was remarkably homogeneous: everywhere one gets much the same sort of pottery, the same types of tomb, cist tombs or earth-cut graves, and similar articles of ornament, the rings, the arched fibulae and the two varieties of long dress pin. This may seem a very unimposing list, but it covers most of what has actually been found, and provides a distinctive pattern which has to be set against that of Mycenaean civilisation.

This is an important point, but it is equally important to note the differences that existed, though one is bound to be cautious when it comes to inferences based on the absence of a particular object. There were certainly some regional differences in the pottery – the popularity of amphoriskoi in Athens and on Salamis as compared with their rarity elsewhere, the complete absence of stirrup jars and bowls from the Ancient Elis tombs – and the popularity of amphorae in these as opposed to their virtual absence in other districts except where it was a case of cremation; and the occasional differences in the use of decoration. As to burials, those of Salamis and Corinth were placed in a contracted position, whereas in Athens they were outstretched, usually on the back. The introduction of cremation in Athens and Salamis was not paralleled elsewhere, except later and in a unique way at Lefkandi. At Argos, but apparently nowhere else, they continued to use chamber tombs for a while. At Ancient Elis they confined themselves to earth-cut graves, which seem to have had stone markers above them in certain cases. In the Argolid the earth-cut graves may precede the cist tombs in time; at Athens the cist tombs were the earlier, and on Salamis there were only cist tombs. There seem to be no clearly observable regional differences for fibulae – there are rather too few, except at Athens. But for the pins one may note that those of type B from Argos are rather different from those of Athens, and indeed from those of Mycenae (see pp. 296 f.).

Geographically, the sites tended to be inland rather than on the coast. For the most part, they coincided with those places where the Mycenaeans had lived, but there is evidence that the inhabitants did not choose to build exactly where their predecessors had – one is bound to wonder in what sort of state of decay the Mycenaean settlements were by then. Whether they also inhabited places never previously used by Mycenaeans it is a little difficult to say; after all, both Ancient Elis and Corinth may yet reveal flourishing earlier settlements, though at Corinth the extensive investigations make such a discovery somewhat unlikely.

It was in any case a matter of organised settlement in communities. We cannot of course say anything about the manner of political organisation, except that there cannot have been any surviving traces of the elaborate system of the thirteenth century, even among Mycenaean communities. How large were the settlements? For most cities it is impossible to say, but the two hundred-strong cemeteries of Salamis and of the Kerameikos in Athens are impressive, and indicate a population of fair size, though not necessarily more than a large village. At Athens, however, there were other smaller groups of tombs all round the Acropolis, some at quite a distance, as well as the pits of the Agora area; if all these belonged to the same community it should constitute a small town, but they may represent a number of hamlets or farms adjacent to the main village. At Argos, too, the community may have been relatively large, as there is more than one inhabited area.

What sort of life did they lead? One does not get the impression of a particularly warlike number of communities, and I would imagine that the Sub-Mycenaeans led a fairly peaceful existence. They were evidently in contact with each other, but there is no reason to suppose that they had many links with the outside world in the early phase – though it is entirely likely that the Athenians enjoyed peaceful relations with, for example, the Mycenaean community of Perati in east Attica (assuming that there was an overlap, which I believe is probable – see p. 81). I should stress that this opinion as to a peaceful existence does not depend on the absence of weapons in the early phase,[9] for it may simply not have been the custom to bury a man's weapons with him (though why there should then be a change in the later phase one cannot explain). One has, rather, the feeling of depressed isolation.

Culturally and spiritually, indeed, this earliest phase of the Dark Ages seems to be about their lowest point. There is little enough material on which to base one's judgment, but my impression is that there was simply no attempt to achieve anything worth while. The pottery was spiritless – neither the potter nor his customer seems to have cared much about what was made – an extremely rare event in Greek lands. The bronzework was, so far as one can tell, quite competent, but there are no refinements. Precious metals were almost unknown. And, finally, there is no evidence that they had any ability to build in stone.

For once, the craftsman's skill and the artistic imagination of the Greeks seem to have been dormant, and I would suppose that there was no incentive. Whether the reason for this lay in the exhaustion after some harrowing experience, or in the continual necessity to wrest a bare living from the land, I do not know. But the underlying spirit was there, as is evident from the major developments that came about in the later phase.

These major developments mostly concern Athens, and I would think that the time involved was not more than a generation. Briefly, they comprise a virtual revolution in the style of pottery, the introduction of iron, and a geographical extension of Sub-Mycenaean culture outwards across the Aegean.

Before discussing these, there is a further development, apparently starting in Athens and Salamis, and also visible at Lefkandi, but which does not perhaps belong entirely to the late phase, nor does it come within the same category as the rest. This is the gradual emergence of cremation. There has been more than one theory regarding the part of the world from which it was transmitted to Athens, but I would prefer to leave this problem aside as unsolved: at least it was practically unknown in Cyprus, which played so important a part otherwise in the late Sub-Mycenaean revival. It had been extraordinarily rare in the Mycenaean and Minoan world down to *c.* 1200 B.C., but it is a fact that it appeared sporadically in certain Mycenaean sites, and in Crete, during the twelfth century – there were as many as eighteen burials of this type at Perati, one on Kos and five in Rhodes, and a few instances in Crete.

[9] I omit the swords from Ancient Elis, as I am not sure whether they belong to the early phase.

In Sub-Mycenaean Athens the first very few cremations may belong to
the long early phase, but they are found with increasing frequency in the
late one, until by the beginning of the Protogeometric period they had
almost completely ousted inhumation as the method of burial for adults.
Salamis had two or three cremations, but the cemetery may have fallen
into disuse by the later phase. At Lefkandi the custom was universal. And
it may be noted that while at first in Athens the same type of tomb was
used as for inhumation, a small shaft being hollowed out at the bottom in
which the cinerary urn (usually an amphora) was placed, at Lefkandi it is
uncertain what happened to the body after it had been burnt in the pyre.

To return to the main developments, the revolution in the pottery has
already been analysed (pp. 41 ff.); there is no doubt that a new spirit is
to be recognised, visible in the more imaginative use of decorative motives
and in the introduction of a number of new shapes. In this, acquaintance
with the pottery style of Cyprus played a great part; and as a result – and
this had no connexion with Cyprus, but was a creation of the Athenian
potter, perhaps one individual genius – the Protogeometric style was born.

The contacts with Cyprus are most probably also reflected in the
introduction of the knowledge how to work in iron, since this metal had
been known in Cyprus since before 1150 B.C. Also, one of the swords was
of Cypriot type. It may be suggested that in fact all the iron objects found
were of Cypriot manufacture, and simply exported to the Sub-Mycenaean
world. This seems most unlikely, on the grounds that certain iron objects
that are found in Athens and Lefkandi at this time, pins and a fibula, have
no counterparts in that metal in Cyprus. It seems to me certain that the
inhabitants of Athens and Lefkandi and probably of the Argolid, to judge
from the iron daggers of the warrior grave at Tiryns, had found out how
to work iron, and I think it is also certain that this involved the mining of
iron ore in Greece itself – there are deposits both in Euboea and in Attica.
There was here, in any case, a technical advance, as in the pottery, but of
a different kind. It is, in fact, the beginning of the Iron Age – a very
modest one, but a beginning all the same.

These two major developments, in the pottery and in the use and
working of iron, involved contact with Cyprus. This need not mean more
than that some Cypriots had now made their way to the Sub-Mycenaean
area (see pp. 340 f.), but in fact there is good evidence that the Sub-
Mycenaeans themselves did in this late phase renounce their mainland
isolation and start to look to the sea. The occasion and reason for this I
shall discuss below (pp. 82 f.), but the momentous fact is that they
extended their culture into and across the Aegean. And by extending their
culture I mean that, in all probability, there was a move of groups of
people from the Sub-Mycenaean area overseas. One such move was, I
believe, to Lefkandi, a site which has already figured prominently in this
chapter – but from where in central Greece they travelled to Lefkandi one
cannot say: hardly from Athens, bearing in mind the difference in burial
rites, and indeed in the pottery (and, most oddly, the innovations of the
Protogeometric style found no acceptance there). But there were other

movements, certainly to Miletus on the west coast of Asia Minor, probably to Naxos in the centre of the Aegean, and even, it seems, as far north as Theotokou on the Magnesian promontory of Thessaly. Of these I shall have more to say later (pp. 83, 102).

All of this, it is clear, adds up to a period of considerable and many-sided activity, at any rate for the Aegean-facing districts and especially for Athens, after a time of relative isolation and stagnation. It constitutes a turning point in the Dark Ages, and may reasonably be placed between 1075 and 1050 B.C., the early phase preceding it having lasted for perhaps about fifty years.[10]

So far, I have dealt in detail only with one area, and that not a very large one, of Greece and the Aegean. I have spoken about the isolation of Sub-Mycenaean central Greece, and I have to a great extent discussed it in isolation, though with a brief and incomplete analysis of the situation in Crete and Cyprus for the purpose of clarifying the ceramic development. It is now time to turn to the other areas, which will not only complete the picture, in so far as it can be completed, but will also place the Sub-Mycenaean area in perspective. And only when this has been done will it be possible to discuss the vital question of the origin of this Sub-Mycenaean, but not Mycenaean, culture.

[10] If anything, these dates may be too high; for example, recent excavations by Mylonas at Mycenae have led him to conclude that the date of the final destruction there was later than supposed, c. 1120 B.C. or after; if this is correct, the Sub-Mycenaean period should start later.

4 The Peripheral Areas

The Central Aegean

This is an extensive area, and the sites concerned, some on the mainland coasts bordering on the Aegean, some on the islands within it, are: Perati in east Attica, Epidaurus Limera on the east coast of the Peloponnese, the islands of Keos, Melos, Paros, Delos, Naxos, Rhodes, Kos, Kalymnos, and Chios (Emborio); and Miletus on the west coast of Asia Minor. In every case the sites are right by the sea or close to it. All were inhabited by Mycenaeans during the twelfth century, but some need no further discussion, simply because our evidence is not sufficient for us to tell how long they survived – such are Melos, Paros, Delos, and Keos (unfortunately, as this is a rare sanctuary site, and there is Protogeometric as well as L.H. III C pottery, but it is not yet clear what happened during the Sub-Mycenaean period).

Those that remain are enough to give us a reasonable idea of the course of events in this area, for not only do they cover the four corners and the centre, so to speak, but they formed a group that had, in the twelfth century, many common features. These features are to be found in the pottery, particularly the Cretan-inspired octopus decoration (Pl. 1) on the stirrup jars,[1] and also in certain vases of a religious type – bowls with figurines on the rim, jugs with painted or fictile snakes curved around them; it may also be significant that cremation burials appeared, not only in chamber tombs on Rhodes and Kos, but also quite often in those of Perati – but nowhere else in Mycenaean contexts at this time, so far as is known.

Each site and region had its own individual traits, but it is clear that there was close and frequent intercommunication. There is no reason for supposing that there was any centralised political control binding this group of communities which had escaped the earlier disasters on the mainland of Greece, but they had common interests. It is tempting to think of them forming a miniature trading empire, for their wares have been found as far apart as Thessaly, south Italy, and Cilicia – though not as yet in Cyprus. Whatever their activities, they gained wealth through them, as is shown by the gold and other objects deposited in their tombs; and many of these objects came from the east Mediterranean, hence they must have had contacts with this area.

This group continued to prosper during at least the first half of the

[1] The Cretan influence may have been greater than one has supposed, to judge from a locally made stirrup jar with typical Minoan – but not octopus – decoration from Epidaurus Limera.

twelfth century, but during the second half it was different. Things took a turn for the worse on the mainland, as witnessed by the final destruction at Mycenae, after which event there was a further exodus to Cyprus. The central Aegean communities may well have been affected by this – and indeed the disasters in Cyprus somewhere round about the middle of the century may also have had some effect, if their livelihood depended on trade (which is not certain, nor is it certain that they traded with Cyprus). There was also evidently some sort of disturbed situation in Crete, possibly connected with the exodus of Mycenaeans mentioned above, and then at the turn of the century there seems to have been a move of some Minoans, again to Cyprus. All this will have contributed to the upsetting of harmony in the central Aegean.

Nor was the trouble confined to their neighbours, for two of the eastern settlements, Miletus and Emborio, were destroyed – I would think perhaps not far from 1100 B.C. The cause of these disasters is unknown, nor is it relevant. What is relevant is the eventual effect on this fairly close-knit surviving group of Mycenaean communities. In all of them, Mycenaean civilisation disappeared, and in most cases it meant the abandonment of the site without any immediate successor.

The question is, how long did these communities survive in terms of the early Dark Ages, the Sub-Mycenaean period? It is a very difficult question to answer. At Epidaurus Limera we depend on the evidence of tombs, and just two or three of the vases found therein appear to be of Sub-Mycenaean type such as are known to central Greece. Then there is the Dodecanese. The chamber tombs of Rhodes have produced nothing even remotely Sub-Mycenaean, nor has the one group of vases from Kalymnos, so on the surface it looks as though these communities may have disintegrated well before the end of the twelfth century. One must bear in mind, however, that there is no particular reason why these islanders should in any way have been aware of, far less imitated, the very degenerate ceramic style of the land-based central Greek culture. Here and on Kos, whose cemeteries have been published but whose settlement has not, occupation may have continued longer than one has supposed, perhaps into the eleventh century. And a similar conclusion is possible for the settlements of Emborio on Chios and of Miletus.

On all these sites Mycenaean civilisation came to a full stop. So also it did at Perati. And here again there was no pottery that could be described as Sub-Mycenaean, but can we reasonably suggest that, as in the eastern Aegean, there was no contact with Sub-Mycenaean communities? Surely not, for Perati is in east Attica, at no great distance from Athens. Even so, I believe that it is perfectly conceivable that the inhabitants would have had no desire to borrow from, or in any way imitate, Sub-Mycenaean pottery (the reverse should have been the case, and a possible reason why it was not I will discuss later, pp. 339 f.); and I think that the likelihood of some overlap between the earliest Sub-Mycenaean inhabitants of Athens and the last of the Mycenaeans who buried their dead at Perati is indicated by the presence of four arched fibulae in the Perati cemetery, objects which are entirely typical of the Sub-Mycenaean period, and never else-where preceding it. A ring with double-spiral terminals, of northern affinities, is also worth noting, as similar ones were found at Athens, Mycenae, and probably Lefkandi.

One site is left, that of Grotta on Naxos. Here, as on Kos, there is an unpublished settlement. There were also, however, a number of chamber tombs in the vicinity, and one of these produced a Sub-Mycenaean stirrup jar, of a kind found in the Kerameikos, and a lekythos which could belong to the same period. Another tomb contained an iron dagger, an object in a metal which, as we have seen, was not normally known to the Greek world before the later stage of Sub-Mycenaean. It would seem that the case for an overlap, possibly considerable, between the latest Mycenaean III C and Sub-Mycenaean is fairly strong.[2]

The overall conclusion is that in the central Aegean area Mycenaean civilisation came to an end on some sites before the beginning of the Sub-Mycenaean period, on others at some time during its course. What I think is likely to have happened is that many of these communities of Myce-naeans persisted in their way of life during the early Dark Ages, but that their prosperity and cohesion were gradually eroded by a number of factors – the instability around them, the disasters to their eastern settle-ments, possibly growing pressure on the western mainland communities, all leading to the disappearance of their outside contacts, and to a general feeling of internal insecurity and very possibly a gradual depopulation, until there were so few left that they moved elsewhere or were in no state to resist any encroachment that might take place. While they remained active and prosperous, I think they represented an obstacle to the expan-sion of the Sub-Mycenaeans of central Greece. I believe that a clear sign of their final dissolution is to be seen in the major developments in Athens that characterised the late phase of Sub-Mycenaean, developments that owed much to contact with Cypriotes.

An equally clear sign is the actual movements of Sub-Mycenaean groups into and across the Aegean. One such movement I have already mentioned (p. 78), the one to Lefkandi, where there was presumably a new settlement (associated with the cemetery) replacing the main L.H. III C settlement, and at no great time, it seems, after its desertion.

Within the central Aegean there are two other instances. First, there is Naxos, where either earth-cut or cist tombs replaced the chamber tombs, at a time while Sub-Mycenaean was still current, from the fact that a lekythos of this style has been found in one of them. This is, of course, rather too slight evidence for definite proof. Time will show: the further evidence is surely there, in the history of the settlement. The excavator distinguished three phases of building: the earliest is Mycenaean, the second – an extension of the first – he called Sub-Mycenaean, and the third, whose walls completely disregarded the earlier foundations and were set on a different axis, he assigned to the Protogeometric and Geometric periods. The vital question is what is meant in this context by Sub-

---

[2] The presence of bird vases may also be a sign of late survival.

Mycenaean; did this settlement contain objects of predominantly Mycenaean type, but coeval with the Sub-Mycenaean period, or were the finds
Sub-Mycenaean in type as found in central Greece? Until fuller publication we cannot know.

If there is uncertainty about Naxos, there would seem to be no doubt
in the case of Miletus. After its destruction – how soon after we do not
know – the site was reoccupied, and the new settlement was no longer
Mycenaean, its earliest pottery being, it would appear, Sub-Mycenaean
in type, such as would be found in west Attica. Which phase of Sub-
Mycenaean pottery is represented I cannot say, but there was not very much
of it, and it was then superseded by Protogeometric pottery. There is in
any case sufficient to show that this new foundation predated the Protogeometric period. And as a sort of tailpiece to this, it is interesting to note
that the earliest vase of a cemetery at Asarlik (see p. 180), on the promontory
of Halicarnassus some distance to the south of Miletus, is a stirrup jar
which looks Sub-Mycenaean. It is not impossible that quite a large group
of people from central Greece crossed over the Aegean and settled on the
coast of Asia Minor. A further conclusion is that the evidence of Miletus
makes a movement in the late Sub-Mycenaean period to the much closer
Naxos a reasonable probability.

The hypothesis is then that the eventual failure of the Mycenaean
settlements in the central Aegean, a gradual process probably completed
by c. 1075 B.C., resulted in new opportunities for those who are distinguished by the use of Sub-Mycenaean culture in mainland central Greece,
both in their ability to contact, and profit from, the Cypriotes and in their
ability to expand overseas themselves. And a subsidiary conclusion would
be that since the Mycenaean communities were an obstacle to expansion,
it is virtually impossible that the new Sub-Mycenaean culture of central
Greece came from them or through them. Nor indeed does anything found
in their settlements or cemeteries suggest that it did.

This is a nice tidy theory: whether it represents the actual course of
events is quite another matter.

South Peloponnese

This area, comprising Laconia and the regions south of the river Alpheios,
needs only a brief discussion. Whereas it supported some of the most
flourishing centres of Mycenaean civilisation during the thirteenth century,
it thereafter apparently lapsed into a deep obscurity, from which the most
intensive field survey has not yet been able to rescue it.

For the earlier twelfth century, we can go so far as to say that the
survivors retained their Mycenaean culture, and were in contact with other
districts of the Mycenaean world. The sanctuary of Amyklai in Laconia
remained purely Mycenaean, as is shown by the votive figurines, human
and animal, and by two examples of the Argive Close Style ware. In
Messenia the tholos tomb of Tragana, not far from Ano Englianos (the

Palace of Nestor) contained pottery which is clearly L.H. III C, revealing some influence of the Close Style. The inland and rather isolated site of Malthi, to the north of Messenia, seems certain to have been occupied at this time. At Palaiokastro, on the Alpheios but so far inland that it is just in Arcadia, a large chamber-tomb cemetery undoubtedly continued to be used after 1200 B.C., but only one vase (a stirrup jar of a style resembling those in the twelfth-century cemeteries of Achaea – see p. 91 ff.) has been published. The district of Olympia, finally, has produced one or two traces of twelfth-century occupation, and reports suggest that there are more, as yet unpublished.

These are the main sites. Surface survey has revealed a few others with pottery identifiable as L.H. III C, but that is all. An indication of the violence of the depopulation may be judged by the fact that in Messenia, whereas a hundred and fifty sites have been located as occupied during the thirteenth century, only fourteen or fifteen can be attributed to the twelfth – even allowing for the inconclusiveness of evidence gained by survey work, such figures must have some significance. Nevertheless, there were some twelfth-century Mycenaean survivors over the whole area, and no trace has yet been found of any new settlers.

Such a situation does not augur well for our knowledge of the early Dark Ages, and matters are made even more difficult with regard to any links with the Sub-Mycenaean culture of central Greece by the complete absence (with the exception of the marginal Palaiokastro) of any evidence from the central inland district of the Peloponnese, Arcadia.

In Laconia, indeed, we seem to lose all archaeological touch with the Dark Ages until the tenth century.[3] It is certain that the sanctuary at Amyklai remained in use throughout the Dark Ages, as the worship of the Mycenaean god Hyakinthos survived into later times, but this fact is derived from the later literary testimony, and continuity cannot be deduced from the archaeological material. In Laconia, then, the course of events, and the character of the material culture of the early Dark Ages, remain completely unknown.

In Messenia, on the other hand, there are a few hints, but they are not easy to interpret. To the north of this district, the settlement of Malthi, mentioned above, produced a number of ribbed and swollen kylix stems, very likely a sign of contact with Kephallenia and Ithaca during the late twelfth and early eleventh centuries (see pp. 88 ff.). From here also came a dagger and knife of iron, which suggest a date not earlier than 1050 B.C., and it is likely that this site was continuously occupied.

In western Messenia the tholos tomb of Tragana contained not only the L.H. III C vases mentioned above but pottery associated with occasional later burials as well – and among these were lekythoi which look Sub-Mycenaean. And on the eastern side, at the head of the Messenian Gulf, a number of possibly Sub-Mycenaean sherds have been published from Kardamyla. These two sites raise the question whether in fact this area

[3] I am omitting Epidaurus Limera which, though technically in Laconia, is in reality part of the central Aegean complex, and has been dealt with under that heading, p. 80.

should not be classed with the other Sub-Mycenaean districts at least culturally, and to that no answer is yet possible. One can argue that the sherds from Kardamyla could be later than 1050 B.C., as the analogous material of the Argolid persisted into the later eleventh century. But the lekythoi from Tragana, with their hand-drawn semicircles, must be earlier. It is not impossible that they developed naturally from the local L.H. III C, and so had no link with central Greece (see p. 251).

Then there are two important sites, Kaphirio and Nichoria, on the west coast of the Messenian Gulf. At Kaphirio it has been reported that there was Sub-Mycenaean pottery, and occupation during the later Dark Ages, the Protogeometric period, is certain. Nichoria, finally, is of the greatest interest. The thirteenth-century settlement was destroyed, probably at the same time as that of Ano Englianos, but in this case a later settlement has been identified in the immediate vicinity, and (as at Kaphirio) it has been said to extend back into the Sub-Mycenaean period – but no details are yet available. As well as this, however, tombs have been found (see pp. 251 ff.); not only was there a tholos tomb, thus indicating the survival of this Mycenaean type, but there were also several cist tombs and pithos burials. All these were, however, Protogeometric in date, so if there was an earlier stage for the burials, it has not yet been found.

It looks as though, especially at Nichoria, there might again be something approximating to the Sub-Mycenaean culture. But one must still be cautious. And the cist tombs are a problem on their own; they certainly do not seem to reflect a manner of burial taken over from the Messenian past – what then was their origin? Was there any connexion, even at this late date, with those of Sub-Mycenaean central Greece? These are questions to which an answer can be suggested only in the light of the evidence from the districts which form the subject of the next section. And we need so much more in any case from the whole of the southern Peloponnese.

The Northern Crescent

The situation to the west and north of central Greece is highly complex, and to understand its relevance one must look back briefly to the second half of the thirteenth century. There is no doubt that Mycenaean civilisation had permeated not only the north-eastern, central, and southern areas of the Peloponnese, but the whole western region as well. From the west there had been an extension to the Ionian islands, that is to say Zakynthos, Kephallenia, and Ithaca – and presumably to Leucas, though so far only few traces have been found of Mycenaean habitation. There was also an extension to the coastal area of the districts of Aetolia and Acarnania, from the mouth of the Corinthian Gulf running westwards and then northwards at least as far as Parga and Ephyra in Epirus. Mycenaean pottery has been found on a number of sites, and the presence of reasonably imposing tombs, both in southern Aetolia and at Parga, indicate actual settlement, and not just casual contact. Generally speaking, however, the Mycenaeans did not penetrate far inland, except in south Aetolia, where at Thermon, just north-east of Lake Trichonis, sherds have been reported to be plentiful. Otherwise, there is little or no evidence of them; and this is not surprising, as the country is mountainous and inhospitable. It would be fair to say that at any rate practically the whole of Epirus, including the plain of Iannina, lay outside the Mycenaean world.

Across the Pindus from Epirus lies Thessaly, where the Mycenaeans, as in Aetolia and Acarnania, had concentrated their settlement on the coastal fringes – that is to say, in east Thessaly. The reason for this is that, while the district was easily accessible by sea from the south, overland travel from central Greece, once one reached Phocis, was rather difficult and mountainous. The nature of the coastal hold on Thessaly was, however, very different from that in Aetolia and Acarnania: Iolkos in particular was a flourishing centre. Furthermore, from there the Mycenaeans had penetrated to some extent over much of the central plain, but their influence may not have gone very deep, since there is good evidence for the existence of a native population, with its own culture, in this region. These inland districts are in any case highly vulnerable to attack or immigration, both from Epirus and from Macedonia; the Mycenaeans were wise to confine their main strength to the coast, thus providing themselves with a safe route for reinforcement and escape.

There remain the districts to the north and south of Thessaly. To the south there is the Spercheios valley, which is a sort of no man's land, and may be left out of account. And then there are Phocis and Locris to the south of this, areas within the Mycenaean sphere – at least so far as Phocis is concerned: our knowledge of Locris is not great. In the thirteenth century Krisa and Delphi in Phocis represented, apart from Thessaly, the northernmost extension of the Mycenaeans in the central part of Greece.

North of Thessaly, finally, is Macedonia, and of this region I shall have nothing directly to say, since it seems to have been out of touch with the south during almost the whole period of the Dark Ages, though the great cemetery of Vergina, first used perhaps c. 1000 B.C., is important not only for the latest stage but also, as will be seen (pp. 218 f.), for the earlier period, on account of its connexion with areas to the north and possible inferences from these links for one or two aspects of Sub-Mycenaean culture. During Mycenaean times in Macedonia, when settlements abound but no cemeteries have been identified, chief interest attaches to the evidence for at least ceramic contact with the Mycenaean world during the thirteenth and early twelfth centuries (if not later), and for the stubbornly persistent local imitation of these wares, even through a time of invasion and flux, down into its own Dark Age. And, as will be seen (p. 213), there was a move of Macedonians into north-east Thessaly probably during the late phase of the Greek Dark Ages. The area is, nevertheless, marginal to my main theme, and will be treated as such.

To return to the areas of the Northern Crescent, I have dealt briefly with the situation in the second half of the thirteenth century. Towards the end of this century there came the great disasters to central and southern

PLATE 14 POLIS, ITHACA. A) Cups and kantharoi. B) Kylikes. *BSA* 39, pls. 6 and 8.

Greece, disasters which shattered the whole mainland Mycenaean world. What happened afterwards in the western and northern areas?

In the west, including the north-west, it does not appear that the full impact of the catastrophe was felt. It is true that the most important settlement known to us, that of Teichos Dymaion (a well-fortified citadel near the coast some twenty miles south-west of Patras, not far from the airport of Araxos), suffered some calamity, but it continued thereafter to be strongly occupied into the twelfth century. Southern Aetolia, across the sea opposite this citadel, also continued to be inhabited by Mycenaeans.

The two most significant areas, however, are Kephallenia and Ithaca on the one hand, and Achaea on the other. In both regions we find that there were more Mycenaeans in the twelfth century than in the thirteenth – that at least is the picture given by investigations until now. These were regions, in other words, to which Mycenaeans fled for safety from other districts. But one striking difference is to be noted. Whereas in Achaea the population remained wholly Mycenaean, on the islands it was a mixed one, partly Mycenaean, partly native and non-Mycenaean.

We can now follow the course of events in these islands, in so far as it is recoverable, down into the Dark Ages. On Ithaca, in fact, a number of excavated settlements enable us to trace complete continuity of habitation, from Mycenaean times, through the Dark Ages, and into the light of history. Two sites in particular deserve attention. The one is Polis, a cave later certainly used as a sanctuary, but whether equally so in this period one cannot be sure. The pottery ranges from thirteenth century L.H. III B (in small quantities) right through local L.H. III C, the principal shapes being bowls, cups, kraters, kylikes, and kantharoi (Pl. 14), the decorative motives for the most part spirals, concentric loops, and hatched and cross-hatched triangles and diamonds – generally simple and predominantly geometric. There is a break after this material, and we could not therefore be sure that the island went on being inhabited through the Dark Ages. As it happens, though, the second site, that of Aetos, provides an overlap with the Polis cave, and continued to be used into the Archaic period. And what is particularly significant is that among the originally Mycenaean-inspired Dark Age material there have been found fragments of a Protogeometric vase which was probably imported from the Aegean, and is not likely to be earlier than c. 1000 B.C. Thus we can be sure that the latest pottery of Mycenaean inspiration continued into the beginning of the Dark Ages – in fact, virtually until renewed contact with the fast-emerging new Greek world.

Here in Ithaca there was little enough to link up with Sub-Mycenaean central Greece, though it is interesting to note that a bronze pin with disk and bulb – perhaps of type A – was found in a probably early context at Aetos. Also, a sword with down-turned quillons, the nearest parallel to the one found at Ancient Elis (p. 74), is reported to have come from this island.[4]

The evidence is thus not of great assistance towards determining links with the rest of the Greek world in the Dark Ages, but it does at least show how the Mycenaean ceramic tradition could persist, and it will be seen to have a rather more than local importance in the later, Protogeometric, phase of the Dark Ages.

The situation in Kephallenia is different, in the sense that all our material comes from cemeteries (concentrated in the southern part of the island, south of Argostoli), but the Mycenaean pottery is precisely, and naturally, of the type found in Ithaca. Unfortunately, it comes to an end with the desertion of the cemeteries, before the later Ithacan stage, but the similarities are sufficient for one to be able to conclude that the

[4] It is now in the British Museum.

PLATE 15 KEPHALLENIA. A) Kylikes. B) Kraters. *AE* 1932, pls. 5 and 6.

Kephallenian tombs were probably still in use at the very beginning of the Dark Ages.

Altogether, the material from these cemeteries is very remarkable, and has received less study than it deserves. The tombs themselves are unusual, caves hollowed out and parallel rectangular trenches dug into them to receive the bodies. The Mycenaean pottery is of considerable interest. It is of an individual style, but shows occasional influence from, and so contact with, the rest of the Mycenaean mainland world of the twelfth century. The Close Style was obviously not unknown, there are links with Achaea, and in general the latest Mycenaean ideas about decoration found their way to the island.[5] The relative popularity of certain shapes of vase differs from that of other areas: stirrup jars were common, as always in tombs, but jugs are far more prominent than elsewhere, and a particular feature is the number of kylikes (Pl. 15) with funnel-shaped bodies – a type of vase which died out in some districts, but not, significantly, in north-west Greece, as will shortly be seen. There is also a fine series of kraters (Pl. 15), with one or two odd connexions: one has a close parallel at Gezer in Philistia, and the highly individual decoration of another recurs in Crete.

This is not the only type of pottery, however, for over ten per cent of the whole consisted of hand-made vases. To find any but wheel-made vases in Mycenaean tombs is almost unheard of, and consequently we can conclude that a non-Mycenaean element coexisted with Mycenaean. Nor is it in itself unlikely that there would be a non-Mycenaean population, for the island lies on the fringes of the Mycenaean sphere.

The marginal nature of Kephallenia is also evident in the number of non-Mycenaean objects other than pottery. There were plenty of necklaces and other artefacts of Mycenaean type, but many of the bronzes (there was no iron) are non-Mycenaean, and show influence from the north. The presence of several violin-bow fibulae suggests that the origin of this dress fastening is most probably to be found on the Adriatic or in Italy, and a curious multiple-loop fibula (otherwise unknown to the Greek world except Crete) certainly has northern connexions, as do many of the spiraliform ornaments. Some of the weapons are such as are more commonly found in north-west Greece than elsewhere. The presence of numerous beads of amber is also an almost certain indication of contact with the north – or, if not, with Sicily to the west. In all these northern or local north-western Greek connexions there is a remarkable contrast to the situation in Achaea.

Kephallenia was then in some sort of touch with the Greek world, through its Mycenaean elements, and also strongly susceptible to northern influences. At present we have no such proof as in Ithaca of continuous habitation down to the time when Protogeometric pottery was finding its way to the general area. This does not mean, though, that there was no continuity; it could be in this case that further tombs, or some settlement, will be found, especially as very similar tombs were still known in Classical times, and there might have been uninterrupted habitation right through the Dark Ages – in fact, it would be surprising if there were not, to judge from Ithaca.

It is in any case likely that the Kephallenian cemeteries survived in use into the early Dark Age phase. Were there any signs of contact with the Sub-Mycenaean area?

[5] Of particular note are the vases and decorative systems that very closely resemble the Sub-Mycenaean style, and on which it arose. Their presence here could throw light on the situation in Messenia (pp. 84f.).

Some of the distinctive features of Sub-Mycenaean culture are altogether missing: there are no cist tombs in Kephallenia, nor any arched fibulae. Nor can one base any conclusions on ceramic similarities, since the common Mycenaean background is sufficient explanation. There are, however, short swords of the same type as one at Ancient Elis – such swords have a wide distribution, but half of them come either from here or from north-west Greece. And it may also be relevant that two amber beads were found at Ancient Elis – certainly not a characteristic feature of Sub-Mycenaean culture, but an indication that at least this site had contacts with the north.

What are really interesting are the three dress pins from one of the tombs of Diakata, all in fact from the same burial trench. One is a roll-top pin, of the kind found at Athens and on Salamis. The second, over forty centimetres in length, has strongly moulded rings at the top, very reminiscent of the Argos pins; and the third, only slightly shorter than the second, has the bulbous swelling towards the top of the shaft and the small nail-like head familiar at Ancient Elis, Mycenae, Lefkandi, and Athens. Such pins are, as we have seen, characteristically Sub-Mycenaean, and it is therefore important to determine their context in Kephallenia. The burial trench in which they were found contained the multiple-loop fibula already mentioned, two hand-made vases, a funnel-shaped kylix, a rather Achaean-looking stirrup jar, and a curious pedestalled bowl; and it had one other vase, a krater whose decoration is reminiscent of the Argive Close Style. If the pins were associated with the krater, it is very possible that they are earlier than any known Sub-Mycenaean pin, and we might have an important clue to the origin of these distinctive objects. Unfortunately, we cannot be sure: there was more than one burial in this trench, but we are not told how many, nor which objects were associated with which body; also, there is such a strong persistence of Mycenaean ceramic ideas that it would perhaps be unsafe to say with absolute certainty that the krater itself must be earlier than the Sub-Mycenaean period. Furthermore, no other such pins are known in this part of the world, or anywhere else in the Northern Crescent, at this time or at any time during the early Dark Ages. But what we are entitled to do is to refer across to the early tombs of Vergina in Macedonia, which contained pins of the type with bulbous swelling which cannot have come from anywhere but north of Macedonia (see pp. 218 f.); a similar origin is therefore probable for the one from Kephallenia (which had many objects of northern type), and so also most probably for those found in the Sub-Mycenaean area.

While the cemetery sites of Kephallenia are within a few miles of one another, those of Achaea are spread over a wide area, virtually encircling the Panachaic range of mountains, and extending some distance eastwards along the south shore of the Corinthian Gulf. On the whole, they keep away from the coastline and prefer the shelter of the foothills; two or three, indeed, are well up in the mountains. Whereas in the thirteenth century we know of eight cemeteries, there are at least fifteen that belong to the twelfth century, the period of L.H. III C, so there is quite a considerable body of material. And burials were almost invariably made in chamber tombs.

As I have indicated above, the contents of the tombs seem to be purely Mycenaean. The pottery shows that the inhabitants, like those of Kephallenia and Ithaca, possessed an individual style of their own. Although there were many features common to the surviving Mycenaeans throughout Greece and the Aegean, peculiarities in shape or decoration occasionally allow us to recognise Achaean vases in other parts of Greece, as for example across the Corinthian Gulf in Phocis, and even as far north as south Thessaly, thus showing that there must have been relatively free movement at that particular time in the twelfth century. (But just when? That is the problem.) The other burial gifts were equally of Mycenaean type, for the most part. There is no sense of wealth, such as is at times encountered in the central Aegean, but it looks as though a reasonable standard was maintained. The whole gives an impression of a fairly uniform entity (more so, really, than the central Aegean), and the very occasional weapons indicate that the communities were prepared to defend themselves.[6]

This preparedness for trouble did not prevent the cemeteries – and presumably the settlements related to them – from being deserted, precisely as in the central Aegean. When discussing Kephallenia, I suggested that the absence of continuity may have been due to our own failure to discover the later stages; in Achaea, in view of the number and wide geographical distribution of the sites, I do not think this can be the case.

The important question for the present discussion is, of course, the time when in this area Mycenaean culture disappeared, but it is worth while first considering briefly what we know of subsequent occupation. Once again, the material comes from tombs. The earliest datable testimony is that of a pithos burial in the north of the district, at Derveni not far from Aigion, probably of the early ninth century (see pp. 248 f.).[7] Then, three sites in the western foothills have produced tombs containing Late Geometric pottery; at Troumbe the tombs were reported to be of the tholos type, but at Pharai and Chalandritsa they were cist tombs, those of the latter site being covered by tumuli. So the gap in time is very considerable. There is, however, just one other group of cist tombs, at Agriapidies close to Chalandritsa, which could be appreciably earlier. One of these contained four mugs, coarse, undecorated, and hand-made. The group cannot be dated, but the primitiveness of the pottery may suggest an early date, possibly well within the Dark Ages.

We can now return to the length of time that the chamber tombs remained in use. This is by no means easy to determine, for the pottery is difficult to date, whether on internal or external grounds. Nevertheless,

---

[6] This is, of course, a matter that can be taken for granted, which makes the scarcity of weapons in tombs of the early phase of Sub-Mycenaean all the more surprising.

[7] A cist tomb at Katarrakhti, in the southern part of Achaea, is reported to contain Protogeometric vases, but these could also be ninth century in date.

PLATE 16 TEICHOS DYMAION. A) Krater fragment. B) KYLIKES. *Pr.* 1965, pls. 174 and 175.

there are a few features which suggest survival on at least two sites right up to the end of the Sub-Mycenaean period. The most persuasive evidence, to my mind, is that of the duck vases (Pl. 4), several of which were found, but only from two sites for certain, those of Koukoura, near the Klauss wine factory in the foothills close to Patras, and Kangadhi, well to the south-west. It is very difficult to dissociate them from those of Athens and Lefkandi and Cyprus, and that means that they should belong to the second quarter of the eleventh century. It looks, therefore, as though the two above sites remained inhabited throughout the Sub-Mycenaean period, as we have it in central Greece; but we cannot speak with equal confidence about the rest. It is very likely that there was a gradual falling off of population, and desertion of settlements, much as I believe took place in the central Aegean. And, as there, the question arises, why did this happen?

For a possible and only partial answer to this we must return to the fortress mentioned earlier, that of Teichos Dymaion (p. 87). It had survived the calamity of the thirteenth century, and continued to be strongly held into the twelfth. Then, however, there was a further catastrophe, and from the fact that this citadel then lay deserted for many centuries, it may be assumed that the destruction was a violent one – and there were indeed signs of a conflagration. The cause is unknown, though the very situation of this fort suggests that its purpose was to guard against menace from the sea or beyond. As to the date, all one can say is that it was probably at least as late as the last quarter of the twelfth century. Some sherds display the distinctive wavy-line motive, found in the Argolid after the final destruction of Mycenae, and so popular in Cyprus at the end of the twelfth century, when it was one of the most characteristic features associated with a new wave of migrants to that island. Furthermore, a complete disintegration of the Mycenaean potter's craft is to be seen in the fragments of a chaotically decorated krater (Pl. 16) – not that chaos is an inescapable criterion of lateness.

I think it most likely that the destruction of this citadel took place near the end of the twelfth century, if not later, and though its cause is not known, the effect must have been considerable on the Mycenaean communities of Achaea – and very likely on those across the mouth of the Corinthian Gulf in south Aetolia, as we shall see shortly. As at Mycenae and as at Iolkos in Thessaly, a bastion had fallen, and security was seriously threatened.[8]

A final point, or pointer, from Teichos Dymaion is that two of the 'destruction' vases (they were affected by the fire) were very plain funnel-shaped kylikes (Pl. 16). Now this is a shape of which only one example has been found in the Achaean tombs; it was, however, very popular in Kephallenia and Ithaca, and it is an extremely significant shape for both the next areas to be discussed, those of Aetolia and Acarnania, and Epirus. These constitute, roughly, the southern and northern divisions of north-west Greece, though to be more exact the division was between those parts inhabited by the Mycenaeans, chiefly along the southern coast, and some way up the west coast, with slight penetration inland in Aetolia as far as Lake Trichonis, and those parts, in the main Epirus, where the culture was essentially non-Mycenaean.

What happened to the Mycenaeans in the twelfth century? Did they even survive into this century in this peripheral area? Here we are, as so often, confronted with the difficulty of interpreting the evidence. The tholos tomb at Parga seems to have been abandoned before 1200 B.C., but had the settlement of Ephyra, where walls have been identified as 'of

---

[8] This is, of course, imaginative and hypothetical, but some latitude of interpretation may be permitted in a period of such obscurity. The further implications of the chronological uncertainty are discussed in the concluding chapter, pp. 336 f.

Late Helladic times', also been deserted by this date? Lack of illustration of the material from most of the other coastal sites to the south of Ephyra and Parga forbids any conclusions. It was reported to the archaeological authorities that a small chamber tomb had been found at Lithovouni, just south of Lake Trichonis, but the only objects recovered were a short bronze sword and a spearhead, of which the sword could belong either shortly before or shortly after 1200 B.C., while the spearhead cannot be as closely dated even as that.

Only two sites have been published in any detail. One of these is Ayios Elias, in south Aetolia, between the Achelous river and the Gulf of Kanali. Here a chamber tomb and four tholos tombs were excavated; the chamber tomb belonged to the fourteenth century, but two at least of the tholos tombs were quite definitely used for burials in the twelfth century, on the basis of the pottery. Survival into this century is therefore established, and will no doubt be recognised elsewhere. And what is of particular interest is that one of the twelfth-century L.H. III C shapes was the kylix; as well as this, though, there were stirrup jars, bowls, and a jug of this period.[9] What we cannot tell is how far into the twelfth century these tombs remained in use – it seems at any rate unlikely that they persisted into the Dark Ages.

The other site is that of Thermon, north-east of Lake Trichonis. Some of the sherds from this settlement should be dated to L.H. III C, but of greater interest is the fact that this was essentially a local, non-Mycenaean settlement – the majority of the pottery is native. We are already outside the Mycenaean orbit, and from here inland and northwards we continue to be so.

The region of North Aetolia, and of Epirus to its north, is one of the most consistently rugged and mountainous in the whole of Greece; the only fertile district would seem to be around Iannina. It plays little part in subsequent history, but it may have some relevance just during the early Dark Ages.

The native population was only marginally aware of Mycenaean culture and developments, and had a rather backward culture of its own, which it persisted in using at least down to the fifth century B.C. This is implied by Thucydides, and is confirmed by the archaeological evidence. In the Iannina area, for example, three main classes of pottery were current, all hand-made; two of them were local, and seem to have continued in use from c. 2000 B.C. down to the end of the fifth century. The third had a much wider distribution, with Macedonian links, as well as being found in south Aetolia, and even at Olympia; this class, which though hand-made was at least painted and decorated, is thought to have appeared in the Iannina plain somewhere towards the end of the thirteenth century, and to have continued down into the fifth. There was one further ceramic strain, in origin Mycenaean, and this also was extraordinarily long-lived: at Kastritsa, south of Iannina, some wheel-made kylikes, reminiscent of the Mycenaean shape, have been given an early fourth-century date.

All this may suggest that any attempt at accurate dating is doomed to

[9] One of the other two tholos tombs had what looks like part of a violin-bow fibula of twisted wire, but this could be earlier than 1200 B.C.

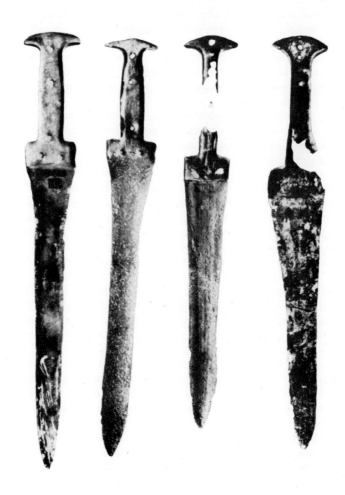

PLATE 17 EPIRUS. Daggers from various sites. *PPS* for 1967, 32, pl. I.

failure, but there are also a few genuine pieces of Mycenaean pottery. The appearance of short swords of the type with crescent-shaped pommel and square shoulders (Pl. 17), as found in Kephallenia and at Ancient Elis, is of importance as well since, first found in the thirteenth century, the type does not seem to have survived the early Dark Ages. A particular variety of spearhead (see Pl. 13), with an almost exclusively north-western Greek distribution, has a similar significance, as most of the examples belong to the twelfth and eleventh centuries.

On the basis of these pointers, we can assign the following material to the late thirteenth or to the twelfth century. The tholos tomb at Parga, in which not only thirteenth-century Mycenaean but also native pottery was found, had a spearhead which may possibly be classed with the type mentioned. A short sword was found at Ephyra, not far south of Parga and also close to the sea (see above for the Mycenaean pottery on this site). North and inland from here, at Paramythia, a cist tomb (note the type) produced a rather earlier variety of the short sword, with sloping shoulders. Yet another, with squared shoulders (as are the others I shall mention) was found at Dodona, not far south of the plain of Iannina; it had no context, but a Mycenaean sherd of *c.* 1200 B.C. was unearthed on the site, in association with what sound like kylix stems. Equally without context was a further short sword from near Kastritsa, east of Iannina, but this area was continuously occupied, and also produced a cist tomb with a stirrup jar which looks to be of twelfth-century date.

Finally, there is a series of three sites, some twenty-five miles north and north-west of Iannina. At Kalbaki there were four cist tombs which contained, in addition to a short sword and spearhead of the types mentioned, an amber bead, bracelets with spiral terminals, bronze tweezers, and native ware. The four cist tombs from Elaphotopos had no weapons (unless one considers as such an extremely fine sickle-shaped knife), but otherwise the pattern of finds was similar to that at Kalbaki, and a date not far from 1200 B.C. may be tentatively suggested. The most interesting object was in any case not a weapon but a bronze finger ring with double-spiral terminals, in other words of the same type as those which have been found in Sub-Mycenaean central Greece. The third site, that of Mazaraki, had only one cist tomb, apparently containing three corpses, and this is reasonably firmly anchored to the end of the thirteenth century by the presence of a stirrup jar; furthermore, it had a remarkable miscellany of weapons, a cruciform sword (probably in active use for a very long time, as the type belongs rather to the fourteenth century), a dagger, two fragmentary knives or daggers, and three spearheads, one of which is of the type so commonly found in this general region.

This evidence is of course most inadequate, but it does seem significant that so many of these swords have been discovered – six, of which five were of the late type with squared shoulders; adding the three from Kephallenia, they make up half of the known examples, and suggest that the inhabitants were fairly warlike. The spearheads lead to the same conclusion,[10] and it may be noted that yet another was found in a tumulus (enclosing cist tombs) at Vajzë, a fair distance to the north-west of Kalbaki, across the Albanian border. It is also evident that the population were not Mycenaean, from their hand-made pottery, but it is also clear that Mycenaean vases, including kylikes, made their way to the inland areas.

Finally, it should be stressed that where in these inland areas the type of grave is known, it is a cist tomb; thus we have tombs of the kind characteristic of the Sub-Mycenaean culture of central Greece, here equally characteristic of Epirus, but at a slightly earlier date. But if one has a link

[10] There were several of different types as well.

in mind, one must remember that the distance between the two areas is considerable, even between the southernmost Epirote example and the nearest Sub-Mycenaean cemetery, that of Ancient Elis. The intermediate stages are missing, unless one may perhaps include the cist tombs of Agriapidies (p. 92) in Achaea, with their hand-made mugs. Nor are there any other apparent links with Sub-Mycenaean, except for the ring from Elaphotopos; and it is perhaps relevant that both the swords found at Ancient Elis seem to have northern affinities (see further on p. 74).

North-west Greece seems then to have had a native culture of its own, which incorporated a few Mycenaean ideas. One apparent extension of this culture has been recently discovered in western Thessaly, and may serve as an introduction to the general area. The site is called Hexalophos, and lies near the foothills of the Pindus about eight miles west of Trikkala. It comprised a tumulus which, when excavated, has so far revealed two cist tombs, one burial in each.[11] Inside these graves were found three or four vases of local manufacture but with decoration recalling, according to the excavator, the pottery of Kephallenia. But this was not all, for there were also several funnel-shaped kylikes (Pl. 18), with ribbed stems – a sure sign of lateness, perhaps even belonging to the eleventh century – and varying decoration. No other kylikes have yet been found in Thessaly, and influence or importation from north-west Greece, or at least through it, cannot be doubted. There were also objects of bronze. Tomb A, in the centre of the mound, contained not only a knife and a spearhead, but a short sword of the type discussed above, so familiar in north-west Greece and the Ionian islands. Tomb B, on the perimeter, had among its metal objects a bronze ring with spiral terminals, a further link with Epirus, and indeed with central Greece as well.

The excavator's conclusions were that here we have a people of a Mycenaean or Mycenaeanised cultural tradition, very probably of Epirote origin, who occupied west Thessaly during the second half of the twelfth century. And there seems no doubt that this is correct, though the date might even be a little later. It would have been perfectly possible for these people to have made their way from the plain of Iannina through Metzovo to Kalambaka and Trikkala; alternatively, they could have taken a more southerly route, starting from the Gulf of Arta. The whole remarkable find sheds light not only on the course of events in Thessaly, but also illuminates the situation in north-west Greece. People were on the move, travelling in an easterly direction, at a time very close to the beginning of the Dark Ages.

Could they have started earlier? At Agrilia, on the foothills of Mt. Chasia, some miles east of Kalambaka, there are more cist tombs. Nothing has been published in detail, but the original report says that there were ten of them, close together, and that they contained mainly local hand-made vases, but also a few Mycenaean ones. The Mycenaean vases were either on their own in separate burials, by the side of other burials which had native vases only, or were found in association with local vases or with hand-made ware

---

[11] The latest report indicates the presence of a pyre connected with tomb A, and makes it clear that there should be more tombs in the unexcavated parts.

imitating Mycenaean. No indication of date was given, but in the report on the tombs of Hexalophos it is stated that the Mycenaean pottery should be dated *c.* 1200 B.C., and that there were weapons as well, including two spearheads similar to those of Hexalophos. It is tempting to suppose that this material may represent an even earlier move from north-west Greece, but there is no hint that the Mycenaean pottery had any such links – and there can have been no kylikes, since those of Hexalophos are stated to have no known Thessalian parallel. Furthermore, as we shall see, cist tombs were already in use in Thessaly during the thirteenth century.

Generally speaking, the situation in Thessaly in the twelfth century, and later, is highly complex. We have already seen, in west Thessaly, that there were new arrivals from north-west Greece, and that the existing local population was susceptible at least to the influence of Mycenaean culture, if not to actual penetration by Mycenaeans (this on the assumption that the Agrilia cist tombs do not represent an earlier move from Epirus). There was yet another intrusive element at a later point, from Macedonia, but before discussing that it will be better to return to the Mycenaeans and try to follow their progress – or rather, their retreat.

There is no doubt that, however numerous the indigenous population was, Mycenaean culture had spread widely over Thessaly during the thirteenth century. During the twelfth century, or L.H. III C, there seems to have been a weakening of this influence in the central inland plain, while it remained, uncontaminated, in the coastal areas – the Pagasaean Gulf and the Krokian plain. Here, indeed, it was surely a matter not of influence but of actual Mycenaean settlements.

More than one factor may have been involved in this recession. It is probable that the disasters on the mainland further south had some indirect effect on those Mycenaeans who lived in Thessaly. There is no question of the district being isolated from the south – for example, a sherd of the central Aegean Octopus Style has been found – but preliminary investigations indicate that the harbour area of Iolkos was little used after 1200 B.C. Inland, it would seem that the main road northwards from Iolkos, past Velestino and on to Larisa, and also the route to Pharsala, may have remained for a while under Mycenaean control. Further inland, it is a little difficult to say: the occasional Mycenaean vase, and the imitations of these, need not mean more than casual contact and the survival of the Mycenaean tradition of pot-making – as is probably the case in Macedonia. It is perhaps significant that at the important site of Gremnos, on the river Peneios and only a few miles west of Larisa, the typical pottery was native Thessalian, and L.H. III C pottery was almost wholly absent.

Secondly, there is the factor of probable unrest in and menace from the regions west and north of Thessaly, one instance of which has already been mentioned. I think there may have been a gradually increasing pressure from these areas, Epirus and Macedonia, throughout the twelfth century. There is no proof, but it is quite possible that the destruction of the palace at Iolkos and the simultaneous temporary desertion of its settlement were due to some invading band from the inland areas. So the Mycenaeans of

PLATE 18 HEXALOPHOS. Kylikes. *Athens Annals* I, 291, fig. 1.

Thessaly may have felt, on the one hand, a sense of insecurity consequent on the catastrophic events further south, and on the other hand they may have had to contend with pressures from west and north of them.

When exactly, or even roughly, did the destruction and desertion of Iolkos take place? This is as yet by no means clear, though it must have been at some time during the twelfth century. The lack of precision is particularly unfortunate, both because this was the principal Mycenaean town of Thessaly, and also because the subsequent settlement, which has impressive stone foundations and continued to be occupied until the Geometric period (in other words, after the end of the Dark Ages) is reported, on the basis of the similarity of the pottery, to have begun its life no more than a generation after the earlier desertion. On the other hand, the excavator states that the characteristic pottery of the new settlement was Protogeometric,[12] on conventional dating not earlier than 1050 B.C. – and it is true enough that the vases so far published from the associated nearby children's cist tombs are of this style (p. 210). It seems to me possible that the gap between desertion and reoccupation may have been appreciably longer than has been suggested.

What then was happening in Thessaly during the early Dark Ages, the time when the Sub-Mycenaean culture prevailed in central Greece? Not a great deal of information can be extracted from the pottery, nor are the settlements and their material at all instructive as yet. Can the types of tombs provide any assistance – as they do in other areas? Unfortunately, they do not clarify the situation, but at least a review of the distribution of

---

[12] See p. 209 for pottery of possibly earlier date.

the main types will show how different conditions in Thessaly were from other districts, and how complex. This review will include not only the early Dark Ages but the periods before and after.

Chamber tombs, so popular in the south of Greece, are surprisingly rare in Thessaly. Until recently, such tombs had been found only at Pharsala and near Iolkos (Volos): two at the former site, and a large group of nearly forty at the latter; and even these were uncanonical, being built of small stone slabs, and those of Pharsala having an entrance at the corner of the chamber. In 1963, however, a group of five were discovered about half-way between Volos and Larisa, of normal type and in use during the fourteenth and thirteenth centuries. So there may be many more, but there is so far no evidence that this type survived even into the twelfth century.

With one exception, that of six cave-like tombs at Homolion, well north of Tempe and practically on the borders of Macedonia – in any case datable no earlier than the tenth century, and more likely belonging to the ninth – burial took place, so far as we know, either in tholos tombs or in cist tombs. One might consequently expect a reasonable chronological distinction, but the opposite is the case.

Both types of tomb were in use during the period down to 1200 B.C. The cist tombs were confined to three sites in the coastal area bordering the Gulf of Pagasae, and appear to range from Middle Helladic down to the thirteenth century.[13] The tholos tombs, dating from Late Helladic II (L.H. II) onwards, are also mostly to be found in this area, but have also been discovered in south-west Thessaly, near Karditsa (one belonging to to the L.H. II period), and also north and east of Larisa, at Rakhmani, where a small one may have been in use throughout Mycenaean times, near Sykourion to its south, where one of the two tholoi dates to the fourteenth and thirteenth centuries, and one at Marmariani, a few miles further to the south. On the whole, the sparse present evidence suggests that burial in tholos tombs was more popular than that in cist tombs. It may also be that cist tombs were more favoured by the native population, but that is conjectural.

After 1200 B.C. the picture becomes very confused. To start with, there is only one case, so far as I know, of tholos tombs being continuously used from earlier times into the twelfth century, and that is at Gritsa, in the south-easternmost corner of Thessaly and relatively isolated: it hardly belongs to Thessaly at all – this is the site that had interesting links with Achaea (p. 92) – and can probably be disregarded. The other tholos tombs, which I discuss below, belong to the post-Mycenaean period, even though they retain in their type the Mycenaean tradition.

As to the cist tombs, there are quite a number. At the head of them, chronologically, stands the Agrilia group of c. 1200 B.C., and the two of the Hexalophos tumulus, not earlier than the late twelfth century; these I have already discussed. Were they the natural successors of the Middle Helladic and Mycenaean cist tombs? This seems unlikely. The Agrilia tombs had, as well as Mycenaean vases, others imitating Mycenaean, and

---

[13] A cist tomb was found further inland, at Chasambali near Larisa, which may also precede the twelfth century.

native ware; and the connexions, ceramic and metallic, of the Hexalophos tombs are clearly with north-west Greece and the north. Also, the tumulus idea was a northern and not a Mycenaean one.

After these in time comes the cist tomb of Theotokou, on the far side of the Magnesian promontory, but here the link may be rather with the south, to judge from the Sub-Mycenaean lekythos and the iron ring that the tomb contained. In fact, this might be yet another example of the outward expansion which, as we have seen, took place in the late Sub-Mycenaean phase (pp. 78 f.).

Possibly contemporary with this are two cist tombs from Retziouni, on the southern foothills of Mt. Olympus – they contained not only native pottery but a vase claimed to be Sub-Mycenaean.

The remainder all belong to the later part of the eleventh century or after, and all are close to the Pagasaean Gulf, with the exception of two at Palaiokastro, fairly easily accessible from the Aegean. Should one trace their origin to earlier Mycenaean cist tombs in this district, or to a gradual move from the west (in other words, to those who buried at Hexalophos), or even to diffusion from the south in Sub-Mycenaean times? Clear connecting links are not visible for any of these alternatives – the pottery of the Iolkos cemetery and other tombs is of Protogeometric type, more akin to that of Lefkandi and Naxos than to that of Athens, but this need not mean that the type of tomb had its origins in the south as well.

The situation is further complicated by the persistence of the use of tholos tombs. The following are all definitely, or reported to be, post-Mycenaean in date. East of Volos, in the Pelion range which forms the northern backbone of the Magnesian promontory, there are three sites with tholos tombs said to be post-Mycenaean. Close to Volos itself, at Kapakli, there is one whose burials may span almost half a millennium, from the late eleventh or early tenth century at least to the seventh. Several, described as of Geometric date, were found at Sesklo, a little to the west of Volos.[14] Travelling northwards, into the central plain, there is a tholos tomb at Chasambali, near Larisa, which was certainly in use c. 900 B.C. Also in this district, north or north-west of Larisa, there is a small group at Chyretiai, just south of Elasson; at Marmariani six tholos tombs spanned the centuries from the eleventh to the ninth; and one at Homolion, the northernmost site, produced pottery whose date is not far from 900 B.C.

All these are situated in the north-eastern section of Thessaly. Only two have been found in other areas: the one at Gritsa mentioned above, in use since Mycenaean times, and re-used in the late eleventh or the tenth century; and one in the foothills of the Pindus, south of the inland plain, whose contents, now lost, were reported to be as late as c. 800 B.C.

In other words, we have here a particularly clear instance of the survival of a Mycenaean type of tomb, almost entirely concentrated in the north-eastern part of Thessaly. Furthermore, at Volos if not elsewhere, burial in tholos tombs was contemporary with that in cist tombs – and although most of the cist tombs at Volos (i.e. Iolkos) contained child burials, one or

---

[14] At least one of these was probably of the tenth century.

two of the later ones did not, so it is not altogether safe to say that tholos tombs were restricted to adults, and cist tombs to children – a judgment which for cist tombs is in any case not valid elsewhere in Thessaly.

Nor do the problems end here. One must suppose the continuance of the Mycenaean tradition in these tholos tombs, and yet no Mycenaean objects were associated with them, with the possible exception of one solitary vase at Marmariani. Nor can one claim natural succession through the pottery, since, again at Marmariani, those vases which seem quite certainly to be the earliest were hand-made, and had links with Macedonia – one can thereafter see the transition from hand-made to wheel-made, in accordance with the new influence of the Protogeometric style. And it is indeed this pottery, probably to be dated not earlier than the late eleventh century, which constitutes the evidence for the further intrusive element mentioned above (p. 99).

It will thus be seen that the picture of Thessaly in the early Dark Ages is obscure, though one can be reasonably certain about a few features. The evidence may be summarised as follows. At least four elements of population seem to be recognisable during the twelfth and eleventh centuries. In the coastal area there were the Mycenaeans, with a harbour and stronghold at Iolkos; their distinctive culture had taken firm root in this area, though they differed from most of the other inhabitants of the Mycenaean world in their apparent dislike of burial in chamber tombs. Whereas in the thirteenth century their influence had extended to the inland regions, the twelfth century shows little evidence of their activities in these parts, except around Larisa, on the main route from Iolkos to the north. During this century also their contacts with the more southerly centres of their world were probably weakened, as a result of the upheavals there shortly before 1200 B.C. At some time in the course of the century the settlement of Iolkos itself was in part destroyed, in part deserted, after which, either late in the twelfth century or during the eleventh, a new settlement arose, in which the Mycenaean tradition was probably preserved in the almost monumental character of the stone foundations, and perhaps also in the pottery. The discovery of a cist-tomb cemetery (which on present evidence cannot be dated earlier than 1050 B.C.) may suggest the admixture of non-Mycenaeans, but the survival of the tholos tomb here and elsewhere in north and east Thessaly should indicate some measure of Mycenaean survival, though not always associated with those of Mycenaean stock, as has been seen above. Only in the southernmost coastal area may the Mycenaean residents have remained undisturbed for quite a while.

Secondly, there was the local indigenous population, probably chiefly confined to the central plain. Except for their pottery, they do not seem to have had any distinguishing features, but there is no doubt of their existence – they were predominant, as we have seen, at Gremnos just west of Larisa. They were prepared, as in Macedonia, to accept certain features of Mycenaean culture.

The other two elements of population were both intrusive. The one came from north-west Greece: whether it is to be recognised as early as *c.* 1200 B.C. in the users of the cist tombs of Agrilia is very questionable, but there is no doubt of its presence at the end of the twelfth century, or the beginning of the eleventh, on the site of Hexalophos – the pottery, the metal objects, and the manner of burial all demand or permit a north-western origin. Whether it subsequently advanced further into Thessaly we cannot be sure, though the later geographical distribution of the cist tombs might be a pointer – and such an extension would be in accordance with the oral tradition (see pp. 322 f.).

The other element was of Macedonian origin, but the time of the intrusion is not clear – perhaps not much before 1000 B.C., in northern Thessaly. These people are chiefly to be recognised in the pottery they used, but for reasons unknown they preferred to bury their dead in Mycenaean-type tholos tombs. The extent of their penetration at this stage seems to have been confined to the northern districts; their later connexion with the coastal area I shall discuss in due course (pp. 213 ff.).

This, it seems to me, is as far as we can go at present. The evidence is too sparse, and the problems of interpretation too great. One final question must, however, be put – were there any links with the Sub-Mycenaean culture of central Greece? So far as concerns the origin of that culture, the discussion below must serve (pp. 106 ff.). But is there any evidence of communication between Thessaly and central Greece during the first half of the eleventh century, and if so was Thessaly at all affected by the late Sub-Mycenaean expansion, as was apparently the case with Lefkandi in Euboea? All we know for certain is that there was some contact, if not more, between central Greece and Theotokou, probably not long before 1050 B.C., and it could be that then some ceramic influence penetrated to Iolkos (as it did in Protogeometric times). But what we cannot use is the fact of the appearance of cist tombs at Iolkos as evidence for a link with Sub-Mycenaean culture. Until we have much more material, and of an earlier date, we cannot rule out the possibility of an alternative origin for these tombs.

There remains one further area, comprising the intervening districts between Thessaly and Boeotia. Whether, strictly speaking, it should be considered as part of what I have termed the Northern Crescent, I am rather doubtful. Nevertheless, it should be mentioned, and this is probably the best place to do so.

Immediately to the south of Thessaly there is the plain and valley through which the river Spercheios runs. There are very few traces of the Mycenaeans here, perhaps not surprisingly since the Spercheios penetrates deep into the range of the Pindus, and the district was thus rather too easily accessible to the non-Mycenaean region; also, it is somewhat inaccessible from the south. What the situation was during the twelfth century one cannot tell: the vases of Achaean type which reach the south-eastern coast of Thessaly may have passed through this district, but alternative routes are possible. The only relevant material comes from Vardhates, on the foothills south of the plain, where a curious type of tomb was found, a rectangular shaft with upright slabs set down the middle, and roofed with large and small slabs. The vases were certainly Mycenaean, and in part belonged to L.H. III C, but whether any could be as late as Sub-Mycenaean is very doubtful.

South again, across the mountains, the situation in the region of Phocis was very different. At Delphi there is no doubt that Mycenaean civilisation survived well down into the twelfth century. The contents of one rich chamber tomb not only show there were contacts with districts to the south and to the east, but included two lekythoi which look Sub-Mycenaean. On two or three sites on the shores of the Corinthian Gulf there is further evidence of occupation into the twelfth century, and of understandable contact with the opposite shore of Achaea. A few vases from chamber tombs at Itea and at Galaxidi have been classed as Sub-Mycenaean, but I am not altogether convinced of the correctness of this. Still, the material at least shows that there were one or two Mycenaean communities in this district which were as long-lived as many of those of Achaea.

Finally, there is the cemetery of Medeon, on the east side of the bay of Antikyra. Here several types of tomb were found. There were rectangular trenches, walled and covered with stone blocks, there were three chamber tombs, all having steps leading down to them, and two covered with slabs, and there were earth-cut graves with stone slab roofing. The first two types were used for multiple burials, and at least some were in use from the fourteenth to the twelfth century. The third type housed individual burials, and the vases they contained are said to be L.H. III C or Sub-Mycenaean. Subsequently (see p. 206), there were numerous cremations in the same area, extending in time at least from the tenth century to the sixth; and from the ninth century onwards there were inhumations as well. But it is of course the earth-cut graves that are of particular importance in the present context. Do they belong with the first two types of tomb, or do they represent something entirely different, and to be taken with the Sub-Mycenaean earth-cut and cist tombs of central Greece? In default of the full report, we cannot say; but at least they lie at no great distance either from Thebes or from the Argolid.

5 The Origins of the Sub-Mycenaean Culture

An attempt has been made in the preceding sections to give a picture of the earlier phase of the Dark Ages in mainland Greece and the central Aegean; and it must be emphasised that in no district is the known and published material sufficient for anything like completeness and accuracy, while in some it remains impossible to get any idea at all of what was happening. Certain points do, however, emerge. The whole situation is set against a previous background of insecurity, and this must not be forgotten. The major disasters of the end of the thirteenth century, with their attendant feature of movements of population, were to a lesser extent repeated, after a short breathing space, during the second half of the twelfth century. The end of this century, and the first half of the next, saw the progressive dissolution of certain Mycenaean communities which had retained their traditional culture, that is to say those of the central Aegean group, of Euboea, of Achaea, and presumably of Phocis. In southern Peloponnese, such evidence as we have suggests the temporary safety of isolation and small numbers. In Kephallenia and Ithaca there was evidently no cause for concern, but here the Mycenaean element had made common cause with the native; continuity is clear, in contrast to the situation in the Aegean. In north-west Greece the coastal Mycenaeans were quite unable to retain their independent settlements; as to the non-Mycenaean peoples of the interior, the situation is that they kept their local characteristics, among which was some superficial acceptance of Mycenaean culture, and there will have been continuity, but there was also some movement of population from the area. Such movement is observable into Thessaly, where the local population of the interior central plains, with the recession of Mycenaean strength on the coast, found itself open to the menace of thrusts both from north-west Greece and, later, from Macedonia. The Mycenaeans themselves, though they held the coastline in strength, nevertheless underwent some disaster at Iolkos, leading to the temporary desertion of this major settlement; thereafter, it is not clear what happened.

This accounts for every district – leaving aside Crete till later – except for the most important of all, that of central Greece, almost entirely surrounded for some time by Mycenaean communities which held fast to an earlier civilisation, while in their own a new culture was introduced. And yet it was the central Greek communities which survived and flourished, and their neighbours who melted away like the summer snows.

I have already said something about the characteristics and progress of these communities, their similarities and their differences, but there is one question of the greatest importance, which could not be even partly answered until the evidence from the whole of Greece and the central Aegean had been outlined and discussed, and that concerns the origin of those who adopted the Sub-Mycenaean culture. Did the communities arise, phoenix-like, from the ashes of their forebears, or are we to conclude that there was an entirely new element in the population?

The answer must endeavour to satisfy not just one or two of the characteristic features of the culture, but all of them – and it may be said straight away that neither solution will be found to be altogether satis-factory. Briefly to recapitulate these main features, they were as follows: the decision to abandon earlier Mycenaean habitation sites and choose different ones of their own – so far as we know; the readiness to locate their burial grounds above and within Mycenaean settlement areas; the decision to abandon the practice of multiple burial (a partial exception being found at Argos alone) and to turn to individual burial in cist tombs or earth-cut graves; the retention of the preceding Mycenaean ceramic style, however simplified and debilitated; the abandonment of the previously cherished adornments of dress coupled with the introduction of new or modified articles, the long dress pins and the arched fibulae. There are other features as well, such as the occasional presence of objects of northern origin, and the curious absence of weapons from early burials – apart from the dubious example of Ancient Elis; these are also worth bearing in mind. The whole impression, whether viewed negatively or positively, is of something radically different from what had preceded it, except in the matter of the pottery.

Or was it really so different? The pottery itself should give us pause, for it is after all a fairly essential feature in the life of the community. Some survivors there must have been: cannot the other features be explained in terms of survival?

On the surface, the greatest change from previous conditions is to be seen in the burial customs. No more chamber tombs, no more multiple burials. But if we look into the earlier state of affairs more carefully, we find that there are cases of burial in cist and earth-cut tombs in Mycenaean times.

It may be pointed out that in the twelfth-century cemetery of Perati, on the east coast of Attica, no fewer than twenty-six earth-cut graves (no cist tombs) were found among the two hundred or so chamber tombs. Might not these be the forerunners of the Sub-Mycenaean type? Such a sugges-tion must be discounted. It is perfectly clear, as the excavator has explained, that the reason for this kind of construction was simply that the cemetery area included a small amount of relatively level ground, and that this was unsuitable for the building of a normal chamber tomb, and so these shafts had to suffice. It was therefore neither a matter of a new fashion nor of an ancient tradition, but of sheer necessity, and no link can be made with the Sub-Mycenaean tombs.[1]

This is not the only evidence, however: there are further instances,

[1] Two points may be added: these tombs belonged to the earlier two periods of the cemetery's use, not to its third and final one; and the excavator got his workmen to try to construct a chamber tomb on the fairly level ground, and it was found to be virtually impossible.

which may be thought to be more pertinent. As to cist tombs, it may in any case be stressed that this type of grave was normally used in mainland Greece in Middle Helladic times, before the Mycenaean age, and at Eleusis in Attica the practice was retained down into the thirteenth century, though the actual type of tomb differed from that current in the early Dark Ages in west Attica, Boeotia, and the Argolid.

In these areas no Mycenaean cist tombs can be clearly allocated to the twelfth century, but for the thirteenth and fourteenth they are to be found on several sites: in the Argolid, at Lerna and Argos, at Asine and, right in the south, at Karakasi; and in Boeotia, at Gla and Orchomenos. Of these, the Karakasi cemetery was evidently a large one, but there is no indication as to its date; elsewhere they are solitary examples.

The evidence for earth-cut graves is much more impressive: thirty-one at Argos, of which nine were not datable, nineteen of the fourteenth century, two of the thirteenth and one (rather doubtfully) of the twelfth; nine at Asine, somewhere within Mycenaean times, and a few at Berbati; four at Voula, on the south coast of Attica, of the thirteenth century where datable, and at least ten at Athens, mostly fourteenth century in date but also of the thirteenth, and one of *c.* 1200 B.C.

Of course, when one sets these beside the great mass of chamber tombs and tholos tombs, and when one notes the fact that most of them belong to the fourteenth century, the evidence seems extremely thin, but the fact that they do appear at all – especially in such numbers at Argos – is of relevance. Furthermore, one can point to similar tombs in other parts of the Mycenaean world, for example Thessaly – and there is an extremely interesting thirteenth-century one at Emborio on Chios, a forerunner of the twelfth-century settlement there. Once again, the total is very small indeed, but sufficient to show that some people did persist in using individual as opposed to multiple burial. And it is also worth mentioning that tholos tombs occasionally contained pits or cist tombs within the floor of the chamber. Can we not then suppose that the Sub-Mycenaean tombs represented a revival of a practice which had never been altogether discarded, and a rejection of the normal Mycenaean system perhaps originally imposed by the ruling class, on the grounds that all that had been finished with? Or could it be something simpler, just a feeling that multiple family burials, in the existing state of insecurity, no longer served any purpose – in which case the trench, stone-lined and possibly stone-covered as well, would be the natural alternative?

As to the dress accessories, it could reasonably be argued that the arched fibulae were logical developments of the earlier – even though un-Mycenaean – violin-bow fibulae, and it has been pointed out that the dress pins of type A (with disk and bulb) had a local predecessor in the sixteenth-century Shaft-grave circle B at Mycenae. As to those of type B, however, examples of which are also to be found in Crete at this time, it has been suggested that they could be a variant introduced from the east Mediterranean, with which area the Sub-Mycenaeans will have been in touch, but not involving any actual movement of people into central Greece, with a similar conclusion of casual contact for those few objects (for example, the votive wheel and rings with double-spiral terminals) of northern origin.

Finally, there is the disuse of Mycenaean dress accessories; here it has been stressed that at Argos anyway these had already gone out of fashion by the early twelfth century, on our present evidence. It would no doubt be explained as a further example of the local rejection of Mycenaean customs, rather as in the type of tomb.

This is a perfectly possible hypothesis (though the suggested origin of the dress pins is not altogether satisfactory, as we shall see), and there is no doubt that such an explanation makes it easier to understand the temporary continuance of burial in chamber tombs at Argos during the early Dark Ages.

But I think that one must not take the rejection of the Mycenaean way of life too lightly, and that it should be realised how thorough it was. We have seen that it meant the discarding of family burial, and the return (if such it was) to a practice which had been only rarely used, except in Argos, and perhaps not used at all, so far as we can tell, since 1200 B.C. It meant the rejection, very likely, of the old manner of dress and the adoption of a new style (this is what the use of fibulae and dress pins seems to involve), and it also meant that these people no longer used the little terracotta figurines which may have had some religious significance.[2] And one must not forget that it also meant (where we have the evidence) the desertion of Mycenaean settlements, and the uncaring use of these settlements for burial purposes. Also, the phenomenon took place not only in part of one community, but totally in a number of communities over a wide area – not necessarily or probably at the same time, of course, but the decision must surely have been taken by the authorities of the community as a whole, with similar decisions in other communities. And all this happened, as I believe, while many communities at no great distance were preserving the Mycenaean way of life uncontaminated. It is indeed so remarkable that I feel it is worth considering the possibility of the arrival of newcomers who fused with, and dominated, the surviving element.

Before investigating this, one must determine whether certain areas can be ruled out as possible originators. In fact there are several. Anywhere to the east of central Greece seems to be impossible, for the Mycenaean central Aegean group formed a barrier, though an increasingly weak one, and neither here nor on the coast of Asia Minor nor in the east Mediterranean do we encounter people who have the appropriate cultural characteristics. Crete may be eliminated for the same reasons (see pp. 112 ff.). Indeed, I do not think that newcomers of the type required can have arrived from anywhere in the Aegean area, and we may then consider the possibility of an overland route.

Nothing in the material known to us suggests that such migrants could have come from the south Peloponnese, but as we have practically nothing to go on it would perhaps be a little unwise to rule it out categorically. What, though, of the western and northern routes of access? Here again

[2] I deal with religious continuity at a later stage, pp. 278 ff.

we must go a little carefully, bearing in mind that at least the district of Achaea, and perhaps also that in the neighbourhood of Delphi, constituted a possible barrier to infiltration in the shape of the surviving Mycenaean communities. Even so, it is worth considering north-west Greece as an area of possible origin; and if one has obvious reservations about the size of population the district could support, one must also remember that the whole of the Greek mainland was seriously under-populated, and even a small group of newcomers was not likely to meet much opposition.

Would it have been feasible, though, for such a group or groups to journey to central Greece from north-west Greece, avoiding if necessary the districts of Mycenaean survival? There seem to be two possible ways, one wholly overland, the other involving a sea-crossing at one point. The first would descend the Spercheios valley and then turn south-east, eventually reaching Boeotia and Attica; the second would follow the modern highway from Iannina to Missolonghi, and at about this point the Gulf of Patras would be traversed, after which the route would turn south, and then east over rather difficult country to the Argolid – it would of course be much easier to continue southwards down the west coast of the Peloponnese, and we may in time find that this did happen, though that would not rule out an eastward move as well.

Is there any indication that such a move took place? All one can say is that there is evidence that these people were on the move, as traces of them have been found in western Thessaly. The final destruction of the coastal fortress of Teichos Dymaion is relevant in this context, since it is most naturally attributable to people coming across the Gulf of Patras. But the date is the vital point, and that has not yet been established; should it be shown to be substantially later than *c*. 1125 B.C., there can then be no connexion with the initial appearance of the Sub-Mycenaean culture, and it might be used as an argument against the idea of people moving into the Peloponnese from north-west Greece at an earlier date.[3]

Assuming, however, that it was possible for these north-westerners to have made their way to central Greece in the second half of the twelfth century, we must ask whether they possessed the right sort of characteristic customs for the inspiration of the new culture. The main point is that they used cist tombs, and were already using them in the late thirteenth century and in the twelfth – and no other type of burial is known. So there is a similarity in tomb type, but one still has to bridge the gap in distance between those of Epirus and the nearest Sub-Mycenaean ones, those of Ancient Elis (and perhaps of Agriapidies, quite undatable) in the Peloponnese, or those of Thebes in Boeotia.

Apart from this, there is not very much to go on. The pottery of the north-west was hand-made, but that is no problem. It would be natural for migrants from this area to adopt the wheel-made tradition they would encounter in the Argolid, Boeotia, and west Attica – it is not suggested that newcomers expelled the existing inhabitants. Their weapons were distinc-

[3] I return to this problem in my concluding chapter, pp. 336f.

tive and characteristic, but then we have nothing from early Sub-Mycenaean to set beside them, though it may be worth noting that a spearhead of the leaf-shaped type is said to have been found near Thebes. Against this, when we eventually encounter weapons in the Sub-Mycenaean area (with the exception of Ancient Elis) they are found to reflect rather the latest Mycenaean developments (see pp. 308 ff.). And the fact itself that weapons have not been found in earlier Sub-Mycenaean graves, whereas they were frequently deposited in the cist tombs of Epirus, must be borne in mind, and could affect our conclusions.

It must also be stressed that the two most characteristic dress accessories of the Sub-Mycenaean area, the arched fibula and the long dress pin, are entirely missing from the earlier cist tombs of Epirus. The question of their origin is, however, an extremely complex one, and I attempt to deal with it in a later chapter (pp. 297 ff.). For the arched fibulae, a local development out of the earlier violin-bow type – itself not Mycenaean in origin – is possible. For the dress pins, on the other hand, the derivation of type A from a Mycenaean pin of the sixteenth century is singularly unconvincing, while the attribution of the east Mediterranean as a source for those of type B is open to considerable doubt, bearing in mind the evidence of Diakata and Vergina (pp. 91, 218 f.). There is also the fact that long dress pins as such, and used in the same way, are known in central Europe long before they appear in central Greece.

That there was contact between the Sub-Mycenaean area and the north, outside the limits of Mycenaean Greece, is shown by such objects as the votive wheel of bronze from an Argive chamber tomb, the Tiryns helmet, and the gold hair spirals of doubled wire found in tombs from Athens and Tiryns. These, except for the wheel, belong to the later stages, but not necessarily so the amber beads of Ancient Elis. And there is one final object, the ring with double-spiral terminals, of which there are examples in Athens, at Mycenae, and even in the cemetery at Perati; and here at least there is a connexion not only with the north in general, but specifically with Epirus, both at Elaphotopos and at Thessalian Hexalophos, where the finds show contact with Epirus.

There is no doubt that the hypothesis of the arrival of newcomers from north-west Greece needs a great deal more solid evidence to support it before it can be accepted as providing the impetus for the Sub-Mycenaean culture. It still, however, seems to me the more likely solution, bearing in mind the almost total rejection of the Mycenaean way of life that it involved, than that which explains matters as the return to earlier practices by that element of the local population previously dominated by the Mycenaean upper classes. One must remember that the population must in any case, at this period, have been very small indeed. And it may be added that the arrival of newcomers is in principle what the oral tradition claims to have happened – a move of people from the north-west, westwards to Thessaly, and southwards to the Peloponnese, such moves being apparently confirmed by the later dialect distribution.[4]

---

[4] The case for a purely local development of the Sub-Mycenaean culture is fully and admirably set out by Snodgrass, *Dark Age of Greece* (pp. 314 ff.).

6 Crete

Before c. 1100 B.C.

The situation in this island is complex, and made even more so by the difficulties of interpreting the evidence. During the thirteenth century it would
appear that the palaces of Knossos, Mallia, Phaestos, and Ayia Triadha
were all occupied – after a fashion. At Mallia only a very small part of the
whole remained in use, and that seems to have been abandoned before
1200 B.C.; as for Knossos, controversy still continues as to the extent and
character of the occupation, but it would certainly appear that there was
some measure of desertion before the end of the thirteenth century. Only
a small part of the two palaces of the Mesara was occupied during this
century, but whether there was any further constriction at or towards its
end is not known.

There are of course other sites as well. The first reports of the excavations of the fine settlement at Chania, in the west, show that there was continuity at least throughout the thirteenth century and into the twelfth.
Elsewhere, however, the picture is a little different. The major part of the
settlement of Katsamba, near Heraklion, was deserted at the end of Late
Minoan III B (i.e. the thirteenth century); south of Mt. Dicte and east of
the Mesara plain, Kephala Chondrou suffered destruction at or near the
end of the same period; a little further east, close to the northern coast,
Gournia did not survive the thirteenth century, nor did Palaikastro in the
extreme east.

There was then a partial recession towards the end of Late Minoan III B,
to judge from the settlement evidence, and this is confirmed by the tomb
material. Two cemeteries near Knossos fell either completely or temporarily out of use at this time, and so did two or three others in this general
area – and much the same picture emerges from the eastern part of Crete,
though at least one cemetery in this region, that of Myrsini near Seteia,
was still in use in the twelfth century.

During the thirteenth century the material culture had remained predominantly Minoan, little affected by Mycenaean, but at the beginning of
the twelfth – in very round figures – there was an interesting development,
in that locally made pottery of early Mycenaean III C type was introduced.
It is similar in type to that which appeared suddenly in Cyprus, and at
Tarsus in Cilicia, and it is difficult to avoid the conclusion that this represents the after effects of the disasters on the Greek mainland (see pp. 20 f.).
It is particularly noticeable at Knossos and at Phaestos,[1] apparently to be

---

[1] Here and at Ayia Triadha supplemented by the occasional terracotta figurine of Mycenaean
type.

connected with a reoccupation at both sites, and very possibly contemporary with a new settlement at Gortyn, close to the foothills a few miles to the east of Phaestos. Furthermore, there are also signs of this Mycenaean ceramic influence in two settlements on the eastern part of the north coast: at Vrokastro, where reoccupation took place after a lengthy disuse, and at Kastri, close to the deserted Palaikastro and its obvious successor. These two latter sites are distinguished by their very strong naturally defensible character. The picture suggested, then, is that the turmoil of the last part of the thirteenth century in other parts of the Aegean may initially have been reflected in Crete by a partial desertion of sites, that a number of fugitive Mycenaeans made their way to the island, mostly fusing with the existing population and resettling or settling anew, but that the feelings of alarm and despondency earlier diffused were sufficiently strong in the east of Crete for the inhabitants to look to their defences.

Their fears were, however, groundless for the time being, for there ensued the period of brief revival in and around the Aegean, the time of the Argive Close Style and of similar remarkable developments at Lefkandi and in the central Aegean group. And the interesting thing is that, at least culturally, Crete played a more direct part in Aegean history than for some time previously. It has been argued cogently that certain elements in the Close Style itself were of Minoan inspiration. Further, there is no possible doubt that the central Aegean Octopus Style was of Minoan origin, and consequently Crete must have been for a while in reasonably close touch with the area concerned. Within Crete itself an elaborate and flamboyant local style, known as the Fringed, was evolved (Fig. 12). It would seem, as a recent writer has stressed, that the loosening and disruption of the Mycenaean political system, originally all pervasive and imposing a fairly rigid conventionality, resulted in the temporary resurgence of the artist's individual imagination.[2]

During the first half of the twelfth century one can speak of a fairly homogeneous cultural unity over the central and eastern parts of Crete (the situation in the west is not yet clear, as the relevant material has not been fully published). This does not mean that there was unity in other aspects. In matters of burial there are indications that central Crete, as far east as the Dictaean range, preferred to retain the chamber tomb, which until the twelfth century had been the favoured system everywhere in the island; east of this, however, it became customary from the early twelfth century onwards to bury the dead in tholos tombs,[3] a custom that persisted for centuries (see Fig. 26 B). Just what this change meant is not clear, but for some while it had no effect on the unity of culture, nor therefore on free intercommunication. While it would be most interesting to know where the Cretan Fringed Style first originated, its distribution all over the central and eastern regions of the island is the more important factor – and it is also significant that it is still a Minoan style, in spite of the intrusive Mycenaean elements.

[2] Professor Emily Vermeule in *A Land called Crete*, pp. 81 ff.

[3] Tholos tombs had indeed been built earlier, but these are generally larger and better constructed, and are relatively few in number.

The revival which this style represents, shared with other areas of the Aegean, was relatively brief, however. The second half of the twelfth century saw the gradual fading of this brilliance, even though the cultural unity, at least in the ceramic sense, still persisted. The stages of the decline, and its cause or causes, are extremely difficult to follow or interpret.

The chief features of this period, very roughly from 1150 to 1100 B.C., may be set out as follows. In the immediately preceding period we had seen evidence of some resettlement or new settlement. Now, at the very beginning of this one, there is another new settlement, that of Karphi, and it illustrates to an extreme degree the easily defensible type, as found at Vrokastro and Kastri. Whereas these were on the coast, Karphi stands some four thousand feet up, high in the north-west corner of the Dictaean range, a desolate and inaccessible spot. This site I discuss in detail later (pp. 120 ff.). Secondly, at some time after the foundation of Karphi, but almost certainly before 1100 B.C., the settlement of Kastri, in the far east of the island, was abandoned. Third, there are signs of a further intrusion of Mycenaeans during this second half of the twelfth century (p. 58). And finally, at the turn of the century, there is evidence that a number of Cretans migrated to Cyprus (p. 51).

All this, taken in conjunction with the deterioration in the pottery generally, suggests some measure of disturbance and unrest. What lay behind it? The existence of purely internal factors of dissension we have no means of assessing, but we can reasonably take into account the situation at the time in Greece and the Aegean, especially in view of the possible intrusion of Mycenaeans into Crete. This is just the time, as has been seen (pp. 24 f.), of further unrest north of Crete: Mycenae, Iolkos, Lefkandi, all were affected; in the eastern Aegean Emborio and Miletus could have been destroyed and abandoned before 1100 B.C.; although the communities of the Dodecanese and the central Aegean certainly or possibly survived till about 1075 B.C. or later, they were already in decline by the end of the twelfth century. It was between 1150 and 1100 that a further group or groups of people from Greece or the Aegean migrated to Cyprus, in sufficient numbers to have a considerable effect on the island's civilisation. And it seems very likely that it was before the end of the century that the Sub-Mycenaean culture established itself in central mainland Greece, whether as a local phenomenon or as introduced from the north-west. All this increases the likelihood that people from the dying Mycenaean world went to Crete to try to find new homes there, and may thus have been at least one of the causes of the unrest in that island resulting in the decision of some Minoans to move eastwards, to Cyprus. Whatever the full story, there is no doubt that for Crete, as for much of the Aegean, the twelfth century ended on a note of depression.

The Eleventh Century

So far, no mention has been made of the Dark Ages in so far as Crete is concerned, whereas in the central areas I have assumed that the period started c. 1125 B.C. It will be evident, however, that in such a disrupted period as this it would be wrong to over-systematise or over-simplify. In any case, the definition of a Dark Age as something with a specific beginning is inapplicable to many districts where there is simply a continuity of decline. It may be that in Crete as well the conditions of the later twelfth century were such as to justify the epithet of darkness, but I have chosen the presumed date of the minor exodus to Cyprus, c. 1100 B.C., as symptomatic of the start of the Dark Ages.

I am also intending to depart from my other chronological dividing point, that of c. 1050 B.C., as separating the early from the late Dark Ages, the latter then extending to c. 900 B.C. This was based on the central mainland Sub-Mycenaean, but it is not valid for Crete, which remained almost entirely unaffected by the circumstances out of which the characteristic Protogeometric of the later Dark Ages emerged. It is still, however, desirable to keep the criterion of pottery, unsatisfactory though it is, and here it appears that the counterpart of Sub-Mycenaean, Sub-Minoan, exhibiting the same feature of simplicity in its general design and linear motives, was dominant throughout the eleventh century – in other words until the Athenian Protogeometric style asserted its influence from c. 1000 B.C. (and a very approximate date it is). Even in this matter there is a difficulty, since the influence of Protogeometric, as will be seen, was more or less confined to central Crete, the eastern districts persisting in the use of the old style of pottery throughout the rest of the Dark Ages. All the same, it seems convenient to make this division between the two centuries.

The west of Crete plays no part in the following discussion, as no material can yet be attributed to this period. I have no doubt that evidence will accumulate in course of time, but as things stand it means that we are confined to the central and eastern districts.

From these, our criterion being the Sub-Minoan pottery (analysed in detail earlier, pp. 57 ff.), the following picture of settlements and cemeteries emerges.

The north central region is represented solely by material from the Knossos area (see Plan, p. 226). Two chamber tombs in the Gypsades cemetery contained altogether seventeen vases, and one of them also produced four bronze dress pins, three with ribbed upper part (Fig. 14), two bronze finger rings, an iron knife with bronze rivets (Fig. 14), four beads (one of which is of amber), and two sealstones. Another tomb, from Ayios Ioannis, produced, in addition to a belly-handled amphora and two stirrup jars, two more bronze dress pins, one of which had an ivory head (Pl. 60), and an iron ring. The earliest grave of the Teke area (tomb Π) had some

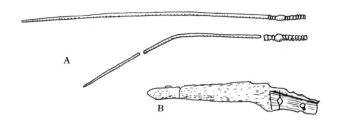

FIG. 14 KNOSSOS, GYPSADES TOMB VII
A) Dress pins; ·26 m., ·22 m. *BSA* 53–4, p. 257, fig. 34, VII 13 and 14.
B) Iron knife with bronze rivets; ·16 m. *BSA* 53–4, p. 255, fig. 32, VII
   12.

twenty vases, a fragmentary pin of iron, and some beads (see p. 229); and at least two stirrup jars from tombs of the main Ayios Ioannis cemetery can be classed as Sub-Minoan, though much of the rest of the pottery is certainly or probably later. A secondary deposit in the very early tholos tomb at Kephala consisted of about fifteen vases. And finally there is the pottery from the shrine of the underground Spring Chamber, nearly twenty vases apart from a quantity of small plain handleless kalathoi (presumably used for libations), a hut-urn, and a terracotta sphinx.

In the south, in the plain of the Mesara, two settlements are known, both of early twelfth-century origin. At Phaestos, where in three or four sectors these later constructions were built over or abutted on to the ruins of the palace, occupation continued into Geometric times. Similar evidence is revealed by a small settlement at Gortyn, which apparently gave way to a temple during the ninth century; the sherds were supplemented by three bronze fibulae, of which the two arched ones probably fall within the eleventh century, though the violin-bow example could be earlier.

As well as settlement material, there are also tombs at Phaestos or close to it. The cemetery of Liliana consisted of four chamber tombs and four trenches, all containing clay coffins in varying numbers; from the pottery one can deduce that they were first used in the twelfth century and continued so into the eleventh, but no further. Most of the objects came from the chamber tombs, and included a number of glass paste ornaments. There is one other, perhaps a chamber tomb, on the slopes of the acropolis of Phaestos, whose contents may fall entirely within the first half of the eleventh century; in addition to thirteen vases there were a hair pin, a steatite button, and two bronze arched fibulae.

The rest of the sites are in east Crete, which I define as everything from the western foothills of Mt. Dicte eastwards. On these foothills themselves, in the southern part, there are the five tholos tombs of Panayia; the rather small amount of pottery included at least some of Sub-Minoan type, but the significant point is that there were also a number of iron weapons. Then, on the north-western side of Dicte, there is the extremely important settlement of Karphi, which I deal with separately. Still within the area of Mt. Dicte, but on its eastern flank, there is the solitary evidence of a tomb at Dreros in the plain of Neapolis. This tomb, which held three skeletons and twelve vases, has been reported to be of the cist variety, but the excavator was in some doubt, and thought that it might have been the lower part of a tholos tomb; whatever the original shape may have been, the construction as preserved differs from that of cist tombs on the Greek mainland and elsewhere.

Gradually moving eastwards one comes to the bay of Mirabello. Close to this is the site of Vrokastro, reoccupied in the early twelfth century, and thereafter continuously inhabited till the Geometric period, as was the case at Phaestos and Gortyn. It should therefore provide good material for the eleventh century, but no stratification was able to be observed, and none of the illustrated sherds can be identified as certainly Sub-Minoan; it is then of no help except as an example of continuous habitation. Fortunately, there was cemetery material as well, a pithos burial of twelfth-century date, the curious 'bone enclosures' which are not earlier than the ninth century, and seven tholos tombs of which four were in use wholly or partly within the eleventh century, the other three being on the whole later. From the four, in two of which partial cremation seems to have been practised, a good selection of objects was recovered. There were thirty-one vases in all, including nine stirrup jars – mostly with airholes – two kylikes with swollen stems and decorated in what must be the final phase of the Fringed Style, two bird vases (Fig. 11; a spout, as always in Crete before the developed Protogeometric period, takes the place of the bird head), and a lentoid flask. Among the other offerings there were six arched fibulae of bronze – one stilted and one of the type with bulbs and adjacent collars, which must surely belong to the tenth century – a bronze pin, several bronze hair and finger rings, a sealstone, a few beads and a number of iron objects, a spearhead, a ring, and two knives, one of which had bronze rivets.

Next there is the site of Kavousi, commandingly placed on high ground east of the bay of Mirabello and, so far as natural defences are concerned, of the same type as Vrokastro. The excavated settlement belonged to the Geometric period, but a number of tholos tombs in the neighbourhood contained vases ranging from the end of the twelfth century at least to the ninth, thus making it difficult to give a precise date to the other objects found, which included bronze arched fibulae and iron weapons.

Finally, there are groups of tholos tombs and a cave burial in the Seteia district, not as yet published in full, still in use in the Geometric period and probably in part going back to the eleventh century.

This is very nearly the sum total of the published material apart from that of Karphi, and it will be evident how exceedingly meagre it is. To give a general account of eleventh-century Crete based on it is not easy, and can obviously be very misleading, on several counts. The scarcity itself of material is one factor, and this includes the completely blank area of west

Crete. Secondly, it is rather misleading to discuss this century as an isolated period, for there is clear continuity with what went before as well as with what came after. And third, it may be extremely misleading so far as east Crete is concerned, since the style of pottery on which our findings are based seems to have remained rather static in this region during the next century and even beyond the time when central Crete had taken over many of the features of the Athenian Protogeometric style. In east Crete one can get Sub-Minoan pottery during the tenth century as well as during the eleventh, and consequently the objects associated with it (including the iron weapons) are equally difficult to date. The whole situation is not made any easier by the lack of stratification on such settlements as are known nor (especially in east Crete, again) by the continued use of tombs for many generations. In spite of these serious obstacles, the following general and provisional summary of conditions during the eleventh century may be attempted, with the Karphi evidence borne in mind.

One thing can, I believe, be stated with reasonable certainty, that the population was not large. This seems to have been the situation in the twelfth century, and there is no particular reason to suppose that conditions were very different in the eleventh. The population was still also predominantly Minoan (though whether this name embraces a number of different racial elements I do not know). As we have seen, it is very likely that people coming from Mycenaean areas had settled in the island on at least two occasions in the twelfth century – their presence being attested by the pottery and the types of figurine. In the eleventh century, the appearance of a Mycenaean type of building at Karphi, though in the minority as compared with the Minoan type (p. 120), may suggest that they still retained their individuality, and the types of dress ornament, to which I shall return later, might indicate some contact with those of the Sub-Mycenaean culture, but one must tread warily. What must be stressed is that nowhere in the regions known to us was there any trace in religious matters of any but the traditional Minoan practices – except in the use of hut-urns, and these are neither Minoan nor Mycenaean.

This does not mean that there was hardly any contact with the outside world. Above all, there are many signs of links with Cyprus (see Pls. 5 and 7 and Figs. 1–11) – which is of course not surprising, in view of the move-. ment of Cretans to that island c. 1100 B.C. The main evidence comes from the pottery (see pp. 60 ff.). In one or two cases there might be an alternative source of origin. The triangular bodies and swollen stems on the kylikes of eastern Crete have parallels not only in Cyprus, but at Asine, and in Kephallenia and Ithaca. The belly-handled amphorae of central Crete are to be found in Sub-Mycenaean central Greece as well as in Cyprus – but my impression is that the particular shape reflects the latter area more closely. In general, indeed, the connexions are clearly with Cyprus, both for shape and for decoration. The flasks found at Vrokastro can hardly have been inspired from anywhere but Cyprus. The bird vases, widely distributed, are linked with those of Cyprus, and the same may be said of one or two other shapes. Nor was the movement all in one direction: the pyxis with high handles came to Cyprus from Crete, and there are of course the goddesses with upraised arms which provide the most cogent evidence for the actual movement of Cretans to Cyprus. And the distinctive decoration of some Cypriot stirrup jars was of Cretan origin (though conceivably *vice versa* in this case).

In metal the Cypriot source is evident. Not only were the clay stands of Karphi modelled on Cypriot bronze ones, but part of the bronze leg of such a stand was found on this site. Then there is the iron knife with bronze rivets, if not of Cypriot origin from somewhere in the east Mediterranean, examples of which have been found at Knossos and Vrokastro. It is indeed more than likely that the knowledge how to work in iron was introduced to Crete from Cyprus, and it might have happened earlier than, for example, in Athens, though the evidence from Karphi, assuming that that town was not abandoned till the latter part of the eleventh century, would not really support this.

Such are the links with Cyprus: one can trace them during the first half of the century, but was there a hiatus in the second half? We do not know.

Were there any other outside connexions? A possible link with Sicily or Italy will emerge from the discussion of the Karphi material. We need not expect that the Cretans had much to do with the moribund Mycenaean communities of the central Aegean. But were there no links with the area in which the Sub-Mycenaean was flourishing up till *c.* 1050 B.C.? Ceramically, it appears not, but ornaments of dress, fibulae, and dress pins, suggest that there may have been. The violin-bow fibulae can be disregarded, as they have been found in earlier contexts both in the Mycenaean world and in Crete. But there were also arched fibulae, notably two from a Sub-Minoan tomb at Phaestos, and several from Karphi. It is just possible to argue that they were introduced from Cyprus, but a Sub-Mycenaean origin is more likely, especially in view of the presence of three dress pins with ribbed swellings in the Gypsades cemetery, whose closest parallels have come from Sub-Mycenaean Argos.[4]

If there were links with the Sub-Mycenaean area, does this not contradict the supposition (p. 82) that that area was cut off from overseas contacts to the east, and so presumably to the south, by the still existing communities of the central Aegean? Not necessarily so, for Sub-Mycenaean culture was still current when they finally collapsed. This remarkable period of Sub-Mycenaean progress and expansion could also have been the occasion for renewed contacts with Crete – but it was only temporary so far as concerned outward expansion, and we have to wait till the tenth century before the next clear evidence of intercommunication.

Finally, there is the internal situation. We have seen that from the early twelfth century the districts of central and eastern Crete used different types of tomb. In the tenth century the eastern region was surprisingly

[4] Perhaps one should not, however, forget a similar pin from Kephallenia (p. 91), especially as the Gypsades tomb contained a bead of amber, a type of object reasonably common in Kephallenia, as being of northern origin, but except at Ancient Elis not found in the Sub-Mycenaean area.

resistant to the impact of the Athenian Protogeometric style, whether from Athens itself or from central Crete, to which it had spread. Are there any further signs of a possible schism between the two districts during the eleventh century? This is a question of some importance, but there is not sufficient evidence to suggest an answer one way or another. There is at any rate no reason to assume that the intercommunication that continued throughout the twelfth century did not persist well into the eleventh, and there is good reason to think that east Crete was just as receptive to outside influences as the central region during the first half of the eleventh century at least. It is a problem, though, which should not be forgotten.

Karphi

I have left this site (Pls. 19–23 and Figs. 9–12) until the end as it deserves consideration on its own, and also because its evidence provides a corrective, and may put into perspective the conclusions that have been drawn from the abysmally sparse evidence of other sites, not only in Crete, but throughout Greece and the Aegean.

There was, first, a settlement. By no means all of it has been excavated, but even so a hundred and fifty rectangular rooms have been identified, on the basis of which, and by comparison with a modern village of similar extent, the excavator (John Pendlebury) thought that the population may have amounted to some 3500 persons. The houses were built of hard limestone, almost entirely in the dry-stone technique. Door jambs and thresholds were made of well-shaped blocks, the doors being placed in certain cases on the long side of the room, as was the normal Minoan custom, and in others on the short side, as was common in Mycenaean Greece. The columns that supported the roof must have been of wood, and only two stone bases were found. As to the roofs themselves, it was reckoned that they must have been flat, with chimneys made out of large broken jars (there was good evidence for this). The houses were mainly of one storey only, but in one or two cases there were cellars. In fact, it was thought that this small town looked very much like the modern Tzermiadha, in the plain of Lasithi below.

Associated with the settlement there was a sanctuary, in the highest spot, an unpretentious building, with an altar and a raised bench for the cult statues found therein.

Below the settlement, at some distance down the hill, there were two groups of tholos tombs, seventeen in one, four in the other. The tombs were small, either rectangular or circular, and were either wholly or partially free-standing – a feature that is noted as being unique to Crete.

These are the basic details, and it may be added that, as no significant rebuilding or succession of superimposed floors was found, the total time of occupation may perhaps not have been more than a hundred years, a hundred and fifty at the most, from about the middle of the twelfth century down to the later part of the eleventh. This is the sort of site that the

PLAN OF KARPHI

archaeologist would ardently desire to find and excavate in many parts of
Greece and the Aegean, in order to obtain any sort of true picture of the
Dark Ages: there are just a few slightly comparable ones, but this is the
best.

Karphi was in the end evacuated peacefully, and therefore one would not
expect many objects of worth to have been left behind; but as it was never
subsequently inhabited (not surprisingly, as living conditions must have
been intolerable during much of the year) what was left remained undisturbed. And in fact we have sufficient to give us a reasonable picture of
the normal way of life in this mountain community, and of its level of
culture, but we must always bear in mind that the most precious and useful
objects of the final stage of occupation will have been removed.

The pottery is naturally the most prolific material, and we have an

PLATE 19 KARPHI. General view. *BSA* 38, pl. 15.

excellent range of several classes of this. The coarse domestic ware is well represented, the usual storage and cooking pots of a community, types which do not vary a great deal from century to century – lamps were found as well. Vases used for religious observances were also common. One of the rhytons (libation vases) is the only vase which from its decoration could belong to the thirteenth century, and was no doubt a family heirloom. Many of the kalathoi and pyxides were probably used for offerings, especially as they were mostly found in rooms connected with cult practices – one kalathos certainly was, as it incorporated inside it a figure with up-raised arms, representing a deity or a worshipper. The tankards may also have had a similar use. Finally, there was the remainder of the pottery, used for a multiplicity of purposes in daily life, and it is in these vases that we can follow the progress and interplay of stylistic elements, the internal cross-currents and the external influences. The shapes are a mixture of traditional Minoan and intrusive Mycenaean or Cypriot, and include very late features such as swollen stems in the kylikes and airholes in the stirrup jars. There is good evidence for contact with the rest of Crete, and this is confirmed by the decoration, which is, for the twelfth-century phase at least, very strongly Minoan with little Mycenaean. The rather pleasing

'open' style was applied to small bowls, while the Fringed Style is to be found on the larger vases – stirrup jars, kraters (a Mycenaean innovation), pyxides, tankards – and even occasionally on kalathoi. It is in fact from Karphi that the finest and most variegated collection of Fringed Style vases has come, and among these are certain highly individual pieces that show that the local potters were rich in imagination.[5] The subsequent descent into Sub-Minoan can also be traced, especially in the triangular motives applied to stirrup jars, and in the general simplification of design on other vase types.

As well as helping towards appraising the domestic and cultural life of the community, the pottery affords in any case the chief evidence for dating. It can be concluded that the town was founded well after 1200 B.C., and that c. 1150 B.C. would be a not unreasonable date. The early Mycenaean III C elements, as known at Knossos and Phaestos in the central zone, and at Kastri in the east a little later, hardly appear at all at Karphi. On the other hand, the Fringed Style is exceptionally strong: the start of this style should be placed somewhere within the first half of the twelfth century, and at Karphi it appears in its most fully developed phase. Its popularity suggests that the town was particularly flourishing in the second half of the twelfth century. The subsequent simplification of decoration, which may

[5] Almost all the pottery was made locally.

PLATE 20 KARPHI. A) Pyxides. B) Tankard. C) Krater. *BSA* 55, pls. 7–9.

PLATE 21 KARPHI. Goddesses. See *BSA* 38, pl. 31.

involve further Mycenaean influence before 1100 B.C. and Cypriot links both before and after that date, is also well attested and it is on the whole likely that Karphi was still inhabited during the second half of the eleventh century.[6]

So much for the pottery; but there is much other material that helps us to visualise the life of the community. The clay stands may be taken as imitations of Cypriot metal stands – and indeed part of one of the bronze struts of just such a stand was found. It is doubtful whether these were altars, but cult objects are particularly well exemplified by the series of splendid terracotta figures of goddesses with upraised arms, evidence of the uncontaminated survival of the Minoan tradition. Numerous other similar objects, some unique, reveal better than on any other site the religious practices of this period, and among these may probably be included several hut-urns (see p. 285), since one found in the Spring Chamber sanctuary at Knossos had a deity inside it – the origin of these is not clear, but at least it is not Minoan.

---

[6] In the detailed survey of the pottery, unavoidably delayed for many years, reference is made to one or two sherds of true Protogeometric style, but these are not described. If it were a matter of compass-drawn circles, the settlement could have persisted into the tenth century.

PLATE 22 KARPHI. Bronze objects. *BSA* 38, pl. 29.

The town produced few traces of weapons, and it may not have been the custom to bury them with the dead, since none was found in any tomb context. Those which were still serviceable will have accompanied their owners when they finally left, and so what remains is rather fragmentary – and invariably of bronze, thus suggesting that at least in this area and for weapons there was no very early introduction of iron-working. The one sword-blade is of a type common throughout the Aegean; on the three daggers there is nothing to comment; the spearhead is apparently a survival of a type current much earlier; and there were three arrowheads.

As well as the few weapons there was a fair selection of bronze tools, awls, saws, chisels, sickles, and a trunnion-axe. These are of course common everyday objects, and it is a sad commentary on our general ignorance that they are almost the only tools assignable to this period.

Particular attention has been paid elsewhere to the ornaments of dress and other personal accessories, and it may be of some significance that the pattern at Karphi is much the same as in central Greece during the early Dark Ages. Rings are in any case to be expected, and these were mostly for the finger (including one with an oval bezel), but four multiple-spiral hair rings recall an example from a late Sub-Mycenaean tomb of the Kerameikos. There were also twelve fibulae, three of which were of the violin-bow type, the rest of the simple arched class – and one of these was of iron.[7] In addition, there was the swivel-pin of a fibula of a type at this time

[7] Iron was exceedingly rare – only five fragments altogether, of which one is part of a knife, and another may be part of a pin or nail. But the metal was used.

PLATE 23 KARPHI. Bronze objects. *BSA* 38, pl. 28.

found as a rule only in Italy and Sicily – one of many small indications of contact with the outside world, in this case not the Aegean. Dress pins, too, were found, but not quite of the types current elsewhere, except for five short ones with bent or roll top, where the inspiration could be Cyprus. In general, these and the fibulae show that the new type of dress they presumably involve had penetrated to Crete – as is indeed confirmed by other sites.

Apart from these there are objects which do not imply any outside influence – for example, the clay and stone whorls, the mortars and pestles, the knives (including three rather delicate ones, perhaps for toilet use), and the short bone pins. All add to the picture of a flourishing community, known to us in greater fullness here than one gets anywhere else in the Greek world at this time.

A small final point is worth making, that from the evidence of clay figurines, tusks, horns, and bones we know some of the domestic animals in use – oxen, sheep, bulls, cows, horses, and (inevitably) goats. We can tell that boars and red deer roamed the forests that must have covered much of this area. And these people cultivated the olive.

Here then we have a community with a recognisable personality. If we knew as much about even half a dozen other communities elsewhere in the Aegean and on the Greek mainland, the study of the Dark Ages would be a more rewarding pursuit. Conclusions denied to us on other sites can be drawn here, simply because of the bulk and variety of the material, some of which is unique, and some unexpected. For instance, one of the most interesting points is the evidence provided for close contact with other parts of Crete, at least for some of the period, and also for overseas connexions.

There remain questions which concern Karphi itself: why did people ever build a town here at all? And what sort of people were they? It has to be realised that the site must have been uninhabitable in the winter, for not only was it so high up, it was also very exposed. Even in early summer the place is bitterly cold before the sun rises.

The usual answer is that it was a city of refuge for those who wanted to escape from trouble elsewhere in the island. But if it is true that they could not live there all the year round, why did they occupy the place at all? And how is it that they were in touch with developments in other parts of Crete, and how is it that objects from outside Crete reached them? It is true that no precious metal of any kind was recovered from Karphi, and it may be a valid conclusion that they had no great wealth, but much the same can be said of the rest of the Greek world virtually throughout the Dark Ages; and in any case the main point is that they were in constant touch with other communities, especially in the early stages.

Another possible theory is that Karphi formed a natural stronghold, a base for the activities of brigands who would descend on unsuspecting communities and travellers in the low-lying areas below. From Karphi one certainly gets a fine view over part of the northern coast (on a clear day it is possible to see Santorin, fifty miles to the north), and the route up to the site can easily be watched and guarded.[8] This theory would explain certain features, and might be a factor in a possible division between central and eastern Crete, for Karphi forms, so to speak, the westernmost bastion of the mountain barrier which constitutes the eastern boundary of the central regions. And yet one does not somehow get the impression of a community that lived on the proceeds of violence.

One of the main features of Karphi is its sanctuary and cult statues. But evidence is not restricted to these, for many other cult objects have been found; nor is it restricted to the sanctuary, for this had a number of dependencies, and what may have been a priest's house with access to it. May one then hazard the possibility that the principal *raison d'être* of the community was the sanctuary of which it was the focus? Did it represent the chief surviving religious centre for the true Minoans? If so, it should then have drawn attention away from the Dictaean Cave, that holy place just the other side of the plain of Lasithi – and it is perhaps worth noting that in the fullest publication of the votive offerings from this cave it is stated that, although it was still visited during the time of Karphi's occupation, 'there are very few objects from the cave which can be attributed with certainty to the Intermediate Period [latest Late Minoan IIIC and Sub-Minoan] or the Protogeometric'.[9]

This hypothesis sounds attractive, but there are difficulties in accepting it. There is no evidence that there was an earlier sanctuary on this spot, and one would have thought that in a world where the greatest sanctity attached

[8] One can get from Karphi to Knossos in a day's march.

[9] J. Boardman, *The Cretan Collection in Oxford*, p. 5.

to places such as caves, such a condition would have been a pre-requisite. Also, it was no longer a centre of worship after the city was abandoned. In fact, the whole situation at the end is odd: the goddesses did not leave with the community (in spite of being provided with movable legs so as to be able to make the descent). One would naturally suppose, in that case, that there would be a good reason for their abandonment – presumably to play the role of divine guardians – but then why was no further attention paid to them? There they stayed, deserted, desolate, and discarded, a prey to the inclemency of the elements. All one can suggest is that they had failed their worshippers.

However that may be, there is yet one further difficulty. Were all the inhabitants of the town true Minoans – as they should be, for this hypothesis to have validity? The appearance of the *megaron* type of room (in other words, with the entrance at the short end) in the most imposing building complex, together with other features, led the excavator to conclude that the community was ruled by non-Minoans (specifically, Achaeans), even though the majority of the inhabitants were Minoan. In that case it is odd that the rulers did not introduce in some form their own religious practices. All of which may lead to the conclusion that the more material one has, the more numerous the problems, but it is at least a welcome thing to have a solid body of material on which to base one's hypotheses.

III

The Late Dark Ages

7 Athens

The middle of the eleventh century has been taken as a turning point between the early and late Dark Ages. This, it must be stressed, is a purely
arbitrary date, and certainly or probably not applicable to most areas of
Greece and the Aegean. In many regions sufficient evidence is not available, but in others, where it is, there is no sign of anything new – for Crete,
indeed, I have felt it necessary to adopt a different system. In general, the
whole area is so lacking in coherence that no single all-embracing turning
point is to be expected, not even within the central mainland Sub-
Mycenaean districts.

The turning point I have chosen is based purely on the creation of the
Protogeometric style of pottery in Athens. It can justifiably be pointed out
that there was a slightly earlier one of greater importance, the opening up
of the Aegean to the Sub-Mycenaean communities, involving not only
group movements in an easterly – and perhaps also northerly – direction,
but also contact with Cyprus. This is a beginning, not an end; and yet I
have placed it at the end of the early Dark Ages.

All this is true, but the following considerations should be borne in
mind. First, the placing of these important developments within the early
phase of the Dark Ages enables us to relate the Sub-Mycenaean area to
Cyprus and so to establish some sort of absolute dating. Secondly, and more
important, this new beginning was in a sense, as will be seen, rather a false
start, as for a while it does not seem to have led to any further developments, and the link with the east Mediterranean appears to have been lost.
The third point concerns the positive reason for accepting the turning
point that I use here: the new Protogeometric style which emerged
definitively at about this time was, culturally and archaeologically speaking,
the characteristic feature of Athenian life for the following century and a
half; furthermore, it was this style that in due course influenced, to a
greater or lesser degree, the other styles of pottery in almost every accessible district of the mainland and the Aegean, thus allowing us to place these
in chronological perspective and to draw a number of other conclusions.

The turning point has, in other words, been chosen with an eye to what
was to come, even though it was the earlier freedom of the seas, and the
attitude of mind that it produced, that made the later developments
possible.

Having equated the duration of this period with the life of the Athenian
Protogeometric style of pottery, the first need is to explain and justify the
chronological limits given, from *c.* 1050 to *c.* 900 B.C.

The date of the start has already been discussed; it is related to the connexions with Cyprus that immediately preceded it, the Cypriot material being itself approximately dated by cross-reference with other areas in the east Mediterranean, thus giving an equally approximate date to the Athenian pottery.

The absolute concluding date must be sought in similar manner, and a very complex process it is. The argument may be summarised as follows. The basic area for purposes of arriving at an absolute date is Palestine, with its established Biblical chronology. A number of settlements have been excavated in this region, and from the pottery found in their respective levels we can refer across not only to Cyprus but in a few cases directly to Greece and the Aegean, and specifically to Athens, the earliest direct link with this town belonging to the first stages of the Geometric style (Early Geometric II). Since this style developed out of Protogeometric, one is therefore within reasonably calculable distance from its end, and it would seem that there should be no great difficulty. Unfortunately, however, the chronology of the settlement levels themselves is a matter of dispute, and it is not until c. 750 B.C. that one comes upon a generally agreed date, one which through the presence of imports from Athens can be accepted as the end of the Middle Geometric phase. It then becomes a question of which alternative system of dating to adopt in order to fix the beginning of Middle Geometric: according to one theory, it would not start later than the end of the tenth century, according to the other it should begin in the middle of the ninth. If it is impossible to come to a decision on the Palestinian evidence, one can still argue on grounds of probability, from the length of time one can reasonably expect the Middle Geometric phase to have occupied. The argument is that, although it is recognised that this covered a fairly long period, to give a hundred years seems far preferable to allowing it a hundred and fifty. On the basis of this I shall assume that it started c. 850 B.C. How long then was Early Geometric? It is agreed that its duration was considerably shorter than Middle Geometric, and a probable life of not more than fifty years has been suggested: so we reach the date of c. 900 B.C. for the end of the Protogeometric style in Athens. This date I shall then accept as approximately correct, adding that, while it could not be appreciably later, an earlier date of up to fifty years cannot be entirely ruled out.[1]

We are then faced with a total of a hundred and fifty years for the duration of the Protogeometric style (and so also of the later Dark Ages). Three main stages of development have been recognised within this style, Early, Middle (or Ripe), and Late Protogeometric. Early Protogeometric is a short phase, and inevitably overlaps the latest stage of Sub-Mycenaean; it is therefore not easy to define. To it I assign those tomb groups (our evidence is almost wholly based on material from cemeteries) whose contents include a preponderance of certainly Protogeometric vases as opposed to survivals of the preceding Sub-Mycenaean or shapes which display the influences of Cyprus. Middle Protogeometric is equally short,

---

[1] The most recent, and fullest, analysis will be found in J. N. Coldstream's *Greek Geometric Pottery*, pp. 302 ff.

representing the time when the style had overcome the experimental stage and established its characteristic features. Late Protogeometric is, on the other hand, very long; in it the established features are accompanied by an increasing number of variations and elaborations, and forerunners of the following Geometric style.

The assessment of the relative length of each phase is principally based on the number of tombs that can be assigned to it; another factor is also rather subjective, the likelihood that the early experimental phase would soon pass, and the equal likelihood that the late phase, with its many variations, would tend to be long. A third factor must also be taken into account. The influence of this style on other districts was massive, and suggests that its superiority was so great that it was bound to affect the work of other potters as soon as it became known. But, as we shall see, the acceptance of Athenian ideas can only rarely be traced earlier than the late phase, even in districts close to Athens. There are of course possible extenuating circumstances such as the force of traditionalism in other areas,[2] but I doubt whether these can often have been very strong; judging from the remarkable diffusion of Late Protogeometric, it would seem that the only compelling reason for failure to adopt the new ideas would be that the district concerned was out of touch (as, for example, Ithaca), and there is no evidence that those bordering on, and within, the central and south Aegean were. I am inclined to think that it cannot have been long before the style became widely known and imitated, and therefore I would conclude that the early and middle phases must have been short. In absolute terms, I would suggest that these together did not cover more than forty years, the late phase thus extending for a century, or perhaps slightly over.

There is no doubt that Athens was the most outstanding town of this period, in itself and in its influence on other communities, and I therefore deal with it first.

For the sake of clarity and ease of continuity, I shall leave the full analysis of the pottery until the end and concentrate first on other aspects of the evidence.

The greater part of our knowledge is, as in the early Dark Ages, based on cemetery material. There are a number of pits and wells, signs of settlement, in the Agora, immediately north-west of the Acropolis (see Plan, p. 136), and there are two areas which seem to have been used for sanctuary purposes, as will be seen, but none of this material has been published in full, and we have therefore to rely on the burials and associated offerings.

One obviously important question is the size of the area in which finds have been made, of whatever nature (Plan, p. 136). The Acropolis may be taken as the central point. Up to the latest phase of Sub-Mycenaean there had been burials on the Acropolis itself (but never before or after), a small cluster of tombs about three hundred yards to the east, and a further group immediately to the south as well. But the main area of burial had been to the north-west: a scatter of tombs within the Agora and its surrounding area, but mostly concentrated in the Kerameikos, over half a mile from the

---

[2] East Crete is a good instance of this, see pp. 118, 235.

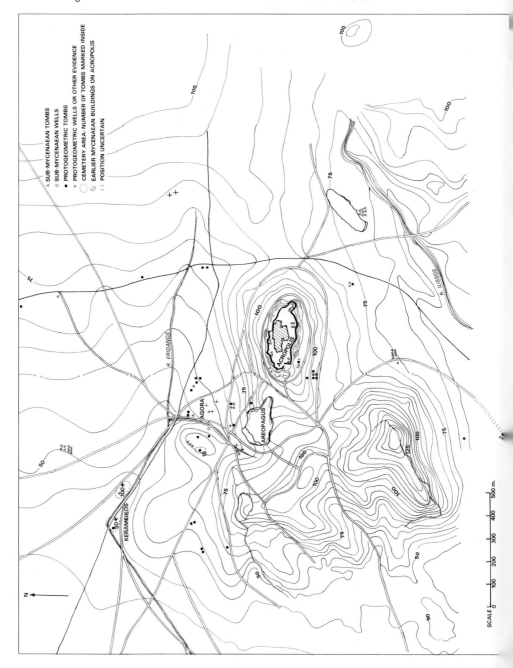

SUB-MYCENAEAN TOMBS
SUB-MYCENAEAN WELLS
PROTOGEOMETRIC TOMBS
PROTOGEOMETRIC WELLS OR OTHER EVIDENCE
CEMETERY AREA: NUMBER OF TOMBS MARKED INSIDE
EARLIER MYCENAEAN BUILDINGS ON ACROPOLIS
POSITION UNCERTAIN

PLAN OF ATHENS

Acropolis. The total area was already fairly extensive, and does not seem to have been greatly enlarged for some while. Graves of the transitional phase to Protogeometric are fairly numerous to the south of the Acropolis, so far nothing else until Late Protogeometric – but the interval, as we have seen, need not be a long one. On the other hand, tombs of Middle (or Ripe) Protogeometric date have been discovered about three hundred yards slightly east by north from the Acropolis, under the modern cathedral, and in Late Protogeometric others have been found a further half mile to the north of this. All these burials could have belonged to one central community, but not so a small group of tombs, of the very latest phase, from Nea Ionia, a good four miles to the north; no doubt this was a separate village – but in close touch with the main area, as the pottery was made in Athenian workshops.

Such evidence as there is of actual settlement is confined to a few sherds from the Acropolis and, as we have seen, to the pits and wells of the Agora area.[3] The two instances of sanctuary deposits, however, are outside the main area and confined to Late Protogeometric: the one is in the Academy district, about a mile and a half north-west of the Acropolis – well beyond the Kerameikos – and the other is high up on Mt. Hymettus, on its western side, representing the earliest material of the sanctuary of Zeus.

To sum up, it seems fair to say that there was a settlement of considerable size at Athens throughout the Dark Ages. The evidence suggests that there was some extension of the community during the Protogeometric period, but one must be cautious: so much that has recently been found has been due to chance discovery, or to the occasion of deep foundation digging in the centre of the modern town that one cannot be sure that the present picture is accurate. We can use the positive evidence, for example that Protogeometric burials extended over a certain area, but we do not know how much larger it may have been, nor whether the earlier inhabited area may not have been greater than at present identified, nor really whether it was not a matter of small groups or pockets of inhabitants rather than a continuous whole – though other evidence, as will be seen, indicates that the latter is the more likely answer.

From the area of extent we can turn to the manner of burial. In the early Dark Ages, down to the latest Sub-Mycenaean, the prevailing custom had been inhumation in cist tombs (see Fig. 28), shaft or pit graves of similar dimensions to the cist tombs, but lacking the slab lining, and occasionally the slab covering as well, and shallow pits used for children and infants. There were also, however, just a few instances of cremation; these consisted of circular pits, which could be lined with slabs, into which was placed the vase which contained the burnt remains of the dead body; either pit or urn or both could be covered over with a stone slab.

The final phase of Sub-Mycenaean saw an increase in cremations, and with this a structural development, the trench-and-hole system (Fig. 29), which persisted throughout Protogeometric and into Geometric: instead of just a cremation pit, a rectangular trench was first dug, and then the circular

---

[3] Protogeometric sherds have also turned up to the east, not far from Constitution Square (Syntagma). The context suggests an area of irrigation.

pit was embedded within it. It would seem that the cremation pyre was situated close at hand;[4] at the end of the act of cremation the ashes or burnt bones would be placed within the urn, together with any personal ornaments or belongings other than vases. The urn would then be placed in its pit, and the debris of the pyre swept into the trench, including the remains of the pottery, either that which had been used in the cremation, or unburnt vases which may have been intended for the use of the dead; the rest of the trench was then filled in with earth. During this closing stage of Sub-Mycenaean, the urn was a belly-handled amphora, used for male and female burials alike, and its mouth was covered by a stone slab or (in one instance) a bronze shield-boss.

So we come to the Protogeometric period, the late Dark Ages. The situation can be dealt with as a whole (and the same holds for Early Geometric), as there are very few variations. It was as follows.

Infants were buried in coarse amphorae – this is a practice so far attested only in Late Protogeometric – and children were inhumed in cist tombs or shaft graves, at times within the settlement area itself.

Adults were almost always cremated, with one or two rare exceptions at the very beginning. The trench-and-hole system was retained throughout; and, as in the latest preceding phase, only the personal belongings (not the vases) were placed in the urn with the ashes of the dead, unless it was a question of a sword, which would be either left outside or bent and wrapped round the outside of the urn, so 'killing' it (see p. 312). As to the type of the urn, a new practice was introduced, that the ashes of men were placed in neck-handled amphorae, and those of women in belly-handled amphorae, until the very end of the period, when shoulder-handled amphorae replaced the belly-handled variety. This system was held to almost without exception: there is no known instance of men being buried in belly- or shoulder-handled amphorae, but on rare occasions a neck-handled amphora could be used for a woman.[5] As before, the urn would be covered with a stone slab, but it became increasingly fashionable, especially in the late phase, to use a small vase instead of the stone slab; and, curiously, two of the very latest urns had a bronze shield-boss (Pl. 25) as a covering – either a revival of a custom found in late Sub-Mycenaean, or, more likely, evidence that this custom was never lost. The burials, finally, normally took place outside the settlement.

There are then just a few variations, just a few exceptions; but the most impressive feature is the uniformity, the going by rules. This is basic and, as will be seen, seems to repeat itself in other matters, and it may reflect the attitude of the community towards their whole way of life. If this is so, then we have to ask whether it was a uniformity of convention or fashion, or was it something imposed by authority? The adoption of cremation for adults is the critical case. The previous convention was that of inhumation for adults – not universal, but extremely widespread. Now there is no reason to

---

[4] It appears that cremation could take place within the tomb itself.

[5] The types of object usually enable us to determine whether the burial was of a man or a woman.

suppose that the progress from Sub-Mycenaean to Protogeometric involved any change in population – all else exhibits continuity, and so in a sense do the cremations. There had already been an increase in the number of cremations immediately before the later Dark Ages, and that itself is significant, for one would think that this could be a matter of very strong convictions.[6] But the almost total adoption of the practice is rather different. This cannot be explained as a new fashion, for one would surely find some old-fashioned exceptions. If burial customs were a matter of tradition or convention, then one is entitled to ask what sort of circumstances can have brought about the change, particularly as tradition was one of the most powerful forces of antiquity. I think that one must admit the possibility that cremation was enforced by whatever authority may have existed – and an authority which must have had religious sanction and competence. But the nature of archaeological evidence does not allow us to go further than treating this as a possibility.

The various types of object other than pottery placed in the tombs were very much the same as those of the earlier period, but there are significant differences as well.

The personal ornaments comprise, as before, bracelets, hair and finger rings, fibulae, and dress pins. Bracelets were rare: as opposed to the three of the Sub-Mycenaean period there is just one pair, bronze, attached to the wrist of a child in a burial of the middle phase. Hair rings were not particularly common, either. They take the shape of multiple spirals, and three of gold, from an Early and a Middle Protogeometric burial respectively, are of interest in that they link up with similar ones from late Sub-Mycenaean graves (p. 67); they were made with doubled wire (see Pl. 60), a northern feature and not found in Mycenaean times, and they are the only objects of gold to have been found in Athens until the appearance of the Geometric style (negative evidence which must clearly be treated with great caution).

Besides these there were six multiple-spiral rings of bronze from two tombs of the late phase; they could have been for the finger, but in the one tomb the excavator considered that they were probably for the hair, and this may have been the case for all six. If they were, then there is only one attested example of a finger ring for the whole Protogeometric period, from the same child inhumation of the middle phase in which the bracelets were found – the ring was attached to the finger bone, and was of bronze. This is remarkable, in contrast to the popularity of finger rings during the early phases of Sub-Mycenaean; on the other hand, it follows on the sharp decline apparent in the latest phase of that period, and one cannot attribute the absence of such rings to chance; furthermore, they reappear in the early ninth century, at the beginning of the Geometric period. Why then this dearth? No certain answer can be given, but there are two possibilities: one is that the use of finger rings simply went out of fashion, the other that the retention of a ring by a cremated corpse was thought un-

---

[6] Not necessarily, though, for there were further fluctuations between inhumation and cremation in later stages of the history of Athens.

PLATE 24 ATHENS (NEA IONIA). Pins (lengths ·36 m., ·39 m., ·21 m. incomplete) and fibulae (lengths ·09 m., ·11 m.). *Hesp.* 30, pl. 27.

suitable. The first is weakened by the presence of one ring in a Middle Protogeometric context, the second by the rings in Early Geometric crema-tions, and by the existence of one in a cremation of the latest Sub-Mycenaean phase – and indeed in Late Protogeometric, if the spirals noted above were finger rings. A third possible explanation, that the lack of rings, usually of bronze, may be connected with an apparent dearth in that metal, I shall discuss later (pp. 316ff.), but in any case, as we have seen, rings could be of iron.

Fibulae (Pl. 24) also virtually disappeared during the latest Sub-Mycenaean phase and Early and Middle Protogeometric, but in this case it was nothing to do with the rite of cremation, since during Late Proto-geometric they have been found not only with two inhumation burials, but with eight cremations, in these associated both with men and women. There are sixteen altogether, twelve of iron, only four of bronze. All except one[7] have basically the same shape (Fig. 34 E): instead of the simple arch usually found in the early Dark Ages, these are stilted, the bow coming up vertically from the catch-plate and then curving over and gradually down-wards to the spring of the pin. The central part of the bow is much

---

[7] An iron fibula of rectangular shape, with flat leaf-shaped bow.

thickened, and on either side, for the bronze examples, there is a bulb with two ancillary collars.[8] The stilting is occasionally found earlier, and the two collars on their own, but the late Dark Age model was an improved one.

Finally the dress pins (Pl. 24), found in much the same numbers as in the Sub-Mycenaean period – there are over thirty, from twenty-three tombs, covering the whole of Protogeometric. These, as the fibulae, are also all of the same type, with only minor variations (Fig. 33 F, G). They have a straight shaft, circular in section, with a heavy spherical bulb near the top, which itself consists of a flat circular disk usually, but not always, surmounted by a small knob. And there is one other feature: while there are only four or five of bronze, and these either from the earliest or the latest stages, the rest, in other words the great majority, were of iron, all except the bulb, which was of bronze; and most of them belong to the Protogeometric period.[9] They are of considerable interest, both for the technique they exhibit, and also because of their occasional appearance in other parts of the Aegean – the Argolid, Kos in the Dodecanese, and Theotokou in Thessaly (see p. 299). Why should this technique have been used? It may be that it was beyond the power of the early ironsmith to make such a pin, as required by tradition and convention. Why then not make the whole pin of bronze, as was done both earlier and later? Was this because, as was hinted in the case of the finger rings, bronze was in short supply during most of the later Dark Ages? There were, too, very few fibulae of this metal. The discussion of this possibility I must leave until the rest of the evidence has been set out, both from Athens and from the rest of the Aegean as well (see pp. 316 ff.). There is, though, another possibility, that the combination of, and contrast between, iron and bronze, once having been tried, was found to be aesthetically pleasing, and became the accepted fashion. Such an explanation is not capable of proof, though it is fair to say that the love of well-proportioned contrast visible in the Athenian-created style of pottery would go some way to support this idea – it is the sort of thing, I believe, which the late Dark Age inhabitants of Athens would appreciate.

Weapons (Figs. 36–39) were found with reasonable frequency – associated with nine burials in all – covering the whole Protogeometric period. There were four swords, two daggers, two knives (assuming that these were weapons), six spearheads, and a solitary arrowhead. All were of iron except for the two spearheads of bronze found with a cremation of the early phase – indeed, there is no known spearhead of iron before Middle Protogeometric.[10]

It is not easy to distinguish the various types, especially for those of iron, where the heavy oxidisation often prevents the recovery of the original shape. So far as one can tell, the swords seem to have been of a kind of characteristic of the latest Mycenaean times (see Fig. 35 and p. 308), except

---

[8] The heavy oxidisation of the iron fibulae makes it difficult to be clear about these details, but they do not seem to be present.

[9] The latest is mid-ninth century, but they are very rare in Geometric.

[10] In only one tomb before the ninth century were a sword and spearhead found together – for the first time, as Snodgrass comments, since the Mycenaean period.

for one variant of this type, from an Early Protogeometric tomb, which is associated rather with Cyprus, and could have been imported from there.[11] The spearheads are more variable in shape, but at least two of them can trace their ancestry back to Mycenaean times, and one of the two bronze ones is similar to a Cypriot spearhead of slightly earlier date. For the rest I have no comment.

The only two items of defensive armour are two bronze shield-bosses (Pl. 25). Both belonged to very late burials and were used, as we have seen, to cover the cremation urn. They were of a slightly different and more advanced shape than the one found in a late Sub-Mycenaean context, and used for a similar purpose. Such shield attachments were not known to the Mycenaean world; the closest parallels to these, and to two others from Tiryns (see p. 69) and Skyros, are to be found in Cyprus: the whole question of the origin of these objects, however, and indeed at times of their purpose, is obscure.

Apart from these objects there is little else, though worthy of mention are the two iron tools (one is a trunnion-axe) from a very late burial, a bird's head in bronze from an equally late, if not later, one, and a hemispherical bronze bowl from the same tomb. On the whole, it is a rather undistinguished collection, with little variety, and gives one very much a Dark Age feeling. The main evidence, however, is still to come, that of the wheel-made pottery, in which the achievements and spirit of the community are best observed.

Before discussing this, however, some account must be given of the hand-made wares, which fall into two distinct classes. First, there were nearly a dozen coarsely made jugs, all associated with female burials; the natural inference from this is, of course, that the women did the cooking, but it is a curious fact that in the Sub-Mycenaean period there were only two which preceded the concluding phase. And such vases are only with the greatest rarity found in Mycenaean tombs.

Secondly, there is a class of hand-made clay objects which falls into an entirely different category, a strange phenomenon which extended from Late Protogeometric into the early stages of the succeeding style. This ware, it must be emphasised, is not coarse but fine (see Fig. 15). The following types are known: beads, spindle whorls, hollow balls; hemispherical bowls with rounded or rather pointed base; little pyxides with narrow mouth, lugs or ears, and tall lid; small tripods and tub-shaped vases; and bell-shaped dolls with short stumpy arms and sometimes legs as well. All have incised or impressed decoration, and display a large variety of motives, such as vertical and horizontal lines, circles, chevrons, lines of dots, straight or in festoons, and zigzags. An even greater elaboration is found in Early Geometric.

---

[11] Notable is the fact that of the four swords two were deliberately bent out of shape (but not the one of possible Cypriot origin), thus rendering them useless; and the custom continued into the Geometric period. A similar practice is known among the prehistoric Germanic peoples, and it has been surmised that, even as the warrior himself had died, so was his faithful companion, his sword, 'killed', and sent to join him wherever he might be.

FIG. 15 ATHENS, HAND-MADE INCISED WARE
JdI 77, p. 97, fig. 15, nos. 6–8, 10–14; p. 98, fig. 16, no. 12.

This is a remarkable collection, and one would like to know two things: what was their purpose, and what was their origin? As so often, neither question can be answered satisfactorily. As to the purpose, one must bear in mind that so far these objects have been found in tombs only, and indeed only with female or child burials; there is therefore a connexion with burial, but I do not see how one can get any further. On the question of

PLATE 25 ATHENS. Shield-bosses (diameters ·174 m., ·114 m.). *Ker.* IV, pl. 37.

origin, one must first ask whether they had any immediately previous history in Athens, and all that one can point to is three pyxides in Sub-Mycenaean contexts, and a few beads and spindle whorls of earlier Proto-geometric times, but even in these, it seems, the type of decoration is rather different, and they can in no way explain the complexity and popularity of the later ware. However, at least this ware did not appear absolutely out of nothing, so to speak. Is there then any comparative material elsewhere which might more naturally have given the impetus to the fashion? The closest parallels are with the beads and in Crete, especially the Knossos area (p. 229), and there is also one small vase in this technique from Phaes-tos in southern Crete (p. 232). There is surely some link here, since the appearance in each area was roughly contemporaneous, but it is not yet possible to say with certainty whether the ideas went from Crete to Athens or *vice versa* – the latter is much the more likely. Apart from this, fine hand-made ware is known in tombs of about this period in Corinth and the Argolid, but one gets vase shapes only, quite different from those of Athens, and a minimum of incised decoration. Outside Greece altogether, it is possible to produce parallels for certain details in other regions, for example the north Balkans and Cyprus, but there seems no clear chrono-logical link. It has also been pointed out that there is a remarkable resem-blance between the incised patterns found on Early Helladic pottery – roughly the third millennium B.C. – and those on the fine hand-made ware of Protogeometric Athens. But no connexion is provable or in any way probable. To prove it, one would have to show that some tombs or deposits of the earlier period had been disturbed in the tenth century, and that the Athenians thought it desirable to copy the incised motives of decoration, but not the shapes: it seems unlikely.

In the above discussion objects of clay other than vases have been dealt with, and it therefore seems appropriate at this point to say something of the clay figurines of animals.[12]

Three of these have survived, sufficient to prove that the Athenian potter was not incompetent in this medium. First there is a rather impressive, though not in any way naturalistic, stag (Pl. 26), found in a very late tomb, and with this may be associated the head and neck of another, without a context. The complete one is quite small, about twenty-six centimetres high, a fat barrel-shaped body with the legs draped round the flanks, a short tail, a long neck surmounted by a not very well-moulded head with antlers; the animal is decorated with a series of rectilinear panels, relieved by zigzags along the top of the back and down the legs. The fragmentary one corresponds closely, in what remains of it, to the complete one.

The tomb in which the complete stag was found was that of a woman, and one is bound to wonder what the significance of this funeral gift was. In this case one cannot know, but the answer is perfectly clear for the third object, belonging to a child's burial: it is a horse on wheels, and was certainly a toy (Pl. 26). He is about eleven centimetres high, with a long tail and a mane; the body is for the most part painted over, but the top of the back is divided into sections of horizontal and vertical stripes. The tomb also contained two cups with high conical feet, and probably belonged to Late Protogeometric, but not to the latest phase of all.

We can now turn to the central feature of the whole period, the wheel-made Protogeometric style of pottery, but first a brief recapitulation, as an introduction.

The time of transition to the Protogeometric style which marks the end of Sub-Mycenaean was one of experiment and consisted of three main elements. First, there were the well-established traditional vase types, made and painted rather carelessly, without any regard to aesthetic considerations either in shape or decoration – the true Sub-Mycenaean, the dead end of Mycenaean. Second, there was the Cypriot element, recognisable in a number of new types of vase, in higher and sharper conical feet, in additional decorative motives, and in the far freer use of decoration in zones and panels, these motives and system being applied to Sub-Mycenaean vases as well. Third, and entirely individual to the Athenian potter, there were the technical innovations, the faster wheel and the invention of the dividers with multiple brushes on one arm for making circles and semicircles. That some new style should emerge from this was reasonably certain, but the direction it would take could not have been predicted.

Essentially, in the opening stages of the new style, it was the Cypriot influence that was rejected. The Cypriot types of vase – the bottle, the bird vase, the ring vase, and one or two others – all dropped out, except for the belly-handled amphora (if it did come from Cyprus – see p. 51). The new motives and the rectilinear zones and panels were rather pushed

---

[12] There is no known instance in Athens of fashioning a human figure – except for the hand-made dolls, which come into a rather different category.

PLATE 26 ATHENS
A) Stag; ·266 m. *Ker*. IV, pl. 26.
B) Horse; ·115 m. *AD* 22, ii, pl. 70.

PLATE 26 ATHENS
c) Cups; ·066 m., ·07 m. *AD* 22, ii, pl. 70.

into the background, though not forgotten. What one gets is a return to
simplicity, in the main based on the traditional Sub-Mycenaean shapes
as transformed by the new techniques of vase-making and mechanical
decoration. It was, however, a very different kind of simplicity from that
of the Sub-Mycenaean period. Not only was the shape of the vase now
considered to be something worthy of careful and aesthetic execution,
but the decoration applied was consciously related to the shape, thus giving
each vase type a personality of its own. The whole effect was enhanced by
the more careful preparation of the clay, and soon by the application of an
extremely fine and lustrous glaze, this being the result of firing the vases
at a higher temperature, and constituting a further technical improvement.

In view of the importance of this style as influencing the work of
contemporary potters in other areas, and for purposes of comparison with
the surveys given of the preceding Sub-Mycenaean, Sub-Minoan, and
L.C. III B styles, it will be best to give a short description of each of the
main types and of its development, to be followed by a general summary
of the style.

NECK-HANDLED AMPHORA (Fig. 1, Pl. 27)

Body ovoid, high neck, slightly concave, flaring out smoothly to an everted
and well-rounded lip; handles rising vertically from mid-shoulder and
then curving over to join the neck just below the lip. Ring base, undercut
(no longer flat as in the Sub-Mycenaean amphorae).

The whole is divided into separate areas by the use of horizontal bands
of paint: lip painted, band at base of neck, narrow bands enclosing a broad
one below the shoulder (to support the main decorated area), three bands
below the belly. General effect clay ground, but the principle of division
persists even in the later stage when the dark-ground system was used, for
the demarcation of shoulder and belly by reserved bands. Exceptional

are late amphorae with two or three broad bands spaced over the body, and no other decoration.

As a rule, only the shoulder was decorated, apart from the bands. To start with, concentric circles and languettes from the neck, but this very soon replaced by sets of semicircles, sometimes flanking a vertical motive (e.g. straight lines and zigzags, cross-hatched panel). There is an exceptional and very late instance of the belly covered with successive panels of rectilinear decoration, and narrow zones of decoration above and below this.

BELLY-HANDLED AMPHORA (Figs. 2–3, Pl. 27)

Body globular, becoming ovoid, high neck, either flaring out into a wide trumpet mouth or slightly concave and coming up to a very pronounced everted lip. Handles set on the belly. Ring base, as for the neck-handled variety.

The system of dividing the constituent parts is also as in the neck-handled amphora. The neck is, however, always painted, and when circles adorned the belly the banding below tended to be that of narrow bands enclosing a very broad one, as for the shoulder – in order to mark out a major field of decoration. Clay ground throughout (apart from the neck), but one very late one has the lower body painted over.

Decoration on the shoulder: at first, concentric circles and languettes, the latter motive persisting briefly into the time when semicircles replaced circles; from then on sets of semicircles, usually unfilled, with occasional intervening motives in the late phase. The very late amphora mentioned above is also exceptional in substituting for the semicircles a thin band of dog-tooth decoration, with a very fine zigzag below the supporting bands. Decoration also on the belly: either a triple wavy line or sets of circles – no chronological distinction can be made between these two motives, but in the latest amphorae the belly can be left unpainted. There are other rare variations in belly decoration. Note the depiction of a horse beneath the wavy lines of one amphora.

The shape disappeared before the end of Protogeometric, and was apparently replaced – at least for burial purposes – by the amphora with shoulder handles.

AMPHORA WITH SHOULDER HANDLES

Body ovoid, becomes more globular, high neck flaring to wide trumpet mouth. Handles set vertically on the shoulder. One amphora has a low conical lid with flat knob on top.

Dark ground. Elaborate linear panelled decoration on shoulder, with subsidiary supporting linear zone, for the two latest Protogeometric amphorae. For the three transitional or Early Geometric vases, decoration on the neck (meander, dog-tooth), and a narrow dog-tooth zone on the belly. Note absence of circles.

PLATE 27 ATHENS (NEA IONIA). Amphorae; ·455 m., ·395 m. *Hesp.* 30, pl. 24.

A rare type, replacing the belly-handled amphora, and found only in the latest stage of the style and the transition to Geometric. Freely used in Geometric.

AMPHORA WITH HANDLES FROM SHOULDER TO LIP

Body ovoid or oval; neck wide or fairly wide, coming up to everted lip; low conical foot. May be provided with low domed lid, with knob at top, and lugs for lifting off.

Dark ground. Decoration varied. Neck may or may not have motives – note the two horses on one example. Shoulder usually decorated (cross-hatched triangles, one case of half-circles), with or without subsidiary dog-tooth zone; one amphora has linear decoration in panels on the belly, with shoulder left clear.

Only seven, so far as I know, all of the late phase. There may or may not be a connexion with a shape that appears (a survival from late Mycenaean) in one of the earliest Protogeometric tombs – those discussed above are, however, about half the size of the earlier one, under twenty centimetres, and indeed considerably smaller than any of the other types of amphora.

PLATE 28 ATHENS
Oinochoe; ·315 m. *Ker.* IV, pl. 15, 914.
Pyxides; ·131 m., ·121 m. *Ker.* IV, pl. 20, 912–13.

HYDRIA

Body as for belly-handled amphora, with appropriate handles; neck as for neck-handled amphora, but one handle only. Low conical foot.

Either dark ground or clay ground, but neck always painted. Decoration confined to shoulder, semicircles as a rule, occasionally some other motive – languettes, cross-hatched diamond panel.

A rare shape, only four known, all of the late phase. Presumably, however, some link with Sub-Mycenaean, where three are known, from the Agora. The height varies between twenty-four and forty centimetres.

ONE-HANDLED JUG (Fig. 7)

Fragments only have been found in Athens. Round mouth, dumpy ovoid shape. Dark ground except for semicircles or cross-hatched triangles or diamonds on the shoulder. Late Protogeometric.

TREFOIL-LIPPED OINOCHOE (Fig. 8, Pl. 28)

Body ovoid throughout most of the period; at the end either a more slender ovoid or rather dumpy and tending towards the globular. Well-pronounced foot. In the transitional stage to Geometric, the vase may be smaller, the neck narrower, and the lower body truncated to give a broad base; but the original shape persists.

Brief trial of clay-ground system, soon becoming and remaining dark ground. The system of band division at first adopted, and never entirely rejected, was the same as for the amphorae, with the main decorative motives, at first circles with languettes, then semicircles, with or without some intermediate vertical linear motive, confined to the shoulder. The group of bands below the belly was frequently dispensed with in the late phase, which also witnessed another and popular development, the abandonment of the shoulder decoration altogether, with the whole body painted over except for a zone round the middle of the belly, consisting of two reserved bands enclosing a zigzag or (less frequently) groups of opposed diagonals. It was in fact a vase whose elegance of shape was its main attraction, and the potters realised that it needed the minimum of decoration.

It was extremely popular as a burial offering, and the shape survived into the Geometric period (ninth century), though by that time the broad-based trefoil-lipped oinochoe, with decoration on the neck, and sets of reserved bands on the body, had become the normally accepted shape.

LEKYTHOS (Fig. 6)

Body ovoid; neck narrow, culminating in a trumpet lip; handle vertical from shoulder to middle or upper neck; pronounced low conical foot.

The development in decoration closely parallels that of the trefoil-lipped oinochoe, with the following exceptions. The neck was almost invariably banded, there is no instance known to me of any attempt to place full circles on the shoulder, and in the late phase two new ideas are found, a cross-hatched diamond motive in between the semicircles and, much more frequently, the replacement of the semicircles by cross-hatched triangles; also, the late feature, on the oinochoai, of painting the whole body except for a zone on the belly is hardly ever found on the lekythoi.

Reasonably popular throughout Protogeometric, this shape disappeared completely at the end of the style.

SKYPHOS (Fig. 9)

Foot, high conical, from which the lower body curves out sharply, then ascending almost straight, finishing with a gentle outward curve to the rim. This is the usual form, but the very earliest feet are not so high; very large skyphoi can have a flaring foot, and the outward curve to the rim can vary to a certain extent. Handles set horizontally on the upper body.

The general effect is dark ground with decoration between the handles, on both sides, but in the early and middle phases, and exceptionally later, the lower body and upper part of the foot can be left unpainted. The lip is always painted.

Apart from the earliest stage, when the style had not yet settled down, and which includes a unique example of compass-drawn semicircles, there are several main decorative systems. First, there is a band below the lip, with a horizontal zigzag immediately below it, and then three sets of concentric circles with bands below, the remainder being painted. This continues throughout. Second, instead of three sets of circles there are two, flanking a central linear motive – usually a cross-hatched rectangular panel, but cross-hatched diamonds and chequers are also found. This belongs to the late phase. Third, no circles, but a succession of rectangular panels showing the interplay of vertical, horizontal, and diagonal lines. This type is found only on small skyphoi, where it would be impracticable to describe circles, and is known in every phase. The fourth is quite different, in that the whole upper body is painted except for a narrow zone between the handles, bands enclosing a rough zigzag. This system has only so far been found in the middle phase, and includes skyphoi whose lower body and upper foot are unpainted.[13] In the late phase there is a similar system, but the motives are different, dog-tooth or formal zigzag.

This is one of the most distinctive of all the Protogeometric vase types, and it is discarded at the end; in the transitional stage to Geometric the conical foot has already been replaced by a much lower one.[14]

[13] There could be some link with, and influence from, the Argolid (see p. 164).

[14] The custom of filling the central circle with some variety of cross seems to be confined to the late phase.

PLATE 29 ATHENS (NEA IONIA). Krater; ·468 m. *Hesp.* 30, pl. 29.

KRATER

As the material is so scarce, and in most cases fragmentary, it is difficult to give any satisfactory description of the stylistic progress.

Early in the style, and probably continuing well into the late phase, the body is very similar to that of the skyphos. The mouth consists of a wide everted lip below which the rim comes down to a sharp ridge to form the connexion with the body. The foot is low to start with, but eventually develops a good conical shape, though it is broader in proportion to that found in the skyphos. Two handles (one case of double loops, and perhaps they mostly were) were placed horizontally on the upper body.

The latest Protogeometric krater yet known has a rather different shape (Pl. 29). It has a high-shouldered body sloping inwards towards the everted lip, and the two handles are set vertically from the top of the body to the lip; the distinguishing ridge has disappeared. Whether this is typical of the kraters of this latest phase one cannot say, but the shape of the body is reflected in other vase types, especially the kantharos.

The system of decoration is dark ground throughout, so far as can be seen, with the main decoration confined to the upper body. My impression is that at first one gets a series of vertical rectilinear panels, that then sets of concentric circles, with or without intervening panels, were used, but at the end there was a return to the purely rectilinear system of panelling within a narrow zone.

In this shape at least one can see the continuance into Protogeometric of the Cypriot decorative system of the late Sub-Mycenaean phase.

HIGH-FOOTED CUP (Fig. 10, Pl. 26)

Foot as for the skyphos, and a similar sharp outward swing for the lower body, the convex curve becoming gradually less pronounced and starting to curve inwards at the junction with the lip, when again a sharp break is made before the gently outcurving lip. Handle vertical from belly to lip.

The general effect is, as on the skyphoi, dark ground. The only decorative motive for most of the cups is a zigzag round the outer lip, but miniature cups may have rectilinear panel decoration on the belly.

Like the skyphos, this type is confined to the Protogeometric style, and in fact the alternative of the flat-based cup makes its first appearance as early as the middle phase, but only completely replaces the high-footed variety at the time of transition to Geometric. This being a smaller vase than the skyphos, the high foot was no doubt found to be even less suitable.

FLAT-BASED CUP

There is little to be said of this vase. It has a high belly, sloping inwards towards a low out-turned lip, with a thick vertical strap handle from belly to lip. It is always painted over, except for a reserved band on the outer lip and horizontal bars on the handle. Very rarely there is a low foot. Except for one which belongs to the middle phase, all are from late contexts, and become the accepted type for the Geometric style.

KANTHAROS (Pl. 30)

Body profile as for the high-footed cup; two vertical handles from body to lip; foot varies, from base ring to high conical, one of transitional to Geometric date being high and ribbed.

A dark-ground type of vase, such evidence as we have suggesting that at first the whole body was painted over, but that as the Geometric period approached, the whole area between the handles was decorated, or else just a small square panel, the main motive being a meander. The known examples all seem to be very late in the style, with one exception which could belong to the middle phase.

PYXIS (Pl. 28)

Body ovoid with low conical foot, or globular with low ring foot. Lip sharply everted. String holes in the lip correspond to similar ones in the lid, a low dome surmounted by a high distinctive knob.

Dark ground. The earliest, of the middle phase – an ovoid one – has no

PLATE 30 ATHENS
Kalathos; ·074 m. *Ker.* I, pl. 71, 579.
Kantharos; ·115 m. *Ker.* IV, pl. 21, 2026.

decoration, but usually there is a decorated zone around the upper belly:
sets of opposing diagonals, chequers and vertical lines, dog-teeth. The lid
has reserved bands, often with an additional dog-tooth zone.

Only the one is known from the middle phase; the rest all belong to Late
Protogeometric. At the time of transition, or Early Geometric, the everted
lip disappears, and the body either remains globular or is lengthened to
give the effect of a whip top: on these there are several zones of decoration,
the main motive being the meander.

The type seems certain to be an invention of the Protogeometric potter.
Heights vary between eleven and fourteen centimetres, and there are also
miniature ones.

KALATHOS (Pl. 30)

A wide and rather shallow bowl. It has a broad flat base, from which the
body rises, as a rule, in a slight concave curve to an offset lip with flat rim,
often with one or more string holes. Very exceptionally the body can have
a convex curve. The vase is either handleless, or provided with one
vertical handle from upper body to lip.[15]

This is a dark-ground type, but always has reserved bands and one or
more zones of rectilinear decoration (zigzag, formal or rough, dog-tooth,
herringbone, alternating diagonals, chequers) – circular motives were
clearly thought to be unsuitable. Rims have groups of bars, and the base
also is decorated (reserved cross, chequers).

The kalathos has so far been found only in the late phase, and continues
in use into Geometric times. Whether any eventual link with the not
unsimilar late Mycenaean kalathoi will emerge one cannot tell.

[15] The plain openwork kalathos is more characteristic of the Geometric style; strangely, its
only earlier appearance is from a well with pottery of Middle Protogeometric date.

MISCELLANEOUS

There are a few unusual types of vase, characteristic of the latest phase of all – it would seem, in fact, that they contribute to an experimental stage leading to the Geometric style, rather as happened at the end of the Sub-Mycenaean period. This is not unnatural, but what is surprising is that one or two of the shapes recall those of the earlier period. The high-handled pyxis in one of the latest Sub-Mycenaean tombs is matched by two which probably belong to the very end of Protogeometric, but these are larger, finer, and rather different in conception. Ring vases[16] and clay boxes are common to both experimental phases, but not found in between – the later boxes are, however, greatly superior to the earlier ones. The fine openwork stands from a Late Protogeometric burial recall slightly the combined tripod stand and bowl of Late Sub-Mycenaean date; the link is tenuous, but more significant is the fact that both, in their respective periods, reflect the influence of Cyprus, an influence also visible in late – but not the latest – Protogeometric in the tripod-loop base of a belly-handled amphora. Apart from these, there are three or four bowls and cups of unique type, all very late.

The whole style may be summarised as follows. The surviving Sub-Mycenaean shapes can be divided into the closed and the open types. In the first category there were the neck-handled and belly-handled amphorae, the trefoil-lipped oinochoai, the lekythoi, and the hydriai, for all of which the major feature was the elegant ovoid body, tending to become even more slender as the style progressed; of these, the belly-handled amphora was discarded in favour of a variant with vertical handles on the shoulder before the end of Protogeometric, the lekythos continued until the end but no longer, and the other three survived into the Geometric period. The open vases were represented, at least in the tombs, by the skyphoi or bowls, and the one-handled cups, and in both cases the characteristic novelty was the high conical foot, which did not outlive the style – it made for a well-balanced profile, a nice juxtaposition of the angular and the circular, but evidently broke too easily, and there were already signs of the appearance of a flat base for the cups, and a much lower foot for the skyphoi, before the Geometric style emerged. A third type of open vase was the krater, certainly of Sub-Mycenaean origin but only very rarely found in tombs: this also was provided with a substantial foot, but its development is at present difficult to follow. The two major shapes which did not survive Sub-Mycenaean were the stirrup jar and the amphoriskos.

As well as these traditional vase types, several new ones were intro-duced. All are most commonly to be found in Late Protogeometric, but some made their first appearance in the preceding middle stage, these being the pyxis, a small ovoid or globular vase with everted lip (which disappears towards the end), and string holes corresponding to similar ones in a lid; perhaps the kalathos (see p. 155, n. 15), of rather conical shape

---

[16] There is also a variant to this shape, a flat circular jug with trefoil lip (other similar ones have been found at Marathon and on Skyros, in Early Geometric contexts).

and flat-based; the kantharos, a variant of the skyphos, with its handles vertical to the lip instead of horizontal on the belly, and a high conical foot, truncated in course of time; and even the flat-based cup, mentioned above as the eventual successor to that with high conical foot. Confined to the late phase are the amphora with shoulder handles, already mentioned, a smallish amphora with handles from shoulder to lip (perhaps a revival of a Sub-Mycenaean shape? cf. p. 33), the jug, possibly the kalathos, and sundry rarities (one or two of which revive links with Cyprus) such as the ring vase, openwork stands, boxes and a high-handled pyxis, which once again herald a transitional period to a new style. A new variety of pyxis, shaped rather like a top, is Geometric rather than Protogeometric.

The system and details of decoration may be dismissed more briefly. The vases of the latest, transitional, Sub-Mycenaean phase were in the main mostly painted over (dark ground), but in Early and Middle Protogeometric there was a tendency to leave extensive areas unpainted (clay ground). This was evidently, however, felt to be unsatisfactory, and the dark-ground system was normally used during the late phase, with exceptions in accordance with the vase type.

Decorative motives were as a rule confined to a small area of the vase, except for the skyphoi and most probably the kraters – but the cups had, almost without exception, just a zigzag line round the outer rim. For the closed ovoid vases the shoulder was the preferred area, and it is only in the later stages that this was abandoned; the belly was used as a decorative area for the belly-handled amphorae, and later for oinochoai when the shoulder was painted over; decoration on the neck is always a sign of extreme lateness. As to the motives themselves, concentric circles and semicircles were by far the most frequently used throughout most of the period, wherever the surface was suitable for them, as on the closed ovoid vases and the skyphoi. There were rectilinear motives as well, however, and as the style progressed these were used as features dividing the circular motives, and eventually took their place, when once again one can get a multiplicity of panels, as in the earlier transitional period, and using much the same kind of motive. It is to this last stage that belongs the introduction of the meander, one of the characteristics of the succeeding Geometric style. On the whole, the Protogeometric style was one in which decoration was used sparingly, a notably sober style, but always very carefully related to and integrated with the shape of the vase; uniform during most of its course, the last phase of all, the latter stage of Late Protogeometric, exhibits numerous signs of dissatisfaction with the previous conventions, and introduces developments both in shape and decoration that were to lead to the Geometric style.

At first sight, the overall impression of Athens in the late Dark Ages is not a very exciting one. It is obvious, and important, that there was a great advance in the technique of vase-making, and an equivalent artistic progress in relating decoration to shape, but the potters soon became set in their ways. There was also an improvement in metalwork, but the same thing happened as with the pottery, and in addition it would appear that there was a temporary recession at least in bronzework. In other words, a substantial leap forward had been taken, but the impetus was not followed through.

Another feature of importance that the evidence permits us probably to deduce is that the society as a whole took on a rather regimented character, and if this deduction is correct it might have a bearing on the cultural and technological situation. A satisfactory state of affairs had been created during, roughly, the second half of the eleventh century, and then either conservatism or higher authority led to its retention. In this case we would have something more than stagnation, though even so the impression would remain of a community that had not lived up to its great promise.

Why, therefore, should such attention be paid to this community? The answer is that it is wrong to consider Athens in isolation; we must rather think of the Athenians in the wider sphere, as one community among many. As soon as we do this, we can see how superior at least the culture of the Athenians was to that of others, both in pottery and in metal objects (the only comparative material available). Nor is this how it seems only to ourselves; it is how the Greeks at the time viewed it, as they were anxious to learn from Athens. The Athenian products, which may seem conventional and a little dull to us, obviously did not give that impression to their neighbours. Furthermore, Athenian influence was, we shall find, chiefly exercised at a time when their culture had become established and set; it reflects the remarkable progress made, and had an almost inevitable effect on nearby, and even on distant, areas. Again it may be that we should bear in mind the probable atmosphere of society; the orderly nature of the community suggested by the standardisation of culture and customs presumably meant a well-organised and strong city which gave it a prestige and a primacy in the Greek world that, when lost, it was not to recover till the fifth century.

The main importance of Athens is to be seen, then, in the wider view, in the influence of the Athenians over other communities. The following sections will, I think, show the truth of this.

8 Attica, Aegina, Keos

The scarcity of material from the rest of Attica is in direct and remarkable contrast to the quantity at Athens, and such material is apparently confined to the Late Protogeometric phase. Not all of it has been published, for example tomb groups from Marathon and vases from Brauron, but even with those the total is extremely disappointing.

As things stand, and as published, there is a scatter of coastal sites. From Marathon, Aliki, and Eleusis, just a few tombs and associated vases; from Thorikos near Laurion, clear traces of a new settlement covering the end of Protogeometric and the beginning of Geometric, in one area of which evidence for the extraction of silver from lead was discovered (see p. 162 for an earlier instance from Argos). Inland, especially in the rich Mesogeia, the region east of Mt. Hymettus, there is so far practically nothing.

The finds, then, are few, of late date, and mostly confined to tombs. The conclusions are consequently also few, but not wholly unimportant. The pottery is very close in style to that of Athens, but of lesser quality; however, we know at least that not all the vases of Attica were made in Athens. The strict uniformity of burial customs noted in Athens was not observed over the rest of Attica: for example, a very late Protogeometric or very early Geometric amphora from Menidi, north of Athens, was associated with an adult inhumation.

These conclusions are valid, but is one justified in arguing from the existence of so very few sites, with so very little material, and from the fact that nothing certainly earlier than Late Protogeometric has been found? The situation, it may be added, remained much the same during the first half of the ninth century, Early Geometric, and it is only in the second half that there is a known increase in the number of sites and in the amount of material. Would it be reasonable to infer that almost the whole of the population was concentrated in or close to Athens, an inland site, especially during the early phases of this period, thereby leading to the further inference that there was still a widespread feeling of insecurity? It seems to me that the success and relative speed with which the Athenian style penetrated the Aegean and south mainland strongly suggest the opposite conclusion. What then of the lateness of the material outside Athens? Here one must bear in mind that what we have is very scanty indeed, and that in any case Late Protogeometric covers quite a long period, probably the whole of the tenth century. On the whole, especially in view of the evidence from other areas, it is fair to say that we have not yet a true picture. Settlements will take some identifying, since solid and enduring constructions are likely to have been negligible, and the discovery of tombs is so often a matter of chance.

With Attica may be taken the two islands of Aegina and Keos (nothing is known of Salamis at this time nor for some while after) because of their proximity and the fact that their pottery is Attic in style.

Aegina has just the one site, by the sea immediately to the north of the modern town. From here we have a few sherds from the settlement, and vases associated with two child inhumations in cist tombs. Finally, there is a large neck-handled amphora of unknown provenance, which may indicate that adults, as in Athens, were cremated, for it is a typical crema- tion urn. Not much pottery is involved, and all of the late phase of Proto- geometric. There are clear links with Attica (Eleusis and Athens) which are only to be expected. Perhaps less foreseeable, but nonetheless of great interest, was the presence of a cup which certainly came from the Argolid, and a fairly clear indication of the way that goods could, and probably did, travel between Attica and the Argolid.

Keos[1] also has one known site, that of Ayia Irini, and the finds were made in an area used both earlier and later as a sanctuary (see pp. 280 f.). The preliminary report states that Protogeometric ware was abundant, and included large vessels; so far only three sherds have been illustrated, from two skyphoi and a cup – all could be of Athenian manufacture.

These two islands may not have produced anything of outstanding interest, but at least they provide evidence for limited sea-going activities, not only of the inhabitants of Attica, but also of those of the Argolid.

[1] There are also two stray vases from this island, an amphora of the early eleventh century, and a Late Protogeometric lekythos.

9 The Argolid and Corinthia

The Argolid

Since Athens, the original home of the distinctive Protogeometric style of
the later Dark Ages, had been one of the main centres of the Sub-
Mycenaean region of the central Greek mainland, it is of importance to
discover what happened in the other major group, comprising the sites
of the Argolid. Traces of the final Sub-Mycenaean experimental phase, so
strong in Athens, are extremely scarce so far in this district, and it may be
that we should infer, provisionally, that the Argolid had at this time
no close links with Athens. This inference I shall assume to be correct, and
in consequence we need not expect that the new Protogeometric style, in
spite of the technical improvements involved, would immediately be
reflected in the creations of the Argive potters.

We have to approach the Argolid, therefore, with the probability that
at least in the pottery, which as usual constitutes our main evidence, the
previous culture survived, overlapped the beginning of Protogeometric in
Athens, and was likely to place its distinctive mark on what subsequently
emerged. We must also bear in mind that on the three main sites, Mycenae,
Argos, and Tiryns, although they had been prior Mycenaean centres, the
Sub-Mycenaean element seems to have been separate from the Mycenaean,
both in type of tomb (with Argos as a partial exception) and in place of
habitation. The same three sites provide the bulk of our knowledge in the
later Dark Ages, and to these can be added Asine, another Mycenaean
stronghold, but which has produced exceedingly little that can be assigned
to the early Dark Ages.

As these sites lie within a few miles of one another – though Asine is
geographically somewhat isolated from the rest – it seems reasonable to
discuss their material as a whole. First, however, some idea must be given
of the extent and nature of the evidence on each site.

Of the four, Argos is the most significant, not only in consequence of the
thorough and extensive excavations carried out in recent years by the
French School and by the Greek Archaeological Service, but also because
it was probably becoming the dominant town of the Argolid. The area
occupied, mainly to the east and south of the Larisa (the acropolis of
Argos), covered a circle whose diameter is not far off a mile – and of course
it may have been larger. In this respect it rivals Athens, though one cannot
be sure that one has not to do with more than one community. What is of
particular importance is that in a number of localities excavation has

revealed traces of settlement, and in two of these several levels could be assigned to this period. No actual house foundations came to light, and this may strengthen the likelihood that work in stone was at a very low ebb. It is probable that houses were generally built of mud brick, as at Old Smyrna (p. 183) and as still happens today – and there is indeed evidence at one spot of a large number of rough bricks. A number of hearths and ovens were associated with the mass of settlement sherds, and in one place there was a most interesting construction (Pl. 31), datable to the earliest phase of Protogeometric (and also to the latest Sub-Mycenaean, see p. 72), the purpose of which was probably the refining of silver from lead, a unique record, except for Thorikos (p. 159), of the working of a metal which is otherwise virtually unknown (two rings from Knossos seem to be about all), and a witness to the extent of our ignorance. The workshop did not long survive, for by Late Protogeometric the area was being used for burials.

A fair number of tombs were found, at least thirty-five, either in small groups or apparently isolated – one says apparently, for in many places the discovery was due to a single small sounding, and considerable areas remain untouched. The burials are dotted over the whole area, never far, to judge from the known instances, from where the inhabitants actually lived. The great majority were cist tombs, but a few of the early ones qualify as earth-cut, as lacking the lining of stone slabs; all were in-humations, but apart from that there seems to have been no uniformity whether in the orientation of the tomb or in the laying out of the dead person. They contained mostly pottery, other objects being extremely rare.

So far, then, the salient features are the large size of the site, the evidence of habitation, the silver-refining workshop, and the retention (in contrast to Athens) of the practice of inhumation. This final point is equally applicable to the other three sites, whose material has come almost exclusively from cemeteries.

At Mycenae the seven cist tombs (three may be earth-cut) overlay the earlier Mycenaean settlement, as did also the few tombs of the Geometric period. They do not appear, as was the case at Argos, to have been adjacent to any contemporaneous habitation. No assessment, obviously, can be given of the size of the community, though I do not think it was large.

One cannot say much more about Tiryns, though here burials were encountered both to the north-west and to the south of the citadel. As at Mycenae, there was no hesitation in using for burials the areas of previous Mycenaean habitation. There were about twenty tombs, the earliest, as at Argos, being earth-cut, cist tombs then becoming the fashion, except for one possible instance of a pithos burial.

At Asine, finally, there was a sizeable cist-tomb cemetery, forty-six tombs altogether, of which only sixteen contained funeral gifts, whether of pottery or of metal – as, however, all these belong to this period it is probable that the rest also do.

Coming now to discuss the finds as a whole, it must be borne in mind

A

B

PLATE 31 ARGOS
A) Construction probably used for cupellation process.
B) Skyphos. Courbin, *Stratification et Stratification*, figs. 7 and 8.

that the evidence is partial and uneven, and to some extent unpublished.
One could wish for an integrated account of the whole area: all I can do
here is to give what I think was the likely situation as to the customs and
culture, so far as possible based on the known and published material, but
remembering that additional material could result in greater or lesser
modifications.

The later Dark Ages in the Argolid can, I think, be divided into three phases chiefly, but not entirely, on the basis of development in the pottery; there is a brief early phase, a long central one, and a fairly brief concluding one.

Of these, the early stage is nebulous. It corresponds to what in Athens would be Early Protogeometric and perhaps to some of Middle Proto-geometric as well. But since it seems likely that during this time the Athenian ceramic innovations made no impact on the Argolid, the pottery we encounter is merely an extension and final survival of the Sub-Mycenaean, the characteristic ware of the early Dark Ages, and so it is by no means easy to decide whether some of it should not in fact belong to this earlier period. One well-stocked cist tomb at Mycenae, discussed earlier (p. 69), may belong to it,[1] with a few tombs at Tiryns (but not including the warrior grave), and at Argos, where the pottery remains largely un-published and thus provides further uncertainty, probably one burial, part of the time when the silver workshop was in use, and the earlier stages of at least two of the areas of habitation. The cemetery at Asine seems definitely not to have been in use as early as this.

We can say, to start with, that the inhabitants probably lived in houses made of mud brick, and certainly inhumed their dead in earth-cut or cist tombs (i.e. with lining as well as covering stone slabs), in other words as individuals rather than as families.[2]

Apart from this, we have to infer what we can from the objects of pottery or metalwork. The pottery they used was extremely undistinguished, virtually bankrupt of ideas both in shape and decoration. The appeal of the stirrup jar had still not completely disappeared, but there are only two, one from Mycenae (Pl. 9, the only vase to show the experimental or 'wild' style found in Athens), and one from Tiryns, which has lost its spout, the opening being where the disk of the stirrup should be. They used lekythoi, cups, and small trefoil-lipped oinochoai with handle reaching above the lip. All these, except the cup, had extremely simple decoration – small languettes, hatched or cross-hatched triangles. Of the larger vases the only one known which may belong to this phase is a neck-handled amphora with good ovoid body, perhaps here reflecting developments in Athens. The vase most commonly in use, however, was the deep bowl, which was either monochrome to below the belly and the lower half unpainted, or was painted over except for a rough zigzag in a horizontal panel between the handles. We find the potters, then, bereft of inspiration, and from this one might be tempted to deduce that the inhabitants lived in a small world of their own, and that their cultural and technological level was low.

When we come to the metalwork, though, the picture is rather different. The cist tomb at Mycenae which contained the stirrup jar mentioned above produced (Pl. 10) bronze dress pins, fibulae, and finger rings (one of which is of northern type). This is the tomb, though, that might belong

---

[1] Possibly two other tombs as well; see p. 166, n. 3.

[2] There may be one case of a cremation at Argos, where a neck-handled amphora was found, but no bones; no ashes either being found, however, we cannot be sure.

FIG. 16 TIRYNS TOMB VI
Pins; ·14 m., ·157 m. *AM* 78, p. 29, fig. 11.

to the earlier period – and I have in fact discussed it within that context – so
it is preferable not to stress its evidence. There are, however, four tombs
at Tiryns which I believe should be assigned to this phase; they contained
no vases, but in them were found altogether eleven bronze finger rings, one
bronze and four gold spirals for the hair (two of the gold ones of a northern
type), two bronze and eight iron dress pins (see Fig. 16). All can belong
typologically to this time; the iron pins can hardly be earlier, as knowledge
of working this metal does not precede the transition from Sub-Mycenaean
to Protogeometric; and the gold spirals, especially those of northern type,
are found in Athens at just this time, the latest coming from an Early
Protogeometric grave. This material shows that gold, bronze, and iron
were all in use, the iron proving that the local smiths were aware of this
recent metallurgical development. And finally there is the evidence of the
presumed silver extraction already mentioned; as we have seen, it must
precede Late Protogeometric, and we are also informed that in certain
cases the sherds associated with it had circles drawn by hand, thus
indicating the very early nature of the context, and at the same time
perhaps implying that other sherds had compass-drawn circles, and so
suggesting that this workshop continued in use not only during this early
phase but for a brief while beyond it.

This is, of course, of much interest, but the evidence as a whole does not
tell us much about the situation in the Argolid. We know that the potters
were rather unimaginative and that the metal craftsmen were decidedly
competent. It looks as though the three communities in question had a
uniform but low culture, simply preserving the *status quo* of the early Dark
Ages. The size of these communities, we can reasonably guess, was small,
but how many more were there? Of the community organisation we can
say nothing, of course. From the metalwork it seems clear that they were
in touch with outside developments, and there is no reason to suppose that
they were isolated. One assumes that they lived in peace among themselves,
and were not disturbed by attacks from outside. But there is no knowing
for certain, nor can one deduce this from the absence of weapons at this
time – or later.

The second phase covers the rest of the period except for its end. As the
division between one phase and another has been made primarily on the
basis of the pottery used, there is no need to expect any startling change in

any other aspect of life. What is likely is that the communities increased in size: it is within this period that the Asine cemetery falls, though that may be a matter of chance; for Mycenae and Tiryns, also, the evidence is not really sufficient; at Argos, however, the signs are that this was the time of expansion of the inhabited area, and its evidence might take the other sites with it. There is no trace of any more solid house constructions. Inhumation continued to be the accepted method of burial, though now the earth-cut graves seem to have given way completely to the cist tombs. We can now see more clearly, since there are many more tombs, that there was no uniformity in matters such as the position of the corpse or the orientation of the tomb. Just one small point of positive interest emerges, that in certain cases, at Asine and at Mycenae, charcoal and ashes were found near the tomb, suggesting perhaps the burning of votive or sacrificial gifts; but this need not be an innovation of this particular phase, nor evidently was it a regular practice. On the whole, things probably continued as they had done, reasonably peacefully.

In one respect, however, this phase exhibits a change which has nothing to do with pottery, and that is in the marked decrease in the quantity of metal objects deposited in tombs.[3] There are no more fibulae, no more gold spirals (nor any other object of gold); bronze finger rings are much less common. Only the dress pins retained their popularity: they were either wholly of iron or, more frequently, had an iron shaft and a bronze bulb – all four sites have instances of this latter type. In fact, this is very much the sort of picture we get in Athens, though there the finger rings are even more rarely to be found, and it may lend support to the theory that copper was in very short supply. Furthermore, the presence of the iron pins with bronze bulbs, so characteristic of Athens, proves that there was a link between that town and the Argolid, with the influence most probably coming from Athens. And of course, the existence of interconnexions is demonstrable from the developments in the pottery.

It is perfectly clear that the potters of the Argolid took over a number of features of the Athenian Protogeometric style in order to help in reorganising and revivifying their own (see Pls. 32, 33). In just a few cases, they decided on close imitation, as we know of cups of Athenian type at Argos and Tiryns and Asine; and on the two former sites we find replicas of the two main types of Athenian skyphoi, that with three sets of circles and the one with two sets of circles flanking a cross-hatched panel. Much of the borrowing, however, was selective, and adapted to local shapes, whether old or new. Thus the high conical foot was fitted on to the characteristic bowl shape of the early phase, and a similar transformation was made to the cup. Compass-drawn circles and semicircles were freely used – in one sense a good deal more freely than the Athenian potters would have allowed, such as in the placing of circles on the shoulders of

[3] Assuming, of course, that I am right in assigning the four tombs from Tiryns to the earlier phase (see above). It may be added that two of the Mycenae tombs contained objects similar to those of the Tiryns tombs, three iron pins, earrings of bronze, and two spiraliform rings, one of bronze, the other of iron; but as we have no details of these, nor of the jug found in one tomb, I have left them out of account.

PLATE 32 ARGOS
A) Two vases. *BCH* 81, 664, fig. 55.
B) Three vases. *BCH* 77, 262, fig. 55.

closed vases, even in the insertion of the circles flanking a rectangular panel complex on the shoulders of amphorae, to which it was not really suitable. The ovoid shape of most of the closed vases could also have reflected Athenian influences.

We certainly get a much greater range of vase shapes now (though, of course, this could be partly due to our ignorance of the early phase). Stirrup jars were finally suppressed. But there are lekythoi, now ovoid and with a highish conical foot, and oinochoai, both with a trefoil lip and with a round mouth. There are small one-handled jugs, and both neck-

PLATE 33 TIRYNS
A) Belly-handled amphora; ·23 m.
B) Cup; ·10 m. *AM* 78, pl. 10, 5; 18, 5.

and belly-handled amphorae, these being smaller than the great cremation urns of Athens.

Then there are somewhat rarer shapes, such as a pyxis with high handles from Argos, an askos from Mycenae, a sort of kalathos with three struts from Tiryns, and again from Argos a shallow three-handled dish with flaring foot which finds parallels, not with Athens, but with Lefkandi in Euboea (p. 44).

On the whole, this local style was a dark-ground one – a belly-handled amphora from Mycenae, with circles on the shoulder, is a very rare example of a clay-ground vase, possibly but not necessarily reflecting an early stage of influence from Athens. And the system of decoration, in spite of the use made of the dividers and multiple brush for circles, was predominantly rectilinear, the favourite motive, almost the hallmark, being the cross-hatched triangle,[4] used either singly or in a complex, such as the hour-glass patterns. It may have some significance for outside contacts, as this motive, and the rectilinear system of decoration generally, were also characteristics of the pottery of the Dodecanese at this time – in fact, two skyphoi from Argos (see Pl. 31) are remarkably close in shape and decoration to some from Kos and Rhodes (cf. pp. 173 f.).

So while the fortunes of the metalsmiths were at a low ebb, those of the potter had revived somewhat; stimulated by the Athenian style, they nevertheless achieved a separate and individual Protogeometric style of their own.

Equally local and individual was the hand-made ware, occasionally found alongside the wheel-made. Chiefly consisting of jugs and trefoil-

---

[4] Well known in Athens, but there is no reason to suppose any borrowing, as it was equally popular in the first phase and indeed in the early Dark Ages.

lipped oinochoai, it was found particularly in the cemetery at Asine, but examples are known on the other three sites as well; and at times the fabric is very good. Though not really comparable to the fine ware of Athens in Late Protogeometric, it is nevertheless an extremely interesting phenomenon, but for whose presence I can suggest no explanation.

The third and concluding phase may be dealt with extremely briefly. It corresponds to the latest stage of the Protogeometric style in Athens and to the transition to Early Geometric, and its main feature is a much stronger influence from the potters of Athens. The cemetery at Asine did not extend as far as this, but there is plenty of evidence from the tomb contents of the other three sites, in particular a fine tomb group from Mycenae. During this phase the local Protogeometric style disappeared, and the potters of the Argolid followed Athenian developments into the early stages of the Geometric style, in strong contrast to the situation we shall find north and east of Attica, in Thessaly, Euboea, and the northern Cyclades. And there came now a reversion to the use of bronze, especially for dress pins, as in Athens, but it is worth noting that the Mycenae tomb mentioned above contained pins and a fibula that are as fine as, if not finer than, anything produced at this time in that town (Fig. 17).

The results of this analysis may be summarised as follows. The district is represented by four sites, three of which are on the coast or close to it, and the fourth a little way inland. It is probable that there was complete continuity of habitation extending not only over this period but throughout the Dark Ages. Such continuity will no doubt become absolutely clear when we have full knowledge of the settlement material, and indeed the preliminary reports of the work at Argos already indicate it. It can in any case be reasonably inferred from the evidence of burial, since the type of tomb remained in principle unchanged throughout, as also did the varieties of personal ornament found in the tombs, with the exception of the curious disappearance of the fibula during the later stages. It is only in the pottery that a fairly radical change can be observed, and this can be attributed to the gradually increasing influence of the Athenian Protogeometric style during the tenth century (quite possibly starting somewhat earlier), but even so there is quite sufficient evidence to show that the previous Sub-Mycenaean tradition retained its hold on the local potters and resulted, until the concluding phase, in an only partial and modified acceptance of Athenian ceramic influence.

The size of the population is difficult to assess. We have good grounds for thinking that there was a major settlement at Argos, probably growing during the later Dark Ages, but we cannot be so sure about the other three sites. There seems to have been a general uniformity of customs and culture, but there was by no means, even on any single site, the rather rigid uniformity such as is found in Athens. Of the internal organisation of each community we can say nothing, nor can we tell whether any settlement controlled one or all of the rest. We can, however, assume from the nature of the material that the communities were in close touch with one another (they are in any case close enough geographically), and the impression is

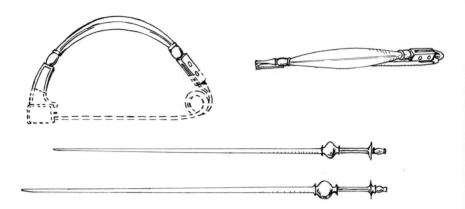

FIG. 17 MYCENAE TOMB G 603
Pins (·15 m., ·168 m.) and fibula (·115 m., as preserved). *BSA* 50,
p. 242, fig. 2; p. 243, fig. 3.

that their life was fairly peaceful and stable. Notwithstanding the relative
security, the standard of living and culture was not particularly high; the
pottery was an improvement on its predecessor – it could hardly have been
much worse – but the scarcity of metal objects during most of the period,
even when compared with that immediately preceding, may indicate a
certain lack either of the raw material or of the skill to work it. In fact, we
are still in the Dark Ages.

So far as concerns external relations, we cannot yet achieve a complete
picture. At the outset there seems to be little evidence of the links with
Cyprus such as existed for a brief while at Athens, nor of any strong link
with Athens itself or with other areas, and yet there is no reason for
supposing absolute isolation – it was during this time that the craftsmen
acquired the knowledge of working in iron, which must have come from
outside. Thereafter, it is clear that communication at least with Athens
was frequent, no doubt via Aegina, where an import from the Argolid has
been found (p. 160), and we shall see later that there are traces of a possible
trans-Aegean movement to the area of the Dodecanese towards the end of
the period, or if not that, connexions of some sort. And there are a few hints
that the people of the Argolid travelled fairly freely within the Aegean –
with three coastal sites out of four, this is only to be expected. Within the
Peloponnese itself it is most probable that close contact was maintained
with Corinthia, and there are a few signs that this district may have been in
touch with the regions to the south and west, but the lack of full evidence
prevents us from being certain.

Corinthia

As opposed to that from the Argolid, the evidence from Corinthia is extremely disappointing, and may be disposed of very briefly. Outside of Corinth there is only one significant group of vases, from a child's tomb at Vello in the western part of the coastal plain. Of the thirteen, seven were hand-made but unremarkable except for their presence, and the rest were what one would expect in the latter part of the tenth century, except for a small multiple vase, which has no parallel at this late stage.

In Corinth itself, where one might expect better things, traces of settlement are limited to a handful of sherds, with circle and semicircle decoration on four, and the rest probably from a single bowl with a zigzag in a panel between the handles relieving what seems to have been an otherwise monochrome vase. Then there were two vases out of context. One, a jug, belongs to Late Protogeometric and is very like one from Eleusis (see Fig. 7); the other, a lekythos, found in a tomb of Roman times, is of the same period, and includes a decorative feature otherwise paralleled only in the Argolid. Both vases have concentric semicircles on the shoulder.

Finally, there is the material from a recently discovered cist tomb, to be dated to the very end of the Dark Ages or (perhaps more likely) slightly later. The tomb itself is unusual, in that at one end it had a separate, and apparently unused, compartment.[5] There were ten vases; the shapes reflect those current in Athens and the Argolid at the time of transition to Geometric, but the general effect of the decoration – except on a fine pointed pyxis, in the shoulder semicircles of a trefoil-lipped oinochoe, and on the pilgrim flask – is one of extreme sobriety. Note should be made also of the narrow panel with enclosed zigzag, on a low-footed skyphos, an extraordinarily persistent feature. There were also five spindle whorls, two bronze rings, and two pins of the same metal, with nail-like head and bulb on the shaft (type A).

---

[5] In five tombs of this type, of the succeeding period, the compartment was used for the funeral gifts.

10 The Dodecanese

From the Argolid, I intend to cross the Aegean to the Dodecanese – not a particularly logical move, it will seem, but it should lead to greater understanding and clarity in the long run.

It was necessary to admit, when discussing the Dodecanese during the earlier part of the Dark Ages, that no certain or even probable information was available. I was able to do no more than suggest that the L.H. III C pottery which had been characteristic of the latest surviving Mycenaean communities might have persisted to the end of the twelfth century or even later, on the analogy of certain sites in the central Aegean with which the Dodecanesians had fairly close connexions.

At that time, the main sites were Ialysos, Kameiros, and Lindos on Rhodes, the Serraglio area on Kos, and Pothia on Kalymnos – all coastal or near coastal. These, except for Pothia, provide the nucleus of our evidence for the later Dark Ages, with the fullest material coming from Kos.

As in so many cases, what we know is derived almost exclusively from tombs. And in this area, as will be seen, the pottery deposited with the dead seems to belong entirely to the late phase of Protogeometric, thus creating a problem in understanding and interpretation, for it involves an unfilled gap of possibly over a hundred years. It seem inconceivable that there should have been so long a period without the islands of the Dodecanese being inhabited. There are, I believe, one or two helpful pointers, but it will be best to discuss the tomb material first, concentrating to start with on the cemeteries sited above the Mycenaean settlement of Serraglio on Kos, within a few hundred yards of the northern coastline.

The cemeteries extended in time from the second half of the tenth century nearly to the end of the eighth, and of the ninety-nine tombs at least twenty (many were undatable) could be attributed to the Dark Ages. The varying types of tomb, the proportion of children to adults, and the quality of the finds, are all of interest. Inhumation was the universal practice. Forty-two of the burials were in cist tombs, all of very young children, and in certain instances vases were deposited outside the tomb as well as inside it. The offerings were of good quality and relatively abundant. Forty-three were 'pithos' burials, in other words in vases, mostly in rough cooking pots, but also a few in wheel-made decorated vases, and in rather larger vases (the pithos properly speaking); all of these were of infants or fairly young children, and with two exceptions – one Protogeometric – the gifts were poor. And there were, finally, fourteen pit graves, eleven of adults, three of older children – and in these the funeral gifts were the poorest of all. All except one were located in the main cemetery, which contained seventy-eight of the total of ninety-nine.[1]

It seems reasonable to conclude that younger children were buried either in cist tombs or in pithoi, with those in the cist tombs belonging to the more prosperous families (a distinction not found elsewhere, so far as I know). These are, however, about the only positive inferences that can be made. We cannot tell how the wealthier adults were buried: in other words, we lack a vital element of the picture, and it is consequently unsafe to look for connexions with other areas on the basis of these burial customs. Finally, the variety of the types of burial found on this site must make us extremely cautious when faced with smaller cemeteries elsewhere: so much has not yet been found.

The pottery – closely related to that of Rhodes, as will be seen – shows us that the inhabitants enjoyed a markedly local and individual style. The latest phase of all, that corresponding to the very end of Protogeometric and the transition to Geometric, may be passed over briefly; the elements of the preceding phase survived, and there was some borrowing from the Early Geometric ware of Athens.

It is, however, the preceding phase itself, the probably long one of Late Protogeometric, that is of particular relevance. Most of the shapes are those familiar to Protogeometric elsewhere, belly-handled amphorae, trefoil-lipped oinochoai, lekythoi, hydriai, jugs, skyphoi, and cups. Of these, the oinochoai and the lekythoi are closest in spirit to the Athenian style, especially one lekythos with decoration of semicircles and a cross-hatched diamond. A hydria, too, with semicircles on the shoulder and full circles on the belly, looks rather towards Athens than to any other area. Even on these shapes, however, the specially favoured decorative system of the Dode-canesian potter, cross-hatched motives arranged in various different ways, is prominent. It is also common on the jugs, but above all is typical of the skyphoi.[2] As to the cups, apart from one with high conical foot, they represent a type (shared with Rhodes) quite on their own, monochrome, flat-based, and straight-sided.

One other motive, tiny languettes dependent from the shoulder of closed vases, links Kos not only with Rhodes but with the East Greek area to the north[3] (p. 181). But to return to the main decorative system, that of rectilinear cross-hatching. Instances of single motives (e.g. the triangle or the diamond) are of course to be found in other areas, including Athens; but can one point to any one region as providing sufficiently close parallels as to have suggested such usage to those potters, or did they invent it them-selves? In Laconia, and even more in western Greece, a rather similar system was used, but the vase shapes are in general quite different. The Argolid is a more likely candidate. The vase types are similar, we have seen that this system of decoration was popular, and there are two skyphoi from

---

[1] I am greatly indebted to Dr L. Morricone, the excavator, for permission to include this account, as well as for other details and illustrations.

[2] Some of these, and the Athenian-type lekythos, are illustrated on Pl. 34, the group of vases from tomb 63.

[3] One or two other connexions with this area will emerge from the Rhodian pottery.

PLATE 34 KOS
A) Anthropoid askos. Higgins, *Greek Terracottas*, pl. 6, A–B.
B) Vases from tomb 63.

Argos which find close parallels on Kos, even to the feature of the reserved band on the high conical foot – but these vases are not typical of the Argive series. I think there was probable interconnexion, and certain other factors suggest that there may have been more than this (p. 178), but I can see no inevitable reason for the potters of Kos to have derived their entire decorative system from the Argolid.

So far as Greece and the Aegean are concerned, there is no other possible source, but before conceding a local origin, it may be that we should look in the direction of Cyprus, whose potters were at this time past masters in the use of cross-hatching in all its rectilinear forms. In both areas the sky-phoi have a similar body profile, and in Cyprus also these vases have at times a reserved band on the conical foot. Furthermore, there are two vase

PLATE 35 Kos. Vases from tomb 10. *PGP*, pl. 30 c.

types found in the Serraglio tombs whose connexions are almost certainly with Cyprus – the one-handled globular flask, of which two are known (both from the same tomb), and the askos, or bird vase, five altogether from as many tombs.[4] This was a shape which in Greece and the Aegean, with the exception of Crete, went out of fashion at the very beginning of the later Dark Ages, but it continued in use in Cyprus. On the whole, the evidence seems to indicate at least some connexion between the two districts during Late Protogeometric, especially as it is strongly visible thereafter. But one should be careful not to assume too great Cypriot influence on the pottery of Kos (and Rhodes), for there were also fundamental differences. Nor can one tell at what date during this late phase the ceramic links were established.

One astonishing tomb group (Pls. 35, 36) may serve to conclude the discussion on the pottery, and introduce the other types of object deposited. In addition to the usual vase shapes, there were several pots with incised decoration – two wheel-made omphalos vases (shallow hemispherical bowls with a low circular convex swelling at the base), two hand-made trefoil-lipped oinochoai with side spout, and a hand-made openwork kalathos. I know of no exact parallel to these, for the incised technique, nor in this period for the omphalos bowls. And they certainly do not belong with the three-handled piriform jar, of Mycenaean III B style, which was also found in this tomb and must have been a casual find from the looting of some much earlier grave.

And then there are the other objects placed in this tomb: three necklaces

---

[4] Four have a trumpet mouth instead of a bird head, the fifth a bird head. For a curious vase with human head and torso, see Pl. 34A.

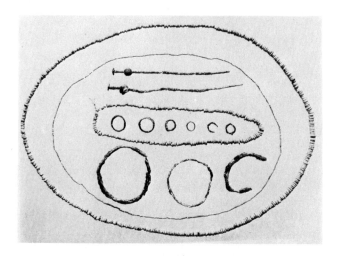

PLATE 36 Kos. Small finds from tomb 10.

made up of tiny disks of faience, three bracelets, six finger rings, and two iron pins with bronze bulb. This is a tomb of some richness, especially for this part of the Dark Ages. The list may be supplemented by what was found in some of the other tombs: no more bracelets, but several necklaces of faience, iron knives, hair and finger rings, of both bronze and gold, more dress pins of the type mentioned, and bronze fibulae, mostly of the simple arched type. To some extent these are, of course, the basic types that one has come to expect, but hardly in such profusion at this time.

The necklaces, evidently not uncommon in this area, as one was found at Kameiros in Rhodes (see below), are otherwise rare. I know of only four, of much the same type – one from Lefkandi, of a much earlier period (*c.* 1050 B.C.), one from a very rich grave at Athens of the mid-ninth century, and two of the tenth century from Knossos. There could – especially on the basis of the faience – be east Mediterranean connexions, but the earliest known one from Cyprus belongs to the ninth century. For the other objects, though the types are familiar enough, one must recall how scarce in Athens and the Argolid rings were at this time, and also the virtually complete absence of the fibula. The use of gold is exceedingly rare elsewhere – and even bronze was sparingly employed; the presence of the gold and the reasonably common usage of bronze on Kos may strengthen the suggestion that there were links with Cyprus during this latest period of the Dark Ages. And finally, the dress pins of iron with bronze bulb are of much interest: typical of Athens, common in the Argolid, and elsewhere found only at Theotokou in Thessaly (p. 208), they suggest a link with one or more of these other places, and the most likely is the Argolid.

One would naturally expect the population of Rhodes to have been greater, and probably more flourishing, than that of Kos – and so no doubt it was, but excavation has so far produced extraordinarily little evidence, at any rate for tombs. At Ialysos, three burials can be assigned to Late Protogeometric or to the immediately subsequent period, while Kameiros produced a further group of three of the same period, and a group of vases said to have come from a tomb. Funerary customs were probably as varied as on Kos. All three burials at Ialysos were in pithoi, one containing a new-born infant, one an adult whose bones had been burnt (so at least a partial cremation), while for the third no information was given. At Kameiros one burial was in a pithos, and another in a stone coffin – no cremation reported. The vases these tombs contained were of similar type and style to those of the Serraglio cemetery, with the addition of an undecorated neck-handled amphora, a shape which can thus be included in the known repertoire. A belly-handled amphora is also of interest: it has the typical Athenian system of semicircles on the shoulder and full circles on the belly, but the latter are connected with one another by horizontal wiggly lines, a feature found elsewhere only, I believe, in the East Greek area, the west coast of Asia Minor (p. 179). The vase also incorporated another typically East Greek motive, tiny languettes pendent from the base of the neck.[5] As well as the pottery, one of the Ialysos pithoi contained an iron spearhead and daggers, and tomb XL at Kameiros had fragmentary bronze fibulae and iron pins (no indication whether they had bronze bulbs), three bronze spirals, and the necklace already mentioned, made up of tiny disks of faience. It is, in other words, much the same mixture as on Kos, though it is satisfactory to find some evidence of weapons.

So far I have concentrated on the cemetery evidence, which does indeed furnish the bulk of the material. We have seen that the period covered was exclusively that of the Late Protogeometric phase (roughly within the tenth century), so our conclusions can bear only on this. The population was concentrated in the coastal areas, as in Mycenaean times, and the same sites were used as previously by the Mycenaeans. Conditions were probably much as in other regions, though one notes the availability of gold, and the reasonable supply of bronze. The potters and metalsmiths were competent, but no more than that. There was certainly no question of isolation, as links are to be found with Athens, with the Asia Minor coast to the north, with Cyprus, and with the Argolid. And in spite of the weapons from Ialysos, these links were most probably of a peaceful nature.

The question now arises, however, were the inhabitants natives of this part of the world, or were they – at least in part – immigrants? There is no connexion with the preceding Mycenaean culture, nor should one expect it at so late a date. The only clue I can offer is the cist tombs of Kos containing inhumations; this could be a yet further extension of the custom that had its origin on the Greek mainland. Now if this usage appeared first in Late Protogeometric, and the absence of any earlier tombs above the Mycenaean settlement of Serraglio suggests that it did, then those who

[5] This motive is also found at an earlier stage in the Argolid.

introduced it cannot have come from Athens nor from anywhere (for example, Caria) where cremation was the custom. The districts of Thessaly and Euboea and Skyros, and perhaps the northern Cyclades, are possibilities, but there are no other known connexions with these areas. In Crete and Cyprus the type of tomb was quite different. There seems to remain only the Argolid, and if there were newcomers, this is likely to have been their place of origin. In the Argolid we get occasional later instances of vases deposited outside as well as inside the tomb, the pottery has certain points of similarity, and both areas used the iron dress pins with bronze bulb. I think, then, that there could have been immigrants from the Argolid to the Dodecanese (or at least to Kos) in the tenth century – and such a move is reflected in the oral tradition. But one still cannot be certain.

Finally, one can now return to the problem mentioned at the beginning of this section, the extraordinary gap between the latest Mycenaean evidence and that of the Dark Age tombs which all belong within the tenth century. It is possible that the gap can be at least partially closed by the extremely meagre settlement evidence. In the area of the sanctuary of Athena at Kameiros a considerable amount of earlier material was found (either settlement or sanctuary in nature), and this included sherds of skyphoi of Athenian Protogeometric type, with sets of circles between the handles – the significance being that this decorative system was most untypical in the period covered by the tombs, and could well be evidence of something earlier. And there is also Lindos, where a small settlement area, which did not survive the Geometric period, produced several skyphos sherds of the same type as those at Kameiros. Thirdly, the Serraglio site itself has produced material which may be suggestive. As I have said, the Late Protogeometric cemetery was situated partly above the Mycenaean settlement (as yet unpublished), but the excavator noted over the whole area the presence of sherds of Protogeometric and Geometric date which did not, in his opinion, come from tombs. There was then perhaps a settlement adjacent to the cemetery, but how far back did it go? The full publication of the Italian excavations, and of the subsequent Greek ones, should solve the problem. And if there was a Dark Age settlement in this area, whose pottery was in part earlier than, and different from, that found in the tombs, then the likelihood of newcomers in the tenth century is perhaps strengthened.

11 Western Asia Minor

There are at present four sites of significance on the west coast of Asia Minor.[1] Two, Asarlik and Dirmil, lie within the peninsula of Halicarnassus, and follow the familiar pattern of tombs without known settlement. The other two reverse this, being settlements with as yet no trace of tombs: they are Miletus and Old Smyrna.

It will be best to start with Miletus, already briefly discussed in a previous chapter (p. 83). As we have seen, the earlier Mycenaean settlement, including its massive fortification wall, was destroyed in L.H. III C – at what precise stage is unclear – and there followed, after an interval, a new occupation, the earliest pottery of which was late Sub-Mycenaean in character. From this time onwards, habitation was continuous, and the settlement extended beyond the area used by the Mycenaeans. The excavator distinguished the Protogeometric period (which included the Sub-Mycenaean phase) from the later, Geometric, level; according to him, the area inhabited in Protogeometric times was not very large, and was thereafter much more extensive. In fact, the find spots of Protogeometric pottery covered quite a respectable area, though not necessarily larger than a village. No house constructions were recovered.

The only published objects are the rather few vases and sherds. From these, one thing at least is clear, the very close similarity to the shapes and decorative motives that one finds in Athens – skyphoi with concentric circles, and an occasional central rectilinear panel, kraters with rectilinear panels, lekythoi with semicircles (one with hour glass filling), and vertical wiggly lines – some of the sherds could come from trefoil-lipped oinochoai – and amphora sherds with languettes and vertical lines on the shoulder. The total is admittedly small, but the important point is that we could have not only the late but the earlier phases of Protogeometric as well, thus linking up with the Sub-Mycenaean. There are, naturally, a number of individual idiosyncrasies, circles with an outline of dots, thick horizontal zigzags, and in particular a light zigzag connecting two sets of circles, found not only elsewhere in this district but also in the Dodecanese. The shape of the almost complete lekythos is much dumpier than that characteristic of Athens. On the whole, however, the parallels with Athens seem remarkable, and it would appear that there may have been continuous connexions between Miletus and Athens during the later Dark Ages – such as

---

[1] Information has now come in of a fifth, a cemetery at Çömlekçi, about 19 miles north-east of Bodrum. Nothing is said of the type of tomb or burial, but the vases are Sub-Mycenaean (or a bit earlier), and at least one is Protogeometric. See Y. Boysal, *Katalog der Vasen im Museum in Bodrum*, I (Ankara, 1969).

are hardly found anywhere else. The inferences to be drawn from this will emerge in due course, but for the moment we can pass on to the two cemetery sites, not far to the south of Miletus.

Both sites are slightly inland, within a few miles of one another. At Asarlik we have already seen that there was some link with Sub-Mycenaean central mainland Greece in the stirrup jar (p. 83). This seems to be the earliest vase in the cemetery, which thereafter remained in use for a long time, well into the Geometric period. From the rather scanty pottery one would conclude that during the later Dark Ages it was, as at Miletus, the Athenian ware that was the direct or indirect object of imitation, with concentric circles predominating – as opposed to the situation in the cemeteries of Kos, just a few miles away across the water (pp. 173 f.). The influence of Athens is by no means as strong as at Miletus, however, and there are local provincial peculiarities.

Several metal objects of personal ornament and weapons were found in these tombs, but usually it is impossible to give them a precise date, and many will surely have been associated with the Geometric burials. Only some fragmentary iron weapons should, from their context, belong to this period.

If one is seeking links with Athens, the fact of universal cremation might be a pointer (again, there is a contrast with the practice on Kos), but it would be a very unsafe one, for the actual types of tomb are entirely different from those of Athens.[2] To this period belong circular enclosures, probably originally covered by a mound of earth, and a kind of tholos tomb, which recalls contemporaneous ones in Crete – they have a passage-way (*dromos*) leading to a rectangular chamber, and are vaulted above. This latter type of tomb persisted in the area until the fifth century B.C.

The second site, Dirmil, consists of a single tomb and its contents. The tomb itself is of the rectangular type with corbelled roof and *dromos*, as at Asarlik. It was reported by the man who found it that there were no bones, so it is very likely that cremation was used. The only objects recovered were six vases, and both individually and as a whole they seem to show very strong influence of Athenian Late Protogeometric (Fig. 18). There were four closed vases: one trefoil-lipped oinochoe, with languettes and semi-circles on the shoulder, rather clay ground; what is probably part of a second one, dark ground, with semicircles with hour-glass filling, flanked by vertical lines of dots, on the shoulder; a belly-handled amphora, neck painted, semicircles with hour-glass filling flanking a solid vertical diamond panel on the shoulder, supported by bands, and the rest unpainted; and a shoulder-handled amphora with decoration as on the second oinochoe, and a zone of dots at the base of the neck. The other two vases were a sky-phos with fairly well-made high conical foot, the body decoration being two sets of circles connected by a zigzag line (as at Miletus), and a fine krater, with double-loop handles, a high flaring foot, and main decoration consisting of three sets of circles with reserved cross filling, flanked by rectangular panels in which vertically set solid diamonds are the chief

---

[2] Also, cremation has been identified in tombs of the Mycenaean period in this area; see *Belleten* 31 (1967), 67 ff. (Boysal).

FIG. 18 DIRMIL, PG TOMB
Krater; ·469 m. Oinochoe; ·32 m. Amphora; ·456 m. Skyphos; ·175 m.
AJA 67, figs. 15–18

feature – there are also groups of tiny languettes attached to the band below
the rim, another typical feature of this district, and found also in the Dodecanese. For this last vase comparison has been made with kraters from
Marmariani in Thessaly (p. 213), but the decoration is Athenian in type,
and it is likely that both this krater and the Thessalian ones derive from an
Athenian prototype. Some local peculiarities (e.g. languettes, dots, and
zigzag) are to be expected, as well as a rather inferior technique to that of
the Athenian potters, but what is astonishing is that the local elements are
so few. I think the whole group is to be dated to Late Protogeometric, from
the presence of the shoulder-handled amphora and the decorative motive
of solid diamonds – but there is no sign of incipient Geometric. If this is
correct, then the larger languettes, more characteristic of the early style in
Athens, must have persisted here into the later phase.

It has seemed worth while giving a fairly detailed description of these
vases, because they form the most distinctive single uniform group in
western Asia Minor, assuming always that the tomb contained only one

PLATE 37 OLD SMYRNA. A) Oval house. B) Neck-handled amphora. *AJA* 66, pl. 96.

burial; but even if there was more than one it is likely that the time covered would not have been great; this tomb is not comparable to the Kapakli tholos tomb (p. 210).

The fourth site is the northernmost one, the settlement of Old Smyrna. It lies at a considerable distance north of Miletus, on a small peninsula which juts out from the coast at the base of the Gulf of Smyrna, with access by sea from Chios, or, more easily perhaps, from Lesbos.

It was, like Miletus, a settlement of considerable antiquity, but its history prior to the Dark Ages was very different, as it appears to have been rather outside the Mycenaean orbit. The characteristic ware was monochrome, and so far the amount of Mycenaean pottery recovered has been negligible – though it is still quite possible that the final picture may produce some modifications.

There is no sign of any destruction, and what we find is that during the Dark Ages pottery of a Protogeometric type (which I assume to have belonged to immigrants) was introduced alongside the native monochrome ware, and that it gradually increased until it equalled the latter in quantity. During this time the settlement seems to have been fairly small; the chief architectural feature is a very small oval house of mud brick (Pl. 37), but there is slight evidence that there were rectangular buildings as well.

The objects associated with this period seem to have been exclusively ceramic, and it is therefore on the pottery that we have to depend. And very little even of this has been published.[3] At Miletus, the illustrated sherds showed close and probably continuous links with Athens, but at Old Smyrna the situation was markedly different – in any case the persistence of the monochrome pottery suggests that there was a fusion between native and immigrant elements.

The important points to establish are, if there were immigrants, where did they come from, and at what time? At present we cannot say anything for certain: we need far more material, and it would be helpful to have some record from other sites as well. It is clear that some of the pottery shows the influence of the Athenian Late Protogeometric ware, but that is not surprising, since it had so widespread an impact.

On the other hand, it has been suggested that the earliest intrusive pottery shows no sign of Athenian influence, and belongs to an early stage of Protogeometric. From this one could deduce nothing about the origin, but one might hesitantly suppose that the date of first arrival could be as early as 1000 B.C. Even so, I believe that 950 B.C. is the upper limit. In any case, it should be stressed that, whatever the source and the time, this was no massive move, but a very small group indeed to start with.

So far, then, we have the following picture. In the southern part of this area, comprising Miletus and the two cemetery sites, the evidence of the pottery shows that there was close contact with Athens, and suggests that at Miletus it covered not only the later Dark Ages but the concluding

---

[3] A neck-handled amphora, reflecting Athenian influence (Pl. 37); a krater and a trefoil-lipped oinochoe, not so close to Athens; and a low-footed skyphos, entirely un-Attic.

phase of the earlier period, and was probably caused by settlers arriving from Athens in the case of Miletus, this being much less likely on the two sites of the Halicarnassus peninsula, where the types of tomb indicate a native population. There was also contact, at least in the late phase, with the Dodecanese, and in fact also with Old Smyrna in the northern part of the district, to judge from one or two local motives of decoration on the pottery. But at Old Smyrna itself an obscure situation allows us to say only that the site was inhabited by an indigenous population, that there was an escalating intrusion starting hardly earlier than the middle of the tenth century, and that there were from then onwards links, direct or indirect, with Athens and probably with other areas as well.

In addition to these four sites there are a few others, all coastal, not necessarily of lesser importance, but whose material is far more scanty. Surface finds of this period have been identified in a few places between Miletus and Old Smyrna, and at one excavated (but not fully published) site, that of Clazomenae. Even north, or rather north-west, of Old Smyrna there has been report of Protogeometric pottery, from the excavations of Phocaea. Otherwise there is no other material of Greek origin or imitation from coastal sites, which can with certainty be assigned to the Dark Ages: not yet, that is to say – but there is no doubt that the whole area would repay further search and research.

One further question deserves to be asked. Was there any penetration inland on the part of the people who used Protogeometric pottery, of whatever type? Coastal footholds are one thing, but settlement inland is another. There is no trace of any such settlement, but there is one interesting body of material that has recently come to light. This is from Sardis, the later capital of Lydia, some fifty miles inland from Smyrna. Here a deep sounding uncovered a level of occupation (including a structure of rubble), sandwiched in between two layers which represented the flooding of the area by the river Pactolus. Within this layer was discovered a small quantity – not more than five per cent of the whole, the rest being local – of sherds adjudged to be of late Mycenaean and of Protogeometric type. Other finds included a fibula which can hardly be earlier than the ninth century. There is clearly a problem as to the type and dating of this pottery. The excavators have provisionally assigned the material to the twelfth and eleventh centuries, but this seems somewhat unlikely. So far as concerns at least the Protogeometric ware, the main feature is that of pendent semicircles on skyphoi and cups, a feature which, as we shall see, cannot in any case precede the very late tenth century, and is most common in the ninth (pp. 185 f.). If this pottery then belongs to the late tenth and ninth centuries – and presumably the fibula would be associated with it – how are we to interpret the pottery of apparently very late Mycenaean type? It is a question to which I have no answer.

12 Euboea, Thessaly and other Areas

A few words of warning and explanation are desirable here. The region covered is not a self-contained one (the area of Macedonia is in any case marginal), but the interconnexions its constituent districts show, from time to time and in varying measure, justify its treatment in a single section. It is not particularly easy to work out a plan which will be both clear and logical. The method I adopt is as follows. First I shall deal with the islands of Tenos and Andros, whose evidence has a bearing only on the latest Dark Age phase and on the earliest succeeding one (thus going beyond my terms of reference, strictly speaking, but justifiably so, as will be seen); this evidence has the chief merit of helping to clarify an important point of relative chronology not covered elsewhere, in particular not for the focal and vital site of Lefkandi in Euboea, which I discuss in some detail after the two former islands. From Lefkandi I go on to a summary of the material from the rest of Euboea, and after that deal briefly with Skyros, which seems best discussed at this point. I then pass to the few sites of Boeotia and Phocis, on the grounds that they show connexions both with Attica and with Euboea – and probably with Thessaly as well. Then on to Thessaly, remembering however that its links with Euboea will have been by sea and not by land, and bearing in mind that the known material is virtually confined to the eastern half of the district. And from Thessaly to Macedonia, finally, in order to demonstrate further connexions, the evidence coming almost exclusively from Vergina.

Tenos and Andros

Not a great deal is known of the Dark Age communities of these two islands, and indeed nothing at all until towards the end of the tenth century, except for one amphora from Andros. This is disappointing, as both are reasonably fertile, and conveniently placed for the trans-Aegean traffic which was surely one of the features of the time.

   The importance of the material is, generally, its illustration of the presence of a separate ceramic strain, shared with that of Athens during the later tenth century and later becoming dominant, and specifically, the light it throws on the evolution of one particular vase type, the low-footed skyphos with semicircles pendent from the rim (see Pl. 45), a type to be found everywhere within the region under discussion throughout the whole ninth century, and having a wide area of distribution outside, the chief witness, in fact, to a flourishing trade based on this region.

There are two main groups, covering the end of the tenth and the beginning of the ninth centuries. The one is of five locally made vases, said to have come from a single tomb not far from the capital of Tenos. Two of them, the cup and lekythos, are very close to Athenian types; another two, a small jug and a large one-handled pitcher, belong to the Euboeo-Thessalian sphere – and so there is a blend of two styles; and the fifth vase, a skyphos, is in the Athenian tradition in that it has a high flaring foot and sets of circles between the handles, but the fact that there are only two such sets, as well as the rather overhanging lip, indicate a breakaway from Athens. This group certainly still belongs to the Late Protogeometric style.

We can now come to the second group, from Zagora on Andros, representing the contents – unfortunately, mixed – of two tombs. One of the vases, a fine shoulder-handled amphora with semicircles on the shoulder, should still precede the end of Late Protogeometric, and is in the Athenian style. Then there are two vases with high flaring feet: the one has the body and rim profile of an Early Geometric Attic skyphos and three sets of circles between the handles; the other is deeper, its lip overhangs more sharply and there are, as on the Tenian vase discussed above, two sets of circles. This one should date perhaps to the borderline between Protogeometric and Geometric (remembering that borderlines can be very elastic). And finally there is a third skyphos, low footed, with overhanging (not offset) rim and intersecting semicircles pendent from it. From our other evidence one would probably conclude that it was later in date than the first two, but not so here, as it has been confidently stated, on the basis of the diameter and number of arcs, that it was painted by the same man as was responsible for the skyphos with two sets of circles – in other words, the same multiple brush was used. And this is the point of particular importance, as it not only shows the sort of way in which the low-footed skyphos developed, but it also places the time of that development as very close to c. 900 B.C. And with this development may surely be taken that of another type, not found in these groups but certainly contemporary, if not indeed earlier, the low-footed skyphos with two sets of circles between the handles.

I have discussed these vases in perhaps rather too great detail, but their importance and relevance will appear more clearly throughout the rest of this section. It may be borne in mind, however, that although these groups help us to understand how and when the low-footed skyphoi developed, they do not tell us where those were first introduced, a question to which I shall return later.

As a postscript to this discussion it may be added that further tombs of the early ninth century from Tenos show how, during this time at least, these islands became more closely absorbed within the Euboean, as opposed to the Attic, sphere.

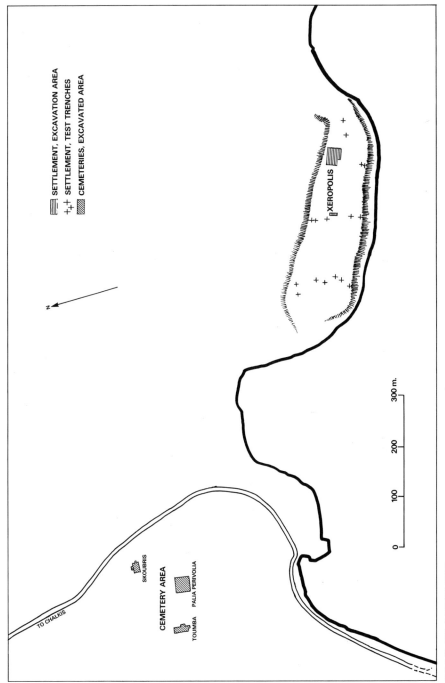

SETTLEMENT, EXCAVATION AREA
SETTLEMENT, TEST TRENCHES
CEMETERIES, EXCAVATED AREA

N

XEROPOLIS

300 m.

200

100

0

TO CHALKIS

SKOUBRIS

CEMETERY AREA

PALIA PERIVOLIA

TOUMBA

PLAN OF LEFKANDI

PLATE 38 LEFKANDI. View of Xeropolis settlement.

Lefkandi

From Tenos and Andros we can go straight on to Lefkandi in Euboea
(Pls. 38–46 and Plan, p. 187). This is one of the key sites of the Dark Ages,
one of the very few where we can observe the course of development almost
uninterruptedly. It has already figured in previous sections (pp. 43 f., 67 f.),
both because its latest Mycenaean settlement probably survived into the
early Dark Ages, and because the community which established itself
shortly after the desertion of that settlement, and unfortunately known to
us until nearly the end of the Dark Ages only from its burials, had links
with the late Sub-Mycenaean communities of central Greece.

   We have therefore to proceed primarily on tomb evidence, but the point
is that the series of burials extended straight through from late Sub-
Mycenaean, say the second quarter of the eleventh century, to Middle
Geometric, which began in the middle of the ninth. Consequently, it is
most desirable to discuss the material as a whole, and most appropriate to
do so in this section, even though it means recapitulating what was said in
the previous sections. Furthermore, as will be seen, this material permits
us to make connexions between Lefkandi and many other sites, not only
Athens to the south, but generally over the whole region, and it therefore
deserves the fullest possible treatment.[1]

   The position is that there are three known cemeteries, very close to each

[1] I would like to acknowledge my deep indebtedness to Professor M. R. Popham, Mr L. H.
Sackett, and Mr P. G. Themelis (of the Greek Archaeological Service) for permission to
mention and illustrate material not yet published.

PLATE 39 LEFKANDI. Finds from Skoubris tomb 38.

other, and a settlement site, Xeropolis, a few hundred yards distant from the cemeteries, originally occupied from Early Helladic to the end of Late Helladic, then abandoned, and only reoccupied after a possibly long interval. The Skoubris cemetery has produced sixty-three tombs and nineteen pyres; all the earlier material comes from here, but it was still in occasional use later. The other two cemeteries were mainly in use from c. 950 to c. 850 B.C.; so far, thirty-five tombs and nine pyres have been found in Toumba, the richer of the two, and in Palia Perivolia forty-seven tombs and forty-six pyres; the total is thus exceedingly impressive. As to the later settlement on the Xeropolis site, it can so far be traced back only to the end of the tenth century, but was then in continuous occupation for two hundred years.

The evidence will be dealt with chronologically. During the latest Sub-Mycenaean phase and the transition to Protogeometric[2] the range of pottery includes many of the conventional shapes found in central Greece at this time, amphoriskoi (with both horizontal and vertical handles), lekythoi, stirrup jars – two only, but that is in accordance with the trend elsewhere – jugs, cups in quantity, deep bowls, small hydriai, and trefoil-lipped oinochoai. Triple vases, hardly known to neighbouring districts, still reflect the Mycenaean tradition; duck vases are a feature shared with Athens – and with Achaea and Cyprus. There are also unusual shapes, such as a sort of

---

[2] A selection of objects is shown on Pls. 39–41.

PLATE 40 LEFKANDI. Vases from Skoubris tomb 20.

squat bottle, a straight-sided pyxis with high loop handles to above the
rim, and a pedestalled bowl, all nevertheless characteristic of the experimental nature of this period, as also visible in Athens (p. 43). The variety
of shapes was not matched by a similar variety of decoration, this being
mostly confined to wavy or wiggly lines, cross-hatched triangles, and hand-
drawn semicircles mostly with half-moon filling. Many of the vases have a
dark-ground appearance (in other words, for the most part covered with
paint), but some are clay ground. The construction of the vases sometimes
leaves much to be desired, but one feature should be noted particularly,
that low conical feet were already in fashion, as in Athens, though they
often look heavy and cumbersome.

It will be seen that the closest comparative ceramic material is that of
Athens, and a similar situation holds with regard to the objects other than
pottery. The personal ornaments were the same: rings (probably including
one with double-spiral terminals), fibulae – arched or stilted, occasionally
with twisted bow, more rarely of the violin type with leaf-shaped bow – and
dress pins of both main varieties, those with bulb and disk, and those with
swelling on the upper shank and a small globular head. And, as in Athens,
iron as well as bronze was used for these objects – one tomb contained
the obviously popular dress pins, as well as rings of gold, similar to those
found in Late Sub-Mycenaean and Early Protogeometric Athens, and of
equal rarity. There is, however, no parallel in Athens for a necklace of
blue faience beads, but this will no doubt have been another instance
of the short-lived contact with the east Mediterranean at this time (p. 78).
Only one weapon was found, an iron dagger, similar to that of the Tiryns
warrior burial (p. 69).

PLATE 41 LEFKANDI. Finds from Skoubris tomb 46.

On the whole, there seem to have been reasonably close links with Athens in the cultural sense. This did not, however, extend to the burial customs. In Athens inhumation in cist tombs was in process of giving way to crema-tion, with the ashes placed in a vase which was then put into a shaft, the trench-and-hole system. In most other districts, inhumation in cist tombs was retained. At Lefkandi there is a curious blend of both systems: cist tombs were carefully constructed, but the corpse itself was cremated in a nearby pyre, and there its ashes apparently remained; on the other hand, the burial offerings were placed in the tomb – in one, indeed, they were placed in such a position as though an inhumed body lay there. It is alto-gether rather strange, but the custom was continued, when pit graves replaced cist tombs, during the later Dark Ages and even beyond.

There is then continuity in burial customs between the early and late Dark Ages. There is also a continuity in types of metal objects in use, though it is a little difficult to be certain, as there are so few of them during most of Protogeometric – a scarcity, especially in the use of bronze, which

A

B

PLATE 42 LEFKANDI. A) Vases from Skoubris tomb 51. B) Enlargement of the 'archer' hydria.

is reflected in much of Greece and the Aegean at this time (see pp. 316 ff.). In the pottery, however, we find certain differences and developments, as well as similarity and continuity.

It is not in fact easy to make a clear division between Sub-Mycenaean and Protogeometric, nor of course should one expect such clarity, especially

A

B

PLATE 43 LEFKANDI. A) Toumba tomb 14 as found. B) Same tomb with vases removed.

as the particular innovations which were so characteristic of the basic Athenian Protogeometric style had hardly any effect at all on the Lefkandiot potters. There are differences, however. A number of shapes dropped out of circulation, including most of the rare experimental ones. There are no more stirrup jars, no more duck vases; it is possible that the lekythos did not long survive, and certainly the triple vase became much less common,

PLATE 44 LEFKANDI. The two amphorae (·424 m., ·378 m.) and the sword and spearhead from Toumba tomb 14.

as also did the amphoriskos with horizontal handles. We are left, basically, with the small one-handled jug, the cup, the skyphos, the pedestalled bowl, the trefoil-lipped oinochoe, and the hydria.[3] The outline of these has become perhaps a bit sharper, and certainly the conical feet were more carefully made. The system of decoration is now almost exclusively dark ground, though particular prominence is given to the habit of leaving the lower body and foot unpainted – a relic of the Granary class of L.H. IIIC, and also still observable in the Argolid in the later period. The decorative motives were even further restricted, vases having either no decoration at all or just a horizontal zigzag or wiggly line – this is strange, as the potters were quite adept in the use of decoration: one hydria, perhaps of Middle

[3] It will be realised that nothing can be said of large amphorae or kraters, as being too big to be deposited in cist tombs, though fragments of the former appear in the pyres.

Protogeometric date, has not only an elaborate panel of zigzags and dog-tooth, but also a representation of two confronted archers, so far as I know the only instance anywhere in Greece during the late Dark Ages of humans being portrayed on a vase (Pl. 42).

And with this, as I have said, hardly a trace of influence from Athens: no single instance is yet known of the use of compass-drawn circles or semicircles.

The period covered by the material from these cist tombs, ranging from Late Sub-Mycenaean to Middle Protogeometric (if not later, as will be seen) is a little difficult to assess in absolute terms. One would suppose that the first burial was not much later than *c.* 1075 B.C., and on the basis of the earliest subsequent material the last one might come down as far as 950 B.C., that is to say well into what would be Late Protogeometric in Athens. In that case, it could be that the tombs with pottery of Sub-Mycenaean character continued in use till nearly 1000 B.C., as they are at present the more numerous; and that would mean a survival longer than in Athens. However, one must also take into account the falling off in the number of metal artefacts, a phenomenon which may have to be equated with what was happening at about the same time throughout much of the Aegean. Also, of course, the present distribution of tombs may not give an accurate picture.

If, though, 950 B.C. is a reasonable terminal date – certainly no lower – for the rather undistinguished Early and Middle Protogeometric pottery of Lefkandi (I speak of Early and Middle simply as denoting probable con-temporaneity with developments in Athens: there is little to distinguish between the two on this site), then we are left with about fifty years to the end of the Dark Ages as here defined. This was a period of considerable change and much importance. One of the main features is the influence of Athenian pottery – similarly visible in other areas at this time. The effect was remarkable. Of the few main shapes current earlier, the one-handled jug persisted, but the pedestalled bowl apparently went out of fashion. More important, the cup, probably the most common tomb offering, was transformed. Previously it was a pleasant little vase, with rather straight sides, a very gently outcurving rim and a low conical foot, painted all over except for a reserved band below the handle, or the lower body and foot unpainted. Now there appears an approximation to the Athenian type, with offset rim adorned by a zigzag, curving body and high flaring foot (Pl. 45). The skyphos, too, underwent a radical change; the process is not yet clear at Lefkandi, though we must suppose that there were vases such as those from Tenos and Andros, discussed above; it will surely have in-volved the use of compass-drawn circles and semicircles, motives now fully accepted by the Lefkandiot potter, and subsequently retained with bulldog tenacity. Trefoil-lipped oinochoai take on an Athenian look, especially the latest Protogeometric development, wholly painted over except for a reserved band with zigzag or alternating diagonal decoration round the belly. Amphorae now, if not earlier, imitate Athenian originals closely, as very probably do the kraters. The lekythos reappears, and for a while the link with Athens is clear. Pyxides with everted rim and kalathoi were introduced into the local repertoire at some time during this period, and the one known hydria, with languettes on the shoulder, looks towards Athens. It is almost a new style, and the Athenian features are dominant.

There may also be links with Athens in the metalwork: some fibulae are of the current Athenian type. Whether we can say the same of two weapons found in one of the tombs, an iron spearhead and sword, is less certain, but the context of their discovery establishes yet another link. The sword had been 'killed', and although not wrapped around an amphora, as was norm- ally the case in Athens, it and the spearhead were associated with two amphorae, one neck-handled and one belly-handled, the former of which contained the ashes of the dead man, and both being placed in a square shaft, the closest approximation that I know of to the Athenian custom (Pls. 43, 44). And there are at least two other instances of urn cremations. This was a definite breakaway, but it may well have been only a temporary one, as the habit of leaving the ashes in the pyre seems to have continued.[4]

As well as the links with Athens, there is some evidence of contact with areas to the east. A fine trefoil-lipped oinochoe with handles rising high above the lip, semicircles with dot fringe, tiny languettes from the neck and a fairly elaborate neck panel, could possibly reflect East Greek develop- ments (c. 900 B.C. ?); and gold objects which appear to belong to a very late tenth-century context may reflect east Mediterranean influence and be a harbinger of much more frequent intercommunication in the ninth century, as will be seen. The likelihood of the early date suggested for these objects is strengthened, it may be added, by the appearance of two vases of Aegean origin (the only ones) at Amathus in Cyprus, assignable to the tenth century; they are a skyphos and a cup, both high footed, certainly not Athenian, and more likely to have come from Euboea or near it than from anywhere else.[5]

Even so, it must be recognised that the influence of Athens – and it may have gone beyond the cultural, to judge from the cremation urns – was the most important new factor at Lefkandi during the second half of the tenth century. It was an influence that was both persistent and transitory. It was persistent in that the Lefkandiots continued to use the ceramic ideas, intro- duced towards the end of the Dark Ages, not only during this period but throughout much, if not all, of the ninth century. It was transitory in the sense that the further developments in Athenian pottery, involving the radical changeover to the Geometric style, had no effect, except minimally, at Lefkandi. And the presence of the cremation urns seems to be confined to the later tenth century. Once the initial Athenian gifts had been accepted, so to speak, the Lefkandiots went their own way. They did not isolate themselves from Athens – one or two sherds of Athenian manu- facture, of early ninth-century date, have been found in the settlement – but they seem to have formed, with other Euboean and north Cycladic communities (and perhaps others), a separate nucleus, in rivalry with

---

[4] Cist tombs, it may be noted, are hardly ever to be found from now on, being replaced by pit graves, with just two or three examples of inhumation.

[5] If the centaur (p. 199) is of Cypriot inspiration, then a further link is provided.

Athens, at least so far as commercial ventures were concerned. This is a matter, however, that will be discussed more fully in the overall review of the Greek world at this time (pp. 348 f.).

Ceramically speaking, this is what happened. The influence of Athens was still evident at the time of transition from Protogeometric to Geometric (assuming that the appearance of a decorated panel on the neck of closed vases is a sign of such influence – but did the idea emanate from Athens?). Otherwise, there are remarkably few Attic Early Geometric features visible in the make-up of the Lefkandiot style, which can more accurately be called Sub-Protogeometric on account of the persistence of Athenian Protogeometric shapes and decorative motives. Nevertheless, there was a breakaway from Protogeometric canons in the two most common vase types, the skyphos and the cup. The distinctive constructional change was the disappearance of the high conical or flaring foot: on the skyphoi it is replaced by a low ring foot, while the cups simply have a flat base. This is the only significant change in the cups, for the rather high rim with horizontal zigzag decoration was retained. From the skyphoi, however, two different types emerged. The first was a shape with gently outcurving lip and the body decoration consisting, as a rule, of two sets of concentric circles. The second, more popular and I think much more long-lived, had a high overhanging rim (in the later ninth century elegantly swept back and then outwards so that it no longer overhung), to the base of which there was attached the main decorative motive, two sets of pendent concentric semicircles, usually intersecting (Pl. 45). The evidence of Andros (p. 186) suggests that in the earliest stage the lip was not offset, but that may depend on exactly where the type was first created – a question to which there is no answer yet, though I think that Euboea is the most likely. These changes, in my opinion, will have occurred very close to 900 B.C. Other developments may include the eventual disappearance of the lekythos shape and perhaps also of the small one-handled jug; on the other hand, kalathoi became more popular – in tombs, anyway.

A brief reference has been made above to pottery found in the settlement, and it is in fact just during this period, from the late tenth century onwards, that we find people once again inhabiting the site of Xeropolis. Whether this was the earliest reoccupation after the Mycenaean town had been abandoned one cannot be quite certain, as only a small area of the site has been excavated; but what we can reasonably conclude is that, if the original reoccupation belonged to an earlier phase, the late tenth century provides evidence at least of an extension of the new settlement.

There are two questions to which one would like to have a precise answer. When did the Xeropolis resettlement, or alternatively the extension of the settlement, take place? I have spoken of the late tenth century, but one would like to get even closer; all one can say is that, I think, the date was very much nearer 900 than 950 B.C. It could even be after 900, but the fairly large number of high conical feet seem to make this a little unlikely. Secondly, was there any connexion between the Xeropolis settlement or extension and the adoption of so many features of the

PLATE 45 LEFKANDI. A) Cups from Toumba tomb 17. B) Skyphos from Skoubris tomb 33.

Athenian Late Protogeometric style? If the later date for the settlement is correct, then there can have been no connexion, of course; even on the earlier date, I rather doubt it, and would prefer to leave it at that.

The answer to the first question is the more important of the two, as from now onwards there seems to have been a remarkable rise in the fortunes of Lefkandi, and the new foundation or extension may be the first sign of a much greater outward activity, leading to substantial prosperity. Not that one can deduce any greater prosperity from the fact of the foundation itself, but what is of interest is that early on, whenever that may have been, a bronze foundry was established, as fragments of the moulds used have been found. One cannot be absolutely sure that such a foundry did not exist even earlier, but one can point to the fact that objects of bronze are not found at all commonly in earlier Protogeometric tombs, and also to the fact that such objects were generally scarce in Greece and the Aegean during all but the latest phase of the later Dark Ages. If the theory of the shortage of this metal is correct, then the return to normal – probably involving the re-establishment of links with Cyprus – will have provided the Lefkandiots with the opportunity to set up this industry, no doubt to their advantage.

The evidence of a growing prosperity, whether based on some bronze industry or the result of some other activity, can I believe be deduced from the increased number of finds other than pottery deposited in tombs between the end of the tenth century and about the middle of the ninth. The emphasis is on bronze rather than on iron, though there are still examples of fibulae and dress pins in iron. But what is remarkable is the quantity of gold. Many of the tombs which span this period (especially those of the Toumba cemetery) contained gold objects, and some a fair number of them. Gold rings are particularly abundant, and as well as these there are earrings, bracelets and beads, pendants and bands, and even a fibula, all of gold, and also gilt iron dress pins. Whether they are of local workmanship or not (some are, others are surely not), the probability is that the metal was imported from the east Mediterranean, and thus an indication of renewed links with that part of the world, confirmed not only by some of the gold objects themselves, but also by the ivory and faience artefacts which now reappear. The picture suggests the fruits either of piracy or trade, and the latter explanation appears by far the more likely, in which case the community must have been thriving and progressive.

Lefkandi was only one community in a region whose trading activities during the ninth century were far-flung, from Macedonia in the north to Syria in the east, and from which activities no doubt sprang the colonies founded in the eighth century by its near neighbours Chalkis and Eretria, but it was surely one of the most important – and the original impetus seems to belong to the end of the Dark Ages, and to be symbolic of their end and the start of something new. It is hardly accidental, I feel, that this site has produced one of the masterpieces of the late Dark Ages, the splendid and unique clay statuette of the centaur (Pl. 46). A figure of great dignity: the modelling of the head is especially remarkable; but, knowing as little as we do, dare we say that it is in advance of its time?

Euboea

There is no known site in Euboea as yet comparable to that of Lefkandi, but a brief analysis reveals a number of points of interest. A valuable surface survey has recently been carried out over the island, chiefly with the prehistoric period in mind, but providing information on later periods as well. So far as concerns the Dark Ages, no trace of habitation, rather surprisingly, has been found in the southern section of the island, nor anywhere along the whole north-facing coastline until the extreme north-eastern tip is reached, where one site has been recorded; on the other hand, four have been identified at the north-western extremity. These five have yielded sherds described as Protogeometric, but this does not necessarily mean that they belong within the Dark Ages: we have seen how this style persisted into the ninth century at Lefkandi, and cannot therefore be sure, without further investigation, that the sites in question go back earlier than this.

There remains the extremely fertile district of the southern coastline in

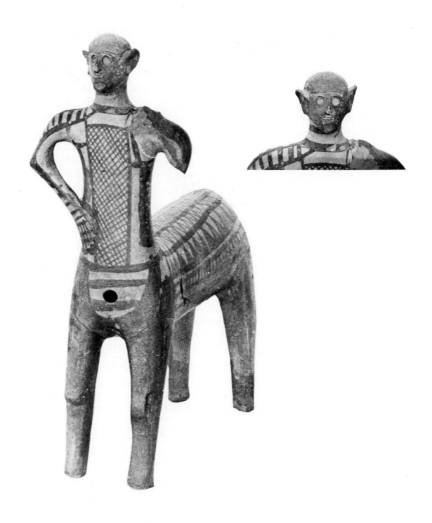

PLATE 46 LEFKANDI. The Centaur; ·36 m. *BSA* 65, pl. 8.

the central part of the island, starting at Chalkis, where the gap between Euboea and the mainland narrows to about fifty yards, and extending eastwards past Lefkandi, through the Lelantine plain to Eretria and a short distance beyond, a total distance of some twenty miles. Near Eretria the vases from a number of tombs probably belong to the tenth century, but at Eretria excavation has as yet revealed nothing earlier than the ninth. The only significant addition to our material comes from Chalkis itself.

No settlement has been found, but a number of vases from tombs show that the site was inhabited at least during the later Dark Ages. There were sixteen vases from seven or eight tombs, and they are of much the same type as those from Lefkandi. The earliest is perhaps a triple vase, probably on the borderline between Sub-Mycenaean and Protogeometric, and an amphoriskos with vertical handles could belong to the same period. Otherwise, the vases mostly belong to Middle Protogeometric or to the beginning of the late phase, and include a small neck-handled amphora with wavy lines on the shoulder, a type not yet found at Lefkandi, a lekythos of Athenian type, and a jug with full circles on the shoulder. The latest group should belong to Late Protogeometric, as it shows the full adoption of the compass-drawn semicircles. Unfortunately, no other finds were recorded from these tombs, which were all of the cist variety – it is of interest that the only properly excavated one contained a child inhumation, so it may be that the burial customs differed from those of Lefkandi, close though it was. In addition to these tombs, it may be noted that two other grave groups provided evidence for the early ninth century.

Skyros

This island, no great distance to the north of Euboea, is not, however, particularly easy of access from that part of Euboea where, as we have seen, the main sites were concentrated. Four groups of tombs deserve brief discussion, all within the small plain north of the modern town, and all cist tombs, with inhumations where identifiable. The first two, consisting of seven tombs altogether, contained pottery ranging from Middle to Late Protogeometric. The vase types are not unsimilar to those of Lefkandi, especially the one-handled jugs, a skyphos, and a hydria with languettes. The cups with their high flaring feet, and the compass-drawn semicircles on a jug, indicate a knowledge of the contemporary Athenian style, but the general effect is of a sober dark-ground system. Of the third group of tombs only one contained any funeral offerings; this was certainly of Late Protogeometric date from its krater – of Athenian inspiration – but the cups it contained look rather towards Thessaly than either towards Euboea or Athens. So far, only this tomb had any significant objects other than pottery, and some of these, curiously, seem to have been Mycenaean in type: they could have come from some looted Mycenaean tomb in the vicinity. Another unusual feature was that while these were inside the tomb, the vases had been deposited outside.

A rather similar practice to this was adopted in the final group of four tombs. In these the finds were the richest of all, and they correspond fairly closely to those of the last period discussed at Lefkandi, thus extending from the end of the tenth century well into the first half of the ninth. Not only are the vases similar in type and decoration, but there is also a comparable wealth of other objects, including gold – though not in quite such profusion.

It is unfortunate that we have not got the full sequence throughout the Dark Ages; similar links with Euboea may have existed for a long while, but more material is needed.

A final small point may be noted, to be borne in mind for future reference, that tombs of all four groups contained hand-made vases suggesting possible contact with Thessaly or Macedonia (pp. 213, 217).

Boeotia

This area, of which far too little is known, is geographically so placed as to be easy of access both from Attica and from Euboea (especially the Chalkis district); since Dark Age links are evident with both, this seems an appropriate place to discuss its evidence. There are three sites only, two of them, Orchomenos and Vranesi, close to each other on the north-western shore of Lake Copais, while the third, Thebes, dominates much of the eastern region.

There is not much from Orchomenos: two skyphoi reflect the familiar Athenian expansion of the tenth century, while for the first half of the ninth a group of vases from a cist tomb exhibits a mixture of Attic and Euboean traditions, the Euboean being confirmed by the presence in another tomb of a skyphos with pendent semicircles.

Vranesi is at once more interesting and more frustrating. This is a matter of a mound, itself unusual for this part of the world, with a sort of cairn of large stones at the centre.[6] From the description, the burials took place in cist tombs, but included examples of both inhumation and cremation, and the period of use was a long one, from within the tenth century to the beginning of the eighth. Unfortunately, the account was insufficiently detailed for one to determine which objects came from which tombs, nor indeed is it known how many tombs there were, though there must have been at least eight. No vase is earlier than the tenth century, but to this period – probably the second half – belong a fine neck-handled amphora with semicircles on the shoulder and a trefoil-lipped oinochoe with dog-tooth decoration round the belly, both reflecting Athenian influence, which is confirmed by a cup with high conical foot which was probably imported from Athens. And if the amphora was used as a cremation urn, the relationship might be more than cultural. The influence of Euboea, as at Orchomenos, is apparent in the early ninth century – yet another skyphos with pendent semicircles.

There were other finds as well. The gold bands are presumably of ninth-century date, but what of the two gold earrings, described as simple spirals, the fragments of shattered bronze vases, and the bronze swords? We cannot tell. The bronze swords suggest an early date (so does the type of earring), but need not precede the ninth century, since one has been found at Orchomenos in a Geometric context.[7]

---

[6] There was more than one mound, but it would seem that only one was excavated.

[7] Snodgrass believes that this was probably 'old at the time of its interment'.

At Thebes we again find a link with Euboea shortly after the end of the Dark Ages, this time in a low-footed skyphos with two sets of full circles on the body. We can also, however, trace the link back to within the Dark Ages: an amphora with wavy lines on the neck, from a pit grave, recalls a vase from Chalkis (p. 201), and a one-handled jug with rough zigzags on the shoulder, from a cist tomb, looks rather towards Euboea than Athens. The Athenian connexion is clear enough from the discovery in another tomb of a Late Protogeometric lekythos which could be an import. These last two vases, it may be noted, came from the cist-tomb cemetery first used in the early Dark Ages (p. 69). We could do with a great deal more evidence from this important site.

On the whole, the slight evidence from Boeotia does no more than confirm what we would expect, links with both Attica and Euboea at least from the tenth century onwards. We are, however, entitled to hope for a good deal more: for example, there should surely be traces at least of some local pottery style. More important, the earlier stages are unclear, and this is a serious gap in our knowledge, especially as they might throw light on the Sub-Mycenaean culture. They might also help us to interpret the extremely interesting material discussed in the next section, that from Phocis.

Phocis

This district, lying to the west of Boeotia, looks more naturally to the Corinthian Gulf than to the Aegean, from which it is separated by rugged and mountainous country; even so, as will be seen, there are good reasons for discussing the evidence of one of its two known sites, Delphi, with that of Euboea and Thessaly.

The main interest at Delphi attaches to the contents of a single tomb (Pls. 47, 48). The tomb itself is of unusual shape for this period, as it seems to have been a small chamber tomb cut into the natural rock, but with no *dromos* leading to it. Two burials were found inside, both inhumations, but with the second of these we are not concerned; much later than the original one, it belonged to the eighth century. The earlier one was that of a warrior, as a bronze spearhead, typical of the twelfth and eleventh centuries, was associated with it.[8] Of the eighteen vases also associated with it, eleven were wheel-made – two amphoriskoi with horizontal handles and two with vertical ones, four small one-handled jugs, an oinochoe, a hydria, and a flat-bottomed jug. The system is dark ground, and except for hatching on one of the amphoriskoi the only decorative motive is rough wiggly lines on the shoulder. One might almost be describing a typical Early Protogeometric tomb at Lefkandi, and I would have thought that there must be a connexion, though whether through Boeotia, or even through south Thessaly, one cannot say. The presence of

---

[8] A closely similar one has been found in another tomb from Delphi, of the twelfth century. It belongs to Snodgrass's standard early type.

PLATES 47/48 DELPHI. Tomb group. *BCH* 61, pls. V and VI.

the hand-made vases is unusual, as such are not normally found at this time, and in any case not in such quantity. They are mostly crude replicas of the wheel-made ware, but include a cup and a strange-looking object which appears to be an imitation of a bird vase. Whatever the conclusion, we have in this tomb a further instance of a group of vases, certainly datable to the early part of the later Dark Ages, to my mind, where the influence of Athenian Protogeometric is not yet visible.

The later stage, represented only by a few settlement sherds, reflects the picture already familiar elsewhere – part of a skyphos which could have

been imported from Athens and three high conical feet from skyphoi, for the tenth century, and several sherds from skyphoi with pendent semicircles for the ninth; but there are also indications of links with Thessaly (jugs with cutaway necks), Corinth, and perhaps even Ithaca, these belonging to the ninth century.

On the whole, strange though it may seem, it appears that the inhabitants of Delphi may during the later eleventh century have had connexions rather to the east than to the west. And it is of course of interest that they came within the Athenian orbit during the tenth century.

The second site is Medeon, mentioned briefly in an earlier section (p. 105). There is evidence for settlement during this period, evidently continuing into later times, but whether also connected with the preceding Mycenaean levels is not yet clear, though the same spot was in use throughout. So far as concerns the cemeteries, although the situation at the end of the Mycenaean period is somewhat obscure, there is no doubt that there was a sharp break in the burial customs at some subsequent point, as inhumation in chamber tombs or in slab-covered pit graves was replaced by cremation in shallow pits, a practice that remained unchallenged until the Geometric period. A comparison may be made with the early custom at Lefkandi, in that these elliptical pits were the pyres on which the dead were burnt, and the ashes left therein; burning was never complete, however, and there is no sign of the accompanying cist tombs such as abound at Lefkandi. Instead, a jug (often one which had seen considerable use as it had been mended in antiquity) was used to pour a libation, and then broken and left in the pyre, which was then covered over with earth.

What we cannot tell until the final publication is at what period this custom was introduced, unfortunately. The only datable material mentioned is three vases, one a jug with close parallels at Derveni and in Ithaca (p. 248), second a small amphora with characteristic western fringed decoration, and third a fine trefoil-lipped oinochoe with sets of semicircles with hour-glass filling on the shoulder, which is typically Athenian Late Protogeometric, but could have come from Corinth. This last vase, if not the other two, takes us back into the tenth century, but the earlier stages, if they existed, remain obscure.

Thessaly

The picture that emerged from the discussion of this region during the early Dark Ages was a rather confused one. There was evidence of a move from Epirus into the western central plain at the end of the twelfth century, if not a little later, but it was not possible to say whether there was any further penetration, nor in what direction. In the inland north-eastern area a group of people, probably of Macedonian origin, established themselves at an uncertain date, perhaps c. 1050 B.C. or even after. The Mycenaean foothold along the eastern coast, it seems, had been gradually eroded away during the course of the twelfth century, but the degree of survival either of the Mycenaean population or of its culture remained unclear, as did the degree of their possible supersession by new-comers whether from the north-west or from the south. The only un-doubted evidence of contact with the Sub-Mycenaean area of central Greece was confined to the remote – from the Thessalian point of view – coastal site of Theotokou. The existence of a later cist-tomb cemetery at Iolkos was insufficient to prove that this type of tomb was introduced from the south in the early Dark Ages. Nor could one connect the later use of tholos tombs with a surviving Mycenaean element, since at least those who buried in such tombs at Marmariani were patently not of Mycenaean stock.

The situation during the later Dark Ages is in some ways simpler, but this is partly, no doubt, due to the relative scarcity of evidence – it is almost an archaeological axiom that the more we know, the more the problems increase in number and complexity. There are very few sites altogether, and even fewer of real significance. In the central plain the only evidence for the western part has to be disregarded, since our information is not detailed enough; in the eastern part, south of Larisa, the settlement at Ktouri has a few sherds of Protogeometric character, and a cist tomb at Palaiokastro produced one vase, and probably a second, since found close to it, which are of either Middle or Late Protogeometric date, and similar to those of the coastal sites.[9] The coast is represented by Halos and Gritsa, well to the south, Phthiotic Thebes, not far from Iolkos (a solitary but interesting low-footed skyphos with full circles), Theotokou, already inhabited in the earlier period, and the central and important site of Iolkos itself. A number of tholos tombs from the Magnesian promontory and elsewhere (p. 102) must be set aside, owing to insufficient information. Inland, in the north-eastern district, we encounter those who probably migrated from Macedonia and buried their dead at Marmariani. Finally there is the site of Homolion, at the extreme north-east of Thessaly, practically on the borders of Macedonia, whose tombs, five cave-like and one tholos, used at the end of the Dark Ages and for some time thereafter, contained gifts which involve interesting Macedonian links. In the discussion below I shall concentrate on four sites only – Halos, Theotokou, Iolkos, and Marmariani.

The main interest focuses on whether the culture and customs found on these sites reflect indigenous elements, or intrusion from the north, or the survival of the Mycenaean strain, or influence (and if so, of what kind) from the south, at any time from Sub-Mycenaean onwards. Such questions are not always easy to answer. Marmariani provides an instance of intrusion from the north, but were native elements involved as well? On the other sites – and in due course at Marmariani – the ceramic influence of Athens from c. 950 B.C. onwards, whether direct or indirect, is beyond doubt, but there are certain earlier local features shared, as will be seen, with Euboea but not with Athens, which have their eventual origin in Mycenaean pottery, and can be interpreted in one of three ways, local developments from local Mycenaeans, diffusion from the late Sub-Mycenaean communities of Euboea (or some other unspecified area), or a parallel development in both Thessaly and Euboea, on the assumption that these districts were closely linked from L.H. III C or Sub-Mycenaean times. The analysis will depend mainly, and rather deplorably, on the pottery, but due weight will be given to other aspects of the material that may be available.

The southernmost site of Halos is of no great assistance in resolving any problems. Here there was a small cemetery of ten cist tombs and one circular enclosure. Inhumation (as everywhere in Thessaly at this time)

---

[9] A cist tomb at Pharsala, with no vases but a whetstone and an iron knife, could belong to this period.

was practised in the cist tombs, but neither bones nor ashes were reported from the enclosure. Most of the cist burials were of children, but only three contained offerings; these belong to the tenth century, their vases showing not only the influence of Athens but also (for example, in the one-handled jugs and flat-based cups) features held in common by Thessaly and Euboea. The pottery from the enclosure should be dated to the early ninth century, and is of interest as proving the survival, at any rate on this site, of the one-handled jug.[10]

At Theotokou the child burial of late Sub-Mycenaean times has already been discussed (p. 102). Of the other two cist tombs, containing adult burials, one is of Early Geometric date, but the second is contemporary with the Halos cist tombs and exhibits much the same characteristics in the pottery. Most of the objects of metal from this second tomb, the bronze and iron rings, the iron knife blade and what may be part of an iron fibula, are fairly standard for the end of the Dark Ages in this part of the Aegean, as well as in Athens. There were also, however, four dress pins, and these have the iron shaft and bronze bulb so typical of Athens – and Theotokou is the only site in the whole complex region at present under discussion where they have been found.

In spite of this interesting point, the material from Halos and Theotokou does not get us much further. There is at least no trace of links with Marmariani – a useful negative inference, as such links are visible in the Early Geometric tomb at Theotokou (though not in the roughly contemporary enclosure at Halos). The existence of strong Athenian ceramic influence in the tenth century is clear, and indicates connexions with the south. The similarity between the local pottery and that of Euboea, and in such metal objects as we have, and the use in common of cist tombs may predispose us to think that culture and customs spread from the south, but even if that were so for the tenth century it would not necessarily hold for the earlier period.

In due course of time the excavations at Iolkos should help greatly to clarify matters. As in Mycenaean times, and as today, Iolkos was the principal port of Thessaly – in fact, one cannot visualise any other. It was the communicating link between the Aegean world and inland Thessaly. It was also well placed to become a flourishing town in its own right, as it stands in reasonably fertile country, and has easy access to the coastal Krokian plain.

These excavations have been very rewarding: to the Dark Ages have been assigned a multi-stratified settlement with good stone foundation masonry and a cist-tomb cemetery. In the neighbourhood further cist tombs and a tholos tomb straddle the Dark Ages and the succeeding period. Of the settlement we can say little except that its excavator believed the date of its establishment to be hardly more than a generation later than the twelfth-century desertion of the Mycenaean site, and that it continued in existence throughout the Protogeometric period. A very small number of its sherds have been illustrated, of late Dark Age date, and

[10] A bronze pin with roll-top head was found in this tomb; there was no other significant object of metal.

PLATE 49 IOLKOS. Vases from tomb XII. *Pr.* 1960, pl. 37 *a* and *b*; 38 *a*.

two complete vases, one of which, a cup, looks Sub-Mycenaean, and would thus be the earliest known vase from the site, though it was reported that the pottery was generically related to Mycenaean. None of this, however, is a sufficient basis for detailed conclusions, and we must turn, as so often, to the evidence of the tombs.

Here the earliest material comes from the cist-tomb cemetery associated with the settlement, containing over forty burials, all of children. The publication is not yet complete, but the information we already have is of great interest. There is the usual disadvantage that the size of the tombs was not such as to permit the depositing of large vases, and the added drawback that the vases were of types considered more suitable for children, but both in shape and decoration there is a remarkable similarity to the local style of Lefkandi, the period covered being possibly Early Protogeometric, certainly the middle phase, and probably continuing some distance into the lengthy late period – no vase yet illustrated goes back to Sub-Mycenaean. There are the customary cups of the Skoubris cemetery at Lefkandi, the small one-handled jugs and oinochoai; also one or two lekythoi and hydriai, and a kalathos with incised triangular decoration. There are the usual conical feet, and the decoration is much the same, a generally dark-ground system occasionally relieved by the habit of leaving the lower body and foot unpainted. As at Lefkandi, decorative motives are extraordinarily sparse, and mostly confined to wavy or zigzag lines, though hatching is found and, on one cup, full compass-drawn circles. Tomb XII, with six vases (Pl. 49), is most instructive, as every vase can be paralleled at Lefkandi, during Late Protogeometric but before the radical developments at the end of that phase; there is even a cup with high flaring foot and a zigzag round the everted rim. It was from this tomb that the kalathos came, thus suggesting that the shape may have reached Lefkandi at an earlier date than we yet have trace of. As well as this there is the negative evidence, no flat or low-based cups or low-footed skyphoi with circles or pendent semicircles, no vases showing the influence of the Marmariani style (see below, p. 213). In its pottery, then, this cemetery covering perhaps much of the later Dark Ages, though not the concluding phase, shows signs of close contact with Euboea.[11] The metal objects, most as yet unillustrated, seem from their description to be typical of the whole Aegean area – bronze and iron ornaments, such as rings, bracelets, and fibulae – but with no necessary connexion with Euboea. Indeed, Iolkos is unusual in retaining in use, beside the arched fibula, an earlier type with leaf-shaped bow; and so far only one dress pin (of iron) has been recorded.[12]

So much for the cist tombs. The main bulk of the material, however, comes from a single tholos tomb, that of Kapakli close to Iolkos; but it is of far less value. The tomb continued in use, for adult inhumations, for hundreds of years, but it was not possible for any accurate information to be obtained either as to tomb groups or as to the relative disposition of the burials. In consequence, the pottery has to be judged on purely stylistic grounds, and the other finds, unillustrated, have to be left out of account altogether.

[11] The contact probably still existed in the very early ninth century, to judge from the contents of two cist tombs (both adult burials) – each had a skyphos with pendent semicircles and a trefoil-lipped oinochoe with semicircles on the shoulder.

[12] Beads of glass paste and of faience were also found: whether these have any significance for comparative purposes I have no knowledge.

PLATE 50 MARMARIANI. Jugs and oinochoai. *BSA* 31, fig. 4, 6; pl. I,
10; pl. III, 42; pl. IV, 48 and 60.

Assuming the close connexion with Euboea and the transmission,
direct or indirect, of the Athenian Protogeometric style, can we say when
this tomb was first used? The small ovoid one-handled jugs, typical of both
Euboea and Thessaly, would suggest that we have to go back at least into
Late Protogeometric; even though they are known later at Halos, they are

PLATE 51 MARMARIANI. Amphorae and krater. *BSA* 31, pl. VI, 77 and 79; pl. X, 141.

much more common in the tenth – and eleventh – centuries. A Dark Age date for the earliest burials is, to my mind, confirmed by vase types which show quite clearly the influence of Athenian Protogeometric. Two fine neck-handled amphorae, clay ground, have full circles on the shoulder, which might indicate a date as far back as Early Protogeometric, but their bases are well undercut, as opposed to the flat early ones of Athens – and one has learnt to expect the misuse of the circle motive anywhere outside that town. The oinochoai and amphorae with semicircles on the shoulder could perhaps belong to the ninth century, but not so, I would think, a splendid krater with high conical foot and four sets of circles between the handles, nor a large skyphos of similar type. On the other hand, there are no cups of the earlier type, and most of the skyphoi have pendent semi-circles. I think it is likely that the tomb started to be used in the second half

FIG. 19 MARMARIANI
Kantharos. *BSA* 31, p. 15, fig. 5, no. 23.

of the tenth century rather than during the first.

As well as the vases already discussed, there are two shapes, first introduced at the end of the Dark Ages, which belong to a separate ceramic tradition: the kantharoi with handles high above the rim (two are hand-made, the rest wheel-made), and the jugs with cut-away necks, all wheel-made. For an explanation of their presence we must turn to the tombs of Marmariani.

This site is entirely different in character from Iolkos, well inland, on the foothills of Mt. Ossa north of Larisa. The material came from five tholos tombs not, fortunately, used over so long a period as the one at Kapakli. As opposed to all the other sites so far discussed, the earliest pottery was hand-made, and seems to show clear links with Macedonia. Of the twenty-nine vases of this type, all but two were jugs with sloping or cut-away necks, or plain or decorated kantharoi, the general effect of fabric and decoration being rather barbaric (Pl. 50 and Fig. 19). That these hand-made vessels were the earliest there seems no doubt, since the two main shapes recur in the wheel-made group.

It would be natural to expect the technique of the wheel to be introduced through contact with those living on the coast, and there is indeed plenty of evidence to show that this is what happened, and that the occasion was sometime during the later Dark Ages, the Late Protogeometric period. Not only was the wheel adopted, but elements of the style as well. Eleven of the seventeen wheel-made jugs with cut-away necks have compass-drawn semicircles on the shoulder (Pl. 50). As at Kapakli, there are neck-handled amphorae with full circles on the shoulder, and oinochoai with semicircles, but above all, the earliest of the splendid series of kraters must be contemporary with Athenian Late Protogeometric (Pls. 50, 51). Only the small one-handled jugs are missing, but they are unexciting vases, and the local potters may have felt no interest in them.

Furthermore, the influence from the coast continued into Early Geometric, visible in amphorae, oinochoai, and kraters, and especially in the flat-based cups and skyphoi with pendent semicircles. On the basis of these, it has been reckoned that the Marmariani tombs ceased to be used in Middle Geometric I, during the second half of the ninth century. The time of first use is, of course, a good deal less certain. It must have preceded the introduction of the wheel, which can perhaps be dated c. 950 B.C. or a little after, and I would think it probable that the earliest burials belonged to the second half of the eleventh century.[13]

The finds other than pottery are of interest, though not easily datable. The hair rings of gold recall earlier ones of Athens and Lefkandi, but similar rings were also found at Homolion (see p. 207), which cannot precede the late tenth century. Finger rings, both of bronze and iron, were massive; the bronze armlets have northern connexions. There was one arched fibula of bronze, and for the first time we encounter spectacle fibulae (see Fig. 22 for the type), three of them, made of iron with a bronze boss, the boss in one instance being plated with gold leaf – these presumably belong to the latest burials (see the discussion of Vergina, pp. 217 ff.). The only two pins were of iron, with cylindrical T-shaped head, a type not known to me elsewhere in Greece. Iron was also the metal used for the fragmentary sword, spearhead, and knives. And finally there were numerous beads, especially of glass (875 were found in one tomb). For comparative purposes one looks north as well as south, though the spectacle fibulae at Vergina, the early examples of which seem to belong to the tenth century and continue into the ninth, were all, with one exception, of bronze.

The situation in Thessaly can be summed up as follows. Nowhere, so far, can the published material be with certainty assigned to an earlier date than 1050 B.C., except probably the lekythos from tomb C at Theotokou and a cup from the Iolkos settlement. There could therefore be a gap in our knowledge covering almost the whole of the early Dark Ages, the latest preceding material being that of Hexalophos in west Thessaly, which might be as late as 1100 B.C. (p. 98). This is an unlikely gap, which could easily be narrowed when we have the full account of the post-Mycenaean settlement at Iolkos. For the moment, however, it is safer to confine our conclusions to the later Dark Ages.

We have also to confine ourselves to two main areas, the eastern coastal district extending marginally inland to the central plain, and the north-east of Thessaly, north of Larisa. This geographical restriction is due to the unfortunate fact that most of the central inland area, and the west, are virtually unknown, though the publication of a group of vases from near Trikkala might give us a clue.

The fact that there are two clearly distinguishable areas is nevertheless important. Along the coast, the inhabitants of whatever their stock (and it

[13] On the analogy of the tombs of Vergina, pp. 217 f., where the usual custom was to provide the dead with one jug and one bowl, one can suggest that there were at least eleven burials associated with hand-made pottery at Marmariani, though of course one has to allow for some overlap after the introduction of the wheel.

may have been a mixed one) seem by the end of the eleventh century to have assimilated the culture, and perhaps also the burial customs, of areas to the south, principally Euboea, and later shared in the wide influence of Athenian Protogeometric pottery. Inland in the north-east, those who used hand-made pottery of Macedonian type can be traced back to the eleventh century. Whether, if they came from Macedonia, their intent was warlike we do not know, though I think it is more likely that they were displaced persons, fortunate in finding thinly inhabited territory to settle in. What is reasonably certain is that thereafter their progress was peaceful. For a while they appear to have been out of touch with the coastal areas, but from the middle of the tenth century there was intercommunication between the two, a matter of great interest. To start with, they assimilated the wheel-made pottery of the coastal communities; they adapted the technique and decorative motives to their own style, and also introduced new Protogeometric vase types. But this was not all, for their pottery in turn had a reverse influence on the coastal region, starting perhaps a little later, say the end of the tenth century, and continuing thereafter.[14]

There was, then, from the middle of the tenth century onwards, peaceful intercommunication and co-operation, and it looks as though in these areas the period of stress which probably characterised the early Dark Ages had been resolved. And this was an extension of the peaceful co-existence with regions to the south, traceable through Euboea to Athens (unless it came direct), and symptomatic of the whole central and southern Aegean at this time. Such conditions certainly appear to have continued into the early ninth century, but thereafter it may be that the Thessalians became somewhat more isolated, at least culturally.

One would like to be able to make some deductions from the type of tombs used. So far as concerns the cist tombs, my belief is that their distribution favours the theory of diffusion from the south, but the point is not provable. There is also the added complication of the distribution over north-east Thessaly of the tholos tombs, reaching to the coast at Iolkos, and thus confusing the issue, especially as such evidence as we have suggests that in this community, until the end of the tenth century, adults were buried in tholos tombs and only children in cist tombs: but is this evidence altogether reliable?

As to the size of the population, we are reasonably safe in assuming that there was a community of substantial size and importance at Iolkos – hardly surprising in view of its past history and the natural advantages of the site. And I think that Marmariani as well could have been a place of substance; the pottery may look barbaric, but it includes some very fine pieces, especially the series of kraters, which still provides the yardstick for other vases of this style throughout the Aegean. I think there is little doubt that such vases were made for a flourishing community. Apart from these two sites, though, one can say nothing.

---

[14] A small point of interest is that whereas most of the wheel-made jugs with cut-away necks at Marmariani had semicircles on the shoulder, there is no instance of this in the Kapakli tholos tomb; perhaps the potters of Iolkos preferred consciously to imitate not only the shape but the decorative system of Marmariani as well.

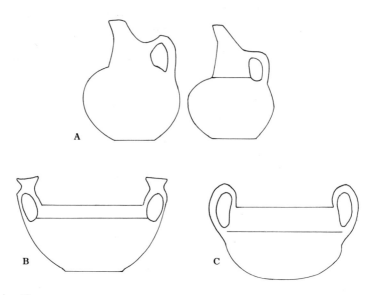

FIG. 20 VERGINA
A) Jugs. *Vergina* I, p. 195, fig. 39.
B) Knobbed bowl. *Vergina* I, p. 203, fig. 42.
C) Kantharos. *Vergina* I, p. 212, fig. 51.

We know, then, something of the internal situation in north and east Thessaly, and the external links with the south are plain enough. There remains the problem of what connexions, if any, the Thessalians had with Macedonia to the north. Nothing can be said for certain except at Homolion, itself almost within Macedonian territory, but such connexions were obviously possible, and in any case a brief discussion of what we know of Macedonia at this time will be found of relevance to the whole region under review.

Macedonia

Macedonia is of only marginal significance as regards Greece and the Aegean during this period, even more so perhaps than it had been in Mycenaean times, and I shall discuss it simply in so far as it sheds light on developments to the south. Its two main features were a very strong native tradition, and a natural outlook towards the north. The latter stages of the Mycenaean period, it is true, had seen a limited infiltration of Mycenaean pottery, and the Macedonians were prepared to continue imitating this for many generations, as we shall see. The twelfth and eleventh centuries, as elsewhere, were times of stress, and there is no doubt that invaders penetrated into central Macedonia down the Axios river, and later into western Macedonia, a separate group probably using the route of the Haliakmon river. There may have been other disturbers of the peace as well, and some such intrusion could have been responsible for the displacement of those whom one finds established at Marmariani in Thessaly perhaps not long after 1050 B.C. – there could even be a connexion with the Haliakmon group. In spite of all this, though, the indigenous features persisted.

When we start searching for links with the south during the Dark Ages, we find that in central Macedonia they were, so far as is known, virtually non-existent. The earliest pottery of southern origin – mainly skyphoi with pendent semicircles – does not precede the ninth century.

Until recently we would have had to admit that the same conditions applied in western Macedonia, but the excavation in recent years of a very large cemetery at Vergina has at last provided us with a fairly clear picture of what was happening in this district. The discussion that follows is confined to the material from this site.

The site itself lies a little south of the Haliakmon river at a point where it emerges into the central plain, and the cemetery consists of a large number of mounds, each of which contained several burials – almost invariably pit graves and universally inhumation.[15]

The time range is from c. 1000 to c. 700 B.C., according to the excavator, so there is an overlap with the later Dark Ages. The material, as I have indicated, suggests that the cemetery was used by people who came down overland from the north, probably along the Haliakmon, but who adopted much of the current local pottery style. The determination of the upper chronological limit is one of the most difficult and important questions, and the evidence as a whole has to be brought into play. Little assistance is gained from the bulk of the pottery, as it was hand-made (Fig. 20), and continued to be so throughout – of 544 vases only 58 were wheel-made. This therefore was no Marmariani: the strength of local tradition was obviously far too great to permit the general adoption of the wheel. And yet it is the wheel-made vases which not only provide vital clues in establishing the chronology but are also of major interest to us, as they involve links with the south.

When was this link established? Most of the vases can be dated firmly to the ninth century – the low-footed skyphoi with pendent semicircles (the most popular), the flat-based cups, the small krater, the oinochoai and feeding bottles, and the amphoriskoi. Even the one vase that was an import – and it is of considerable interest that the others were all made locally – is more likely to be of ninth than tenth-century date (it is a low-footed skyphos with two sets of full circles between the handles). There are, however, three vases which seem likely to be contemporary with Late Protogeometric in the south, and so to precede the end of the Dark Ages

---

[15] I confine myself almost wholly to the mounds excavated by Professor Andronikos, because they apparently cover the earlier periods of use. Some of Dr Petsas's finds, however, are among the earliest.

and take us back into the tenth century. These are a skyphos with highish flaring foot, the area between the handles banded, and the lower body and foot unpainted; a cup with high flaring foot, and a zigzag just below the outswung rim; and a remarkable pithos used for practising the multiple-brush technique. It may be that one or two of the other vases also belong to the tenth century, but one cannot be certain.

Whatever the time of the first regular contact between Macedonia and the south, it would be a noteworthy event, but particularly so if it was – as it could well be – towards the end of the tenth century, for this is just when we had occasion to conclude that the community of Lefkandi was entering on a flourishing period of activity, to be related to a time of considerable commercial expansion for it and the surrounding districts (see pp. 198 f.). If the first contacts belong in fact to this time, or indeed to some other, we then have to ask whether they may not rather have been in the first instance with Thessaly, overland or by sea. This is perfectly possible, but my impression is that such evidence as we have suggests that the area of Euboea, Skyros, and the northern Cyclades was the more likely source. One small point of comparison may belong to the early ninth rather than to the late tenth century: at Vergina we have an example of a flat-based cup with slightly offset rim with zigzags round it – this is not only absolutely typical of Lefkandi, but has so far been found nowhere else except at Vergina. If the link was specifically with Euboea, then this could be the origin of a relationship that was eventually to lead to the extensive Euboean colonisation to central Macedonia in the eighth century and later. It may be, too, that communications were not only in one direction: there are jugs with cut-away neck in ninth-century tombs at Lefkandi, and other similar hand-made vases of both tenth and ninth-century date in the tombs of Skyros. For these, however, a Thessalian origin or inspiration would be equally acceptable.

This is one significant possible conclusion, but the cemetery of Vergina affords other material of interest, especially in the earliest burials. The wheel-made vases discussed formed, as I have indicated, an essential point in the excavator's chronology, as he was able to show that a number of objects must precede their first appearance, so leading him back to a date of c. 1000 B.C. for the first use of the cemetery. Most surprisingly, there are two pyxides of Mycenaean inspiration, the one wheel-made, the other hand-made. It is extraordinary to find such survivals, and the later the date the more unlikely; but no use is made of this argument, as the context of the two vases is not helpful.

More cogent is the presence of several dress pins (Fig. 21) of a type which further south has not been found later than c. 1050 B.C., that with slight swelling on the shank and small head, such as is found at Lefkandi, Athens, Mycenae, and Ancient Elis in the early Dark Ages. There are also a few rings with double-spiral terminals (Fig. 21), of equally early date when found in the south. At Vergina they are never found in association with wheel-made vases, and can reasonably be supposed to be earlier and so to take the first tombs back into the early tenth century, possibly to

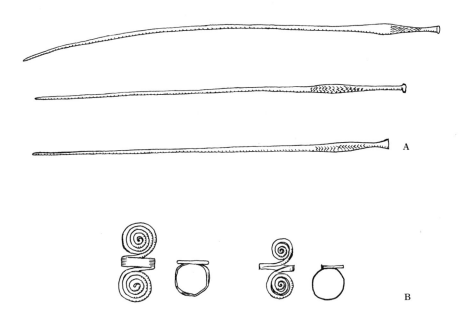

FIG. 21 VERGINA
A) Pins. *Vergina* I, p. 234, fig. 74.
B) Rings with double-spiral terminals. *Vergina* I, p. 238, fig. 78.

1000 B.C. Further interest attaches to them in that they form part of the northern-inspired tradition which characterised many of the bronze objects from this site, and would thus help to confirm the ultimate northern origin of such pins and rings when found in the Sub-Mycenaean contexts of central Greece.

Yet another feature is the fibulae with arched and often twisted bow, especially when taken in conjunction with the series of later spectacle fibulae (Fig. 22), which the excavator was able to show were introduced towards the end of the tenth century. Since these spectacle fibulae very soon became the only acceptable type of brooch, the arched fibulae which they replaced must be earlier, and contemporary with the dress pins and rings discussed above. Again, it would suggest a northern origin for the earliest appearance of this type in the south.

A further point of interest is the quantity of iron weapons, swords, spearheads, arrowheads, and knives. The context does not always permit precise dating, and one cannot be sure whether they reach back to the early tenth century, but there is a strong possibility that they did, and it

A

B

FIG. 22 VERGINA
A) Arched fibulae. *Vergina* I, p. 232, fig. 70.
B) Spectacle fibula. *Vergina* I, p. 228, fig. 67.

has been argued that the profusion is such that it is not easy to accept a southern Greek origin for them. It is known that there are very early traces of iron-working in central Macedonia, possibly even from the twelfth century onwards, and one may reasonably deduce that there was a flourishing local industry. And one other deduction: this was a warlike community – and the first clear example of one.[16]

Finally, the mounds themselves and the burials they contained: there is, to my knowledge, nothing exactly comparable in Greece and the Aegean. The mound at Vranesi had a sort of central cairn of stones, not known at Vergina, and both inhumation and cremation were practised; in the mounds of the central plain of Naxos, in use from the later ninth century onwards, cremation was the custom, as opposed to universal inhumation at Vergina. If anywhere, the connexions are with the north.

[16] For a much fuller and better discussion, see Snodgrass, *Dark Age of Greece*, pp. 253 ff. He prefers a lower date for the first burials in the Vergina cemetery.

13 The Central Aegean

We have now more or less circumnavigated the Aegean. The mainland coastal areas, whether European or Asiatic, have been dealt with in so far as they are relevant. A few islands have been discussed, notably Euboea, Andros, Tenos, Skyros, and the Dodecanese. There still remains Crete, which may be deferred for the moment. There also remains, however, a large number of islands, large and small, comprising the Cyclades of the central Aegean and the eastern group north of the Dodecanese. These should be of much interest, both in themselves, and as helping to clarify the various interconnexions between east and west, but on the whole they have produced little of worth.

It is not easy to present the evidence in a clear or logical fashion, but I shall attempt to proceed both chronologically and geographically. First, though, one can discard quite a number of the islands. There are those which have produced no evidence whatever, comprising the majority of the Cyclades, most of which are small and so barren as hardly conducive to settlement; the absence of any material from Syros or Mykonos is, however, surprising. Here we are left with Amorgos, Thera, Melos, Siphnos, Paros, Naxos, Delos, and Rheneia. In the eastern group of islands we can similarly dispense with Icaria.

More depressing than this, the two large and fertile islands of Chios and Lesbos have produced nothing beyond a handful of sherds showing that there must have been some contact with the Greek world to the south and west of them. Nor are excavated sites entirely lacking, but Antissa on Lesbos is related rather to Asia Minor, Emborio on Chios has divulged no trace of habitation in this period (see p. 20 for the late Mycenaean settlement), and Kato Phana, a sanctuary site near it, belongs mainly to later times. It is true that these two islands lie rather to the north of the direct routes across the central Aegean, but it is extremely difficult to believe that we have anything like the true picture, especially bearing in mind the situation and material of Old Smyrna, which lies beyond them (see pp. 183 f.). The two obvious settlement sites are those of the modern capital towns, Mytilene and Chios, and these have not yet been investigated: it is there that a start could be made.

We now have only Samos from this group, to be added to the eight of the Cyclades; nor have some of these much to offer, but some points of interest emerge.

We are confronted not only with a general lack of material, but also with an almost total absence of evidence for the first phase of the period, Early and Middle Protogeometric. One island alone has produced such evidence, and that is Naxos, the largest of the Cyclades and centrally situated: this may then be taken first. The site concerned is just north of the modern capital of the island; the settlement, known as Grotta, lies right on the shore – in fact the encroachment of the sea created great difficulties for the excavator – while the tombs, assuming that they were associated with the settlement, were not far inland on higher ground. The Dark Age cemetery area, the successor of the Mycenaean one, was much disturbed by houses of the Roman period, but it was established that it consisted of pit graves dug into the natural rock. In the preliminary publication, wherein the vases from the tombs were illustrated, the three vases from one are not only such as might be found at Lefkandi, but can confidently be dated to the Early Protogeometric phase: one is a feeding-bottle with basket handle, dark ground except for two wiggly lines round the belly; another is a lekythos with low conical foot and hand-drawn semicircles with a half-moon filling on the shoulder; and the third is a cup with highish conical foot, fairly straight sides, and compass-drawn circles below the rim. It is thus clear that the Naxians knew of the recent Athenian innovations, and it is also clear that, as in the Argolid and as at Lefkandi – and possibly linked to it – they were evolving an independent style, based on the late Sub-Mycenaean pottery of those who took over from the surviving Mycenaeans (see pp. 82 f.). This is confirmed by the only two vases from the settlement to have been published, little one-handled jugs with wiggly lines on the shoulder, and the lower body and foot unpainted. Once again, such vases would not be out of place at Lefkandi, but are unknown to Athens: an Early or Middle Protogeometric date can probably be assigned to them. By Late Protogeometric, things may have been different, as the single vase from the second tomb is a trefoil-lipped oinochoe of Athenian type, but that is not surprising in view of the tremendous impact that Athenian pottery made in the tenth century.

Such is the highly important evidence from Naxos, and one can only await with eagerness the full publication of the settlement, including its relation to the earlier Mycenaean settlement which it overlies. It is in any case of great significance that we find the inhabitants occupying houses of rectangular construction with fairly solid stone foundations, a rare phenomenon in a period overshadowed by cemetery material.

On the neighbouring island of Paros, one could also wish that more was known of the settlement (no house constructions identified) and sanctuary area excavated there. We have to rely on a small number of sherds, representing nevertheless a fairly wide range of shapes – skyphoi, cups, amphorae, and kraters. These show an entire dependence on Athens; their date is certainly or probably Late Protogeometric (the krater sherd, though, has been claimed as belonging to the middle period). Such evidence does not, of course, exclude the possibility that the earlier situation was as on Naxos; but it confirms the picture of the powerful influence exerted by Athens in the tenth century.

The exiguous evidence from Melos and Siphnos indicates a similar dependence on Athens, and here the dependence persisted into the Early

Geometric of the first half of the ninth century. An isolated skyphos from Thera, found in a much later tomb, is very like one from Melos, and both could be imports from Athens. The southern group of the Cyclades most probably, then, came within the exclusive sphere of Athens during the last phase of the Dark Ages. The easternmost island of Amorgos, however, had links both with Athens and with the Dodecanese at this time.

The excavations at Miletus (p. 83) had suggested the existence of close relations with Athens, starting in late Sub-Mycenaean, and continuing through Protogeometric. The situation on Naxos may lead to hesitation in accepting complete continuity, since it lies on one of the main sea routes to Miletus, but there is at least no problem for the tenth century, to judge from the evidence of Samos. Excavation has concentrated on the great sanctuary of Hera, and from here the few published sherds seem to show clear links with the Athenian style (one of them, indeed, could be Early Protogeometric). Most recently, investigation of a sanctuary near the ancient capital has revealed further Protogeometric sherds, among which were included conical feet and part of a skyphos with three sets of circles, and a zigzag below the rim – a familiar Athenian type.

Finally we come to the islands of Delos and Rheneia. In these islands there is no Dark Age material prior to Late Protogeometric, and that is disappointing. As to Delos, the few Late Protogeometric sherds show the same close contact with Athens as throughout the Cyclades, and no further comment is needed. But in the early ninth century, whereas in the southern islands Athenian Early Geometric ceramic influence persisted un-challenged, a rival element appears on Delos – or rather on Rheneia, in the earliest material from the Purification Trench, the place to which centuries later all the contents of the tombs of Delos were transported. Pottery of Athenian type is indeed found, but alongside it there are vase types, notably amphoriskoi with vertical handles and low-footed skyphoi with two sets of circles or, above all, semicircles pendent from the rim, which are typical of Euboea, Skyros, and eastern Thessaly, and of Tenos and Andros.

Finally, the contents of a tomb on Rheneia, an amphoriskos with vertical handles and a high conical foot from a skyphos (probably Attic), give a good idea of the mixture of the two ceramic strains at the very end of the Dark Ages.

To sum up on this whole region is by no means easy, and no conclusions can be accepted as firm. We are hindered by the absence of material from many of the islands, and by its extreme scarcity in many more. The fact that we have to depend solely on pottery is a further drawback – no other artefacts have been recorded. The almost total lack of evidence for the early stages of the period is yet another disadvantage. The salient points are as follows. In the early stages, one coastal community on Naxos en-joyed a culture and customs rather different from that of Athens, but ap-parently closely associated with that of Lefkandi, suggesting a similar state of affairs in the north-western Cycladic group for which we have as yet no evidence. Whether this affected the situation at Miletus in Asia

Minor we cannot tell. During the tenth century, from which most of our evidence comes, the predominant feature was the influence of the Athenian Late Protogeometric style, and this covered the whole area. Whether this influence went beyond that visible in the pottery, and may not even have involved actual migration or colonisation, we have again no means of knowing, but it seems possible that certain settlements, as for example those in Siphnos and Paros, did not exist earlier than this century. It is in any case easy to understand the links with the coast of Asia Minor, and how Athenian pottery was able to have its effect on central Crete, where imported vases are also found (pp. 229, 234). Assuming at least the existence of a trading element, it would seem that the Athenians were the main commercial power in the Aegean during much of the tenth century.[1] At the end of this century, however, and during the early ninth, it would seem that the influence of Athens, still dominant in the southern Cycladic group, was faced in the central and north-western islands with competition from some other area, extending from Euboea to east Thessaly, but probably centred in Euboea.

---

[1] It may be noted in passing that there is no intervening trace of the connexion which may have existed between the Argolid and the Dodecanese (pp. 173 f.).

14 Crete in the Tenth Century

The pattern of sites during the tenth century is very closely similar to that of the eleventh, with two major exceptions. The town of Karphi, I am assuming, had been abandoned by *c.* 1000 B.C. (or, if not by then, very shortly afterwards); the significance of this event, I must stress, can only be understood if one knows, which one does not, why the town was built and continued to be lived in. Secondly, there is a brief glimpse of light from the west, in the cemetery of Modi, which could in part belong to the latter years of the tenth century. There is then one loss and one gain, and the loss is the greater.

In the analysis which follows I shall take first central, then western, and finally eastern Crete.

Central Crete

There are three main centres of habitation, as in the eleventh century: Knossos, Phaestos, and Gortyn. These have provided material of both settlement and cemetery type, and I shall discuss them first, though a few other sites have produced some scraps of evidence, mostly from tombs.

So far as concerns the settlement material there is unfortunately nothing to add to my earlier remarks (pp. 115 ff.). At Knossos the situation remains obscure, while at Phaestos and Gortyn one can only as yet say that the known settlements persisted throughout the tenth century and into the ninth.

The tombs, on the other hand, are very instructive. At Knossos, whereas the few Sub-Minoan graves so far identified lie mostly to the south of the Palace,[1] in the Gypsades cemetery, the tenth-century Protogeometric ones are to the west and north. There are two main groups: to the west, in the Fortetsa cemetery, three tombs are certainly within this period, and three others extend from the late tenth to the early ninth century; over a mile to the north of this, at Ayios Ioannis, six of the eight tombs belong wholly or partly to this period. Apart from these there were two other tombs, one in the Teke area, one on the west side of the Kephala ridge, which probably represent further groups. At Phaestos, there is one tomb on the Palace hill (Mulino), and another about two miles to the south-east of it. And there is one tomb at Gortyn, used from the very late tenth to the mid-ninth century.

The first point of note is that both at Knossos and Phaestos it must have

---

[1] Just one is north-west of the Palace, associated with later tombs (the Teke area).

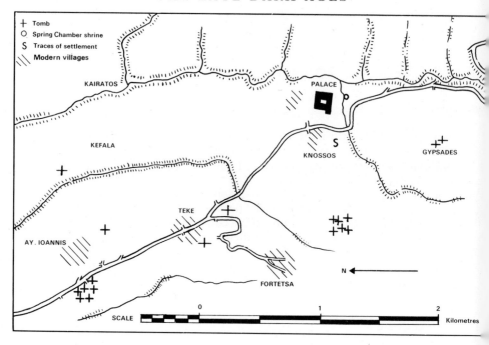

PLAN OF KNOSSOS

been a matter of more than one community – there could have been several in the Knossos area (see the plan), to judge from the combined cemetery and settlement evidence.

Next, the types of tomb. At Knossos all burials were placed in small chamber tombs cut into the soft rock. At Phaestos, the type of the one on the hill is not clear; the other, at Petrokephali, was an almost square shaft a metre deep. At Gortyn, finally, we have the finest known example of a Protogeometric tholos tomb, a very interesting find, as such tombs are otherwise, except for nearby Kourtais, confined to the eastern region.

The manner of burial involves a substantial change from preceding practice in central Crete. Previously there are only two instances of cremation, one from Liliana near Phaestos, of twelfth-century date, and a probable one in the Teke area (second half of the eleventh century?). In the tenth century, however, cremation became the rule, with the ashes placed in various types of vase. In the Mesara, at Gortyn and at or near Phaestos, there are no exceptions: the tholos tomb at Gortyn contained several such urn cremations, while at Petrokephali, with five burials, and at Mulino, with three, it was noted that the bones were half-burnt. In the Knossos area, cremation was also universal in the Fortetsa cemetery, but the single tombs in the Teke area and on the Kephala ridge contained inhumations, and both inhumation and cremation were practised quite indiscriminately

PLATE 52 KNOSSOS (AYIOS IOANNIS). Amphorae from tomb VIII. *BSA* 55, pls. 32 and 33.

in the Ayios Ioannis cemetery, even in two cases within a single tomb – as is also the case at Vrokastro (p. 235). This example of simultaneous use of both customs is of course of importance, and should be a warning not to build too much on the manner of burial; on the other hand, the change to universal cremation in the other cemeteries demands some explanation. It is tempting to associate it with the marked influence of the Athenian Late Protogeometric ceramic style, and to conclude that it was introduced from Athens, but if the earlier tomb of the Teke area, where the vases are purely Sub-Minoan, contained a cremation, such an explanation is unlikely. And since at Vrokastro in the east the cremations can in no way be associated with Athenian influence, it seems that we must reject this link with Athens. Unfortunately, I can offer no other explanation.

For the offerings deposited with the dead[2] it will be best to separate the Knossos area from the two sites in the southern plain. First, at Knossos, there is quite a reasonable number of vases,[3] illustrating on the one hand the continuance of the Sub-Minoan tradition, and on the other the influence of Athens. Most of the vase types are of local origin – cups, kraters large, small, and miniature, stirrup jars (a symbol of Cretan conservatism, as they go on till the middle of the ninth century), bowls with horizontal handles, kalathoi, open vases with vertical handles from shoulder to lip, including pithoi, some of the trefoil-lipped oinochoai, the belly-handled amphorae and the neck-handled ones; also the pyxides with almost vertical sides, collar neck, and two horizontal handles rising vertically

[2] The custom seems to have been to place all objects, including vases, in the cremation urn, as opposed to Athens, where the vases remained outside it.

[3] See Pls. 52, 53 for a small selection.

FIG. 23 KNOSSOS, FORTETSA TOMB VI
Detail of goats and ships on a krater. *Fortetsa*, pl. 135.

above the shoulder – and another type with everted lip, vertical handles to
the lip and usually a cup attached to the shoulder. This accounts for more
or less all the known shapes, and even if one cannot discover parallels in
Sub-Minoan, comparative material can be found in late twelfth-century
contexts, as for example at Kastri. These vase types reflect not only the
true Minoan shapes, but also the earlier influences from outside Crete – the
kalathoi and kraters from the Aegean, the belly-handled amphorae and
the pyxides with excrescent cups from Cyprus, for example. In general, this
is a clay-ground style, the shapes being deeper and more elongated than
previously, and there being a strong tendency towards a flat base, though
the kraters of all types have a low conical foot. The decorative motives are
on the whole sparse and undistinguished, as often as not just a horizontal
zigzag or wiggle, although the stirrup jars can still have elaborate linear
decoration on the shoulder, and the potters were perfectly capable of
imaginative effort, as in the two confronted Cretan goats on a small krater,
with two ships on the other side (Fig. 23).

One further decorative motive may be added to the list, compass-drawn
circles and semicircles, and here we come to the Athenian side of it. Full
circles appear regularly on the shoulders of neck-handled amphorae (not
semicircles, as would be the rule in Athens), on kraters, and occasionally on
kalathoi. Semicircles are extremely rare, and may indeed not have been

used before the ninth century, as for example pendent ones on a very late stirrup jar, and a frieze of alternating standing and pendent sets on a fine large krater from Ayios Ioannis.

There seems to be no other decorative feature attributable to Athens, but its influence can be observed in the neck-handled amphora, with the handles to the neck instead of to the lip, as was the earlier tradition; it can also be seen in the neck profile of some of the belly-handled amphorae, and it seems very likely to me that the general elongation of the closed vases had its origin in the typical Athenian ovoid profile.

On the whole, however, the debt to Athens was slight and rather grudging, and on this evidence it could be questioned whether it came directly from Athens at all. The answer to this is provided by four imported vases found in two tombs of the Fortetsa cemetery. One of them, a belly-handled amphora having on the shoulder sets of semicircles with triangle filling, did not come from Athens, but the other three, two skyphoi with high conical foot and circles flanking a cross-hatched panel, and a lekythos with cross-hatched triangles on the shoulder, certainly did. The lekythos is Late Protogeometric, and so presumably are the skyphoi; as a group they not only prove that the influence on the local pottery came from Athens, but also ensure a tenth-century date for its appearance. One can perhaps go further, and suggest that the time was early rather than late in this century, as there is no evidence for the last phase of Athenian Protogeometric, such as has been found in many areas; nor indeed did the Early Geometric developments have any effect on Crete. But, as at Lefkandi, what elements they incorporated they retained in use for a long time.

Another possible or probable connexion with Athens may serve as an introduction to the types of object other than pottery. The link appears in the clay beads with variously incised decorations found in both areas. Only two are known from the Fortetsa cemetery, but some two hundred and fifty were found in one of the tombs of the Ayios Ioannis group; and they are very close to those which were specially fashionable in some Late Protogeometric tombs in Athens, there in conjunction with hand-made vases and figurines of the same technique (pp. 142 ff.). Similar beads, as we shall see, were found in other parts of Crete, but are almost unknown elsewhere.[4] At first sight, it would seem likely that this type of bead came from Athens to Crete, particularly as there were some in Athens in contexts earlier than Late Protogeometric. As, however, similar beads were found in the Sub-Minoan tomb Π (p. 116), whose vases show no trace of the influence of the Athenian pottery style, it would be safer to leave the question of origin open.

The weapons I shall discuss below. For other artefacts (Pl. 53 and Figs. 24, 25) we have the following picture. Of bronze, four fibulae and several dress pins and finger rings; an armlet and a belt; three shallow bowls and a cauldron; and a tripod stand with a cauldron that fitted on to it. Of iron, several dress pins. Of gold, two pins and a dozen rings; five beads with spiral grooves forming part of a necklace; pieces of foil and leaf, in-

[4] Others have been found at Eleusis, and perhaps Lindos and Delos.

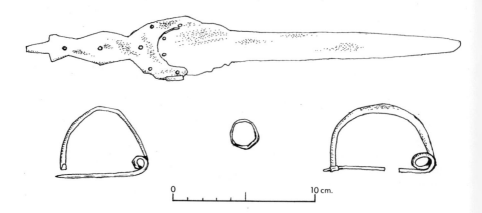

FIG. 24 KNOSSOS, AYIOS IOANNIS TOMB VIII
Dagger, fibulae and ring. *BSA* 55, p. 141, fig. 9, nos. 16–19.

cluding a small shell covered with gold leaf. Of silver, two finger rings. Of lead, a small figurine of a lion. Of ivory, a pendant and part of a pinhead. Of faience, a ring and two necklaces. Of bone, two pins.

Considering the relatively small number of burials and the period under review, this is an astonishing collection. It is clear that bronze was in reasonable supply, and so presumably was gold; and the silver rings are the only known examples of objects of this metal throughout the Dark Ages.[5] Some objects are of a type one would expect: the fibulae, where verifiable, were of the simple arched type; the dress pins, though short, have the bulb and small head known elsewhere – but no examples of the Athenian speciality, with iron shank and head and bronze bulb. Others, such as the lion of lead, the bronze tripod stand and cauldron, the ivory pendant and the faience ring and necklaces, certainly or probably came from the east Mediterranean. And the gold-covered shell shows the special, though obscure, importance attached to these objects, found in tombs elsewhere in Greece and the Aegean. In general, one gets the impression of flourishing communities in peaceful contact at least with Athens and the Aegean to the north, and to the east with the Levant. The one disadvantage, and it is a serious one, is that we cannot determine to which part of the tenth century they belong, though it is reasonably certain that some come from the middle rather than the end of it.

This outwardly peaceful picture may have to be modified in the light of the weapons the graves contained, since several tombs produced one or more of them (Fig. 24 shows a dagger). Except for a spearhead of bronze, all were of iron; it is not easy to distinguish what is what, for in two or three

[5] But not entirely unexpected, in view of the evidence at Argos and Thorikos for the extraction of this metal (pp. 159, 162).

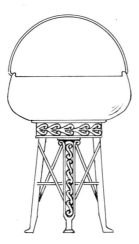

FIG. 25 Knossos, Fortetsa tomb XI
Cauldron and stand; ·24 m. *Fortetsa*, pl. 138.

cases there was just a corroded mass of iron, but there were three swords, and a fairly large number of spearheads and pikes. Of these, particular interest attaches to the pikes: they are long weapons, rectangular in section, of a type peculiar to Cyprus, and there known only within Cypro-Geometric I, in other words *c.* 1050–950 B.C. Almost certainly imported from Cyprus, they are a clear witness to the continuation, if not strengthening, of links between the two islands, and in consequence it is likely that a number of the other objects mentioned above also came from Cyprus.

The three tombs in the south of Crete, two from the Phaestos area and one from Gortyn, can be dealt with more briefly. The number of vases is fairly large – two dozen from Mulino, nearly eighty from Petrokephali (Pl. 54 shows a few), and an unspecified but obviously considerable quantity from the many cremation urns in the tholos tomb of Gortyn. The period covered is, I would say, the tenth century and the first half of the ninth. Generally speaking, the Sub-Minoan and Protogeometric elements are the same as those found in the Knossos area: in other words, there is the same persistent background of tradition, and the acceptance of Athenian Protogeometric features follows the same pattern; there must therefore have been close links between north and south central Crete. The homo-geneity is particularly impressive in the kraters of all sizes – not only the miniature bell-kraters, which become standard equipment throughout Crete – in the pyxides with collar necks, in the cups with their curious bi-partite dipped technique, and the stirrup jars. There are of course a number of individual pieces,[6] but they do not affect the general picture.

[6] Note particularly a krater with associated stand from Petrokephali: its decoration, more elaborate than is normal, is surprisingly close to a vase of not unsimilar shape from Modi in west Crete (see p. 234).

PLATE 53 KNOSSOS (AYIOS IOANNIS)
A) Gold and silver rings, tomb V. *BSA* 55, pl. 39.
B) Necklace, tomb V. *BSA* 55, pl. 39.
C) Stirrup jar, tomb V. *BSA* 55, pl. 38.
D) Cup, tomb VIII. *BSA* 55, pl. 36.
E) Stirrup jar, tomb VIII. *BSA* 55, pl. 37.

As already stated, Protogeometric features were adopted or adapted in
very much the same way as in the north of Crete. Additional points worthy
of note are the use of semicircles on the shoulders of several of the Mulino
vases (a motive almost entirely disregarded in the north), and the presence
of a trefoil-lipped oinochoe at Gortyn, whose shape is closer to the Athenian
type than any other in Crete. There were also, as in the north, a few instances of pendent semicircles: one is tempted to suggest contact with the
Euboeo-north Cycladic area of the early ninth century,[7] but one cannot
be sure. Finally, among the few hand-made vases was a small one with
incised circles and vertical lines (Pl. 54), in the same technique as the beads
found at Knossos (p. 229); since the tomb in which this vase was found also
contained beads, it seems likely that they too were of the same type.

With regard to finds other than pottery, objects intended for personal
use or decoration were disappointingly few: a bronze violin-bow fibula
from Mulino and the beads from Petrokephali, mentioned above, seem to
be about all. Weapons, on the other hand, were as plentiful as in the

[7] A low-footed skyphos with pendent semicircles was found in a tomb near Knossos, published
by Payne.

PLATE 54 PETROKEPHALI. Selection of vases from a tomb. *Ann.* 19–20 (N.S.), 358, fig. 216.

Knossos area; they are all of iron, and include swords and spears. As well as these, a number of iron tools were found in the tholos tomb at Gortyn.

So much for the main sites of central Crete, in the sense of those known to us by excavation and publication. There are however others, of varying importance, which help to fill in the picture of occupation. Half a dozen have been identified in the central plain near Heraklion or along the northern coast, and no doubt there are many more. The evidence is mostly of the cemetery type; all burials, so far as is known, were in chamber tombs, and the only certain instance of the manner of burial was cremation – this at Tylissos, south-west of Heraklion, the burnt bones being placed in a hemispherical bronze bowl, and the other finds consisting of a stirrup jar, two fibulae (one of a type that can hardly precede the late tenth century), and two pieces of iron which probably belonged to a small knife. The vases from the various tombs were all of the kind that one finds in the Knossos area.

The only settlement close to Heraklion, Amnisos, has not been published in full, but there seems no doubt that it was occupied throughout this period. There is also another settlement, Kalochorio Pedhiados, about fifteen miles further east and a little inland, reported to have been occupied in the tenth and early ninth centuries.

One would expect some evidence along the main ancient route from Knossos to the south, and this there is. Reports of Protogeometric material have come from Arkhanais and from a site to the south-east of it. To the south-west of Arkhanais, and on the old road leading to the Mesara, a tomb group from Kanli Kastelli contained a high-footed skyphos of Athenian fabric, the southernmost export from Athens yet known. High in the hills above the southern plain, the sanctuary of Prinias was probably in continuous use from the twelfth century onwards, and a stray krater from a tomb in the vicinity was painted by the same potter as made a krater found at Petrokephali. And some of the vases from the tholos tombs of Kourtais, in the foothills not far from Gortyn, could belong to the tenth century, though most are much later.

Finally, a brief note may be made of the tholos tombs at Rotasi, in the eastern sector of the Mesara, which are reported to have contained vases of this period; but these may go rather with east Crete.

West Crete

Our detailed information is confined to one site only, that of Modi, west of Canea, where a group of tombs was excavated. Several types of tomb were in use, as there is record of two rock-cut chamber tombs, a burial under an overhanging rock, four rectangular shafts, and isolated pithos burials; and both inhumation and cremation seem to have been practised.

Of nearly eighty vases over half were either of the miniature bell-krater type, dipped and the lower half unpainted, or a rather similar shape but with vertical handles from belly to lip and decorated rather differently. This latter shape is probably derived from a much larger vase, of which one has a high flaring foot and the other two the favourite Cretan flat base; it is one of these whose decoration, a pattern of opposed curves set vertically, is so closely paralleled at Petrokephali near Phaestos – a motive also found on two other large vases. Other shapes include pyxides with ribbon handles, cups, oinochoai, jugs, pithoi, an amphora and two four-handled vases. Decorative motives, apart from that already mentioned, are most prolific on the larger vases, usually combinations of cross-hatched triangles and diamonds in panels or in series. Compass-drawn circles were found on only one vase.

As well as the pottery there were other finds, including a number of bronze fibulae, one of which was of the arched type, and iron tools. And once again, just as in central Crete, there were many weapons of iron.

The chief difficulty is the date of these tombs and their contents, whether in relation to one another, or in relation to the material from the rest of Crete. The internal chronology will, it is hoped, be cleared up in the final publication; as to external links, there is no doubt that the potters were aware of developments in central Crete, from the popularity of the little bell-kraters, but the decoration is often highly individual. My impression is that, though some of the vases belong to the tenth century, most would fit more comfortably into the ninth. In this case, the Athenian style will have made no impact on this part of Crete; but were there no connexions with any other areas? The decoration seems to be unrelated to any either preceding or contemporaneous Cretan style (admittedly we know nothing of earlier stages in this part of the island), and looks closer, for example, to that of the Argolid, though in this case neither the typical shapes nor the Athenian influence on this district find any echo at Modi. Perhaps we may find a clue in south or west Peloponnese or even in Kephallenia, when we come to know more about these areas.

East Crete

Since the persistence of the Sub-Minoan style of pottery into the ninth century makes it often impossible to distinguish between the eleventh and tenth-century evidence, little need be added to what has been said in the earlier section (pp. 116 ff.). Pride of place was given to the site of Karphi, but it is reasonable to suppose that it must have been abandoned, if not in the eleventh century, at latest in the early tenth. Of the other sites, only four were discussed in any detail, the five tholos tombs of Panayia, the single tomb of Dreros, the settlement and cemetery of Vrokastro and the tombs of Kavousi. A bare mention was made of tholos tombs and a cave burial covering four sites in the Seteia district. In addition to these, there are two tholos tombs reported as Protogeometric, from Kritsa, west of Ayios Nikolaos.

In contrast to central Crete, the prevalent custom was to use tholos tombs, though there are cave burials in the Seteia district. Inhumation, also, was the normal manner of burial; cremation was not unknown – in particular there are the cremations, together with inhumations, at Vrokastro, and evidently there were instances of this practice at Berati near Seteia – but it was far less common than inhumation.[8]

One of the chief negative features of the pottery is the near complete absence of any sign of Athenian Protogeometric influence. An amphora from Vrokastro has a Protogeometric look, but it almost certainly belongs to the ninth century. The only two vases which both appear to be in the Protogeometric tradition and may belong to the tenth century come from a tomb at Kavousi, as yet unpublished; so there may not have been a complete isolation, nor was there from central Crete, for the miniature bell-kraters, found in some quantity, prove that there was a link. In general, however, the pottery was simply a survival and extension of the earlier Sub-Minoan style.

As to the other objects, mention has already been made of the iron weapons of Panayia, of the fibulae, rings, dress pin, knives, and spearhead

[8] There are also the cremations of the cemetery of Olous, on the bay of Mirabello, but the material is rather puzzling, and I have omitted any discussion of it.

from Vrokastro,[9] and of the fibulae and iron weapons found at Kavousi (p. 117). For the rest, the Kritsa tholos tombs contained bronze fibulae and pins, and some iron tools; and many fibulae are recorded from the tombs in the Seteia district, as well as necklaces with beads of glass paste or cornelian, dress pins, two gold rings, and weapons mostly of iron. Just how many of these fall within the tenth or even early ninth centuries, as opposed to the periods before or after, one cannot say, but obviously some must. One is entitled to draw attention once more to the prevalence of weapons, but that is about all.

Summary

The geography of Crete, with its three great ranges, the White Mountains, Ida, and Dicte, encourages separateness but does not enforce it, except perhaps for certain areas along the south coast. Communication by sea is always possible in reasonable weather, nor do the mountains constitute an insuperable land barrier. The tripartite division I have made in the preceding discussion does nevertheless seem to reflect the actual state of affairs during this period, even allowing for the poverty and unsatis-factoriness of our evidence. Greater knowledge may no doubt reveal further subdivisions, and on the other hand it will also probably show that the distinctions already made are less clear-cut than originally supposed, but I do not think it will lead to an obliteration of these divisions.

The material from the west is the most slender and unsatisfactory, as it is confined to a single cemetery of uncertain date at Modi in the distant plain of Chania.[10] There are no other sites (except Eleutherna, a few miles to the east of Rethymno, the reports from which are in no way illuminating) until the central region is reached, nearly a hundred miles to the east. Nothing can be deduced from the tombs themselves, which are varied, nor from the burial customs, and we have to depend entirely on what is known of the style of pottery. Here it is evident that we have something entirely different, at least in the system of decoration, from that current in other parts of Crete, and for whose ultimate source we might even have to look outside the island. This is the only evidence that western Crete was culturally separate from the other regions, but it also contains the proof that there was no complete isolation, since the distinctive miniature bell-kraters were as popular here as in the rest of Crete (but never found outside it), and there is also the remarkable similarity in decoration between certain of the vases of Modi and one found at Petrokephali in south central Crete.

As opposed to the west, the central and eastern regions are much better known, and the distinctions between the two seem valid both on internal and external grounds. On internal grounds we can set the use of chamber

[9] To which must be added a bronze tripod stand, similar to the one found at Knossos, probably of the late tenth century, and presumably showing contact with Cyprus.

[10] There have been reports of settlement and tomb material at Vrises, not far from Modi, but details are lacking.

tombs and cremation in central Crete against the tholos tombs and in-humation of east Crete. Both criteria need qualification: tholos tombs are known in southern central Crete, perhaps not earlier than the late tenth century; there are instances of inhumation in central Crete, in the Knossos area, and of cremation in the east, not only at Vrokastro but at Olous and on one site in the Seteia district. But on the whole these seem to be excep-tions to the general pattern, a pattern in which centre and east go separate ways. Then there is the pottery of the two regions: in both there is the common Sub-Minoan tradition, and both have the small bell-kraters mentioned above, developed during the tenth century and constituting a definite link;[11] but there is a substantial difference in that the Late Proto-geometric style of Athens had a clear influence throughout central Crete but only a minimal effect in the east. This concerns not only the internal situation, in that the style developed in the centre of the island was not transmitted to the east, but also the external, in that direct contact with Athens, as confirmed in central Crete by imported vases, is not reflected in the eastern areas. One must naturally be cautious in making deductions based on this, both because of the relative lack of evidence and because the failure of Athenian pottery to attract imitation or adaptation in any particular area does not prove that there was no contact with that area; but at the same time, it has a bearing on the attitude of receptiveness, and in this east Crete was much less receptive than central Crete.

Athenian products were not the only external ones to reach Crete: one must also take into account the links with the east Mediterranean, parti-cularly Cyprus. So far, interestingly, there has been little further trace of the ceramic interconnexions which are to be found in the eleventh century, and we have to turn to other types of object. For these, northern central Crete (but not the southern area, so far as I know) offers a good deal of evidence – the bronze tripod stand with its associated cauldron, perhaps some of the other bronze vessels, the iron pikes, the lead lion, the objects of faience and ivory; eastern Crete, on the other hand, can only produce the bronze tripod stand and the faience from Vrokastro. Can this evidence be used to support the idea that the communities of east Crete were on the whole unreceptive to contacts from outside? Hardly so, for on the one hand the evidence from Vrokastro proves that these contacts did exist, and on the other hand we have no detailed information as to the nature of the finds on the remainder of the sites.

There are then many instances where one has to admit to uncertainty, and it is clear that east Crete was isolated neither from the outside world nor from central Crete; even so, there are differences between east and centre – but it would be dangerous to speculate on what they meant.

Putting aside the divisions, what else can be said? In the context of the general picture of the late Dark Ages in Greece and the Aegean probably the most significant feature of Crete, as particularly exemplified in the finds from the Knossos area, is precisely the links with the east Mediterranean – a feature which it shares with the Dodecanese (pp. 174 ff.) but which seems

[11] Beads with incised decoration were also found in east Crete: this is surely an internal rather than an external link.

to be absent until the end of the tenth century from the regions to the north, the central Aegean, and the Greek mainland. But here again a note of warning should perhaps be sounded: I have throughout spoken of tenth-century Crete, but it is extremely difficult, if not impossible, to decide whereabouts in this century objects belong, and I could not prove, for example, that any of the objects which show links with the east Mediterranean precede the late tenth century. On the other hand, given the history of continuous contact with Cyprus at least from *c.* 1100 B.C., the probability is that there was no break. If there was a break it was rather in the discontinuity of influence of either pottery style over the other.

What then of the contacts between Crete and the regions to its north? In the eleventh century these were illustrated, so it would seem (p. 119) only by the dress pins and fibulae; there is no other comparative material, and it is possible that for a while, though there is no reason therefore to conclude that there was any lack of communication, neither area had any effect on the other. During the tenth century, the borrowing was mostly from Athens and in particular from its widely diffused style of pottery, thus replacing the slight Cypriot influence of the eleventh century.[12] The incised beads may also be another instance of a tangible connexion, but the interpretation is a little difficult, as we have seen (p. 229). The popularity of cremation as the burial custom of central Crete in this period, is not, however, attributable to contacts with Athens; the earlier instances, and its use in areas where there seems to have been no link with Athens, rule out this idea – nor is the manner of cremation similar, in the sense that while in Athens certain vase shapes only were used as the urns, and the accompanying vases were placed outside it, in Crete a variety of vessels, and not only of clay, could be used, and vases as well as other funeral gifts could be placed in the urn.

Besides this, the Cretans may have been, and probably were, in contact with other areas of the Aegean – there is some slight evidence for this. But whatever happened, they seem always to have been the receivers, never the givers.

Internally the picture – at least that provided by central Crete – is one of peaceful and fairly flourishing co-existence, with possibly an increase in the population. This one can deduce from the way in which Protogeometric features spread from the north to the south (the natural direction, confirmed by the distribution of imported vases – four near Knossos, one at Kanli Kastelli in the centre, none yet in the Mesara), and to a certain extent from the number and geographical position of the settlements involved. Is it, though, consonant with the one phenomenon common to the whole of Crete, the relatively large number of weapons deposited in tombs? Surely this implies some preoccupation with war, either internally or externally? This is a difficult question. It is true that a few of the sites in east Crete were located in easily defensible positions, but this is not universally the case,

---

[12] It will be pointed out that the Mycenaean influence on the local pottery in the twelfth century was explained in terms of actual intrusion. In this case the technical excellence of the Athenian pottery is sufficiently good reason for its partial adoption.

nor should it apply to central Crete, where intercommunication was apparently both easy and frequent. Was there any fear of attack from outside? There is no evidence for it, and a reasonable amount of evidence against it. I would suggest that the simplest explanation for a prevalence of weapons lies in the nature of the Cretan himself – an independent and a wary man, always ready to resist any intrusion on his rights, and to take vengeance should they be violated. The existence of some measure of internal dissension cannot be ruled out.

Finally, a point which deserves stressing. In spite of the divisions within the island, it must be thought of as a single entity, and as such a unit it was inward, not outward, looking. It did not cut itself off from the outside world, but the movement of ideas and people and objects was, at any rate during this century, always towards Crete and never away from it. It was becoming entirely self-sufficient, relatively unconcerned with what people were doing elsewhere. And these were characteristics which it was to retain for many centuries.

15 The Western Regions and Laconia

So far, the districts I have discussed have been those which bordered on the Aegean; and furthermore, their outlook and interests were linked with each other through the Aegean. They comprise the main part of the inhabited Greek world, but not quite all. The remainder will be discussed in this section, their chief characteristic being that they look elsewhere than to the Aegean. Laconia is the first of these districts – rather surprisingly, as it has an Aegean seaboard; then I deal with Ithaca, with Aetolia, and thirdly with the whole of the western Peloponnese, regions which may be expected to have a non-Aegean outlook. Certain districts I have to pass over, as producing either nothing during the later Dark Ages, or so little that it has no value – such are Arcadia, Kephallenia and others of the Ionian islands, and north-west Greece as a whole. Those I deal with can hardly be said to constitute any sort of a unity, but there is some evidence that they had dealings with one another, and this may justify the treatment of the whole area as a very loose whole.

Laconia

In the survey of the early Dark Ages it was unfortunately necessary to admit that there was no material of any sort, from settlement, tomb, or sanctuary, or even from surface investigation, from anywhere within this district. To suppose a complete blank in habitation would be unnecessary and unrealistic – what, for example, would we know of Euboea without Lefkandi, only recently excavated? In Laconia itself, in fact, there is the site of Amyklai where we know from the literary sources that the earlier god Hyakinthos continued to be worshipped into historical times; and yet there is no archaeological evidence between the L.H. III C material of the twelfth century and the later artefacts which, as we shall see, can hardly precede 1000 B.C. As there was continuity of worship, what has happened to the offerings of the early Dark Ages? Which of course suggests another side to the problem: can we be sure that we would recognise what we are looking for? However, with sanctuaries there are other possibilities; at Amyklai worship might for some time have taken the form of simple libations, in which case nothing would have survived.

The site of Amyklai also provides our main evidence for the later Dark Ages. The material, it must be stressed, did not come from an actual sanctuary building, as none such was recovered either for the latest

Mycenaean period or for the Dark Ages; it consisted of pottery and other objects which had either been thrown away from the sanctuary or had in course of time been washed down the hill on which the temple stood. There is a definite stratum, fairly thick, and this contained not only the late Dark Age material, but some Mycenaean pottery and figurines as well.

Both in the pottery and in the types of votive offering the late Dark Age shows a very sharp contrast with Mycenaean times. Whereas in the twelfth century they dedicated clay figurines of goddesses or worshippers and animals, in the tenth century or later the offerings were of metal, including two spearheads of bronze.

As to the pottery,[1] the great bulk came from open vases, skyphoi either shallow with flaring lip or deep with a high, vertical lip and prominent belly, and kraters and cups related in shape to the deep skyphoi. In these, and on the closed vases as well, the use of horizontal grooves to mark the distinction of lip and body, or some zone of decoration, is a prominent feature not found elsewhere. As to the decoration, the cups and a few of the skyphoi seem to have been completely painted over, but for the most part use was made of the panel system, and the cross-hatched motive was almost universal, triangles, rectangles, and diamonds, with just very occasional sets of concentric circles (no semicircles were found), always very cramped and generally only three or four circles to each unit.

In contrast to the open vases, closed shapes were rare – a miniature hydria with cross-hatched triangles (the only complete vase), and a few sherds of jugs and trefoil-lipped oinochoai. These, as I have said, share with the open vases the propensity for grooves; and there is another common feature as well for most of them, a very lustrous metallic-looking black to black-brown paint.[2]

So far, the whole style, though it embodies features and motives found outside Laconia, is extremely individual and has no obvious links with any other yet discussed. The same may be said of the two vases,[3] a hydria and a neck-handled amphora, recovered from Mavrovouni, near Gythion (the chief harbour of Laconia). Most of the pottery from the sanctuary areas of Sparta was also of the same type as that of Amyklai, but two pieces are different, a sherd of a skyphos with band enclosing a zigzag between the handles, and a trefoil-lipped oinochoe with conical foot, painted over except for two sets of sharp-angled zigzags on the upper part of the belly. The latter vase recalls a shape popular in Athens and elsewhere at the end of Protogeometric and in Early Geometric; the sherd reflects rather the kind of Protogeometric ware found in the Argolid, and in both cases the influence may have come from that area.

In this discussion of the pottery I have moved away from Amyklai to two other sites, Sparta and Mavrovouni. And in fact, apart from surface sherds on two other sites, this is the sum of the material known. And it is

---

[1] Pl. 55 shows sherds from Amyklai and Sparta.

[2] Most of the sherds with the circle motive do not have this metallic lustre.

[3] With them was associated a piece of an iron weapon, probably a spear, and there is little doubt that they formed part of the contents of a tomb.

PLATE 55 LACONIA. Sherds from Amyklai and Sparta. *PGP*, pl. 38, 1–9.

not only the lack of material that is remarkable: not a single tomb, except
the presumed one near Gythion, has been identified; and, except for this
and for the two sites known only from surface investigation, all the material
seems to have come from sanctuaries.

There is also a serious problem of chronology, and to explain this
we must return to Amyklai. Above the stratum which contained the
Mycenaean pottery and what has been called Laconian Protogeometric
there was another with Geometric pottery, and this cannot be dated to
before the second half of the ninth century, and indeed the earliest material is
probably much closer to 800 than to 850 B.C. And this picture is confirmed
by the evidence from Sparta. This means that a good deal of the pottery discussed above, ascribed to the late Dark Ages, falls outside the Dark Ages
altogether, according to the criteria adopted in this book, and belongs to the
ninth century. It could even be argued, on the grounds that the style is
hardly likely to have remained unchanged for more than two generations,
that it belonged entirely within the ninth century. The trouble is that not
only is this style completely divorced from any Mycenaean antecedents, it is
also isolated from other contemporaneous styles. The only clue seems to

be the use of the concentric circles, as combined with cross-hatched panels, suggesting possible contact with the end of Athenian Protogeometric. But even here there is no certainty, as the concentric circles still figure in the subsequent Geometric, and the system of cross-hatched panelling need not, I feel, necessarily be related to any tenth-century source in the Aegean area. On the whole, it is likely that this Laconian style did go back into the tenth century, and so into the Dark Ages, but I would not be at all confident that any of it is earlier than 950 B.C.

Assuming that some of the material falls within the Dark Ages, the conclusion must be that Laconia as a whole may have been relatively isolated from any contact with the Aegean – an isolation that covered not only the late Dark Ages but apparently much of the ninth century as well. Links even with the Argolid seem to have been slight. As will be seen, there could be connexions with other areas of the Peloponnese, but this is a matter better left till their evidence has been discussed.

Ithaca

We have seen that in Laconia, slight and unsatisfactory though the evidence is, we have moved rather outside the Aegean orbit, into a different world which resisted whatever the Aegean had to offer culturally not only during the Dark Ages generally, but even, it appears, deep down into the ninth century; to find common ground is exceedingly difficult.

North and west, and so further away from the Aegean, it may be expected that the same conditions will hold, unless it be found that the sea routes westward through the Corinthian Gulf facilitated the expansion of ideas as the Aegean undoubtedly did. This, however, did not happen until the eighth century, long after the end of the Dark Ages. The whole region of the west Peloponnese and of the islands that adjoin it, and of what we know of north-west Greece, remained isolated – and yet still an integral part of the Greek world.

The evidence so far available is slight and patchy in the extreme, and the corresponding problems of interpretation considerable, very much in the same way as in Laconia. There are nevertheless sufficient interconnexions within it – and indeed occasionally with Laconia, to merit a discussion of the area as a whole. There is no logical or ideal system of proceeding, but it will probably be clearest first to deal with that district where we have a certain link both with the earlier Mycenaean, and with later developments as evidenced by renewed contact with the Aegean – that is to say, the island of Ithaca. As was seen in an earlier section (p. 88) the material came principally from the sites of Polis in the north and Aetos in the centre, and was almost exclusively confined to pottery, the style evolved being the natural outcome of the local twelfth-century ware, as found in Ithaca and in the neighbouring island of Kephallenia. The settlements, that of Aetos overlapping and succeeding the deposit of the Polis cave, then provide witness of continuous occupation until the first substantial renewal of

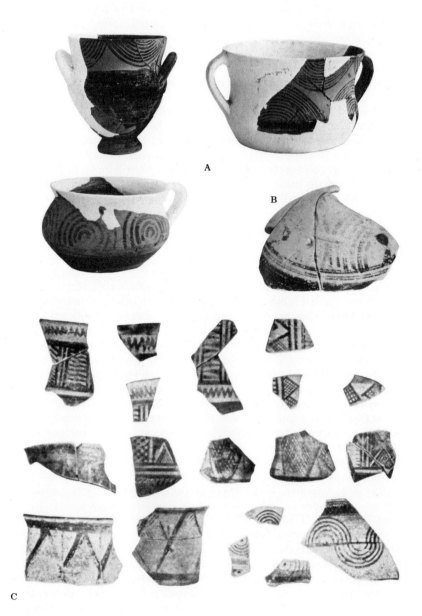

PLATE 56 ITHACA, AETOS
A) Open vases. *GGP*, pl. 47 *a–c*.
B) Fragment of lekythos. *PGP*, pl. 37, 84
C) Sherds. *PGP*, pl. 37, 19–35.

contacts with the Aegean world in the shape of Corinthian pottery; as, however, this did not occur till after 800 B.C., we are faced with an even longer interval than in Laconia. Once again, all we have is the pottery (apart from fragments of four violin-bow fibulae of twisted bronze wire which should surely belong somewhere within the Dark Ages), and so it is on an analysis of this that we depend for a picture of a very long period indeed, of some two hundred and fifty years.

The open vases (see Pl. 56) are in the majority, as is usually the case in settlements, and the most distinctive of these are the kantharoi, in other words bowls with two vertical handles. The feet are conical or flaring; the bodies have a characteristic double curve, the concave element, rising to the lip, being offset by the handles. A few of these vases were painted over except for a reserved band round the belly (probably the earliest), but the more favoured system was cross-hatched triangles or diamonds, occasionally panelled, right up to the lip or at least covering the shoulder area. Concentric circles and semicircles are found, but are not common.

With these may go the high one-handled cups with rather similar but straighter profile. An early one has a low foot and is painted over except for a reserved band enclosing a zigzag round the belly (a late Mycenaean motive which is known in the twelfth-century tombs of Kephallenia), but later ones can have the elaborate rectilinear decoration.

As well as these cups, there is a rather shallow, squat type with flat base. The lower body, and sometimes the whole, is painted over, but the outer rim may have a zigzag (a motive normally associated with Athenian Proto-geometric cups, these however being of an entirely different shape), and one cup has concentric semicircles on the shoulder.

Deep bowls or skyphoi can be divided into two types: one is close to the late Mycenaean deep bowl, and tends to be monochrome, but the other is tall and has a very high flaring-lip unit, the outer part of which may be decorated with pendent concentric loops, hand-drawn.

There are also a few krater fragments with well-moulded rims and ridges, usually horizontal handles, and low feet or flat bases; the decoration is generally panelled and rectilinear, but there are a few instances of the use of concentric circles or semicircles.

Finally of the open vases there are the kylikes, the descendants of a local late Mycenaean shape, with triangular bodies and usually with heavily ridged stems. As a rule banded, there may be, exceptionally, a series of zones of decoration, cross-hatched triangles and zigzags. They would seem to be more common at Polis than at Aetos.

Of the closed vases, the large jugs are the most significant (Pl. 57). The lower body was usually painted over, but the shoulder was decorated, and so also at times was the neck. The same combinations of cross-hatched triangles and diamonds, fringes, vertical zigzags, and double-axe motives, in series or in panels, are to be observed as on the kantharoi and kraters, though there are one or two examples of the use of concentric semicircles.

This brief account must suffice for what can be called the Ithacan Proto-geometric style, the only pottery series in the west of Greece to have a recognisable predecessor, in local Late Mycenaean III C, and successor, in the eighth-century Geometric pottery of Corinth as adapted to the native style. In spite of this advantage, its relative stylistic progress is not easy to interpret.

That its creation owed nothing to Aegean developments is clear enough; many shapes and most of the rectilinear motives (singly and in complexes) find parallels in the Kephallenian tombs as well as in earlier contexts in Ithaca itself. There is admittedly nothing like the kantharos in Kephallenia, but the idea could have derived from the large vertical-handled kraters – there seems nowhere else from where it might have come. The conical feet that are a feature do not need to have been imported from Athens, as they were already developing locally at an earlier stage. Nor is it necessary to look to the Argolid for the origin of the occasional Granary class motive of a wavy line encased within a reserved panel, as that had made its way to Kephallenia by the late twelfth century (and we have seen how remarkable a distribution it had over the Aegean world and outside it). Definition as Protogeometric as opposed to Mycenaean is not easy, but can be expressed negatively by the disappearance of certain shapes, notably the stirrup jar, and decorative motives such as spirals, and positively by the rather sharper and different contours of certain vases, and especially by the more elaborate use of the rectilinear motives – as opposed, for example, to Lefkandi where the similar stage saw the general repression of decoration: in Ithaca they were not afraid to build on their past.

The inception of the style was, then, purely local. And the impression is that the further development was to a great extent that of native ideas. If it were entirely so, then we should have considerable difficulty in relating it to contemporaneous styles in other parts of the Greek world. Fortunately, however, the appearance of compass-drawn concentric circles and semi-circles shows that there was no complete isolation during the later Dark Ages of the tenth century, and that this technical innovation, which exercised so extraordinary an attraction on all who came to know of it, made its way to Ithaca.[4] But nothing else much was adopted – unless just possibly the zigzag on the outer rim of cups, and the chequer-board motive – and there was no attempt to use the circles in the way that the Athenians would have done. Nor do they seem to have introduced any vase shapes from other areas; the absence of most of the characteristic Athenian Protogeometric vase types surely proves that the Aegean had no particular impact on this part of the Greek world.

It appears to me that the compass-drawn circles and semicircles were introduced during the tenth century rather than later,[5] but the Ithacan Protogeometric style persisted throughout the ninth, and once again there was little borrowing, it seems, from any area of the Aegean. The only feature I can suggest is that of applying decoration to the neck of jugs.

[4] How did it arrive? Obviously by sea, but through the Corinthian Gulf or all the way round the Peloponnese? I favour the latter, on the Messenian evidence (pp. 250 ff.).

[5] The presence of part of an imported lekythos, with semicircles and hour-glass filling on the shoulder, strongly supports this (Pl. 56).

So far, I have stressed that Ithaca had very little to do with the Aegean. That does not mean, however, that it had few links with areas closer at hand. There was, indeed, as will be seen, a fairly close ceramic relationship with Aetolia and certain areas of the west Peloponnese, at least during the ninth century and perhaps even during the tenth, though the further back one tries to go the more difficult it is to identify such links.

To start with, there are just a few points of contact between Ithacan pottery and that of Laconia. This is visible not in the shapes (we know far too little about Laconia), but in the decoration, in particular in the popularity of the closely packed cross-hatched motives, and in one or two small but significant details. There is a greater family resemblance between Laconian and Ithacan Protogeometric than between the former and any Aegean style, and it must indicate the direction in which those who inhabited the Spartan plain looked, but one must be careful not to overstress this, and also to remember that the evidence from Laconia is most unlikely, as we have it, to precede the tenth century – and perhaps mostly belongs to the ninth.

These connexions may serve to tie up ends left loose in Laconia. As well as this, however, and of greater immediate importance, the Ithacan pottery style can be used as a spring-board from which to launch into the districts of Aetolia and the west Peloponnese: the latter districts must surely have served as intermediary between Ithaca and Laconia.

These districts, then, comprise Aetolia, Achaea, Elis, and Messenia (including Triphylia), and I shall deal with them in that order, not the most satisfactory chronologically speaking, but the best to illustrate the links with Ithaca. In them the type of evidence reverts to that to which one has become almost too accustomed, tombs and their contents.

Aetolia

Evidence from this region has so far been limited to the coast, specifically the Gulf of Kanali and two sites on it. The material is thus slight, but what there is, is of interest.

At Calydon a pithos burial was found, containing a tall kantharos, a shape very close to those of Derveni in Achaea (discussed in detail on p. 249), and also related to Ithacan shapes.

Secondly, an unknown number of pithos burials were discovered at Kaloyeriko, a few miles west of Calydon. The one vase illustrated is a fine krater, with horizontal side handles but otherwise similar in shape to the tall kantharoi. Its decoration, a panelled complex of vertical fringes and zigzags, and cross-hatched diamonds and triangles, all supported by a zigzag band, is precisely the sort of thing typical of Ithaca and Derveni in Achaea (see Pl. 57). Other vases not illustrated included oinochoai, amphoriskoi, skyphoi, and cups. Also, it is reported that bronze fibulae and dress pins, and a bracelet, were found: the types are not yet divulged, but could be very important for comparative and dating purposes; there is only

A   B

PLATE 57
A) Oinochoe from Derveni. *GGP*, pl. 48*j*.
B) Lekythos from Aetos. *GGP*, pl. 47*f*.

one comparable group in this area, that from somewhere in the north
Peloponnese (see p. 250).

Achaea and Elis

The most obvious link between Ithaca and the west Peloponnese is that
shown (Pl. 57) on the one hand by a jug from Aetos in Ithaca and on the
other a trefoil-lipped oinochoe from a pithos burial at Derveni in Achaea,
not far inland from Aigion, on the south shore of the Gulf of Corinth. The
details and system of the decoration on the respective shoulders of these
vases are remarkably similar.[6]

In addition to the oinochoe, there were eleven other vases associated
with the Derveni burial (Pl. 58). The one hand-made jug needs no further
comment, though it is interesting to find such a vase in company with the
wheel-made. The skyphos with low foot and reserved bands empanelled
between the handles may recall one or two Corinthian vases of the early
ninth century; on the other hand, a bowl with high pedestal foot has been
thought to be rather later. An ovoid jug, the neck and mouth of which have
been lost, is the only vase to show compass-drawn circles – not very happily
placed on the shoulder, but important as witness to the existence or survival

[6] A jug from Medeon, across the gulf in Phocis, has very much the same decoration (see
p. 206).

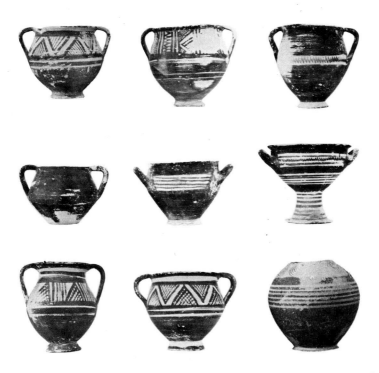

PLATE 58 ACHAEA, DERVENI. Vases from tomb. *GGP*, pl. 48 (except *j*); *AJA* 60, pl. 5, fig. 38, no. 52.

of the Protogeometric styles of the Aegean. The rest are all kantharoi, and of considerable importance, for comparative purposes, for the whole area comprising the west Peloponnese, Ithaca, and Aetolia. There are two main types, tall and broad; all have angular vertical handles and all except one, broad, monochrome and flat-based, have low conical feet. As to decoration, two of the tall kantharoi have a reserved panel round the belly (one is filled with a zigzag) and are otherwise painted over, while the third has cross-hatched triangles on the shoulder, separated into panels by groups of vertical lines. The other three, all broad, also have rectilinear decoration on the shoulder, two dovetailing cross-hatched or hatched triangles, the third, in which the decoration is taken right up to the rim, a series of panels, including fringes, vertical zigzag, and cross-hatched triangles.

Such is the group from Ďerveni, and its date is rather the beginning of the ninth century than earlier or later, so just beyond the Dark Ages, though in this area the end of the tenth century did not perhaps have any great significance.

As I have said, the kantharoi are the most helpful. On the one hand, the broad kantharoi are closely allied, both in shape and manner of decoration, to those of Ithaca and Aetolia at this period, and thus confirm the link already noted above, between the oinochoe and the jug. On the other hand, we shall find variations of the shape right down the western coast; the rectilinear motives, and the system of applying them, are also fairly typical of the whole area, and we can even note a parallel with Laconia, in the practice of placing cross-hatched triangles in panels.

One other significant tomb group is probably, but not certainly, from Achaea. The objects, now in the archaeological collection at Mainz, are simply said to have come from a tomb 'in North Peloponnese'. They include a tall kantharos, similar to those of Derveni, with cross-hatched triangles on the shoulder and a rough zigzag on the neck, and three other vases, none easy to date. As well as these, however, there were several objects of bronze, five massive armlets, two long dress pins with swelling on the shank and incised rings above and below it, and three fibulae, slightly stilted, with swollen arches and strengthening collars on each side, such as are fairly typical of Late Protogeometric Athens (see Pl. 24). In view of the rarity elsewhere of finds other than pottery, these bronzes are of the greatest interest, but the date is unfortunately not certain: assuming that a single date should be given to all (itself not certain), I think that the late tenth century is the most likely, and in that case the survival of the earlier type of dress pin is remarkable.

This concludes the evidence from Achaea, apart from the possibly very early cist tombs of Agriapidies (p. 92); that from Elis is even more slight, unfortunately, and there is nothing leading on from the Sub-Mycenaean cemetery of Ancient Elis (p. 74). All we have are two sites from the region of the river Alpheios. The one is Ayios Andreas, at the mouth of the river, and here the one illustrated vase may belong to the early rather than to the late Dark Ages. The other is Salmone, a little way inland, and this produced another pithos burial which contained four vases, a kalathos (a very rare shape for this part of the world), two oinochoai, one of which had a fringed-triangle motive on the shoulder, thus linking up with Ithaca and Achaea, and finally yet another of the tall kantharoi. The date could be much the same as that of the Derveni burial, and thus the evidence from both Elis and Achaea tends to be late, apart from that which belongs to the early Dark Ages, thus leaving an extremely undesirable gap.

Messenia and Triphylia

This region forms the fairly compact south-western part of the Peloponnese. The northern boundary follows the line of the modern railway and road, across from Kyparissia to the upper reaches of the fertile plain that extends southwards to Kalamata, with the range of Taygetus providing the eastern border. So Elis and Arcadia lie to the north, Laconia to the east; but the most prominent feature is the long coastline.

One has to travel a fair distance southwards from the sites at or near the mouth of the river Alpheios before one reaches any further trace of habitation that can perhaps be attributed to the later Dark Ages. There are two sites involved, one that of Rizes, a few miles north of Kyparissia, the other being Malthi, a little way inland from Rizes, above the valley leading eastwards from the coast. The latter is a well-known settlement with a long life, extending far back into prehistoric times; all that can be said is that the ribbed and swollen kylix stems, and even more the one or two iron objects, suggest that the site continued to be occupied into the Dark Ages (see p. 84). As to Rizes, we have simply the contents of a pithos burial found by chance – and they are not easy to date. They consist of seven small vases. Four were small hand-made jugs, parallels to which can be found in twelfth-century Kephallenia – and no doubt elsewhere, as the types are not uncommon. The other three were wheel-made cups, fat-bellied and flat-based, two with angular handles; they were wholly painted over except for the area immediately under the lip, in one case left clear, in the other two decorated with a rough zigzag, and the only comparable pieces seem to be cups found in Ithaca, probably of late Dark Age date.

So far, the evidence is slight and uncertain, the reverse of promising. Southwards again, there are two further sites in central Messenia which are of greater interest, though that does not mean that their material is necessarily easier to interpret. They lie within a few miles of each other, and close to the Palace of Nestor, Tragana to the south, and Kokevi to the south-east of it. Each is represented by a tholos tomb, but whereas the one at Tragana had originally been built in the fourteenth century, that of Kokevi was constructed in the later Dark Ages.

To take Tragana first, there was obviously a considerable period of use, not entirely continuous, as there is no thirteenth-century evidence, but possibly continuous from the twelfth century to the tenth. That is to say, there seem to be sufficient inhumations to cover the whole of this latter period, but the associated pottery is too scanty to prove that they did; and this is particularly frustrating, as it is the nearest we get to possible continuity in all Messenia. While the early Dark Ages were slightly uncertainly represented by a group of lekythoi (p. 84), for the later period we have to be content with a small group of sherds, mostly from bowls or skyphoi with a narrow reserved panel between the handles enclosing either a rough wavy line or a zigzag (influence from where and at what period?) or sets of compass-drawn semicircles – a very unusual use of the motive on this type of vase, and unlikely to precede the tenth century. The shape of these vases is as difficult to determine as that of the origin of their decoration, but it looks as though there were two types, the one more full-bellied than the other. Apart from these there was a narrow-mouthed bowl, and this had the uncommon decorative system of alternating standing and pendent loops; I would not like to hazard where in the sequence it should be placed.

The greater amount of material, as well as the fact of a tholos tomb being built in the Dark Ages, make the Kokevi tomb extremely interesting, even though only half of it was preserved. One inhumation was noted and the finds included parts of an iron knife and dress pin,[7] a bronze ring, and two buttons, one of which was of steatite – a not unusual collection, though the steatite button may be an intrusion from some Mycenaean context, the whole region being honeycombed with Mycenaean sites. And there were six vases. Two of them were amphorae; the one, belly-handled, with almost spherical body, looks early, and so does its decoration, simply bands enclosing a rough zigzag both round the neck and belly; the other was a rather dumpy neck-handled vase with high neck and heavily moulded outturned lip, and this one seems relatively late, to judge from its shoulder decoration of compass-drawn circles flanking a cross-hatched diamond. Of the two bowls, the one was relatively deep with low conical foot, painted over except for a narrow reserved panel between the handles – a rather similar type of vase would in the Argolid probably be dated to the early stages of Protogeometric; the other has the same decorative system but is shallower and bellies out much more strongly, probably a local variation. The lower part of a rather biconical jug has concentric loops on the shoulder and bands below; there is nothing at all closely comparable to it. And lastly, there is a vase which resembles in shape the tall kantharoi found at Derveni and elsewhere; it seems to have had only the one vertical handle, and the decoration is confined to a small zigzag panel just below the lip, but even so this may be a reflection of the characteristic west Peloponnesian and Ithacan type. I would think it likely that this tomb belongs to the later Dark Ages.

So far, there has been practically no sign of the cross-hatched rectilinear decoration so typical of the other regions already discussed in this general area. As, however, dovetailing cross-hatched triangles are the only known motive of surface sherds from Kaphirio, their absence from most sites may be accidental.

Kaphirio is the southernmost of a number of important sites grouped round the Messenian Gulf. Preliminary reports suggest that there was continuous occupation here throughout the Dark Ages, but this awaits verification. A little to its north lies Nichoria, also on the coast, at the point where the main road from eastern Messenia turns inland to the central district. This is where we would expect a site of note, and our expectations have been fulfilled. The very impressive Mycenaean settlement came to an end at about the same time as most of the other settlements of Messenia (see p. 85). Thereafter the inhabitants are found occupying another site close by: whether or not there was continuity of habitation remains to be seen, and as major excavation is now taking place we should before long be in a position to know. So far, our knowledge is confined to cemetery evidence. A brief preliminary report mentions six cist tombs, built in the dry-stone technique and apsidal in shape, containing a large quantity of Protogeometric vases ('oinochoai, amphorae, etc.') and some bronze pins. One vase only has been illustrated, a rather dumpy belly-handled amphora with cross-hatched triangles and panels on the shoulder, but this is of no great assistance. In addition to the cist tombs, a number of pithos burials are

[7] There was also part of the spherical head of another dress pin, of iron coated with bronze.

PLATE 59 MESSENIA, NICHORIA. Skyphos and oinochoe from tholos tomb. *Athens Annals* I, 208, figs. 3 and 4.

said to have been found near them, and to have contained Protogeometric pottery. Whether the two types were used contemporaneously or whether the pithoi were subsequent to the cist tombs is not clear.

There was, furthermore, a third type of tomb in use, and that was the tholos tomb. Only the one has so far been found, but it was constructed during the Dark Ages, and a fairly full account of it has recently been published. Quite a small tomb – as most of the Dark Age tholos tombs are – it contained four inhumations, three of which had been swept to one side, the fourth being laid out in an extended position (but, curiously, with the elbows bent) covering most of the available space. And in addition to this it is reported there was an unspecified number of cremations; according to the excavator they were later than any of the inhumations, a useful chronological pointer, especially as they constitute the only evidence for this kind of burial in the whole of the western and southern Peloponnese; unfortunately, only one vase, and that only possibly, was associated with them, a one-handled jug with cross-hatched triangles on the shoulder.

All the other vases and metal objects (of iron) belonged to the inhumations. The last inhumation had with it four vases and a dress pin. The pottery (Pl. 59) is of great interest, particularly a fine trefoil-lipped oinochoe, mended in antiquity and thus revealing the value attached to it, with globular body and rope handle; it is dark ground except for the upper belly, which is banded, and the shoulder, which has compass-drawn sets of semicircles flanking vertical zigzags. Then there was a small jug which also had sets of semicircles on the shoulder. The other two vases were skyphoi, painted over except for a narrow panel between the handles, one of which enclosed a zigzag; their shape, deep and full-bellied with low out-turned rim, seems to be peculiar to this part of the world, and has a resemblance to the kantharoi in the body profile.

The other inhumations[8] had vases of much the same type – three skyphoi with panels (two enclosing zigzags) between the handles, one of which had, like the oinochoe, been mended in antiquity, and two jugs, the one undecorated, the other painted all over except for three sets of semi-circles on the shoulder. The whole group is most instructive and, if we could be absolutely sure that the jug with cross-hatched triangles was, as is supposed, later, could have valuable stylistic significance. In any case the clear and rather surprising connexion with Aegean Protogeometric developments, as visible in the semicircles, indicates that these inhuma-tions almost certainly belonged to the tenth century, and the presence of iron objects would agree with this.

Finally, a curious minor feature of this tomb may be mentioned, the presence of a bird sacrifice on the left wall of the entrance; unfortunately, we do not know with which burial it was associated. So, in general, the finds from Nichoria, even as yet known, are of the greatest importance.

The rest of the evidence can be dealt with more briefly. On the opposite side of the gulf from Nichoria, the settlement of Kardamyla has produced sherds from bowls with wavy lines or zigzags in panels, possibly a little earlier than those from Nichoria, but still perhaps datable to the later Dark Ages. Then we come to the rich plain at the head of the gulf, where the modern Kalamata is situated: this should be a very promising area, but so far we have only a little material from the ancient site of Thuria. From surface exploration came a few sherds said to be of Laconian Proto-geometric type, no doubt to be expected, as we are close to Laconia, though the barrier of Mt. Taygetus is not inconsiderable. And, more important, six vases were recovered from a tomb of unspecified type; few details have been given, but one of the vases was a skyphos with a conical foot and decoration of concentric circles, strong confirmatory evidence of links with the Aegean. Furthermore, numerous high conical feet are reported from the final site, Volimnos, other sherds including concentric-circle and cross-hatched motives. Here it is the actual position of the site that is significant, as it has rather the character of the 'refugee' sites of Crete, lying isolated and high on Mt. Taygetus to the north of Kalamata; there is no record of any occupation earlier than the tenth century, and one is bound to wonder what was the cause of its foundation.

Such, then, is the evidence from the south and west Peloponnese and from Ithaca and Aetolia; the material from the few sites being generally so slight and the period of time covered so great, it has seemed advisable to describe the finds in much greater detail than would otherwise have been necessary or desirable.

To give a summary account of this area whose only common feature seems to be a negative one, a relative independence of the Aegean world, and which is far from being a coherent entity, is extremely difficult.

The main trouble is internal, though. It is only in Ithaca that we can follow the complete sequence of events, and even then one has to depend

---

[8] With these were also associated fragments of two iron knives, and an iron ring.

on the usually fragmentary pottery; in Messenia there are at least a few sites whose material can confidently be ascribed to the later Dark Ages, however obscure the early period is; but the greatest difficulty is manifested in Aetolia, Elis, and Achaea, just where one would most welcome a fully documented story. Take away the early cemetery of Ancient Elis (p. 74), a vase from Ayios Andreas, and the cist tombs of doubtful date from Agriapidies in Achaea, and all that remain are four tomb groups which at the very earliest cannot precede the late tenth century, and two of which are far more likely to belong to the ninth. And the situation in Laconia – note the absence except at Mavrovouni of any tomb groups – is almost as bad. The only connecting link is at the lower end, and that brings one down to the end of the ninth century; consequently, a good deal of the material classified as Laconian Protogeometric must belong to the ninth century, and there is no way of telling how much of the tenth century was also covered – extreme caution might even suggest that none of it was.

The consequence of this is that we can only discuss the area as a whole from the latter part of the tenth century to the end of the ninth, the time, however, during which there may be rather little material from Messenia. And it is true that there are ceramic interconnexions visible between the various districts during this period. They seem to be strong between Ithaca, Aetolia, Elis, and Achaea, both for shape and for system of decoration; on the basis of decoration but not of shape we can see that there were also slight links between these districts and the Protogeometric style of Laconia; and both for shape and decoration there are some links between Messenia and the regions to the north, up the west coast of the Peloponnese.

For the last set of links, it may be that they are stronger than yet known since, as I have said, we know little for certain of Messenia in the ninth century. If we could place a definite date on all the pithos burials found the whole way up the western Peloponnese, from Nichoria in the south to Derveni in the north, and across the Calydonian Gulf in Aetolia, we might be able to suggest an even closer relationship. When found in other regions, their upper limit seems to be the late tenth century, and those in this area which are datable (Calydon, Kaloyeriko, Derveni, and Salmone) have a similar limit. However, we do not know the dates of the remainder – the one at Rizes sounds earlier – nor is this an altogether satisfactory criterion.

All this, in any case, only just impinges on the Dark Ages at their latest point, and it would be unsafe to conclude that similar links existed during the greater part of our period. Nor is there any other criterion than pottery. It is tempting to point to the cist tombs of Nichoria, and to suggest that this usage came about as a result of a gradual earlier move of people down the west coast of the Peloponnese (see p. 110), but there is no evidence yet to support it – only a plausible likelihood, even if one takes into account the Ancient Elis cemetery and the Agriapidies group.

So the idea of some internal cohesion within the districts of this area during most of the Dark Ages is purely hypothetical. Are we even justified in claiming that they had in common a resistance to the cultural influence of the Aegean? So far as Laconia, Aetolia, Achaea, and Elis are concerned, it is fair to point out that such influence was, during the ninth century and probably the late tenth, of a minimal nature (one or two features may indicate relations with the Argolid and Corinthia), and it is a possible argument that if there had been significant earlier influence directly or indirectly from the Athenian Protogeometric style it would have left some trace on the later pottery, as for example in the area of Euboea and the northern Cyclades, and that the absence of any trace suggests that there was in fact no earlier influence.

In Ithaca and Messenia it is different. We have at least some evidence, and each district must be treated separately. Neither was entirely un-affected by Protogeometric developments in the Aegean. Ithaca was the less influenced: local shapes and decorative systems were retained through-out; the compass-drawn circles and semicircles were introduced, but they were adapted in a rather clumsy fashion, and there is hardly any other feature of Aegean origin to which one can point. In Messenia, however, the effect may have been considerable: there are the high conical feet, and the use of circles and semicircles was much more conventional – for example, the full circles on a skyphos, the semicircles on the shoulders of jugs and of a trefoil-lipped oinochoe.

Then there arises the question of the source of the influence. For Ithaca it is impossible to tell, but in Messenia there is another factor to be reckoned with, the bowls or skyphoi with just a narrow panel between the handles, either left blank or enclosing wavy lines or zigzags. This was a system particularly favoured in the Argolid, and it may be that the relations were with that district for the more purely Athenian features as well; but one cannot be sure, and there may have been more than one source. Wherever it was, it was somewhere in the Aegean, and it must have been transmitted by sea, with the slight alternative possibility that it came overland from the Argolid, through Arcadia.

There is very little else that one can say about this area. The finds other than pottery are not very enlightening. No weapons have been found except in Laconia, and fibulae only in Ithaca, in the Kaloyeriko tomb in Aetolia, and in the late tomb from somewhere in the north Peloponnese, tombs which also contained armlets and dress pins. Other dress pins, both of bronze and iron, have been found in Messenia, but their type is not clear. Messenia, strangely, has produced the only objects of iron (there are knives as well as pins), but this may reflect no more than the absence of Dark Age material (except the latest stage) in the districts already men-tioned, and in Ithaca the fact that we are dealing with settlement deposits, wherein metal objects are seldom found.

Was the area well populated? How can one tell? Personally, I think that the inhabitants were very few – and there is in any case no doubt that they were far fewer than in the thirteenth century – but future research may prove otherwise. Was the atmosphere one of peace? Again, there is no certainty, but the continuity from Mycenaean times visible in Ithaca suggests strongly that the islanders were left undisturbed, and the contacts with the Aegean in the later Dark Ages, naturally not great in Ithaca, but reasonably strong in Messenia, lead to the likely conclusion that outside relations were on the whole peaceful during this time. But what happened in Laconia and in Elis and Achaea? My impression is that the inhabitants of Laconia, in contrast to those of Messenia, were self-isolated or at least self-dependent, their interests if anywhere within the Peloponnese, and hardly at all with the Aegean. For those of Achaea and Elis the obviously close links with southern Aetolia and Ithaca probably from the tenth century onwards indicates a peaceful community of interests, possibly extending to Messenia, and is one of the most significant features of the period, but unfortunately the lack of evidence prevents us from knowing at what earlier stage these interconnexions were formed.

IV

The Material Evidence

16 Settlements

The importance of this aspect of the archaeological picture needs no emphasis; its fragmentary and unsatisfactory nature during the Dark Ages is, therefore, extremely depressing. There is no doubt that what has been identified represents a fraction only of the actual state of affairs – the number of cemeteries or smaller groups of tombs unconnected with any known settlement makes this clear – but what is particularly discouraging is that we cannot estimate the size of the fraction: do these settlements represent a quarter, or a tenth, or even less, of the total? This is a major defect, and there are other lesser ones; the reasonable course seems to be to discuss briefly the actual information that can be extracted, in the hope that this, taken by itself and in conjunction with the situation before and after the Dark Ages, will provide some sort of helpful clue.

Over the whole of Greece and the Aegean there are fewer than thirty sites on which settlement material has been recognised. For the most part our only evidence of such is a deposit of pottery – not that this is to be despised, for it provides the basic material for purposes of identification, and when stratified can tell us when the settlement was established and how long it lasted, whether or not it linked up with the preceding period, whether it survived the Dark Ages.

There were, however, a number of instances (about a dozen) where some construction was associated with the pottery – houses or house walls, circular pits and wells, hearths and ovens, for instance. But in only one case was there a complete settlement, Karphi (see Plan, p. 121) – and that owed its unchanged survival till modern times to the fact that few in their right senses would ever dream of living there. For the rest, one speaks of a 'settlement', but in fact what one means is that two or three houses have been uncovered, or a scatter of unrelated house walls, or a hearth – the almost wholly obliterated debris of a forgotten age.

From these we get the following information. For hearths and ovens, and for the construction probably intended for the extraction of silver from lead at Argos, baked clay seems to have been the usual material.[1] For the houses themselves it was a matter of stone or brick, or both, with wooden supporting features. Stone is encountered more frequently than brick – in the Cretan sites, at Old Smyrna, Grotta in Naxos, and Iolkos – but only on the last-named site does one get superior workmanship, with fairly massive and well-dressed blocks. Generally the workmanship was poor and the blocks small, such as would be removed by later builders –

---

[1] Stone could be used for the hearth, as at Gortyn.

which would partly explain why so few stone foundations have survived. Bricks, rectangular and rather crudely fashioned of clay or other soil and straw, are known only from Old Smyrna and Argos, but it is quite likely that they were used more commonly than stone. It was a simple and well-known method of building – familiar to the Mycenaeans, from whom it was presumably derived – and perfectly satisfactory for normal purposes, but even more liable than stonework to later removal, and a material that tends to disintegrate in course of time.

The one building of note partly constructed of brick so far known to us is the small single-roomed oval house at Old Smyrna (Pl. 37). Apart from that, the impression given is that houses with stone foundations were rectangular, or roughly so, and such houses probably had flat roofs (this seems to have been established for Karphi), while oval houses, or houses with curved ends, may rather have had sloping roofs, thatched. In any case, the main point is that buildings, except perhaps at Iolkos, were small or fairly small, and of relatively poor workmanship, which is after all what one would tend to expect.

There is, so far as I know, no evidence of any fortification wall built during the Dark Ages. The nearest one in time is perhaps the mid-ninth-century wall of Old Smyrna, which had its lower outer face and a fill of stone, the remainder being of brick, the whole being fairly massive, as the base was four and three-quarter metres in width. This is the sort of defensive wall that Dark Age people might have built, but the fact remains that there is no indication that they ever did. Bearing always in mind the fragmentary state of the evidence, it still looks as though fortifications were very rare in this period. The masons of the time, as has been seen, were not very competent; the communities must often have been too small to undertake any substantial defence works, and, for that matter, there will on many sites have been Mycenaean citadel walls still standing and usable.

It must also be stressed that use was made of places well defended by nature, as in Crete. Certain settlements, however, had no defences, artificial or natural, for example, Grotta on Naxos, and Iolkos, and presumably Athens, though one could always withdraw to the Acropolis. In these cases, I am inclined to think that peaceful conditions as well as lack of manpower and technical ability could account for the absence of fortifications.

Emphasis has been placed on the small size of most communities: is this justified? With so little to go on, there is no absolute proof. At the same time, when the matter can be tested it does appear to be so, and one can use the evidence of later conditions to demonstrate it, in other words where, on an extensively investigated site (as, for example, Miletus and Old Smyrna), the area in which Dark Age deposits or associated constructions have been noted is much smaller than in the following Geometric period. On the other hand, just a few communities were relatively large. The only clear example of one from actual settlement evidence is Karphi, which the excavator estimated could have held a population of 3,500. Use may also be made of the size and extent of the burial grounds:

this leads us to believe that Athens had a large and growing population (assuming that it was a matter of a single community, which is not provable, though there was probably at least a centralised rule), and most likely Argos as well, where there are several settlement deposits of the time in addition to a wide embrace of tombs; the size of the cemetery at Lefkandi suggests a population of unusual size, and it is possible that there may have been a large concentration at Knossos, though in this area it is likely that there were at least two or three communities. In spite of these examples, it still seems true to say that not only were there few settlements but that most of them were extremely small, a judgment not uninfluenced by the conditions of the immediately preceding period, that is to say the extraordinary denudation, in the sense of settlements and population, of many regions as compared with the proliferation of the thirteenth century. Such a conclusion is of considerable significance for our whole understanding of the Dark Ages, and does not depend solely on the settlement material, as will be clear; but this material is one of the principal factors in establishing its probability.

So far, I have discussed Dark Age settlements without chronological distinction, but these can occasionally be made, and can be revealing. In this respect, tomb evidence, unless the cemetery is extensive and one knows that its extent has been thoroughly determined, is of much less value.

The main point of importance is whether we can establish the date of the original occupation of a site. This has a special bearing on the question of continuity with the preceding Mycenaean age, and the evidence as we have it provides the remarkable result that nowhere, except in Ithaca, at Grotta on Naxos, and possibly at Iolkos, have we got continuity of settlement between the latest Mycenaean and the early Dark Ages. Mycenaean sites were often used, but not precisely the spots which the Mycenaeans had lived in; the clearest example is at Argos. There is one major exception to be made, and that is in Minoan Crete, where settlements reflect a break not at the outset of the Dark Ages, but earlier, towards the beginning of the twelfth century; it is an exception that emphasises even further the situation in the rest of the Aegean and in mainland Greece. Interpretation is, however, not easy, and there are still far too many gaps in the evidence. It did not mean the disappearance of all of Mycenaean stock, but something of note took place, to distinguish the new from the old. And once the Dark Age settlements were established, they seem to have continued to be inhabited throughout this period and beyond (there are, as always, exceptions, and Karphi is an obvious one).

Not all the known Dark Age settlements, though, had their origin in the early phase. Several do not precede the tenth century, and some cannot trace their origin beyond c. 950 B.C. The central Aegean provides examples of these, on Siphnos and Paros, and it may be that we have a similar situation in the Dodecanese. Another example is that of Thorikos on the east coast of Attica, where the late tenth and early ninth-century material rests on virgin soil. How significant is this? Again, one must be cautious.

If, for example, we had only the main settlement at Lefkandi, we might conclude that there was nobody living there between the early eleventh century and *c.* 900 B.C., but the presence of the nearby cemetery proves that there was a community, either in some part of the settlement mound not yet examined, or else in the immediate vicinity.

In this way, also, the evidence from settlements is relevant and important in building up the picture of the Dark Ages, but one must always be careful not to go beyond the small amount of material that we have.

Can the pattern of settlements help us to discover what factors influenced the people of the Dark Ages in choosing the sites they did? What did they look for? Bearing in mind the usual reservations due to lack of evidence, one or two points may be suggestive.

There are the obvious natural features – somewhere within reach of good water, somewhere where a living could be made from the soil, or from the sea, or from both. These may be taken for granted, but they need not have been of first or determining importance.

It is noticeable that many, if not most, of the sites were those previously occupied by Mycenaeans, even though not necessarily on exactly the same spot, as we have seen. One possible, and even probable, reason for this is that at least part of the Dark Age population on such sites was of Mycenaean origin – always assuming that the gap was not too great. It is not, however, the only possible explanation. The natural attractiveness and facilities of the site may always have been the decisive factor, especially, for example, for sites with a good harbour, as Iolkos. Also, it could reflect our own limitations; some sites have certainly been investigated primarily because of their importance as Mycenaean centres – such as Mycenae and Tiryns – and here the Dark Age discoveries have been an incidental by-product of the course of thorough investigation.

There is a third important factor, to be put beside that of natural resources and that of familiarity in the sense that some may have had their ancestral roots in the place, and this is the factor of security, and it could have been overriding in an age of small communities, when at least at the beginning people must have lived in the shadow of earlier decades of anxious and disturbed conditions, far too close for comfort and in certain areas very likely still to have been persisting. It would be natural for such a factor to be decisive in the early years, and I think it probably was, though we still have too little evidence for certainty.

What happened later? Here we may distinguish between danger from the sea, and peril from the land. If there were danger from the sea, then one would expect settlements away from the coasts, and one can say with reasonable confidence that this was rare; most of the settlements are coastal, not only within the Aegean, but even along the western shores (though here, admittedly, the evidence belongs rather to the tenth century than earlier); and, as we have seen, they were undefended. A question mark has been placed against Attica, on the grounds that so few Dark Age sites have been identified on the coast. This is indeed true, and surprising, but I do not feel that it meant that there were any dangers from the sea.

The fact that Athens was situated a few miles inland in no way prevented her inhabitants from ranging freely and widely over the Aegean.

If, on the other hand, there was cause to fear attack from the land, whether from near or far, the first consideration, as the inhabitants would seem to have been unversed in artificial defensive works, would be to seek a place of great natural strength. All one can say is that there is no evidence that more than the normal precautions, such as held for many centuries, were taken. In many places there was a stronghold at hand if need arose, but people did not live in these strongholds. The only district where one can perhaps recognise an overriding desire for security at all costs is eastern Crete, and even here it is not certain. On the whole, the pattern of settlement, as other aspects of our evidence, reflects a quick return to relatively peaceful conditions.

17 Tombs

Mycenaean and Minoan

During the long period preceding the emergence of the Dark Ages one can distinguish many minor variations in the tomb types and burial customs of the Mycenaeans and Minoans; over and above these, however, the main lines are fairly simple and clear, and the picture is reasonably uniform.

As a rule, multiple burial was practised, in tombs large enough to hold several bodies, providing (as was the case) that there was no compunction in sweeping one set of bones aside to make room for a later burial. It is a fair assumption that in this system each such tomb belonged to one family rather than being in communal use, since the burials were successive over a long period. The two standard types of multiple tomb were the tholos tomb and (far more common and widespread) the chamber tomb (see Figs. 26, 27); they are to be found everywhere within the Aegean world.[1]

To say that multiple burial was regular and that tholos and chamber tombs were standard does not mean that no other kind of burial was known. There are, indeed, numerous instances of tombs whose purpose was to hold individual burials, thus recalling and no doubt preserving the system that had been in force yet earlier, in Middle Helladic times. These tombs were long and rectangular, very like those familiar to our own age; cut into the soft rock and usually holding not more than one body, they could be just plain trenches, occasionally covered with stone slabs (pit graves), or they could have a lining as well as a covering of stone slabs (cist tombs). They have not the characteristic Mycenaean feel about them – nor the variety of finds, for that matter – and so tend to escape notice; careful investigation, however, has revealed their presence in small numbers in most districts (not Crete), and on one or two sites, notably Argos and Eleusis, they are prominent. What should be stressed, though, in view of later developments, is that the evidence we have indicates that they were less frequently used as time went on: during the first three-quarters of the twelfth century they are of extreme rarity.

The manner of burial was almost invariably inhumation, and this can be taken as standard Minoan and Mycenaean practice. Cremations were not altogether unknown, however, and (in contrast to the individual graves) the closer one comes to the Dark Ages the more there were. Before the twelfth century they were rare,[2] but during the last generations of true

[1] In Crete they were often used rather for the purpose of individual burial – not always so, but this may serve as a further distinction between Minoan and Mycenaean.

[2] Among them are the extremely interesting examples from Müskebi in western Asia Minor, possibly of significance for the origin of the custom.

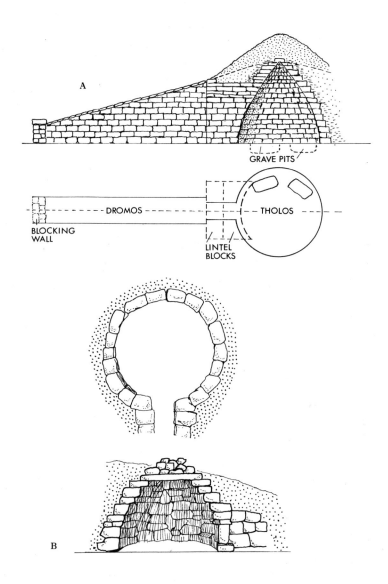

FIG. 26 THOLOS TOMBS
A) Wace and Stubbings, *Companion to Homer*, p. 483, fig. 49.
B) Erganos. *AJA* 5, p. 272, fig. 6.

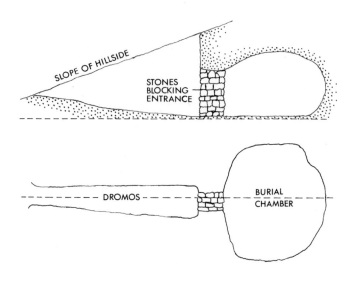

FIG. 27 CHAMBER TOMB
Wace and Stubbings, *Companion to Homer*, p. 482, fig. 48.

Mycenaeans one encounters a minor flood of them in and around the
Aegean. Their presence is one of the connecting links between Perati in
east Attica and the Dodecanese: always found in chamber tombs, and
associated with inhumations, the ashes were either left on the floor of the
tomb or, more usually, placed in a small vase. Cremations of this period are
also known in Crete, the circumstances tending to vary from site to site.
Obviously one should not overstress their importance, exiguous in
number as they are beside the inhumations, but the practice is more
prominent in the twelfth century than earlier, and some could be contemporary with the earliest Dark Age ones. And one point may be noted
for later reference: their close association with inhumations suggests that
there were neither family nor religious objections to the practice.

Dark Age Developments

The major development, that in which the previous exception became the
rule, was the adoption of individual burial, and with it the corresponding
rejection, except in Crete, and in a few other areas only temporarily and
partially, of multiple burial. At the outset, in the early Dark Ages, the two

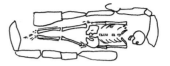

FIG. 28 CIST TOMB
Asine, tomb PG 11. *Asine*, p. 131, fig. 113.

types of tomb best suited to individual interment, the cist tombs (Fig. 28)
and pit graves, were confined to a fairly compact area of central mainland
Greece – west Attica and the Argolid, Boeotia, Corinthia, and Elis. Their
almost universal take-over in these regions is one of the positive symptoms
of the Dark Ages, and they also constitute one of the distinguishing
features of the new Sub-Mycenaean culture, which was in many ways
radically different from the old Mycenaean civilisation still persisting in a
number of adjacent areas. There are variations in details of use and practice,
which I shall discuss below, but they are relatively minor and do not
detract from the significance of this phenomenon as affecting several
districts at about the same time.

It follows that it is of the greatest importance to know why this change
from multiple to individual burial took place in this particular area and at
this particular time. Most unfortunately, there is no certain answer: the
two alternatives, newcomers from north-west Greece or a local revival of
an old tradition, half submerged under Mycenaean orthodoxy, I have
discussed elsewhere in conjunction with the other types of evidence that
have to be taken into account (pp. 106 ff.), and it will be seen that I prefer
the theory of new people, dominant in a mixture of old and new, in spite of
the present geographical gap in the evidence and other difficulties. The
whole atmosphere of the period seems to have been conducive to movements of people, and it is in any case altogether likely that the Sub-
Mycenaean cemeteries of Salamis and the Kerameikos involved immigrants, since we have almost nothing for the immediately preceding
period.

The second stage of the adoption of individual burial, covering a much
wider area, occurred gradually, starting just before the end of the early
Dark Ages, and continuing well into the late phase. During this time the
custom spread to most other districts, at the expense of the Mycenaean
multiple tombs that had predominated until then. In certain regions it
seems to have involved the total rejection of multiple burial, as for example
in the central Aegean, so far as our present information allows us to go;
it appears to have been the rule in the Dodecanese and on Naxos at least

till the end of the Dark Ages (*c.* 900 B.C.), and the same rule held for the north Cyclades, Euboea, and Skyros. In a number of districts, such as the western Peloponnese and Laconia, lack of evidence forbids any definite conclusion, but in Thessaly and Messenia individual burial, though present, did not prevent the revival (or perhaps continuation?) of multiple burial. Generally speaking, except for Crete, and for south-west Asia Minor which is rather marginal, there is no district of Greece and the Aegean which has produced cemetery evidence of this period, where no individual burials have been found, and in almost all such burial became the standard practice.

One is of course faced with the same questions as for the first stage of adoption: how and why did it happen? Did submerged elements among the Mycenaean communities take over or were there further movements of people into these other areas where the Mycenaean inhabitants had become so enfeebled in strength and numbers that they were either in no state to resist intrusion or else abandoned their homes and left the land unoccupied? The answer is no doubt neither single nor simple, but at least the trans-Aegean diffusion is likely to have been due to an actual movement of people.

Whatever the answer or answers, the dominance of individual burial is a remarkable phenomenon, and a feature connecting most districts, at first the central ones and then on a much wider scale, consequent on the rejection of Mycenaean culture with its multiple burial. But one must be careful to realise that beneath the surface of this broad connecting link there were variations, factors dividing one community from another rather than binding them together. A brief analysis, again on the basis of the two stages of diffusion, is desirable and instructive.

During the early stage, when the area affected was relatively small and compact, the variations were few. The type of tomb itself varied from district to district, and from site to site: earth-cut with covering slabs at Ancient Elis, cist tombs on Salamis and at Thebes, both types in the Argolid and at Athens – one may indeed wonder whether this was a distinction of real significance. Nor was there any agreement on the disposition of the body – contracted for Elis and Salamis, outstretched in Athens; and while there were a very few cremations in Athens and Salamis, none is found in any of the other districts.

In the second and later stage the variations are greater and more complex. So far as concerns the original area, things seem to have remained much as before in the Argolid, but in Athens (and perhaps extending over the whole of Attica) there was no such simple continuation: for the rest of the Dark Ages, and even beyond, inhumation was, for adults, replaced almost universally by cremation, the ashes being deposited in a special amphora, and the amphora in a pit, all very tidily (Fig. 29). So one gets a considerable innovation, but at the same time inhumation in cist tombs was retained for children[3] – and this distinction was further accentuated apparently by allowing children at least to be buried inside

---

[3] There was even a third category, infants being buried in vases (pithos burials).

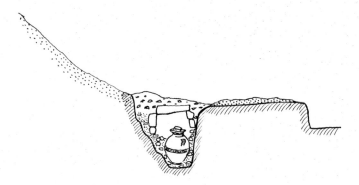

FIG. 29 CREMATION BURIAL
Athens, Early Geometric, Agora. *Hesp.* 18, p. 281, fig. 2.

the area of settlement, while adults were allocated to cemeteries outside. In all this, it may be noted, there is no sign of multiple burial, but it is curious to find at Nea Ionia, a few miles to the north of Athens, evidence of what clearly looks like a family plot, with both cremation and inhumation burials.

Some aspects of the Athenian pattern can be matched in other settlements, but never all of them together. The nearest parallels outside Attica to the manner and details of cremation are to be seen in two tombs of the middle or late tenth century at Lefkandi, but these were entirely exceptional, and may even mean that those buried were Athenian. On other sites where cremation was commonly practised, the system is quite different. Such are in any case few; leaving aside Crete for later discussion, there were in the Dark Ages only three of importance, Vranesi in Boeotia, where our information is totally inadequate and so of no use, Medeon in Phocis, and Lefkandi itself. At Medeon cremation was universal at least in the tenth century if not in the eleventh (see p. 206), but the grave, a shallow elliptical trench, was the actual pyre; there the ashes and partly-burnt bones were left, and the trench was then covered over with earth. At Lefkandi there were rather similar pyres, the ashes of the dead remaining in them, but the process was much more thorough, and there was an additional phenomenon that cist tombs and, later, pit graves were built simply to house the offerings to the dead, a curiously illogical practice, not certainly paralleled elsewhere. In any case the differences between these cremations and those of Athens are obvious.

As one moves north, one leaves the sphere of cremation behind (not that one can properly speak of a definite sphere). Already at Chalcis, a few miles from Lefkandi, it seems likely – on rather poor evidence – that one is back in the familiar world of cist tombs containing inhumations. This is certainly true of Skyros; here, however, we encounter a further eccentricity not yet mentioned, that in certain cases vases were left outside the tomb, with the more personal objects deposited inside it.[4] The same, or a similar, custom has been found on some other sites:[5] just once at Lefkandi; occasionally in the tombs of Kos; in the Argolid, but not yet before the ninth century; and also occasionally at Iolkos in Thessaly (the earliest examples). It is an odd distribution; there could be, and very likely are, links between Kos and the Argolid, and also between Skyros and Iolkos, but hardly between the one pair and the other.

The link with Iolkos brings us to that site, where we get an apparent connexion with Athens in the way of dealing with children as opposed to adults, inhumation in cist tombs, probably in the settlement area. For the adult dead, however, two customs were in vogue, and neither finds a parallel in late Dark Age Athens; one can have individual burial in cist tombs or multiple burial in tholos tombs. Both are represented in other Thessalian communities, though never simultaneously, as they appear to have been at Iolkos.

The fact that one encounters multiple burial in tholos tombs in Messenia as well as in Thessaly (but hardly anywhere else except in Crete) might suggest a connexion, but it can surely be only a coincidence. To start with, the Thessalian tholoi were in use over a far longer period of time. Apart from that, there are differences in other aspects: at Nichoria, the best-known cemetery site, there are also cist tombs, but they are apsidal in shape, not rectangular; and there is a yet further tomb type, the pithos burial, unknown to Thessaly.

Though the pithos burial is alien to Thessaly, it may provide some connecting link between Messenia and certain areas not so far mentioned, the districts north of it up the west coast of the Peloponnese, and Aetolia across the mouth of the Corinthian Gulf. Other types of tomb of the period in these districts are quite remarkably rare – just a few cist tombs from two sites in Achaea, and those not easily datable. It could be a genuine connexion – and other evidence would not rule it out – but one must remain cautious, as there are still so very few of these pithos burials known; and in any case most if not all belong to the end of the tenth century or to the ninth: the earlier situation, apart from the Sub-Mycenaean cemetery at Ancient Elis, is completely obscure.

If there were a link of some sort, then one might expect to extend it to the Argolid, where just one or two pithos burials may belong to the end of the tenth century, becoming fairly popular in the succeeding century. However that may be, it is clear that the characteristic late Dark Age burial customs of this region were simply a continuation of the earlier practice – inhumation in cist tombs (Fig. 28), and much more rarely in pit graves: no cremation, no multiple burials. And the same seems to be true from the very small amount we know of Corinthia.

With Corinthia and the Argolid we have completed a circle and ex-

[4] Perhaps an echo of the custom in Athenian cremations of placing the personal objects only within the ash-urn, the vases staying outside?

[5] Not always the same, as in some cases vases were placed inside the tomb as well as outside.

cluded a whole district, that of the Dodecanese, of which unfortunately our knowledge is confined, apart from the time of Mycenaean survival, to the tenth century. The evidence of the pottery suggests that there might be some link at least between Kos and the Argolid, and the burial customs of the Serraglio cemeteries on Kos would not altogether rule this possibility out – inhumation in cist tombs and pit graves, and in pithoi or smaller vases; no distinction between children and adults in the place of burial, but a clear difference in the type of tomb, as the few adults were all buried in pit graves. The picture is, however, seriously incomplete, for the burials of only the poorest adults have been recovered (pp. 172 ff.). And, finally, Rhodes. Not many tombs can be attributed to the Dark Ages, but there is such a medley of different types and customs that once more one has an entirely individual picture.

This has been a lengthy and rather complex survey, its main purpose to show that, apart from the general prevalence of individual burial, uniformity is almost entirely lacking. No community seems to have had precisely the same burial customs as any other, and in some communities more than one custom was in use. The conclusion is twofold: this type of evidence cannot be used to show inter-community links; it can, on the other hand, be used to show that each community had its own individuality and personality.

So far, the main stress has been on individual burials and their permutations. More needs to be said, however, of multiple burials, which I have already mentioned as recurring in Thessaly and Messenia in tholos tombs. In these two areas there may have been a genuine survival of Mycenaean practice, but as we have not yet found any such tomb in continuous use from Mycenaean times into the Dark Ages, it may be no more than a revival resulting from the later local discovery of these extremely distinctive constructions; in Messenia a Mycenaean tholos tomb was re-used in the Protogeometric period, and in Thessaly those who buried in tholos tombs at Marmariani, and who were certainly not of Mycenaean stock, might either have re-used earlier tombs or have copied such noted in the vicinity.

However that may be, it is good evidence of a readiness to return to multiple family burial – a tholos tomb at Kapakli near Iolkos continued in use for centuries – and there is evidence from other districts as well. At Delphi there is what appears to be a chamber tomb (if so, the only one of the Dark Ages not obviously associated with Mycenaean survivors) whose contents may belong to the middle of the eleventh century; this, however, though suitable for multiple burial, was not used as such. And at Vranesi in Boeotia there are multiple-burial tombs of a type not yet mentioned, mounds covering a number of individual graves, the earliest of which fall within the tenth century, and probably include cremations.

These mounds had, it seems, a northern and not a Mycenaean pedigree. The most distinctive group is the enormous cemetery at Vergina in Macedonia, whose first use may go back to c. 1000 B.C., and whose affinities are with areas further to the north. In Albania, however, there are much earlier mounds than these, and presumably from this area or near it came the people who built a burial mound of the late twelfth or early eleventh century at Hexalophos in western Thessaly. So to the limited revival of Mycenaean types of tomb must be added the occasional and sporadic influence of multiple burial of a northern type. The known mounds are, however, exceedingly few, and for the Dark Ages confined to the mainland.[6]

There remains one area, Crete, where multiple burial was a matter neither of revival nor of limitation, but continuous and unlimited. The same types as had been current in the Minoan period, tholos and chamber tombs, persisted throughout the Dark Ages and beyond. There is no doubt as to the reality and force of survival in this island, of which the burial customs are but one proof. But, just as in the mainland and in other parts of the Aegean, there are variations in detail – and there was one major division, that between the chamber tombs of the centre and the tholos tombs of the east, which goes back to the early twelfth century and may have some significance (see p. 113).

During the Dark Ages themselves only one fundamental change took place, and that was the introduction of cremation on a large scale, mainly in the centre, but also to some degree, increasing as time went on, in the east of the island. Only at Athens, Lefkandi, and Medeon was cremation practised on such a scale; one is bound to wonder whether there may not have been a connexion at least with Athens, especially as cremation became almost standard in central Crete at about the same time as Athenian Protogeometric vases influenced the potters of this region. Such a link is, however, unlikely: the practice of cremation appears in contexts quite independent of the pottery influence, and the way in which it was carried out differed from that of all three of the above-mentioned sites. The ashes were deposited in a container (as opposed to Lefkandi and Medeon), but these could be of any shape, and need not even be of clay (as opposed to the Athenian uniformity), and there was no particular rule – as there was at Athens – as to what objects should or should not be deposited in the ash-urn. And of course in Crete we are dealing with multiple, not individual, burial. So there is no necessary connexion, and we should probably look for a local origin, not unnaturally in view of the earlier known examples.

One final feature of interest in Crete is that on two sites, at Knossos and Vrokastro, tombs of this period contained both inhumation and cremation. So just how important was the difference between the two? The answer may surely vary according to the community and the period. In the Aegean in late Mycenaean times cremation was tolerated beside inhumation; in central Crete in the late Dark Ages, inhumation was tolerated beside cremation; in late Dark Age Athens, cremation was right for adults, but not right for children; at Lefkandi one supposes that it was right for both adults and children; but in many communities and districts crema-

---

[6] Rather more in the ninth and later centuries; Achaea on the mainland, Naxos and Ikaria in the Aegean (these two with cremations). The two tombs of uncertain, but possibly early, date from Agriapidies in Achaea may have had a covering mound.

tion was just not the done thing at all. So the difference was of importance, but of a varying one. The variation is particularly noticeable in Athens itself according to the period, for the community gave its loyalty at times to the one, at times to the other; but whichever they did must have been of importance to them at the time, and one is left wondering at the reason behind their fluctuating decisions. It was not religious; it was not a matter of change in population (as this quite clearly stayed as it was), so it must have been some social or even political pressure unknown to us.

To sum up on the preceding discussion, I have concentrated on what appeared to me to be the main features, on the one hand the massive adoption of individual instead of multiple burial, and on the other hand the multiplicity of customs that can be comprised under the chief headings. The demonstration of these features is a simpler matter than their interpretation. There is no doubt as to the significance of individual burial, in that it enables us to see a clear division between the respective cultures of the Mycenaean and Dark Age worlds, and suggests a measure of discontinuity. To have seen this, however, does not mean that we can understand it; all that it has been possible to do, in the light of such other evidence as we have, is to suggest possible explanations and state a personal preference (pp. 106 ff.). The explanation of the localised adoption of cremation is even more uncertain; no clear connexion can be made between the sites where it occurred on a considerable scale, and we can consequently suggest no valid reason for the appearance of this phenomenon.

The multiplicity of customs, even though it emphasised the important fact of the individuality of each community, led to the negative conclusion that it was impossible, in the state of our present evidence, to show that the introduction of any custom on a number of sites meant that there was some common origin for that custom. For that to be possible we should have to have a general concordance of customs as between one site and another, and this is not forthcoming.

How then can we use what is in fact one of the main types of evidence for the whole period? Perhaps the most important conclusion to be derived from the discussion above is the danger of using tomb evidence by itself, either in its various subdivisions or even as a whole, especially in the sense of making positive inferences. Fortunately, there is usually the additional assistance of the objects deposited in the tombs, objects which themselves help to put a relatively accurate date on the tombs, without which we should not even be able to start interpreting. An undated tomb is useless: a dated one may be of use.

In spite of this rather pessimistic conclusion, there are occasions when the tomb material can give useful and valid information, either on its own or with very little assistance from other material. For one thing, to know what the burial customs were adds to our knowledge of the Dark Ages; if we knew as much about settlements and sanctuaries the whole picture would be much clearer.

Another matter where the tombs by themselves (assuming we can date them) are of importance is in the building up of a pattern of settlement where, as far too often, no evidence of actual settlement has yet been recognised. People live not far from where they bury their dead, therefore a cemetery is evidence of a community; but if only a few tombs are known, it may have been a very small community indeed. On the other hand, our conclusions about the size and importance of Athens depend much on the number and distribution of tombs.

Other aspects are not so rewarding. Surprisingly, very few deductions can safely be made about religion, even though there were no doubt numerous connexions. Once again, the very many-sidedness of the evidence is a stumbling block; and when one finds that the distinction between inhumation and cremation can hardly be explained on the basis of religious beliefs, one is hard put to it to discover what custom may have religious significance. It is likely that the evidence of post-burial offerings, burnt or unburnt, is relevant for this, but it is so slight that it seems impossible to use it. There is just one reasonably certain deduction from burial customs, the firm belief in some sort of after-life; the objects deposited with the dead, whether inhumated or cremated, were such as would accompany him in his further journeying.

One would have hoped that an analysis of the skeletal remains would greatly assist in establishing racial origins, but differences of opinion among the experts make any conclusion unwise. Furthermore, analysis has to be confined to inhumation, and so a whole class of burials, the cremated, is ruled out.

Inferences as to the economic structure depend not on the tombs, but rather on the objects deposited in them, and these are a separate matter: the tombs do no more than provide the essential receptacle.

Where the tombs and burial customs, whether considered on their own or in conjunction with other evidence, can make a contribution is towards the understanding of the social structure – or at least towards an understanding of its complexity. The strict organisation, or its opposite, of a community can to some extent be reflected in the uniformity or diversity of the tomb types and burial customs; the orderly siting of the graves of the early period in the Kerameikos and on Salamis, for example, has led to the suggestion of some community organisation, and a similar inference is probably derivable from the uniformity of burial customs in Athens of the later period. But can one also argue from fluidity of customs to lack of social or political organisation? This seems doubtful, for burial would normally be strictly a matter for the individual or for the family. It is in any case desirable to take into account as many types of evidence as one can muster, in addition to that of the tombs.

The instances and circumstances under which burial was permitted within the bounds of the settlement (intramural) would be well worth study, in view of the rarity of this in Mycenaean times, but the general scarcity of settlement evidence robs such a study of most of its significance. Where, however, it has been identified, as in Athens and probably in Iolkos, it seems that children were those mainly affected. Does this perhaps mean that until a certain age children were not considered true members of the community? Such an inference is very possibly strengthened by the fact that at Athens and on Kos, and also to some extent at Iolkos, the type of tomb differed for each category. On the other hand, there are sites (for example, Halos, and Serraglio on Kos) where children and adults were buried in the same cemetery.

In general, the attitude towards the family as a whole might be expected to be reflected in the burial customs. One might suppose, for instance, that the change from multiple (in effect, family) to individual burial has some significance, but one cannot prove that it had. This is, indeed, typical. We are faced with a situation, a particular set of circumstances, which either directly or indirectly affects some aspect of life during this period; we are given a fact, or else an inference is made possible; but for the most part we have to leave the fact unexplained, the question unanswered.

18 Sanctuaries and Cult Places

Little information, except for Crete, which must in any case be dealt with on its own, will be found in previous sections about places of worship. The evidence is very slight, but the subject of religious practices is one of the most important for any period and area of the ancient world, and it seems best to assemble what can be known in this separate section.

The Dark Age World Excepting Crete

Much of the evidence comes from known sanctuaries of later times, and here one must ask how far the presence of Dark Age material on a spot later used as a shrine constitutes evidence of cult use as far back as our period. This is a difficult question to answer; one must in any case be able to show that there was an uninterrupted sequence thereafter until the first undoubted use as a shrine, and if possible one must produce other features indicating religious use in the Dark Ages.

First, a group in which there is no significant material earlier than the Dark Ages. In Athens, over a mile to the west of the Acropolis, a sanctuary of Geometric times was found, and associated with this a very large deposit of Protogeometric vases of the later tenth century; the considerable number of complete vases makes it certain that these were votive offerings, and this area must therefore have been used as a shrine in the concluding phase of the Dark Ages. Then, a local sanctuary of Zeus was discovered near the summit of Mt. Hymettus, and the precinct revealed sherds of Late Protogeometric date onwards; these also must have been connected with the cult, since this is under no circumstances a suitable spot for a settlement. In Laconia, three of the sanctuaries of Sparta, the Chalkioikos, a Heroon, and the Artemis Orthia temple, all contained sherds (at the Heroon a complete vase) which may go back to the tenth century. It seems likely that these mark the earliest period of worship. Next, there was a good deal of Protogeometric pottery in the area of the later temple at Aetos in Ithaca, with a full sequence thereafter; this is also a possible instance. Finally to Rhodes, where on the site of the temple of Athena at Kameiros the large dump of votive rejects included some tenth-century sherds and a few simple arched fibulae; the case for a Dark Age cult here seems reasonably strong, and would be certain if we could be quite sure that the fibulae (obviously votive gifts) belonged to our period.

We can now come to the sites where there were not only later sanctuaries,

278

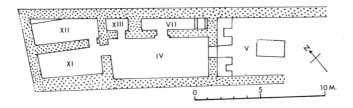

FIG. 30 AYIA IRINI, PLAN OF TEMPLE
Hesp. 33, p. 327, fig. 2.

but also material of Mycenaean times as well as Dark Age material. The first two are the great national sanctuary areas of Delos and Delphi, and clear evidence would be most welcome, but is unfortunately not forthcoming. For Delos a strong case has been argued for the existence of three sanctuaries of the Mycenaean period, on the basis of good buildings of this time, one of which underlay the temple of Artemis, was isolated from other buildings, and contained valuable objects, the second also being isolated, and the third very close to a later temple. If even one of these was a sanctuary it is important, but unfortunately the Dark Ages are particularly poorly represented on this small infertile island – no Sub-Mycenaean and only a scatter of sherds of Late Protogeometric type, some of which, however, came from the area of the temple of Artemis. It may be that the Artemision was a cult place continuously from the tenth century onwards, but one is not yet justified in extending such practice back into the early Dark Ages, even though the underlying Mycenaean construction was a sanctuary. At Delphi no Mycenaean buildings of certainly religious nature were found, but beneath the foundations of the sanctuary of Athena Pronaia nearly two hundred terracotta 'goddess' figurines were unearthed, and it is probable that there was a Mycenaean shrine on or near this spot. A dozen figurines of the same type were found in the area of the main temple of Apollo, but we are still confronted with the problem of showing continuity. As on Delos, there are a few tenth-century sherds, and in the area of the temple of Apollo they are succeeded by Geometric pottery in quantity; but, and this is significant, it was associated with houses, and these were of a domestic and not religious kind – in other words, there was an interruption in cult use, and this is the sort of evidence which leads to uncertainty in other cases. From the known material, cult practice in the Dark Ages is more likely on Delos than at Delphi, but it still only goes back to the tenth century. On the other hand, this does not constitute proof that there was no immediately earlier such use.

If Delos and Delphi are relatively disappointing, the three following sites have produced more convincing evidence. The sanctuary of Hera on

Samos was one of the most important in the Greek world; here again a very small quantity of Protogeometric sherds was found, but the case for religious use in the Dark Ages depends not on these, but on an extremely interesting series of votive terracotta animal figurines. These I shall discuss more fully below, but the point of significance is that stylistically some of them seem to belong to the Dark Ages and, even more important, they represent a type of offering that has its origins in late Mycenaean times, and thus there could be continuity.[1]

Next, at Amyklai near Sparta, a stratified deposit was found below the sanctuary area, and it was this that produced the bulk of our evidence for Laconian Protogeometric pottery (pp. 240 f.), and though much of it must fall within the ninth century, it is reasonable to assign some to the tenth; and its votive character appears to be clear. So far, the material shows that there was some religious cult in the Dark Ages, but no more. In the deposit mentioned, however, there were also a few Mycenaean sherds, a terracotta 'goddess' figurine and fragments of a votive animal, both Mycenaean; and other parts of the site produced many more figurines of these types, mostly datable to the twelfth century.[2] So there is proof that the area was used for religious purposes in the concluding phase of Mycenaean history, and it will be noted that in one spot the Mycenaean and Dark Age material was closely associated, although the value of this is lessened by the fact that the deposit represents a situation of disturbance, even allowing for a very general chronological stratification. However, there is no continuity between the two periods of offerings – this is absolutely clear from the fundamental difference between the two styles of pottery, and the virtual impossibility of dating either the Dark Age material earlier than 1000 B.C. or the Mycenaean later than 1100 B.C. So we seem once again to be faced with the same problem, lack of evidence for the early Dark Ages. Fortunately, this is one of the rare occasions when we are able to make use of the literary testimony: there were in fact two sanctuaries here, the one to Apollo, the other to Hyakinthos, both in use in Classical times, and of these Hyakinthos is an undoubted pre-Greek deity. It means that Hyakinthos continued to be worshipped, and therefore that there was no interruption; the archaeological evidence is in consequence inadequate and misleading. This could obviously have some bearing on the situation in other sanctuaries.

Finally, there is the temple at Ayia Irini on Keos, which deserves rather more detailed analysis (Fig. 30). Originally, a shrine was built in the fifteenth century, corresponding to Room XI, and to this belonged some remarkable terracotta statues. The site was then damaged by earthquake, and the temple was remodelled during the fourteenth century, but during the thirteenth and twelfth little or no use was made of Room XI, the concentration being on Rooms IV and V. Then, however, it would seem that this

[1] Mycenaean constructions and pottery have been identified on this site, but I do not know whether they can be shown to have any cult significance.

[2] The animals (usually bulls) are related stylistically to those of the Heraeum on Samos.

latter area fell into disuse, for the next stage sees the re-use of Room XI: the earliest pottery, and there is plenty of it, is Late Protogeometric – in other words of the tenth century; there was not much material which could be assigned to the ninth, but there is good evidence for the eighth and seventh, continuing on till the sixth and fifth, by which time it has been established that there was here a shrine to Dionysus. Had this god been worshipped since the Dark Ages, and was he also worshipped here in Mycenaean times?[3] The answer to the first question is a very probable yes, in spite of the decline in material during the ninth century; to the second I am not sure, in view of the apparent transfer of the sacred area from one room to another, previously long disused. But whatever the truth, I believe that the Dark Age inhabitants must have known and recognised the sanctity of the building.

The one major sanctuary area not yet mentioned is Olympia. The difficulty here is that pottery, especially of the earlier centuries, is extremely rare, as it was evidently the custom to make votive offerings of metal, and it is by no means easy to date such objects securely. For example, there is a fine series of bronze tripod cauldrons, and it has been claimed that the earliest of these belong to the Dark Ages – but this is by no means universally accepted. There is a great mass of other votive gifts, but I do not feel competent to say whether any of them must be dated within our period. In any case, the few scraps of Mycenaean pottery (no figurines have yet been found, as at Delphi) give no promise that a shrine of those times ever existed.

The results of the discussion so far are exceedingly tenuous. It has been established that there is evidence for cult places and practices during the Dark Ages. This could of course have been deduced without any evidence at all; in fact, even what we have is confined to a very few sites, is not always with certainty demonstrable, and belongs almost invariably to the late Dark Ages, and usually to its concluding phase. The one useful point is that it can be shown that there was then continuous worship into later periods.

We cannot even be sure what the shrines were like. The dearth of stone-built constructions of any sort is a known feature of the Dark Ages, and of those that remain none, to my knowledge, can be identified as a sanctuary. This does not mean that there were no buildings to house the objects of veneration, for with continuous subsequent worship such would have been destroyed to make room for something more ambitious. Even so, it seems more than likely that sanctuaries were open-air affairs. At the sanctuary of Hera on Samos the earliest temple proper, dated to the eighth century, was preceded by altars in the open, and the same system could have held elsewhere. This supposition is supported by evidence from Crete, the open-air sanctuary at Ayia Triadha, dated to the twelfth century and possibly continuing later, and from Cyprus, the sanctuary of Ayia Irini.

What deities were worshipped? Here we have at least some evidence.

[3] The name has been identified in the Pylos Linear B tablets, but not in any religious context.

To take the certain or probable instances, there is Zeus on Mt. Hymettos, Apollo at Amyklai, Hera on Samos, Athena at Kameiros and Sparta, Artemis at Sparta and perhaps also on Delos, and Dionysus on Keos. And there is just one pre-Greek deity, Hyakinthos, worshipped both in Mycenaean and later times at Amyklai. On the whole, a fairly representative selection.

In what way did men worship these gods? On this we have no information, but one can say something about the gifts they offered. For the most part, there will at least have been simple libations, the pouring of some acceptable liquid, after which the vase containing it might be left there, either whole or broken. The usual kind of vase for this would be a bowl or cup, and this is precisely what we find in quantity at Amyklai, though it does not seem that this pattern was always followed elsewhere. There is no reason to suppose that during the Dark Ages special types of vase were used for religious purposes, and this is unfortunate, for if such had been the case and we had found them on the sites concerned, it would have been welcome additional proof of their use as places of cult.

There are, though, one or two instances of objects made for dedication at some shrine. At Amyklai, for instance, with the pottery were found certain objects of metal, including two bronze spearheads, fragments of iron weapons, and part of the leg of a bronze tripod, presumably offerings to Apollo. It may indeed be that certain gods demanded certain types of offering; for example, fibulae were dedicated to Athena at Kameiros – but obviously there may be other explanations.

Another class of object which was certainly made for use as a votive offering, though not necessarily exclusively so, was the terracotta figurine, whether human or animal. There is no doubt that this was the purpose of the series of bulls with wheel-made bodies which are a feature of the Heraeum sanctuary on Samos. And this is of great interest, for they were equally a feature of the late Mycenaean shrine at Amyklai, so we have an instance of religious survival from Mycenaean times, and it is clearly worth further discussion.

During the later Mycenaean age the most popular kind of votive figurine was not animal, but human, a woman with upraised arms, possibly representing a goddess, possibly a devotee; figurines of this type are found in sanctuaries, and in tombs as well (was the corpse provided with some votive offering for use on his or her arrival in the other world?), but they vanish with the collapse of Mycenaean civilisation, and are unknown to the Dark Ages. Towards the end of the thirteenth century, however, men started to make the wheel-made terracotta animals – chiefly bulls, but other animals as well. On the Greek mainland they are known, apart from Amyklai, at several sites in the Argolid, including Mycenae, at Athens on the outer slopes of the Acropolis, and apparently at Delphi and Thebes, where datable belonging to the time when Mycenaean civilisation still survived. Furthermore, similar figurines now made their appearance in Crete and Cyprus, and the tradition of their manufacture continued for some centuries. These, it has been surmised, were originally introduced to the two islands by migrants fleeing from the late thirteenth-century catastrophes; whether that is true or not is by the way, the point of immediate interest being their survival into Dark Age Greece. There seems no doubt that those of the Samian Heraeum are in the same tradition, as there are significant points of resemblance to twelfth-century bull figurines from Amyklai. It is also likely that the tradition continued in Athens, as the painted decoration (of dotted semicircles) on a bull from the south slope of the Acropolis would suit the sub-Mycenaean style. This is not conclusive, for there is a very thin dividing line between the latest Mycenaean and the earliest Sub-Mycenaean, and there are in fact no known later wheel-made bulls from Athens. On the other hand, the same technique is still to be found in the stag (see Pl. 26) which came from a late tenth-century grave in the Kerameikos, and indeed in the Lefkandi centaur (see Pl. 46). It could also be argued that these last two pieces reflect the renewal of Cypriot influence, but the possibility of local survival cannot be completely ruled out, especially as a fragment of an animal, said to come stylistically between the stag and the latest bull, has been discovered (a surface find).

The later part of this discussion has concentrated rather on the question of continuity, and a brief summary may be given. For continuity of religious beliefs and practices from the Mycenaean age, there is the evidence of the Samian Heraeum, mentioned above; the knowledge that a Mycenaean deity continued to be worshipped in later centuries at Amyklai is even more cogent, for it depends on the literary testimony, and detailed archaeological investigation has not revealed it, showing instead a gap of at least a hundred years – if this could happen here, it could also have happened in other areas; thirdly, there is the obvious fact that there were people of Mycenaean descent in Greece and the Aegean during our period. The argument against is more in the nature of a warning that one cannot always assume continuity simply because a cult place used by the Mycenaeans was at some later time also so used. Delphi is a case in point: and there are two not yet mentioned, as they have produced no Dark Age material – the shrine of Apollo Maleatas near Epidaurus, where there is a gap between Mycenaean and Geometric, and the cave of Pan, not far from Marathon, which revealed nothing between Mycenaean and the fifth century B.C. In other words, one must have very strong evidence before accepting continuity of worship in any individual shrine. And one further possible pitfall may be mentioned. The appearance and diffusion of the Homeric epic during the eighth century gave rise to an intense interest in, and veneration of, the great heroes of the past. The remains, still visible, of the great Mycenaean palaces and tombs obviously belonged to these heroes; and so you could get sacrifices to them in their tombs – and there is evidence that shrines were built at about this time on the presumed sacred spots: a particularly good example is a shrine of Agamemnon at Mycenae itself, the earliest pottery being of the late eighth century. Consequently, one can get a sort of artificial continuity, and so care must be taken.

To conclude, it should be made quite clear that the limitations of the evidence available during the Dark Ages prevent us from getting even a semblance of the true picture. On so many sites – even Athens and Lefkandi – we have almost nothing but tombs, which are of minimal assistance towards the understanding of religion. Settlements are exceedingly few, and their identification often depends solely on a deposit of pottery, with no trace of any building; and even where there are house constructions, only a fraction of the settlement has been uncovered. There is no reason for not believing that every village or town had its communal sanctuary; admittedly these may have been of a very primitive kind, and almost every trace of them is likely to have been erased by succeeding generations, but there should still be something which one must hope that excavation will reveal in course of time.

Crete

So far, the evidence under review has tended to show how extremely difficult it is, on archaeological grounds, to establish continuity of religious practices from Mycenaean times into and beyond the Dark Ages; it was concluded, however, that in view of the extreme scarcity of material assignable to our period, whether of shrines or objects associated with them, it would be rash to assume any large-scale discontinuity, especially when one bears in mind that many communities must have included people of Mycenaean origin.

In Crete there is much less uncertainty. The Dark Age links with the Minoan past are manifested in most aspects of the material remains, and the following analysis will make it clear that cult continuity was one of the major features, both from the shrines themselves and from the votive offerings.

In Minoan times, as Hutchinson wrote in his *Prehistoric Crete* (p. 218), 'the holy places were peak sanctuaries, cave sanctuaries, spring houses and domestic shrines'. Examples of all of these have been identified in Dark Age contexts. Karphi may be said to qualify as a peak sanctuary, though its use was confined to the life of the settlement. In the second category there is the Dictaean Cave, which was held sacred not only during Minoan times but well on down into the historical period – offerings certainly datable to the Dark Ages are very few, but they do exist. A cave at Patso, in the Amari district, has produced a similar picture.

There is only one known example of the use of a sacred spring in the Dark Ages, but it is an important one, the Spring Chamber attached to the Caravanserai building south of the Palace of Knossos. This shrine (Fig. 31), originally built in the sixteenth century, was still in use as such in the Sub-Minoan period of the eleventh century, even though the building it formed part of had long been deserted. At this point, however, it was abandoned.

The principal features of the late Minoan domestic shrines are that they were small and simple, of oblong rectangular shape, with an entrance at one of the narrow sides, and at the further end a ledge for the cult objects.

Of the Dark Age shrines, the temple of Karphi has the ledge (and cult objects of pure Minoan type, as will be seen), but the entrance was in the long side, and there may have been no roof. A closer example seems to be the small sanctuary of Pachlitsani Agriadha, near Kavousi in east Crete, apparently built in the twelfth or eleventh century, and attracting votive offerings from then until the sixth century B.C. Furthermore, the Cretans went on constructing shrines in this way, since the earliest temples of Dreros and Prinias, dated to the eighth and seventh centuries, still recall the latest Minoan ones.

To what extent there is real significance in the continuance of use of this very simple kind of shrine one cannot be sure – and it should be borne in mind that similar ones are not unknown to the end of the Mycenaean world, as for example at Asine – but at least it is evidence of a positive type, not available elsewhere in the Greek world during the Dark Ages.

Such is the evidence for the type and architecture of Dark Age shrines. One other may be added to the list, the open-air sanctuary at Ayia Triadha near Phaestos, but this has, so far as I know, no Minoan predecessor.

The objects associated with cult practices may be divided into two classes, the figures of the deity concerned, and votive offerings in the shape of clay animals (there are of course other types of votive offering and cult objects, but these for the most part I disregard).

In the Mycenaean world, the terracotta figures and figurines of deities or worshippers had no Dark Age descendants; in Crete it is very different. During the thirteenth century, if not earlier, the main deity was a goddess, portrayed with upraised arms, and it was precisely this goddess who dominated the succeeding centuries. Those of Gazi, west of Knossos, have been dated to the twelfth century; the figurines of Prinias belong to the twelfth or eleventh centuries, the period covered by the most spectacular goddesses of all, the ones of Karphi (Pl. 21), some three feet in height. The little eleventh-century goddess who inhabits a hut-urn,[4] found in the Spring Chamber at Knossos, belongs to the same family. And similar figures were still being made in the tenth and ninth centuries, at Kalokhorio in the Pedhiadha plain, and at Phaestos. Finally, it may be noted that it seems to have been this type of goddess which the Cretans took with them when a number migrated to Cyprus c. 1000 B.C., and that the type remained long in use in that island. There could, I think, be no better proof of the persistent survival of Minoan cult practices, and the objects that often accompanied them, such as the curious snake-tubes and the rhyta, are of similar Minoan ancestry.

Mention has already been made (pp. 282 f.) of the votive animals, especially bulls, and also of their presence in Crete and the possibility that they were introduced to that island by immigrants from Mycenaean territory. In fact it is not easy to establish the chronological priority of mainland Greece, since both here and in Crete they chiefly flourished in the twelfth century,

---

[4] These hut-urns have no Minoan precedents, and were introduced during the twelfth century from somewhere unknown, surely outside the island – but they were still suitable dwelling places for Minoan goddesses.

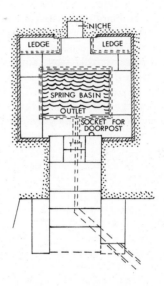

FIG. 31 KNOSSOS, PLAN OF SPRING CHAMBER SHRINE
P. of M. II, i, p. 125, fig. 60.

with uncertain thirteenth-century antecedents; their presence in Cyprus in the early twelfth century, but not later, leads one to prefer the theory that these, and so probably also the Cretan ones, both stemmed from people fleeing from the mainland disasters at the end of the thirteenth century.

However that may be, it is their subsequent history in Crete that is the important point. At Ayia Triadha they made their appearance in the open-air sanctuary that apparently succeeded a shrine in which the goddess with upraised arms was worshipped, and has been dated to the twelfth century, perhaps continuing into the eleventh. A similar date has been tentatively assigned to those found at nearby Phaestos, where the context is unclear. The votive animals of the cave at Patso are also of this period, but they are absent (maybe significantly) from Karphi. A few have been recovered from the Dictaean Cave, but the main proof of their continuity throughout the Dark Ages comes from evidence from the ninth and later centuries from Kavousi and Vrokastro, and from sanctuaries at Gortyn and near Lato.

There is then ample proof that Minoan religious customs, and perhaps also practices introduced by immigrants at the beginning of the twelfth century, persisted into and beyond the Dark Ages, and dominated them;

and further instances could be added. So in the matter of continuity this aspect of the archaeological evidence is of considerable positive value for Crete.

There are no doubt many other conclusions of importance for religious thought and ideas, but these would involve a general survey of Minoan religion, which would be out of place here. Superficially, one encounters a much more concrete sense of religion in Crete than in other areas of the Greek world, but that is surely due to circumstances. In Crete we have been fortunate; elsewhere, with so much of the material confined to cemeteries and their contents, we have not.

19 Pottery

Such emphasis has been put on the pottery found on Dark Age sites, and so much built on it, that it may seem unnecessary to discuss it further. It is, however, precisely because it has had to bear the weight of so many conclusions that one should analyse most carefully how valid our inferences are.

Pottery is interpretable in two basically different ways, either as the main, and sometimes the only, means of enabling the archaeologist to build up a chronological sequence, or as material which provides information on the conditions existing at the time it was made, and on its users. The first is essential, and its value not to be doubted; the second, many-sided, may need a more cautious approach.

Without the pottery, our approach to the Dark Ages would be as obscure as those ages themselves. It has three outstanding virtues: it is found everywhere, it is liable to regular stylistic change, and it is indestructible. It provides our relative chronology, and it is by reference to preceding and succeeding styles of pottery that we determine whether a site was inhabited during the Dark Ages. Since we are concerned with a considerable area, and therefore many districts and more sites, the internal relationship is established almost always, and in any case in the first place, by cross-references between the pottery of one region and that of another. The importance of its use in this way can be exemplified by the problems that arise when it fails us. For example, in eastern Crete there was a remarkable persistence of the Sub-Minoan style of pottery, and it was not superseded until well on into Geometric times, perhaps two generations or more after the accepted end of our period: what then should be placed within the Dark Ages? A similar example appears in Laconia; there is no known previous style on which to attach what is called Laconian Protogeometric pottery; there are no obvious links with the main area, the Aegean, where the pottery gives us a safe sequence; the style which follows on can hardly be dated earlier than 800 B.C.; how much of the Laconian Protogeometric can then precede 900 B.C. (taken as the end of the Dark Ages) or, even if it does, how can one tell how long before?

The pottery found on a particular site places that site in chronological relationship to others. And it does more, as it equally determines the relative date of the other objects associated with it, so that as a result they themselves can very occasionally be used as chronological aids. An obvious example is that by the use of the basic pottery we can determine roughly when and where the working of iron was introduced to Greece.

So far, the emphasis has been on relative chronology, and of course the more frequent the stylistic variations, and the more numerous the ceramic links between district and district, the more detailed and clear a picture we get. There is, however, another consideration, that of absolute chronology. Here, as we have seen (p. 134), there are no written records available within the Aegean area throughout the Dark Ages, and the nearest area where such can be found is the east Mediterranean. Some link or links must therefore be sought between the Aegean and the Levant, either directly, or indirectly through Cyprus. The result is, as earlier indicated, the establishment of the dividing line between early and late Dark Ages as *c.* 1050 B.C. through Cyprus and thence, perhaps a little shakily, to the Levant; the establishment of an approximate date of *c.* 1125–*c.* 1100 B.C. as the beginning of the Dark Ages in the central mainland area, computed on the probable interval of time elapsing after the start of L.H. III C and the links between this and Philistine pottery, whose dates are at least based on absolute chronology; and the establishment of a likely date *c.* 900 B.C. for the end of the Dark Ages, inferred from the assumed length of time occupied by Early and Middle Geometric pottery, wherein cross-references are to be found in Palestine. And the whole system depends fundamentally on the pottery.

To sum up, in an age without written records, the pottery provides the archaeologist and historian with the fundamental means of calculating relative and absolute time, the absolute element being by far the more arbitrary.

It is obvious, therefore, that the importance of pottery in this respect is vital; and there is a rather natural tendency to expect it to give equally vital information about the conditions of the period. We must then try to be as clear as possible as to how far it really can help us.

One initial point must be stressed, that during the late Dark Ages vase-making and vase-painting provided the main outlet for artistic expression – the early Dark Ages I would exclude, as it does not seem to me that such a term can be applied to Sub-Mycenaean pottery. But with the Athenian Protogeometric style art was created anew, so to speak. There was no scope for works of architecture or sculpture or of major scenes of painting, nor were the metalworkers capable of making use of such opportunities as they had; consequently the potters had the field to themselves for a long time, and their medium was held in such high esteem that it retained its supremacy, and attracted great artists, for many centuries.

Now this artistic development, as such, surely reflects a change in atmosphere in Athens, but that I will deal with later, and will first discuss the conclusions which can be deduced from its diffusion.

It is an undoubted fact that many Athenian vases of this style found their way to other districts, and that elements of the style were incorporated by potters elsewhere over a wide area. What does this mean? Take the case of actual exports, first. This means that the vase in question had to be brought from Athens, whether by the donor or the recipient. In Crete, for example, there are two skyphoi and a lekythos at Knossos; another skyphos was found at Kanli Kastelli, well inland. At least the skyphoi can hardly have held any useful or valuable contents, and so must have been prized for themselves. This surely argues, at the lowest, free intercommunication at this time, and an artistic appreciation in the place where the vase arrived as well as in the place of origin, such as is not likely to have come about during a time of continuing flux and stress.

The fact that the Athenian style was imitated reinforces the conclusions based on imports, and the more widespread the imitation, so one gets a more general picture of intercommunication, in this case by sea, at least throughout the central and southern Aegean. How did the potters of the various districts come to know of the Athenian style and the technical improvements it involved? It is extremely unlikely that they themselves engaged in travel, and consequently they will have depended on what they saw in their own towns. This sounds a rather unnecessary assumption, but it can be shown to be not unfounded. The main technical improvements were a faster wheel and so a greater ability to produce a taut, clear profile, and for decoration the pair of dividers with multiple brush to produce circles and semicircles. Now the non-Athenian potters were clearly not very proficient in imitating the vases themselves – this appears particularly in the failure to reproduce the high conical foot which was one of the main features in Athens. On the other hand, they had no difficulty with the circles and semicircles; but I would think that there was no need to have expert instruction in this – once seen, it should be quite easy to work out how it was done. Also, however, there was often a failure to appreciate the principles of the decorative system that the Athenian potters had evolved, of the idea of relating the decoration of a vase to its shape: the placing of full circles on the shoulders of closed vases is an example. I would suggest that a fair amount of Athenian pottery found its way to other districts, and that the local potters copied and adapted from what they saw.

The Athenian Protogeometric style provides the best and clearest example of impact on other styles, due to its superiority. There are, however, other possible instances of lesser influences and interconnexions which, if proved, would lead to fuller understanding – so far, we have only been able to show with certainty that the Athenians were in touch with other regions, not that these were in touch with one another. In such cases, one has to proceed rather more cautiously, and often one needs a good deal more material than is available: an instance of the difficulties that may arise will be found in the attempt to analyse the elements contributing to the pottery of the Dodecanese (pp. 173 ff.). On the other hand, the late material from the west Peloponnese, Aetolia, and Ithaca, clearly shows an interconnexion of developments.

Even greater caution has to be exercised in the early Dark Ages, for here we are faced with pottery which stylistically derived from that current in the final phases of Mycenaean civilisation; one must be sure that an apparent link or borrowing is neither a manifestation of the common heritage, nor an independent development. For example, the custom of leaving on an otherwise monochrome bowl a narrow panel between the handles, and painting a wavy line or zigzag within: this goes back to the twelfth century in the Argolid, and the evidence shows that it persisted there for long into the Dark Ages. But when one comes across examples of this in Messenia, where we are so ignorant of the preceding stages, are we justified in assuming that the idea came from the Argolid? Why should such a rather elementary decoration be imitated? One needs a sufficient range of material, and one needs to demonstrate reasonable accessibility; and it is also helpful if one can show that the style from which the borrowing may have been made was superior in technique, though this is not essential. One should also be reasonably sure that the ceramic features concerned cannot have been evolved from a previous style, or independently conceived, or borrowed from some other area. Given these conditions, one can·then suggest intercommunication between one site or district and another, and that this was of a peaceful nature. On the other hand, one must not infer, simply because there were no ceramic links, that there was no intercommunication. Positive, not negative, evidence counts.

So far I have supposed that pottery provides proof of intercommunication simply in the nature of trade, or visits for other purposes. None of this must be thought to involve any migration, any transfer of people, whether on a large or a small scale. There are, however, instances when that can reasonably be shown to have taken place. It can be said to have happened if the pottery of one site, newly occupied or reoccupied after an interval, closely resembles that of another site or district, and basically different, in case of reoccupation, from what had preceded it. The best example of this is to be found at Miletus (p. 83), in spite of its distance from the central Sub-Mycenaean area. Another example is Lefkandi, where the reoccupation pottery is sufficiently different from that of the abandoned settlement to suggest that there was no link, and at the same time very similar to that of the nearby Sub-Mycenaean districts. In such cases, the less attractive the pottery, the stronger the probability of migration. But if it is of high quality, we may be left in doubt. For instance, in certain islands of the Cyclades the earliest known and only Dark Age material consists of the odd vase or sherds which are either tenth-century imports from Athens or close imitations of Athenian Late Protogeometric: but I would hesitate to say this proves Athenian settlement. In general, it is desirable, in order to show movement of population, to have as much material as possible, and to be able to point to other links, such as burial practices. The evidence of the pottery is fundamental and necessary, but one must be careful not to build too much on it.

Another aspect of pottery, when thought of as linking area with area, is its use for carrying commodities. This must be borne in mind, even though it cannot lead to the identification of any particular commodity. We do not know, for example, what jugs and amphorae contained; we can do no more than guess what sort of commodities may have been transferred from one place to another. Grain and oil are the most likely, but there is no proof. However this may be, it leads on to another consideration. We have seen that vases could be a commodity in themselves; we assume that other vases were useful as containers – other communities must have had some way of familiarising themselves with, for example, the Athenian Protogeometric style which they freely imitated, and this seems as reasonable a way as any. The situation being so, is it not acceptable evidence for trading activity? There are no doubt other explanations, but this one seems the most likely. And it may be added that it was an activity that was basically maritime.

The pottery of the Dark Ages is, then, not only the basis on which we depend for our chronology, but also provides us with the means for establishing that there was intercommunication between certain districts, and gives a clue as to the type of links that existed. As well as this it should be able to tell us something about the community in which its makers worked.

The first point concerns the potters themselves, and their status. During the Dark Ages – and this was surely a legacy from the Mycenaean world, never entirely forgotten – the potters were professional craftsmen. This is not a matter of plain, usually coarse, domestic pottery, but of something quite different (even in the early period); the potters made their living by the exercise of their craft. How then were they paid, in a community that had no knowledge of the use of money? I feel it can hardly have been arranged on the basis of an exchange of gifts, as is visualised for the heroes of the Homeric epic, for that seems too casual a criterion. There must have been a well-organised system of barter, with recognised equivalent values for the various products, whether natural or manufactured. We may speak of Dark Ages, but it is clear from the position of the potters, and indeed also of the metalsmiths, that we are faced with at least a few substantial communities, of urban rather than village character, containing groups of artisans as such – and probably, in the case of Athens, a group of traders responsible for the distribution of the potter's creations.

Further inferences on social and economic conditions are, even though not necessarily confined to Athens, at least best exemplified there. Ceramic evidence for increase in prosperity is somewhat uncertain. The only vase shape which may be significant is the pyxis; it is very likely that it was used for perfume, and if so may indicate a rise in the standard of living in the later Dark Ages, when it first appeared. It may also be that the multiplicity of vases in the latest Protogeometric tombs of Athens means a growing prosperity on the part of some, but that is a rather modest conclusion.

More important, and more debatable, is the role played by the pottery in the hypothesis of the great feeling for organised uniformity in Athens. Over a fairly long period in the late Dark Ages one finds much the same kinds of vase, with much the same type of decoration: if they were all the products of a single workshop, that would explain the situation to some extent, but I would think it more likely that there were two or three, in which case the homogeneity is remarkable. To this may be added the uniformity of the vases used in burials, in the sense that the urn for the ashes was invariably an amphora of unusually large size, with one type of amphora normally reserved for men, another for women. Other aspects of the evidence contribute to the notion of a sort of regimented situation, but much of it depends on the pottery.

Finally, something more insubstantial. It seems to me that a community gets the type of pottery that reflects its circumstances and mentality. Apply this to Athens, and one gets the following picture. First, one encounters a depressed and debased style of pottery, the Sub-Mycenaean. The potter took little interest in what he was making, and it would seem that this echoes a cultural disregard (whether natural or induced by circumstances one cannot tell) on the part of the community. Then comes the period of the opening up of the seas, the contact with Cyprus. Out of this there emerged the Protogeometric style, not a copy of the Cypriot, but something entirely new and self-created. This surely implies a community with renewed confidence in itself. And the way in which the new style developed, especially its insistence on proportion and correct relationship between shape and decoration, likewise probably reflects the Athenian mentality as a whole at the time. This is not to say that the style was formed in answer to some public demand, of course, nor does it mean that the credit did not belong primarily to the potter; but it could have been an answer to an unspoken need, to some potential quality in the Athenians.

20 Dress and Dress Accessories

No representation of what the Dark Age people wore is known to us. For Mycenaean times we have at least some idea of the dress of the upper class from frescoes, men and women depicted on vases tell us what was the correct clothing for hunters, warriors, and mourning women, and the terracotta figurines may provide further clues as to female dress. We also know a certain amount about what men and women wore from the eighth century onwards, again from the depicting of human beings on vases and also from figurines, but this time also from the poets Homer and Hesiod. Of the two poets Homer is deliberately archaising, one must assume, but one cannot be sure to what degree. Hesiod, who wrote not later than the seventh century, describes contemporary fashions for men in winter in a passage worthy of quotation:

> Then put on a soft cloak [chlaina] and a tunic [chiton] to the feet to shield your body – and you should weave thick woof on thin warp. In this clothe yourself so that your hair may keep still and not bristle and stand upon end all over your body. Lace on your feet close-fitting boots of the hide of a slaughtered ox, thickly lined with felt inside. And when the season of frost comes on, stitch together skins of firstling kids with oxsinew, to put over your back and to keep off the rain. On your head above wear a shaped cap of felt to keep your ears from getting wet.

Unfortunately, one cannot accept either the Mycenaean evidence or that of the eighth century and later as a true account of Dark Age dress. The Mycenaean is the nearer in time, but the subsequent changes were so radical in other matters that we cannot be confident that there was continuity in dress – and indeed, as will be seen, there must have been at least one fundamental change. The later evidence is the more likely to reflect the true picture, but the distance in time is great, and fashions change. Most recent research has concluded that while in Mycenaean times men normally wore a short tunic and cloak, and a kind of loin cloth, from the Dark Ages onwards they discarded the latter but retained the tunic, which could be short or long, while instead of the cloak they seem to have had an enormously long and enveloping shawl or plaid, to judge from an eighth-century vase representation. As to women, the Mycenaean world shows them wearing a long close-fitting dress, which later evidence indicates that they retained; on the other hand the heavily flounced skirt and short jacket went out of use during or at the end of Mycenaean times. From the Dark Ages onwards a new standard item of apparel made its appearance, known

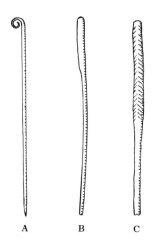

A   B   C

FIG. 32 DRESS PINS
A) Roll-top. Athens, Sub-Myc. *JdI* 77, p. 87, fig. 5, 1.
B) Spatulate. Athens, Sub-Myc. *JdI* 77, p. 87, fig. 5, 6.
C) Spatulate. Argos, L.H. III C. *Nécropoles de la Deiras*, pl. 24, 5.

as the *peplos*: this, it has been suggested, was formed by sewing together a number of lengths of material, so that one got something about the shape of a blanket, then doubling it over and sewing the short ends together; the wearer would then step into this, would fasten it up on each side of her neck, and then bring the two 'wings' downwards in front so that they joined at the waist, where they were fastened.[1]

So much for what may have happened. So far as the present work is concerned we have to depend on such objects that were not perishable – in other words, not only have we no reproductions of the human form, but no fabric has survived except in minute quantities and attached to metal. The most important of these objects, as providing a radical change from earlier Mycenaean times, are the long dress pins. Equally important, they have often been found in pairs, in the position they would have had in lifetime, one over each shoulder. In most cases they were associated with women, and it has reasonably been deduced that they formed the shoulder attachments of the *peplos*. There were, however, instances where they were found singly, and also where they were associated with male burials (on the chest but not on the shoulder), so it must be assumed that they could be used in other ways as well. But the main point is that this evidence supports the idea of a significant innovation in female dress, the *peplos*.

The dress pins were not the only dress fasteners: there were also the

[1] The main evidence for this comes from Iron Age burials in Denmark, therefore much later, but it is argued that it can be traced through Europe to Greece. The subject is discussed fully by I. Hägg in *Tor* (1967–8), pp. 81 ff.

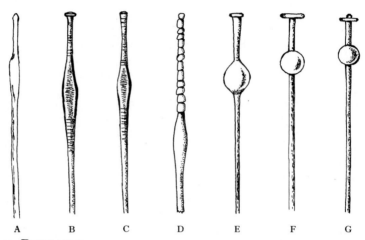

A   B   C   D   E   F   G

FIG. 33 DRESS PINS

A) Slight swelling. Knossos, Ayios Ioannis, Sub-Min. *BSA* 63, p. 213, fig. 4, B4.

B), C) Bulbous swelling. Athens, Sub-Myc. *JdI* 77, p. 86, fig. 4, 2 and 11.

D) Ring mouldings. Argos, L.H. III C. *Nécropoles de la Deiras*, pl. 24, 3.

E) Globe. Athens, Sub-Myc. *JdI* 77, p. 83, fig. 1, 8.

F) Globe. Athens, PG. *JdI* 77, p. 99, fig. 17, 2.

G) Globe. Athens, PG. *JdI* 77, p. 94, fig. 12, 6.

fibulae, the brooches – or, more accurately, safety pins. These were not an innovation of the Dark Ages, as they are very occasionally to be found in Mycenaean contexts, but from the Sub-Mycenaean period onwards they became far more common, especially in the developed arched type. They were associated with both men and women, and it is not so easy to see exactly how they were used. It has been conjectured that they were fasteners for tunics, or alternatively for cloaks and shawls – the latter explanation is the more plausible, as the evolution of the shape and the gradual strengthening of the bow suggest that they were intended to hold together a substantial fold of cloth. It has also been suggested that where they are found in quantity they may have been used to fasten the shroud. Whatever their purpose, however, they too seem to represent some new practice.

These were the only objects which can be called dress accessories.[2] Their importance for the Dark Ages, however, goes beyond their use as such, as a careful study of types and distribution reveals.

The pins were a common feature of the early Dark Ages in the main area for which we have satisfactory evidence, central mainland Greece, and also in Crete (one must remember that in a number of other districts the true Mycenaean culture probably still persisted, and that long dress pins

---

[2] There are also the bronze studs, which probably belonged to belts, from Vergina in Macedonia. These I pass over, as the area seems to have been out of contact with the Greek world during all but the very latest phase of the Dark Ages.

have no place in these). There were quite a number of different types of these pins: these, and their origin, form the chief topic of discussion.

Two of the types, the short roll-top pin (perhaps not used for the same purpose as the long pins) and that with a flat and slightly widened upper part of the shaft, are only rarely found (Fig. 32). Of the roll-top pin there are two in the Salamis cemetery, one in the Kerameikos. The other is represented by one from Argos and one from Athens. For both, a Near Eastern origin has been confidently suggested.

Apart from these there are two main types, A and B (Fig. 33). Type B has more than one variation. The simplest form, with just a very slight swelling towards the top of the shaft, is known only at Karphi and at Knossos;[3] it is tempting to think that it was from this that the other variations developed, but I doubt whether this was the case. The most popular variation has a small nail-like head as well as the bulbous swelling at the top of the shaft, and this can be traced throughout the central mainland area, with minor local differences, but has so far not appeared in Crete. Finally, there is a type with no head but strongly marked ring-like mouldings (as opposed to the shallow incised rings which may appear on the other variation) above the elongated swelling as far as the top of the pin, and also for a short distance below it. Two of these were found at Argos, and two in a tomb in the Gypsades cemetery near Knossos. Two more of this type, of very late Protogeometric date and much more sophisticated, were found in a tomb group from somewhere in the north Peloponnese (p. 250), but on the whole dress pins of type B did not survive into the late Dark Ages. The origin at least of the variety interestingly shared between Argos and Crete has also been given as the Near East, on the grounds that a not unsimilar one came from a tomb of this, or possibly an earlier, period at Gezer in Palestine.[4]

Pins of type A, like some of type B, had a small nail-like head but, instead of the elongated or bulbous swelling at the upper head of the shaft, a globe. There were no variations, and the type was confined to the central Sub-Mycenaean area during the early period. The only development – and it was an important one – was that at the very end of the period, in Athens and at Lefkandi, some of the pins were made of iron, not of bronze. This was the type that was to dominate the later Dark Ages, and my impression is that it was a later, locally evolved, and more efficient development of the other main type. It has however been suggested that its source is to be sought in remote antiquity, in the long bronze pins with crystal globes of Shaft-grave circle B at Mycenae.

It will be evident that one of the important questions concerns the origins of these essentially non-Mycenaean accessories, and so far the claims of the east Mediterranean seem to be strong for the two rare types and for one of the variations of type B. Two further pins of this early period, not yet mentioned, tend to strengthen such claims. The one is from a late Sub-

[3] These sites also had pins without any swelling at all.

[4] Macalister, *Gezer* II, 84; III, Pl. 133, n. 19.

Mycenaean tomb at Athens, is of iron and has an ivory head; the second (Pl. 60) was found in a Sub-Minoan tomb in the Knossos area, a very long slender bronze pin with no swelling but a rectangular section at the top of the shaft and, again, an ivory head. Links are indicated with the east not only in the iron but more especially in the ivory.[5] It is therefore of some interest that a similar pin should have been found in Cyprus, the main source of connexions with the Aegean: of bronze, with ivory head, it comes from a tomb at Kourion and is dated to about the mid-eleventh century.[6] Could one even suggest that the whole idea of such dress pins came from Cyprus?

Other evidence, however, indicates that the case for primary or substantial influence from the east Mediterranean is by no means proved. First, it is curious that three pins, two of which are of types for which an eastern origin has been claimed, were found in a tomb in Kephallenia in association with L.H. III C pottery (p. 91) and so very likely of twelfth-century date. Furthermore, Kephallenia is more noted at this time for its northern connexions than for any contact with the east. But this does not prove that the pins came from the north; not only have no pins been found in any other tombs here or in north-west Greece, but it is by no means impossible that there was some link between Kephallenia and the east. The Gezer cemetery, mentioned as producing one of the varieties of pin of type B, also revealed a krater[7] which both in shape and decoration is remarkably like one from Kephallenia (belonging to a class characteristic of that island). Was there a link? Which way did it go? At any rate it is a little unsafe to use the evidence of these pins by themselves. Secondly, the tenth-century tombs of Vergina in Macedonia contained a few pins (see Fig. 21) with small heads and elongated swelling on the shaft, similar to one of the variations of type B, and in origin almost certainly northern. This suggests a northern source for at least one type of pin, but does not exclude eastern influence in other cases.

To suggest that there are two separate and far-removed sources for the long dress pins seems an improbable answer. Perhaps one should, after all, conclude that all the types were evolved locally, as experiments – though the theory of a far earlier origin for pins of type A seems unlikely in view of the enormous time interval. If one says this, however, then one surely has to consider the actual use for which these pins were intended, and this will have been the new type of dress already discussed. Can this also have been a local development? I do not know, but due weight should be given to the placing of the pins, one on each shoulder, and to the fact that long bronze pins (though none of precisely the types found in the early Dark Age of

---

[5] Ivory is extraordinarily rare otherwise in the Dark Ages: another iron pin, with ivory head and bulb, from a Protogeometric cremation in Athens, an odd and unexplained object from a Sub-Mycenaean tomb in the Kerameikos, and a pendant, certainly of east Mediterranean origin, from a tenth-century tomb at Fortetsa (p. 230).

[6] Now and later there are a few examples of all-bronze pins which seem to belong to type A, in that they have a globe on the shaft.

[7] Macalister, *Gezer* II, 180; III, Pl. 163, n. 2.

Greece) were worn in just this way by the people of the Tumulus Culture of central Europe for centuries before their appearance in Greece, and that they continued in use later as well. No such characteristic similar use is known in the east, so far as I know.

The discussion has been lengthy, since it has a bearing on the vital matter of the origin of the whole Sub-Mycenaean culture. One cannot pretend that it has been successful in dispelling the obscurity, unfortunately. The other points of interest derived from the study of the pins are reasonably clear: the evidence for intercommunication within central mainland Greece (not in any doubt) and very possibly between Knossos and Argos (but just when?); and the appearance, at the end of the period, of iron as an alternative to the otherwise universal bronze.

The later period can be dealt with much more briefly. As stated, type A became dominant. In Athens (Fig. 33), the construction of the head of the pin was improved: instead of a rough nail-like shape there was now a flat circular disk, its size more in proportion to the globe below. At the end of the period a small finial knob was added to the disk, and the ninth century saw a further elaboration of this finial, as well as other ornamental additions, such as incised decoration and collars above and below the globe. Generally, iron replaced bronze (at least for the shaft of the pin – see below) until the very end of the Dark Ages, when bronze came back into favour again, though iron was still used in Early Geometric times.

These pins were on the whole shorter than those of the early period, and the type, or something similar, is to be found in many areas of Greece, though rare as yet in Thessaly,[8] and virtually unknown in those districts, such as Laconia, where we have no cemetery evidence.[9] They have been found both in Crete[10] and the Dodecanese, and provide further proof of the frequent and peaceful intercommunication of the period, and of a culture that originated in the central mainland area.

It is likely that in certain districts we can even narrow down the area of origin to Athens, in view of one refinement not yet mentioned, namely that while the rest of the pin was of iron, the globe was made of bronze. This remarkable, and evidently artistically pleasing, combination was characteristic of Athens, so much so that it must surely have been invented there. Consequently, it is fair to conclude that where such pins have been found in other regions, in the Argolid, at Theotokou in Thessaly, and on Kos, they are most likely to have come from Athens, or at least to have been inspired by the Athenian type.[11] It confirms the eminence of Athenian craftsmen, already so clear in the pottery, though later developments show that in

[8] Only one, of iron, from the child cemetery at Iolkos, which nevertheless had a number of fibulae; was the age a factor here? For Theotokou, see below.

[9] Ithaca has one of bronze.

[10] Those wholly of iron from Knossos include a new development, the globe becoming biconical; similar ones in bronze from Vrokastro may be later than our period.

[11] This type of pin remained in occasional use in Athens till c. 850 B.C., so it is not inescapably a Dark Age criterion by itself.

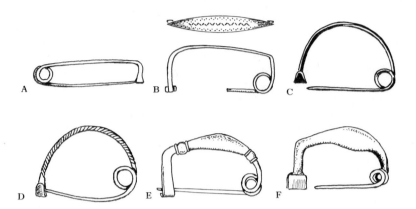

FIG. 34 FIBULAE
A) Safety pin. Mycenae, L.H. III C? Blinkenberg, *Fibules Grecques et Orientales*, p. 46, fig. 9.
B) Leaf-shaped bow. Athens, Sub-Myc. *JdI* 77, p. 87, fig. 5, 7.
C), D) Arched. Athens, Sub-Myc. *JdI* 77, p. 83, fig. 1, 4; p. 87, fig. 5, 13.
E) PG bronze. Athens. *JdI* 77, p. 108, fig. 26, 3.
F) PG iron. Athens. *JdI* 77, p. 108, fig. 26, 17.

metalwork at least the Argolid soon came to rival Attica, but whether before the end of the Dark Ages is not clear.[12]

Fibulae (see Fig. 34) differ from dress pins at the outset, as they already had a Mycenaean background, and so may be said to constitute an element of survival, even though not of Mycenaean origin themselves. The violin-bow fibula (the earliest type) has been found in most parts of the Mycenaean and Minoan world, though in small numbers.

This type of fibula can be subdivided into the 'safety-pin', which seems to be the simpler and earlier form, and that whose characteristic is a leaf-shaped bow, sometimes incised. In the Mycenaean age, the distribution of the simpler type appears to be confined to the Ionian islands, the Peloponnese, and the south Aegean, whereas the leaf-shaped type had a wider, but rather less numerous, diffusion.

In the early Dark Ages the 'safety-pin' version was still in use in Crete, but nowhere else, to my knowledge.[13] A few fibulae with leaf-shaped bow were also found in Crete during this period, but otherwise appear only in areas north of the Peloponnese. There are two from Athens, and at least two from Lefkandi (see Pl. 41). And, which is surprising, they were still in use in the late Dark Ages in Thessaly, as is proved by their discovery with Protogeometric child burials at Iolkos (Pl. 49) – as unfortunately we have

[12] The discovery of evidence for bronze-working at Lefkandi, *c.* 900 B.C., may indicate the growing importance of that area as well. For the Argolid, see the discussion of the fibulae, p. 302.

[13] I omit the fibulae from Aetos in Ithaca, as they have a small catch-plate, a feature not otherwise paralleled, and are difficult to date.

no earlier evidence of fibulae from this region, we cannot tell whether this is the survival of previous usage or whether it was introduced by people from further south, e.g. from Euboea (see pp. 103 f. for the general problem here). This later persistence suggests, however, that the type must have been more firmly entrenched in this general area than could be deduced from the very small number known to the early period.

However this may be, there is no reason to doubt that the other main type, the arched fibula, was much the more popular. Furthermore, the great probability is that it was a creation of the early Dark Ages, probably within the central Sub-Mycenaean area; either that, or it was introduced from the north.[14]

These fibulae are to be found everywhere in tombs that can be attributed to this period. As with the dress pins, it was a time of experiment, though there is no such sharp difference between types; the variations that could occur are well exemplified by the collection from tomb 108 of the Kerameikos in Athens (Pl. 8), but whether similar variations were prevalent everywhere one cannot tell. Again, as with the dress pins, the very latest phase of the period saw the first signs of the use of iron instead of bronze, but only at Lefkandi, and not at Athens, a difference which conceals a rather more radical one, namely that no fibulae at all have been found in the latest Sub-Mycenaean, nor indeed in the earliest Protogeometric, Athenian tombs. There are three possible explanations of their absence: that fibulae lost favour for some time as a fastening, that bronze was in very short supply (odd, if this phase includes the time of Cypriot influence; see pp. 316 ff. for further discussion) and that, as is true, it was not easy to make a fibula of iron, or that it is a matter of chance. I would not like to say which is right.

The situation in the late Dark Ages is by no means clear. In Athens, as with the pins, an improved design made its appearance; the bow was stilted at the catch-plate end, and was thickened in the middle, on either side of which thickening there was a bulb flanked by two rings or fillets, at least in the bronze ones; the spring was double rather than single. This type persisted into the early ninth century, iron being much more commonly used than bronze in the Protogeometric period; furthermore, it was, with one exception, the only type in use, thus supporting the evidence of general uniformity visible in other matters (pp. 138 f., 157 f.). What we do not know, however, is whether so far as the fibulae were concerned the uniformity covered the whole of the late Dark Ages, due to their absence in the early stages.

In other areas we are hampered by the unevenness of our evidence, occasionally by the failure to illustrate the fibulae reported as found, and also by certain problems of relative chronology, in particular the difficulty of identifying any but the latest phase of the Dark Ages.

North of Athens, the situation at Lefkandi is that the use of fibulae, so prevalent in the last stage of Sub-Mycenaean (in complete contrast to

---

[14] I regard the few arched fibulae from chamber tombs (Perati, Argos) as contemporary with this period.

Athens), most likely continued in the early stages of Protogeometric; after that one cannot yet tell for certain, but both iron and bronze fibulae were current at the end of the Dark Ages, including an excellent example in bronze of the Athenian advanced type (Pl. 60), but the simpler type was still used.[15] In Thessaly, the small fragment of an iron fibula from Theotokou is in line with the previous evidence, but those from the child cemetery at Iolkos were of bronze, either arched or, as already mentioned, of the earlier type with leaf-shaped bow; these seem to have been in use throughout the late Dark Ages. And at Marmariani we encounter for the first time the spectacle fibula, of iron and evidence for contact with areas to the north (see Fig. 22); these, however, are not likely to precede the ninth century.

Across the Aegean we have evidence only from Crete and the Dodecanese, where all the known fibulae of the period are of bronze. To this there seems no exception; also, almost all were of the simple arched type. No exception again in the Dodecanese, but it is not impossible that four from a tomb at Vrokastro, of the advanced Athenian type, could belong within the tenth century.

So there is little uniformity as between district and district – and the evidence from the Peloponnese is the most surprising of all. With three exceptions, there are no fibulae assignable to the late Dark Ages – and furthermore, the exceptions (bronze, and of the type common in Athens) all come from the one tomb.[16] But from other sites, absolutely nothing. This is not a matter of lack of evidence, for the Argolid produced a fair number of tombs, and there is material for this period from Messenia, and a few tombs in the western districts. Dress pins are known, but not fibulae. Can this be accidental? For the west and north-west it may rather be lack of knowledge on our part; it is probably from Achaea that the three known fibulae came, and it is significant that fibulae – of what type we do not yet know – have been found in recently discovered pithos burials in Aetolia, where the tenth and ninth-century culture and customs seem closely allied to those of the west Peloponnese. In Messenia and the Argolid it could be more than accident, but one should still be cautious; at Mycenae, for example, no sooner had the tenth century given way to the ninth than one finds a fibula of remarkably fine and elaborate technique, and although the associated vases are very close indeed to those of Athens of the same period, they were locally made, and there is no reason to suppose that the fibula, and the two dress pins of equal workmanship, were not native products as well (Fig. 17).

Meaningful inferences are not easy to suggest. So far as concerns the technique, it is exceedingly likely that the Athenians led the way (as we know they did in other matters), but there is reason to believe that by the beginning of the ninth century, if not before, the craftsmen of the Argolid were their equals, and further discovery could produce similar evidence from other areas. Certain regions may have preferred to retain the simple arched type, but in Thessaly there are traces of an older conservatism in the

---

[15] The iron fibulae were often so corroded that it is impossible to reconstruct the type.

[16] I have assigned this to the very late tenth century (p. 250), but it could be a little later.

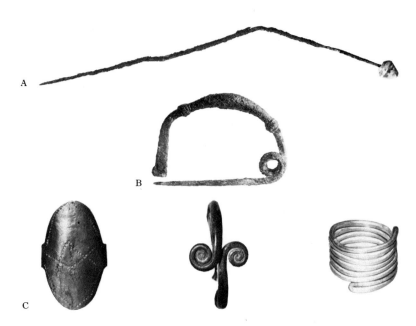

PLATE 60
A) Dress pin from Knossos (Ayios Ioannis). *BSA* 63, pl. 54*g*.
B) Arched fibula from Lefkandi. *BSA* 65, pl. 11*c*.
c) Gold finger ring and hair spiral; bronze finger ring with double-spiral
terminals. *BSA* 64, pl. 34*a–c*.

survival of the violin-bow fibula with leaf-shaped bow. As to the metal, the
one point which probably has significance is that in Crete and the Dodecanese bronze was always used,[17] as opposed to its normal supersession,
until the final Dark Age phase, by iron in the areas from Athens northwards. This could be the result of continued communications with Cyprus,
and is a factor to be borne in mind in the question of the availability of
bronze (pp. 316 ff.). Finally, as to the scarcity or absence of fibulae, whether
in Athens during the early stages of the Protogeometric period or in the
Argolid during the whole of it, it seems safer not to commit oneself until
much more evidence is available.

Of the personal ornaments, as opposed to ornaments connected with the
dress, the finger rings were the most common. A number of different kinds
could be used: with overlapping ends, or completely circular; of wire, or a
thin strip, or much more massive, and the outer part curved. Whether a
close study of these would reveal regional or chronological differences I do

[17] Tholos tomb II at Vrokastro had an iron fibula, but one cannot say whether it belonged to
the Dark Ages.

not know, but am a little doubtful. There are, however, two unusual and distinctive types which call for brief comment, and both went out of fashion after the early period. One, the ring with oval or rather angled bezel (Pl. 60), reflects the Mycenaean tradition. This has been found, in bronze, in the Sub-Mycenaean cemeteries of Salamis and the Kerameikos;[18] in gold, there is one of unknown provenience of probably the same period, and two from Crete, the one from a twelfth-century tomb at Mouliana, and the other from a tholos tomb at Vrokastro whose chronological limits are not easy to determine. The second type of ring, with double-spiral terminals, has a clear northern ancestry; apart from central European examples, these rings have been found at Vergina in Macedonia (possibly tenth century), in a tomb at Hexalophos in Thessaly which may be dated c. 1100 B.C., and associated with an even earlier cist burial at Elaphotopos in Epirus.[19] Consequently their appearance in our area in the early Dark Ages, in the Kerameikos and at Mycenae, and probably at Lefkandi, is of great interest. All these are of bronze, and there is another, of unknown provenience (probably Athens), in the Elgin Collection of the British Museum (Pl. 60).

These rings are, then, predominantly of bronze, and so are most of the others of the early period; at or near the end of it, though, rings of iron are known from Athens, Corinth, and Theotokou – precisely as happens with the pins and (far more rarely) the fibulae. Iron was also used, as might be expected, during the late Dark Ages. Those we have are almost exclusively from sites to the north of Athens – but it should be noted that there is an almost total absence of rings of any metal from Athens and Lefkandi. In the Argolid, on the other hand, rings were still fashionable, and were all of bronze, while from Messenia just one bronze and one iron ring have been reported.

A different picture altogether is to be seen in the Dodecanese and Crete. In both, rings were reasonably commonly used; in the former, they were either of bronze or gold; in the latter, Vrokastro produced rings of bronze and one of iron, but at Knossos gold, astonishingly, seems to predominate – just a few of bronze, none of iron, and two of silver, these being the only known artefacts in this metal during the Dark Ages.[20] Furthermore, the presence of gold in these two regions is in sharp contrast to its absence elsewhere, except in the earliest phase of the later period at Athens and Tiryns, and then only used for hair rings, as noted below.

Other types of ornament can be dealt with very briefly, though they help, when taken as a whole, to fill in the picture. Hair rings or spirals are mostly found in the central mainland area, chief interest attaching to a type made

[18] An oval bezel of bronze has recently been found in a Sub-Mycenaean tomb at Corinth; oddly, the ring with which it could be associated is of iron (p. 69).

[19] A further one has recently been reported, from a chamber tomb at Amphicleia in Locris. The finds are not yet published, but are said to include very late L.H. III C pottery and fibulae of violin-bow and arched types. See Iakovidis, Perati, vol. II, 293 n. 5.

[20] There was also a unique ring of faience, confirming other evidence for contact between Crete and the east Mediterranean.

of doubled wire which is of northern origin or inspiration (Pl. 60). The few examples of this type seem to cover only the middle of the eleventh century, are known from Athens and Tiryns, and are usually of gold – they are, indeed, almost the only objects of gold assignable to the early period or to the beginning of Protogeometric. Bracelets made of bronze are rare, with no particular chronological or geographical limitations. Necklaces seem also to have been rare, though stray beads turn up from time to time on many sites. Those of faience are of particular interest, as the material suggests contact with the east Mediterranean, and it is therefore not surprising to find such at Knossos, on Kos (see Pl. 36), and on a Rhodian site, all of the tenth century;[21] what is more unexpected is that one was found in a late Sub-Mycenaean tomb at Lefkandi – this is presumably another manifestation of the brief contact with Cyprus at this time, though so far as I know none has been found in such an early context in that island.

[21] A necklace of faience from Athens is only slightly later, but just within the Geometric period. Lefkandi has also produced some of the ninth century.

21 Armour and Weapons

The analysis of dress accessories was preceded by a discussion on the type of dress, but such a discussion is not possible for armour and weapons.

We know, in fact, so little about armour that all can be summed up in a few paragraphs. To start with, we have no idea how a warrior protected himself against attack except by the use of helmet and shield. Between the early twelfth century and the eighth there exists no figure or figurine of a warrior, nor any representation of such in vase painting, with the single exception of the two confronted archers at Lefkandi, where in any case the figures were drawn in such a rudimentary fashion that it is difficult to build much on the head coverings they seem to wear.

Comment is confined to helmets and shields, both of course essential elements of armour. For helmets we have only the bronze one from Tiryns, of the middle of the eleventh century, an object which may have northern connexions (Pl. 11, and see p. 111). It is obviously impossible to say whether this was in any way typical. If any deduction at all is to be made, it is that helmets of metal were not in common use, and that a head covering of leather was the more customary.

It is also reasonably certain that the shield was similarly made of some perishable material, since here our only evidence is that of a number of metal fittings, bosses, presumably attached to the centre of the shield. These were basically similar in shape (Pl. 25), but capable of slight variations. It has indeed been doubted whether they were used as shield attachments at all, and the probable answer is that very similar types of object could be used for more than one purpose,[1] but the actual context in which some were found proves that they were warlike accoutrements and therefore most probably belonged to a shield. There are not many: the earliest Aegean ones may be the two from Mouliana in Crete, of the twelfth century; otherwise they fall into two rough chronological groups – at the end of Sub-Mycenaean, one associated with the Tiryns warrior and one from Athens; at the end of the Dark Ages, two from Athens and one from Skyros.[2] Their origin is obscure; none has been found in a Mycenaean context. Their presence in a Cypriot warrior's tomb of the early eleventh century, even though they are later than those from Mouliana, may suggest that the idea came from Cyprus, especially as there are a few later examples

---

[1] Those of Vergina in Macedonia were dress accessories for women. See on this question Snodgrass, *Early Greek Armour and Weapons*, 37 ff.

[2] It is perhaps worthy of note that none of the Athenian bosses was associated with any weapon; they were used simply as covers for the ash-urn.

FIG. 35 SWORD. Mycenaean cut-and-thrust type.

from this island. They were probably not in regular use, or more would surely have been found associated with weapons.

Weapons are slightly more revealing, but not a great deal, and there are the usual chronological and geographical gaps that lead to uncertainty. We can at least, however, establish what kinds of weapon were in use, and we can sometimes point to Mycenaean or Minoan predecessors, though it is only in the case of the latter that any sort of continuity is observable, since in the Sub-Mycenaean area of central Greece, except for the sword and dagger of the Ancient Elis cemetery, themselves very difficult to date, we have no record of weapons being deposited in tombs until the very end of the early Dark Ages.

The weapons can be classified as follows. First, swords and daggers, those over half a metre in length qualifying as swords, those shorter than this being daggers.[3] Then there are the pikes (only found in Crete) and the spears, which in fact means the metal part of the weapon, the spearhead. It is also known that bows and arrows were used but, as will be seen, the evidence for them is extremely slight. Finally, there are a number of knives, which merit brief discussion even though not all of them will have been used for offensive purposes.

It will be best to dispose straight away of the bows and arrows, as there is so little to say about them. Four barbed arrowheads have been found, three of bronze from the settlement of Karphi, so belonging to the early period, and one from a late tomb in the Kerameikos at Athens. Two bows are depicted on an early tenth-century hydria from Lefkandi (Pl. 42), both with an exaggerated double curve as though the bow was extremely flexible, and the archers in the act of shooting. So bows and arrows were used: that is all; no conclusions can be drawn as to the frequency of their use, or even as to their purpose, though at Lefkandi it will surely have been a matter of warfare.

Nor is there any need to delay for long over the knives. Bronze ones are extremely rare, so far found only at Karphi in Crete.[4] Those all of iron are relatively few, scattered here and there over most of the Greek world, and not sufficiently distinctive in type to give rise to useful inferences.[5]

[3] A further subdivision has been made for daggers, as to whether they are short swords or dirks, but it will be simpler to disregard this distinction here.

[4] The Dictaean Cave sanctuary has many, but I do not know whether they belong within the Dark Ages.

[5] The three in Athenian tombs were associated with weapons.

Finally, there is a small class on its own, of iron but with the handle rivets of bronze;[6] specimens have been found in the later Mycenaean material of Perati and Lefkandi, and in Crete in Dark Age contexts at Knossos (Fig. 14) and Vrokastro; probably imports from the east Mediterranean – they are known both in Cyprus and in Syria – their chief interest lies in the strong support they give to the argument that iron was introduced to the Aegean from this quarter.

Swords and daggers and spearheads may be dealt with together, as being the standard weapons, and for the most part of types current in the latest stages of Mycenaean civilisation, which may thus provide an introductory background.[7]

The latest Mycenaean swords were, with a very few exceptions, of what is known as the Naue II type (Fig. 35); fashioned in such a way that one could both cut and thrust with them, they were therefore superior to earlier kinds of sword, and it is extremely likely that they were introduced to the Mycenaean world from the north, an attractive theory being that they were brought by mercenaries. These were all of bronze: in iron, they were to be the characteristic sword of the Dark Ages.

Daggers of the same type, cut-and-thrust, were virtually unknown to the Mycenaeans; far more common was a weapon with square shoulders (Pl. 17), one variety of which was centred on Crete (where it also appeared as a sword), the other variety having its main distribution in the north-west of Greece, Kephallenia, and the fringe areas of Aetolia and Epirus, but with one found as far afield as Perati. This type, however, failed to survive except for one specimen in the Ancient Elis cemetery, possibly indicating a backward state of affairs in this district, especially as the only other weapon, a sword, was of a Mycenaean type not found in any later context (Pl. 13).

A similar fate seems to have befallen one of the distinctive types of Mycenaean spearhead, with blade described as lanceolate (Pl. 13), a type with very much the same distribution as that of the square-shouldered dagger; there is no known example of it in the Dark Ages. Apart from this, there are not many spearheads on the latest Mycenaean sites, but such as there were seem to have been the predecessors of some found in our period – and, as opposed to the swords and daggers, they continued during the early Dark Ages and even a little later to be made of bronze.

The actual catalogue of Dark Age weapons is hardly impressive.[8] There are the two from Ancient Elis, already mentioned; Athens (Figs. 36–39) has produced the largest number, about a score from a dozen tombs, covering the whole period from late Sub-Mycenaean to the end of Proto-

---

[6] The technique has been explained by Snodgrass, *Dark Age of Greece*, p. 217. If the rivets were of iron, they would have to be closed when red-hot, which the early smiths may have found difficult to do; with bronze rivets this would not be necessary. It could thus be a sign of earliness; on the other hand, the same technique is known later, and is not confined to knives.

[7] There are also the pikes, but these have no Mycenaean precursors, and are only to be found in Crete.

[8] For illustrations of some of these, see under the sites concerned.

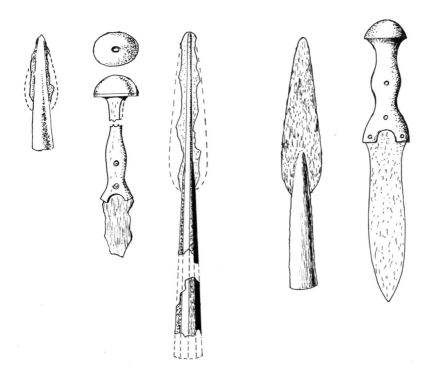

FIG. 36 Spearheads and dagger
Athens, Kerameikos, PG. *JdI* 77, p. 89, fig. 7, 2–4 (tomb A).

FIG. 37 Spearhead
Athens, Kerameikos, PG. *JdI* 77, p. 90, fig. 8, 1 (tomb 34).

FIG. 38 Dagger
Athens, Kerameikos, PG. *JdI* 77, p. 90, fig. 8, 7 (tomb B).

geometric; one tomb only on each site covers the weapons from Delphi, Skyros, Tiryns, Argos, and Ialysos, and in the substantial Lefkandi cemetery only one sword, one dagger, and two spearheads have so far been found. In Crete, on the other hand, a fair number of tombs on sites all over the island produced weapons, the majority being spears; swords were scarce, and there are a few iron pikes, of Cypriot origin, from Knossos; it is not always easy, however, to determine the type of weapon, for sometimes they were inextricably corroded together. Finally, a small number of weapons were found at Kapakli and Marmariani in Thessaly, and at Asarlik in Asia Minor, but these could belong to the ninth century.

What conclusions may be drawn from this meagre and scattered body of evidence? The first is, surely, that under the circumstances it is dangerous

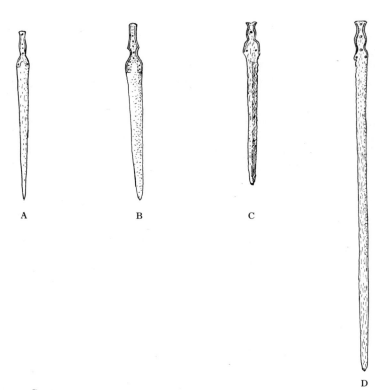

FIG. 39 SWORDS
Athens, Kerameikos
A) PG (Cypriot import?). *JdI* 77, p. 91, fig. 9, 4*b* (tomb E).
B) PG (Cypriot import?). *JdI* 77, p. 91, fig. 9, 7*a* (tomb 2–N).
C) PG. *JdI* 77, p. 91, fig. 9, 1*a* (tomb 6).
D) PG (this sword was 'killed'). *JdI* 77, p. 92, fig. 10, 1*a* (tomb 28).

to accept any conclusions as certain or as representing the whole. We cannot have anything like the true picture, though we may come somewhere near it in Athens. Even so, there are a few useful pointers, a few inferences of a tentative nature.

To start with, the Mycenaean heritage seems not to be in doubt. This need not be a matter for surprise; there were, I think, many communities of Mycenaeans which survived into the early Dark Ages, and there were also mixed communities, both Mycenaeans and others of non-Mycenaean stock. Even if such newcomers as there may have been were in the majority, or else in political ascendancy though in the minority, they may have found that the weapons used by the Mycenaean survivors were more efficient than their own, in so far as these were different. It is in any case a feature of continuity which may be set alongside the pottery.

On the other hand, it is also right to stress the existence of weapons which originated in or reflected some other area than that of the Mycenaeans. We have seen that the daggers and spearheads that were characteristic of the north-western fringe of the Mycenaean world did not survive, and so can have made no impact. If we look in the opposite direction, however, towards the east Mediterranean, there are items of interest. In Athens, two of the swords, the one of the end of the early period, the other probably near the start of the late period, have clear Cypriot associations, and so has a spearhead of the same transitional phase (see Figs. 36, 39). Also, the iron pikes which made their way to Crete – but no further, so far as we know – were of Cypriot type, if not origin.[9] And, most important of all, the very metal, iron, of which most of the Dark Age weapons were made, was the result of knowledge that came from the east Mediterranean.[10] This, how-ever, is a matter of wide significance and some complexity, which I deal with more fully below (pp. 315 f.).

Any survey of this sort should be able to make some comment on the kind of armament generally in use, and on the attitude of the community towards warfare. It is just here that the poverty of the material deprives such comment of much of its value. To say that warriors used swords, daggers, and spears, and occasionally knives, is a conclusion of a rather ele-mentary and obvious kind, and a similar one can be drawn from many other periods and areas, including those preceding and succeeding the Dark Ages. Was it, however, the custom for a warrior to have only one weapon, or an assortment? At Knossos there are two burials where the warrior had a number of weapons, but in most cases in this island it proved impossible to determine the distribution; the Tiryns warrior had two daggers and a spear. At Athens, the best documented, a combination of dagger and spear seems to have been popular, but there are instances of swords on their own, one case of a sword and a knife and one of sword and spear,[11] and in two tombs there was just a spear. One tomb, finally, had a dagger, a knife, and two spears. So there was no uniformity, and it is probably safest to conclude that the same situation held elsewhere.

Inferences as to the warlike nature of a community, or its opposite, are equally a matter of uncertainty. It is reasonable to assume that every com-munity had its warriors, but I cannot see that any of our evidence indicates the existence, for example, of a warrior class – it is in fact most unlikely, as most of the communities were surely far too small for such a separate class

---

[9] Snodgrass, *Dark Age of Greece*, p. 253, thinks it possible that other weapons in Crete (perhaps later) may also reflect Cypriot types.

[10] The iron weapons at Vergina are probably an exception to this, but this site and its problems are marginal, and I have mentioned them only in so far as they impinge on the districts to the south – see pp. 217 ff. A good and full discussion is given by Snodgrass, *Dark Age of Greece*, pp. 253 ff.

[11] This combination, familiar to the Mycenaeans, only reappears in the tenth century; it is also found in one of the Athenian type cremations at Lefkandi (Pl. 44).

to exist. I have noted (pp. 238 f.) that in Crete weapons have been found rather more frequently and regularly than elsewhere, and that conditions may have been more unstable, but other evidence leads to a different interpretation. If anywhere, a martial outlook is to be found at Vergina in Macedonia; that is outside my sphere, but it has its use in leading to the possible conclusion that other communities were not particularly warlike. Even this, though, is probably an unsafe inference, for we do not know whether it was the invariable custom to provide the dead warrior with his weapons. Particularly with swords and daggers, made entirely of metal, there may have been many instances where there was a handing down from father to son. May not the absence of weapons deposited in tombs over a period simply mean that metal, whether bronze or iron, was in short supply, the weapon therefore having of necessity to be made to last as long as possible? How can we possibly tell under what circumstances it was felt right to bury with the dead man one or all of his weapons? How are we to interpret, for that matter, the curious habit, known so far only in Athens and at Lefkandi, of 'killing' the sword (p. 142, n. 11)? If it was thought to be of possible use to the dead in the other life, why bend and distort it to such an extent that it was obviously useless to him wherever he was? Or was the sword thought to have a life all of its own, to be extinguished when its owner died? These questions, like so many others, seem unanswerable.

22 Metals

Gold

There is no evidence that this metal was available locally either to the Mycenaeans or to their Dark Age successors; gold is indeed found in the Aegean area, but the main sources were in Thrace and Macedonia, on the fringes of or outside the Mycenaean world – the lesser deposits in the Cyclades were evidently unknown. Consequently, the presence of objects of gold in Greece and the Aegean means that either the objects themselves or the metal had come from elsewhere.

In Mycenaean times gold artefacts were by no means uncommon, and are thus a witness to the power and outside contacts of this civilisation. It is extremely likely that the gold came from the east Mediterranean, both from the known links with that area in other respects, and because there (above all, Nubia) was one of the chief sources of the metal. After the late thirteenth-century disasters the supply was very much less, the known objects being virtually confined to the communities of the central Aegean group, which preserved their contacts with the east for a while during the twelfth century.[1]

During the Dark Ages gold was even scarcer than before. There is nothing until the end of the Sub-Mycenaean phase (unless some of the objects from the latest Mycenaean communities round and in the Aegean belong to this time). Then, at the end of this phase and into the beginning of the next but no further, a matter of probably not more than a generation, there is some evidence: hair spirals from Athens and Tiryns, hair spirals or earrings and a finger ring from Lefkandi, all within the area where there was temporarily renewed contact with Cyprus. So, it would seem, these objects are yet further proof of such contact; but not all of them, for some of the hair spirals were of a northern type.

After this brief flowering there followed a complete dearth until the very end of the Dark Ages, everywhere except in Crete, which evidently retained its long-standing links with the east Mediterranean, and probably also in the Dodecanese, so far as we can tell from the available evidence. Elsewhere, however, nothing, and this certainly suggests strongly, though does not absolutely prove, that most of Greece and the Aegean was isolated from the sources of gold.

---

[1] There was of course communication with Cyprus, but the situation here was also rather disturbed, and gold objects less common than earlier.

Silver

Mines from which silver could be extracted are to be found in much the same regions as for gold, Thrace, Macedonia, and the Cyclades, and there were also the mines of Laurion in Attica. In the Mycenaean period, however, there is no evidence that any of these deposits were known, and in any case, and in contrast to gold, artefacts of silver are very rare indeed except at Perati, and the metal was thus not normally imported from the east Mediterranean or elsewhere.

The Dark Ages present, superficially, an even more gloomy picture, since the only datable objects – probably of the late tenth century – are two finger rings from a tomb near Knossos. One would then naturally assume that the local sources were just as unknown as to the Mycenaeans, but two recent discoveries of probable traces of the extraction of silver by the process of cupellation prove that this is a false assumption; the one was at Thorikos, a few miles north of Laurion, and is to be dated *c.* 900 B.C., while the other was at Argos, a construction apparently in use during the latter part of the eleventh century. It is hardly necessary to stress that we must suspect any conclusions based purely on the absence of artefacts. This evidence, however, suggests that the process of silver extraction was probably known to the metalsmiths at least of the Argolid and of Attica.

Bronze and Iron

There are deposits of iron in Greece, and also of copper, one of the two constituents of bronze, but not of the other constituent, tin. Before the Dark Ages no use was made of the iron deposits, and iron itself was, until the second half of the twelfth century, regarded as a precious metal, for a reason that will be explained below. There is slight evidence that the local sources of copper were tapped, but for all practical purposes bronze was imported in the form of ingots from the east Mediterranean, presumably from that great centre of copper, Cyprus.

Since iron came into the same category as gold and silver, bronze was thus the sole and staple utilitarian metal – all weapons and tools, and a considerable number of other types of object, were made of it. As it had all to be imported, any dislocation or diminution of the source of supply could create serious problems. This is precisely what started to happen at the end of the thirteenth century, consequent on the general turmoil which affected not only the Aegean world but the east Mediterranean as well. Although there were intermittent movements of Mycenaeans to Cyprus, the reverse flow was clearly much less, and it is doubtful whether many more bronze ingots travelled to the Aegean. It is likely that there was a distinct shortage of bronze, but it need not have been unduly serious, because the population itself was very much smaller, and because it was possible for the smiths to melt down and recast utensils that were of no further use – a practice amply confirmed by the number of bronze founders' hoards found during this period.

This situation persisted into the Dark Ages and lasted for most of their early phase during which, as we have seen, there was still some unrest, and the remaining Mycenaean communities were, at least in certain cases, progressively weakened to the point of inanition. Then, towards the end of this phase, there came the definitive renewal of contacts between Cyprus and central mainland Greece, as evidenced by the pottery. It would be natural to expect this to be the occasion for the arrival of further supplies of bronze, but that is precisely what does not seem to have happened; instead, there came about the introduction of iron.

This was a metallurgical event of the first magnitude, not only for Greece and the Aegean but for the world as a whole. As we have seen, iron was until *c.* 1200 B.C. a precious metal; this was not due to its natural attractiveness, nor to any lack of deposits, but simply because until this time the knowledge of how to work it had been kept a closely guarded secret, confined to the smiths of the region of Kizzuwatna, a province of the Hittite empire which was probably situated in the south-east corner of Asia Minor.

It was the collapse of the Hittite empire that led to the general diffusion of iron-working, but this was bound to take time. The techniques indeed were entirely unfamiliar, involving skills beyond those of the bronzesmith. The first stage of the process, the heating of the ore to a certain temperature, would present no difficulty. Then, however, came the vital stage of carburisation, whereby the metal was hardened, and this was something new, as also were the two further processes, of quenching the carburised metal, then of tempering it by reheating and subsequent cooling, both of which needed a great deal of experience in selecting the correct temperature.

Once the technique was mastered, the plentiful supply of the ore, together with the hardness of the finished article, meant that iron became a utilitarian metal, an alternative to bronze, or an addition to it. It must not, however, be thought of as superior to bronze, as it has been shown that a number of bronze tools and weapons were harder than their iron counterparts. In fact, in areas where bronze was easily accessible it is a little difficult to understand why the new metal made any headway at all – there could be two answers, that the novelty was in itself an attraction, and that the craftsmen must have envisaged the possibility of further technological progress as time went on.

To return to the course of events, it will be evident that iron-working will have been introduced to the Aegean from the east, and there is little doubt that the immediate source was Cyprus, where iron objects have been found, datable to the early twelfth century as well as thereafter. Their presence did not by itself mean that transmission of the technique to the Aegean would be inevitable, especially in view of the disturbed nature of the period. The first step was that a number of iron objects (weapons, knives, and ornaments), made in the east Mediterranean, were exported to the Aegean; this was the situation in the latter part of the twelfth century and the early part of the eleventh. The momentous stage involving the actual transmission of the technique, and also involving the recognition of iron deposits in Greece itself, did not take place until near the end of the early Dark Ages, and was for a while limited to Crete, presumably the inhabited regions of the Dodecanese and the central Aegean, and certainly the Argolid, Athens, and Lefkandi in Euboea.

The main criterion for the local adoption and working of the new metal is its regular use, instead of bronze, for cutting implements, in other words weapons and tools, and in this respect the time coincides more or less with the beginning of the late Dark Ages, the Protogeometric period (not even then for spearheads, perhaps because – as Snodgrass suggests – the sockets were more easily made of bronze); a start was probably made slightly before this, however, to judge from the appearance of a few iron dress pins, fibulae, and rings in Sub-Mycenaean contexts.

The establishment of an iron industry in the areas named is, then, the predominant feature of the middle of the eleventh century so far as useful metals are concerned, and it will no doubt have been a particular advantage that iron deposits were locally accessible.

In the following stage, which may continue into the second half of the tenth century, the manufacture of iron artefacts was further extended, in bulk and slightly in area, but what now catches the attention is the rarity of objects made of bronze, so pronounced that it has led Snodgrass[2] to the conclusion that over most of Greece and the Aegean there was a serious shortage of bronze. This is an extremely interesting hypothesis, and one which deserves careful consideration; if proved, it would mean that most areas will have been isolated from the source of bronze, that is to say, Cyprus.

In his exposition of the theory Snodgrass distinguishes three geographical groups. In the first he places. Crete which, because of the continued use of bronze and from other evidence, he rightly considers still to have been in touch with Cyprus. To Crete may be added the Dodecanese, I would think, as it was equally accessible to Cyprus; our evidence suggests that there were links, but unfortunately what we have is more or less confined to the later tenth century, and Snodgrass prefers to connect this cluster of islands with his second group.

Besides the Dodecanese this latter group consists of Athens, the Argolid and Thessaly, and south-west Asia Minor, its peculiar characteristics being the prominence of iron-working and the extreme rarity of bronze objects. In fact the evidence from south-west Asia Minor, from Asarlik only, is somewhat fragile and uncertain, and it is better to omit it, and so far as Thessaly is concerned the material is confined to the coastal area. On the other hand, Euboea may now reasonably be added to the list, from the clear evidence of Lefkandi – and this is what one would expect. In effect, then, it is an important group, covering the central Aegean beyond Crete, extending northwards to the coast of Thessaly, and including the Aegean-facing areas of Attica and the Argolid.

[2] *Dark Age of Greece*, pp. 237 ff.

The third group consists of the other districts, away from the Aegean, to which knowledge of the iron-working process had not penetrated. These areas, for which our evidence is very slight, Snodgrass envisages as backward or isolated from the second group, the bronze objects therein revealed being of the heirloom type or the results of the melting down and recasting of such stocks as were still available. The implication is that this group was much more sparsely populated than the other two.

For what reasons is it suggested that bronze was in short supply? The arguments are based on the situation in the second group, and one has to concentrate on this: should the case for a shortage of bronze in this area seem convincing, there must have been a similar shortage in the more remote third group, which may then be disregarded. During the time in question, which is put at $c.$ 1025 to $c.$ 950 B.C., iron replaced bronze almost universally for 'working' or practical objects, in other words the weapons and few tools that have survived. This itself is surprising, since bronze could be just as effective a metal for such objects. But ornamental artefacts were involved as well. Here one has in any case to take account of the curious absence of fibulae and rings from Athenian tombs of the time, and similarly of fibulae from the burials of the Argolid; such as have been found, however, tended to be of iron,[3] and it was only gradually, towards the end of the Dark Ages and at the beginning of the Geometric period, that bronze recovered its dominion. Dress pins, on the other hand, which continued throughout (no doubt essential to the type of dress in fashion, see pp. 294 ff.), were regularly made of iron, the only occasional feature of bronze being the globe, an Athenian creation.

The theory cannot of course depend solely on these arguments; it must also be shown that there were no traces of contact between this group and the east Mediterranean in other respects after the transition to Protogeometric, and this Snodgrass makes a good case for, the one or two exceptions being perhaps understandable as heirlooms from the previous period, as for example an iron and ivory pin in a Protogeometric cremation tomb in Athens. There are, for instance, no gold objects anywhere until the closing years of the Dark Ages, although they continue to be found in Crete and the Dodecanese. To this it may be added that there was no further ceramic contact until the later tenth century – surprising in view of the situation in the middle of the eleventh.

Such then is the theory of bronze shortage, leading to the conclusion of complete isolation of the major second group from the east Mediterranean, and of a further relative isolation of the third group from the second. The latter point, involving the question of the relationships, or lack of such, between the non-Aegean and the Aegean districts, may be postponed till the concluding chapter. The dissociation between most of the Aegean and the east Mediterranean is the important problem. Are there any objections to the theory? I would say that there is nothing that rules it out of court, but there are factors that lead to hesitation in accepting it.

The main obstacle arises from the developments in central mainland Greece at the end of the early Dark Ages, the time of Cypriot links with this

[3] A more intractable metal for fibulae than bronze, it should be added.

area, as seen both in the pottery and in the introduction of iron. This is the time when in Athens, where the links are clearest, fibulae and rings became extremely rare, and when iron started to be used for dress pins. In other words, objects of bronze, plentiful earlier, went out of fashion just when links with Cyprus, the main source of bronze, were resumed. Admittedly the contact was temporary, but this is surely rather odd. Is it not possible that when the local inhabitants learnt that they had iron deposits in their vicinity, and had found out the various processes involved in working it, that they simply preferred for a while to use the new techniques and the metal to hand? In other words, may it not have been a matter of choice rather than of necessity? An instance of this during the Protogeometric period could be the iron pins with bronze globes; it is quite possible to make shaft and globe all of iron, as such exist, so the addition of the bronze globe was the result of personal preference, not necessarily a sign of bronze shortage.

If it is true that iron had the attractions of novelty and easy availability, then bronze may not have been inaccessible. There is, however, the other evidence, which cannot be other than negative, of absence of contact with the east Mediterranean. The lack of ceramic links is not a very cogent argument, for once a style such as the Protogeometric has emerged, there would be no interest in further outside influence – on the other hand, one might expect some exchange of vases between the two areas of the central Aegean and Cyprus, and this does not happen till towards the end of the Dark Ages; Athenian exports have not yet been found further south than Crete, and the eastern influence of the style stopped at the Dodecanese. The lack of objects of ivory and gold during most of the later Dark Ages could be explained as evidence of relative poverty among the communities concerned, that they had nothing of sufficient value to exchange, but this is not a very satisfactory argument, as the evidence tends to suggest a rise rather than a fall in prosperity after the middle of the eleventh century. Furthermore, there is the positive evidence of links between Crete and the Dodecanese on the one hand, and Cyprus on the other. It seems very likely, therefore, that there was extremely little contact between Snodgrass's second group and the east Mediterranean, but it might be going too far to call it an absolute isolation.

The final stage, the concluding phase of the Dark Ages, can be dealt with very briefly. What it shows is that bronze started to be used more frequently for dress ornaments, and this trend continues strongly during the first stage of the next period, together with an increasing flow of gold from 900 B.C. onwards. Contact was then resumed with the east, and this obviously strengthens the theory of preceding lack of such contact.

V

Later Literary Accounts

23 The Oral Tradition

In the haze of hesitancy and supposition that characterises this book it is gratifying to be able to make a statement of whose correctness one can be confident, and that is that the later literate Greeks had little or no knowledge of the Dark Ages. There is consequently no need to spend overmuch time in enlarging on their ignorance.

The art of writing had been lost to the Greeks for nearly half a millennium, and was recovered only during the eighth century, in other words over a hundred years after the end of our period. Whether this recovery gave immediate rise, in terms of the communities, to anything but the most elementary keeping of records is most doubtful, as will be seen later, but it is certain that there existed a substantial body of memories of the past, the oral tradition.

The earliest collection of this material was the monumental Homeric epic, to be placed, it is thought, round about 700 B.C. Assuming that it reflected a genuine tradition for the most part (however much misplacement and tendentiousness may have accrued), it is clear that a large number of stories had been transmitted, and this is confirmed by other information emerging from later writers. None of it, however, had anything to do with the Dark Ages, but centred on the events of the latter part of the Mycenaean age, and in particular the war against Troy. And before considering the significance and consequence of this, it may be noted that when later Greeks came to give a precise date to these events, they were not far out in their calculations. Herodotus, for example, gave it as his opinion that the Trojan War took place about the middle of what we call the thirteenth century, and from the general situation revealed by archaeology and certain other evidence this is just about when it could have happened – assuming, of course, that it did happen: in any case, the disastrous events towards the end of this century make it extremely improbable that there could have been such a war after 1200 B.C. Just how the Greeks made their calculations is not known. They were certainly not based on their own records, and a reasonable suggestion has been made that some knowledge may have been obtained from the accurate and long-standing chronologies of some east Mediterranean country, perhaps Egypt.[1] Whatever the source, it was believed, and led to much trouble, as will appear.

[1] Not the Israelite king list, as one later writer was able to claim that the Trojan War was contemporary with the reign of Solomon, which belongs to the early tenth century.

To return to the Homeric epic, this confined itself to the Mycenaean *fin de siècle*, made no attempt to go any further, and conjured up a vision of an age of heroes on familiar terms with the Olympian deities. Historically speaking, this was most unfortunate, for the epic made so tremendous an impression on the Greek world that there was thereafter a tendency to accept it as something historically inviolable, which it did not set out to be, and to regard it as providing the splendid ancestry in which all Greeks must seek their origins if they were to represent themselves as true Greeks. There arose a compulsive desire for relationship with a Heroic Age which came to an end over four hundred years before the writing down and diffusion of the epic.

Homer himself was in no way concerned with the intervening period, nor indeed was Hesiod, that expert on mythology and everyday conditions in Boeotia, who probably composed his works a little later. One thing, however, is worthy of note: it has been well observed that for Hesiod there had been a gradual deterioration of the state of affairs from the earliest times, with no conception of a Dark Age from which there had by his time been a considerable recovery – for him, matters were still in process of going from bad to worse.

From Homer and Hesiod we can pass straight on to the fifth century and to the two major historians of the time, Herodotus and Thucydides. And the first, and disturbing, fact we find is that, to judge from what Herodotus says – and it is amply confirmed by other authors – no clear knowledge existed as to when Homer and Hesiod themselves lived. If such obscurity clouded these two major figures, who belonged to the time after the re-introduction of writing, and so long after the end of the Dark Ages, what hope was there for accurate knowledge of those ages?

Neither Herodotus nor Thucydides wrote a general history of Greece from the earliest times: Herodotus' main theme was the Persian War, that of Thucydides the conflict between Athens and Sparta. In them, however, will be found many references to previous events, and their testimony is of great value for three reasons, that they were among the first of the historians, that their works have survived entire, and that they were scientific in their approach.

Both made occasional reference to the Heroic Age, and it is of interest that of the two Herodotus appears to be the more sceptical. What Thucydides did contribute, however, was a brief account of the development of Greece from Mycenaean times, of which the part after the Trojan War is the most relevant for us. First he mentioned a relatively short period of eighty years, during which there was general disturbance, many changes, upheavals in towns resulting in those ejected founding other towns. Two specific dates were given: the Boeotians came down from Thessaly and settled in Boeotia sixty years after the fall of Troy; twenty years later the Dorians together with the Heraclids gained control of the Peloponnese. With these events we are still only on the fringe of the Dark Ages, and thereafter the whole vast period down to the middle of the eighth century is described in a few words, to the effect that Greece eventually settled down peacefully only after a very long time and with great difficulty, instances of the settling down being the settlement by the Athenians of Ionia and most of the islands of the Aegean, and the colonisation of parts of Italy and Sicily by the Peloponnesians. The whole is considered to be a gradual and very slow process of improvement, with no thought of the Dark Ages, as defined in this book, forming a trough in between two civilisations of far higher standard.[2] In general, and even allowing for the fact that brevity was of the essence, it is clear from this and other indications that very little information indeed was available.

What was known, or at least believed, can be divided into two categories, for which some of the evidence is to be found in these two historians. The first category is that of movements of people. To begin with, only the Greek mainland seems to have been affected, groups travelling in a southerly or easterly direction, from outside or just inside the Mycenaean sphere: such were the Dorians and Boeotians, mentioned above, and other tribes such as the Thessalians, the Dryopes, and the Aetolians. Subsequently, and related to these, there were three major movements across the Aegean. The Dorians, from their Peloponnesian strongholds, chiefly Laconia and the Argolid, spread across the southern Aegean to Melos (its settlement placed by Thucydides as still within the late twelfth century) and Thera, to certain parts of Crete, to the Dodecanese, and eventually to the Asiatic mainland opposite. The northern island bridge was the route taken by the Aeolians, both from Thessaly and Boeotia, and they settled mainly in north-west Asia Minor, though they claimed the important island of Lesbos. The central Aegean and especially the adjacent coasts of Asia Minor were occupied by Ionians. Herodotus is our fullest witness for these last two, and it will be seen that, according to him, the Ionian move, though originating from Athens and consisting largely of Ionians, included many others, from Achaea and Arcadia, from north-west Greece (the Molossi), from Boeotia, Phocis, and Euboea, and even Dorians from Epidaurus in the Argolid. All this is of course of the greatest interest, if accurate – and the later known distribution of the various Greek dialects supports it; but, except for the earliest movements, the length of time involved could, for all we know, be considerable.

Further information on this point is given by the second category, which consisted of just what one might expect, lists of kings of the various towns, the chief of which, as already found in Herodotus, was the Spartan king list. And in course of time, if not from the beginning, certain of these kings or their relatives and connexions, including descendants of the heroes of the Trojan War, were believed to have been involved in one or other of the movements.

All this sounds most promising, and one would expect to be able to proceed to an accurate and helpful reconstruction of the sequence of events by a careful study of the several kings, their interconnexions, and the movements related to them or claimed as having taken place during their reigns. Most unfortunately, the evidence does not stand up to close analysis,

[2] Also, it may be noted, Thucydides took the opposite view from Hesiod, for whom things just went on getting worse.

and many inconsistencies are exposed. An extreme example may be taken. Temenos was one of the three Heraclid leaders who with the Dorians seized the Peloponnese, according to the conventional Greek chronology at the end of the twelfth century. He had a grandson called Rhegnidas, who gained control of the little town of Phlius; this would be not much later than the middle of the eleventh century. This event, as we are told by Pausanias, resulted in the departure to Samos of the leader of the opposition party in Phlius, Hippasos; and Hippasos was the great-grandfather of 'the famous sage Pythagoras'. Pythagoras should then have been living at the end of the tenth century, and so, one might think, one has an admirable Dark Age situation: until, that is to say, one discovers that Pythagoras belonged to the middle of the sixth century, a difference of no fewer than three hundred and fifty years. Such an example, of course, reaches the limits of absurdity, but there is evidently something seriously wrong.

What happened? To my mind, the major fault lay in the attempt to achieve genealogical contact or connexion with the Heroic Age where none existed – or at least where no records of any kind existed. A city of any importance had to trace its ancestry to a hero – if possible, to a demi-god. The worst offender was Sparta. The Dorians and their rulers had nothing to do with the Trojan War – that was agreed; so the kings had to provide themselves with an ancestor within the Heroic Age, and they selected one of the greatest, Heracles. And so one gets lists with Heracles at the apex; there is more than one version of the two royal families' genealogy, and one or two curious names crept in, but the result is that, when one comes to count up the extent of years involved, one finds that one is confronted with an average of forty years to each generation. Lower this even to the normal three generations to a century (and I doubt whether it could have been more), and all touch with the Heroic Age is lost, and we are barely within the closing years of the Dark Ages for the original twin kings who seized control of Laconia.

This conclusion has profound consequences when one considers the chronology of the many movements of population. It affects the whole question of the arrival of the Dorians in the Peloponnese. The balance of probability must be that they were in no way connected either with any of the disasters of the end of the thirteenth century or with the further decline in the twelfth. This applies not only to the Spartan element, but to those related members of the Heraclid family who supposedly gained power in Messenia and the Argolid – and over districts they later came to control, such as the towns and districts neighbouring on the Argolid, and Megara. And one must surely go further, and deny the traditionally high dates given to the diffusion of the Dorians across the Aegean. The dates of the other two trans-Aegean migrations, the Aeolian and Ionian, should also be questioned in so far as their leaders are in any way linked with the Homeric heroes.

So, it seems, there is good reason to reject all or most accounts of links with Mycenaean Greece, together with the high chronology of the movements of peoples, and the venerable ancestry of royal families. But this does not mean that there is no virtue in any of the oral tradition: we are prepared to accept that Homer's epic is based on the genuine transmission of folk-memory, so we should equally accept the possibility that something was known of the intervening centuries. There will surely have been fairly accurate lists of kings, written or remembered, father to son; on a calculation of three generations to a century – and one cannot go further – many go back into the tenth century, and so into the Dark Ages. There seems every likelihood that some movements into and within the Greek mainland, and across the Aegean, took place as tradition said they did; but it is perhaps safer in their case not to try to link them with any personalities, and so their datings are more uncertain – at least, though, if we can find reasonable archaeological grounds for any such movement, we are probably justified in paying regard to what the tradition tells us of the groups who took part. All, therefore, is not lost; but of the conditions prevailing in the Dark Ages later Greek history can tell us virtually nothing: there were kings, there were movements of people (the reasons for whose movements are irrecoverable) – but that is all.

VI

The Human Factor:
Interpretation and
Hypotheses

24 The Greeks of the Dark Ages

To this point I have concentrated on giving the evidence that has come down to us in clay, metal, stone, or other material – all the outward trappings and manifestations of those who lived and died during this age – and I have made some attempt to correlate them and to assess their historical validity. Occasionally, but all too rarely, I have sought to penetrate to the people themselves through such artefacts and constructions as have endured to the present day. In this chapter I shall try to recapture, however dimly, the atmosphere of the Dark Ages, to see the Greek world as some sort of a whole, progressing through a period of over two centuries. To do this without going beyond the evidence is of course impossible, and what will emerge will inevitably be an imaginative picture, though related as closely as possible to the known facts. I shall sometimes go beyond the facts, but endeavour not to go contrary to them.

What sort of conditions faced the communities of Greece and the Aegean at the outset of the Dark Ages? One factor at least was unchanging, the physical world. The main habitable areas are comparatively few, and often rather small, and the rivers are navigable only by lesser craft, and not even these all the year round. The soil is reasonably fertile in some of the plains, but in most cases it is thin, lavishly interspersed with boulders and outcrops of rock. Greece is, in other words, a poor country, imposing strict limits on the size of population it is able to support, and for most a place where one has to struggle for a living. But if there are not many plains, there is certainly an abundance of mountains, and these are the dominating feature of the landscape wherever one is – one cannot get away from them. They are indeed the main deterrent to unity; they encircle one, and hem one in, and lead to isolation. Travel between one habitable district and another is difficult and at times extremely arduous. As soon as one gets anywhere near the foothills (and as a rule this is not a matter of more than a few miles) the land becomes rutted with deep gullies; then one comes to the numerous spurs which thrust outwards, and thereafter one is faced with the barrenness of the mountains themselves, so often with little vegetation and no water. To travel even what looks like a short distance on the map means constant windings and deviations over perpetually rough ground. The natural thing to do was to stay in one's own small habitable area, and not to attempt an overland journey. One might then suppose that the mountains at least provided good protection: unfortunately, this was not so, as, though difficult to cross, they were by no means insuperable. Now this would not matter under stable conditions, such as those which held under the Mycenaean empire at its height, when in fact a surprising degree of unity was achieved. But once let there be some calamity, once one could no longer be sure whether those across the mountains were friends or foes, the sense of insecurity would only be increased by a barrier that was no real protection, that could conceal an invader until the last possible moment.

This was very much the situation at the time the Dark Ages started, and for many communities had been so for quite a time before. It might then seem that things were about as depressing as they could be, but two further factors have to be reckoned with. In the first place, although the mountains could not keep a determined invader out, they could act as an avenue of escape, and their very fastnesses could give protection. And secondly, there was a factor not yet mentioned, one almost as dominant as the mountains – the sea.

The sea is even more of an encircling element than the mountains. Greece must, for its size, have one of the longest coastlines in the world, and it has innumerable islands, both large and small, especially in the Aegean. For so many Greeks it provided the chief means of their livelihood, whether by its products or as a broad and limitless road of communication. Far more than the land, indeed, the sea was used as a means of getting from one district to another, and in case of overland attack on those regions which had a coastline – and most of them had – afforded a way of flight. But the sea also had its own perils. Storms can arise with frightening suddenness (as the Persian fleet found to its cost some six hundred years later), and the number of safe anchorages was strictly limited, and their safety would in any case depend on the quarter the wind was blowing from. The sea itself might destroy the ship; or if that hazard was avoided, there could be equal danger from land – no one who has travelled the Greek seas will forget the sheer cliff faces of island or mainland, the long stretches of steep and barren mountain. Even without this, the insecurity of the times would be a deterrent, especially in cases of journeys to the mainland. Finally, although at the time of the main disasters at the end of the thirteenth century and for some time into the twelfth the sea clearly was a protection, who could tell how long it would continue to be so?

Did nature provide any other hazards? So far, I have stressed the geographical features, by themselves and in relation to the prevailing feeling of uncertainty, but I have said nothing of climate. Now climate is one of the keys of Greek life – in summer, the harsh brilliant atmosphere, the strength-sapping heat of a relentless sun, the perpetual background of the cicadas, the scent of herbs, and all the other unforgettable sounds and smells; in winter, the rain and the bitter coldness of the wind. For some, an enchantment and an inspiration; for most, a never-ending battle not only against the land but against the elements as well. That is how it is now, but was it so then? In my first chapter (p. 22) mention has been made of the theory that there was a drastic change of climate during the course of the thirteenth century, whereby in many regions the winter no longer brought the reviving rain, and that consequently there came a catastrophic drought which accounted for all the disasters at the end of this century and led to the vast exodus from the land. It is a theory which receives not a little support from contemporary documents of Ugarit in the east Mediterranean, which speak of natural disasters;[1] and Professor Rhys Carpenter, its originator, believes that these conditions of drought persisted throughout the Dark Ages. If all this is true, then the country must have been able to support only a tiny population, and those who lived in it will have faced even greater hardships than one has supposed, and the whole pattern of settlement will have been affected in many areas, as well as the outlook of the wretched inhabitants. So far, however, it does not seem to me that any convincing proof of this theory, as applied to Greece and the Aegean, has been provided, and certain factors cast serious doubt as to its validity. Even if it should be true for the end of the thirteenth century, there is no reason to suppose that it was also true for the end of the twelfth century onwards through the Dark Ages. I shall proceed on the assumption that the climate was little different from what it is now, but if it was not, then we shall have to re-think our ideas.

One other general consideration must be borne in mind. Account must be taken not only of the geographical and climatic conditions, but also of the way man had made his mark on the landscape. This was a particularly important factor at this time, especially on the mainland. Here there were very few communities, mostly of very small size, the houses poorly built and hardly a trace of fortification. But this was not all. A bare hundred years earlier, almost within living memory, the main inhabitable areas had overflowed, not only with villages, but with towns, palaces, mighty fortified citadels, great monumental tombs, and wide and well-built roads. Now all was empty of life, but the visible remains will still have been everywhere, overgrown but not obliterated, a stark reminder to those who survived, or indeed to any newly arrived, that they lived in the shadow of a not far distant greatness, occupants of a lonely land, but a haunted one. How can this have failed to have an effect on the spirit, and contribute to the depression which is so manifest in the culture as a whole?

It would seem that all the conditions suitable to a Dark Age were there. Not only had the situation deteriorated with extraordinary rapidity, but there seemed no prospect of improvement; the temporary recovery had been an illusion, only leading to further insecurity. And with this there was the isolation imposed by the landscape.

Conditions and attitudes varied, of course, from district to district, and in accordance with the particular group one is dealing with. For a fuller understanding one must then discuss these variations in greater detail. Inevitably, however, one is faced with the problems of a Dark Age which owes its definition as such almost as much to our lack of knowledge as to the characteristics of the age itself. And there is one enormous area where not even the most fertile imagination can hope to recapture the atmosphere at the end of the twelfth century, comprising the whole of the central and southern Peloponnese – Arcadia and Laconia, Messenia and Triphylia,

---

[1] Furthermore, the archaeological evidence suggests the existence of a severe drought at the time of the city's abandonment in the early twelfth century.

and Elis except for the enigmatic cemetery at Ancient Elis, the type of whose tombs and contents forces one to discuss it with central mainland Greece, and yet as an entirely separate problem. It is more than unfortunate that this area should have to be excluded; it must be true that here the depopulation was extreme, but it was not total, and much may have been happening of which one knows nothing – and one loses the cross-references which may have been provided with other areas.

The first group are those who lived in and around the central Aegean, those who held fast to their Mycenaean traditions and who had emerged relatively unscathed from the earlier troubles. That they had thus escaped was, I am sure, due not to their own efforts, but to their good fortune in living in out-of-the-way places or protected by the sea. They were lesser people, of no great strength, but I think they had one great advantage that led to their continued survival and relative prosperity: I believe that their very position had meant their playing a considerable part in overseas trade; and as the sea routes, whether within the Aegean or outside it, to the east Mediterranean or to south Italy, were still open, they were capable of taking advantage of this. If it was only a matter of the objects found in their tombs and settlements from outside the Aegean their activities could be interpreted as piratical rather than commercial, but the latter explanation seems demanded by discovery of pottery typical of their group (especially the stirrup jars with octopus decoration) in other areas than their own.

It was probably mutual advantage, by no means all based on commercial interests, that drew them together. I cannot see that it is likely that they had any political cohesion, nor any concerted policy to defend themselves in case of attack – which would in any case have been impossible, as they formed anything but a natural geographical group, with a very few communities based on the remoter parts of the Greek mainland, one (Miletus) on the coast of Asia Minor, and an assortment of islanders extending over a very wide area. Their weakness was in fact greater than their strength, and in any case there were some, such as the Lefkandiots of Euboea and the inhabitants of Melos, who appear to have stood apart from the main group.

Now in almost every instance the communities of this scattered area appear to have come to an end before the close of the early Dark Ages, and some indeed perhaps at its very outset or even before. For the most part we have no evidence of continuity whatever; and whether or not there may in a few communities have been continuity, the characteristics that had identified them as Mycenaean disappeared without trace. This is a remarkable phenomenon, and one is bound to speculate as to the causes.

We have to remember always that these people had no internal strength. Circumstances had permitted their survival, but these were no longer favourable. Contacts with Crete do not seem to have persisted long after the middle of the twelfth century, for some reason that may have to do with the internal situation there. Then, shortly before the beginning of the Dark Ages, there was further trouble at least in the Argolid, a final destruction at Mycenae, and apparently one at Argos as well. This need have had no direct effect on our group, except of course to revive feelings of nervousness; but one of the main results of this trouble was undoubtedly a further exodus, certainly to Cyprus, probably to Crete as well. The fugitives will have had to go through the central Aegean, and so the communities will in this sense have been involved, and it is perfectly possible that some of their number will have joined the migrants. One would not think that trading activities with the east Mediterranean would have been in any way lessened, but they will have felt that one of the remaining bastions on the Greek mainland had fallen, and that they were even more insecure. The further migration of a group of Cretans to Cyprus, dated to *c.* 1000 B.C., may have had some effect, too. But perhaps the worst blow came in two events which proved that they themselves were no longer safe, the destruction of Miletus and of Emborio on Chios – the sea no longer afforded any sure protection (and the eastern communities will always have seemed the safest). Unfortunately, it is not possible to say precisely when these two calamities occurred, except that at Miletus the town fell before the end of the early Dark Ages, and that at Emborio the pottery suggests a late date in the twelfth century.

This then was the situation either at the beginning of the Dark Ages or somewhere during its early phase for those Mycenaean communities which had survived. In the western part, the mainland settlements will have felt great anxiety at the renewed unrest, and may have been affected by the establishment of the Sub-Mycenaean culture. The same attitude probably held at Lefkandi, too accessible from the mainland for comfort – their pottery showed a marked deterioration in the concluding stages, and it is perhaps significant that the last known contact with the outer world, the iron knife with bronze rivets, of probable Cypriot origin, was found in the penultimate period of settlement. In the east the destruction mentioned will have produced a profound reaction, and must have given rise to particular anxiety in the Dodecanese. The north Aegean was evidently unknown territory, and in the south Crete had its troubles. It is perhaps no accident that the one community that probably survived with little dislocation throughout the Dark Ages was that of Grotta on Naxos, a central island, least liable to be affected by the unrest and disasters mentioned; and yet here, too, the typical Mycenaean chamber tombs gave way to pit graves or cist tombs at the time of transition from the early to the late Dark Ages. Altogether, there are many factors which may have contributed to the gradual weakening and final dissolution of these communities, but I think one of the most important was in their inherent nature, that Mycenaean culture had no deep hold over them. They did not feel that they had any tradition worth perpetuating; they no longer believed in themselves, and they were unfitted to repel the fresh dynamism of the Sub-Mycenaean element of central mainland Greece.

These considerations may go some way towards explaining why they failed to survive or to transmit their culture, but it is still most unclear what happened to them, especially where there are no traces of destruction. It is reasonable to suppose that many will have left of their own free will at various times; some probably went to Cyprus, and one wonders whether others may not even have settled in south Italy, where there are known links with the Dodecanese. On Naxos it seems possible that many remained, but were joined by others from the mainland. A lot depends on whether radical changes in culture and customs necessarily involve a change of population, or at least a fair amount of newcomers, and I do not see any clear answer to this. In many cases, however, the evidence suggests a definite discontinuity, and one's impression is that much of the central Aegean will have become either severely underpopulated or almost completely depopulated during the early Dark Ages, leaving a gap for others to take advantage of.

Crete forms a group, so to speak, entirely on its own, and is the only island capable of doing so. The whole background is different from that of the rest of Greece and the Aegean. In the Mycenaean areas, one gets the impression of a culture, not actually superficial, but imposed from above on a number of disparate districts. The Cretans had the older civilisation, more deep-rooted than the Mycenaean, and there was a real unity. In their case there had also been catastrophe and decline, but it had taken place some time before, and the effects had not been so violent. There would be none of the overshadowing feeling as engendered by all the visible remains on the Greek mainland. There had been a recession, but it had not altered the fundamentals of life, and the Cretans still held tenaciously to their Minoan traditions, a self-contained conservative society, well able to look after itself, on the whole uninterested in outside events.

This was the situation *c.* 1200 B.C., at about the time when a number of fugitives made their way to the island. After this, things were different, and rather complex. One of the results was that Crete was drawn to some extent into the life of the rest of the Aegean; the characteristic vase of the central Aegean group, the stirrup jar with octopus decoration, originated in Crete, and the appearance of the gaudy Fringed Style may have been due to these outward-looking contacts. There were also connexions with Cyprus, though these are a continuation of previous links. It looks as though the Cretans took good advantage of the limited recovery, and that their situation was better than before. Internally, though, the picture is rather different. It is surprising how many new settlements traced their origins to the early twelfth century – the annexe to Phaestos, Gortyn, Vrokastro revived, Kastri as the alternative to the abandoned Palaikastro, and Karphi as the latest.[2] All, whether near the sea, in the plain, or in the mountains, were in varying degrees easily defendable. It may also be observed that the distinction between the chamber tombs of central Crete and the tholos tombs of the eastern region dates from this time. Notwithstanding the homogeneity of the culture, as mainly visible in the pottery, was all well with the island? There seem to be undercurrents of trouble, and one wonders whether the newcomers were a disrupting influence.

It is in any case clear that there were internal problems in the second half of the twelfth century, some of which were no doubt related to the

[2] One would particularly like to know what happened at Knossos, but the picture is not at all clear.

worsening situation in the rest of Greece, indirectly as reflected in the failure of the central Aegean group, directly as yet more fugitives arrived, perhaps after the troubles in the Argolid. There is a general cultural depression, much as elsewhere. And the culminating point was surely the departure of a group or groups to Cyprus *c.* 1000 B.C. These were true Minoans, to judge from the goddesses they took with them. Was this a forced move or a voluntary act? It is so difficult to envisage Cretans abandoning their homes, leaving the island which was everything to them.

However that may be, there were many who stayed (though I doubt whether the population was at all large); and in spite of certain new elements from outside Crete, and of a gradual transformation of the old order, the main traditions were retained, and there is a continuity such as is not to be found anywhere else. Their roots were too deep for it to have been otherwise. What I think one finds in Crete is neither the hopeless depression that could have characterised the central Aegean group, nor the dynamism of the central mainland, but a sort of inertia.

We can come now to a further group of Mycenaeans – and an extremely interesting one – who inhabited the district of Achaea, the north-west corner of the Peloponnese. This region is even more mountainous than most, but it has a good coastline, and excellent plains around Patras and in the southern section. The population will have been more mixed in its interests as opposed to that of the central Aegean and the Ionian islands, which must have been largely seafaring. The events of the end of the thirteenth century were certainly of concern to these Mycenaeans, directly inasmuch as the main coastal fortress (and the only significant settlement known to us in the whole area) of Teichos Dymaion suffered some damage, indirectly as it was to this region that many fled – if we can trust the archaeological picture at present available. The atmosphere at this time is likely to have been one of some apprehension, but it was evidently felt that the mountains afforded adequate protection.

In spite of this, the first half of the twelfth century was one of peace and recovery, which is of considerable interest in this part of the Greek world, supposing that there had been attacks from north-west Greece. The evidence shows that links were maintained with the Argolid and also with Kephallenia (so there was maritime activity); as well as this, there were no doubt connexions across the Gulf of Patras with the Aetolian coast (Teichos Dymaion recovered from whatever disaster had befallen it), and vases of Achaean type have been found not only in Phocis but as far afield as south Thessaly. So the inhabitants will have recovered much of their confidence, and they certainly had an internal cohesion, but they give the impression of people who wanted peace and quiet – which is of course not surprising. Not particularly prosperous, they yet retained all their Mycenaean characteristics.

What was the situation at the beginning of the Dark Ages, and during its early phase? It is reasonably certain that at least a few of the communities survived practically the whole of the early Dark Ages (even though such a conclusion rests mainly on a single vase type, see p. 93), but then they all disappear without trace, like most of those of the central Aegean group. A number of questions can be asked. What effect did the final disasters in the Argolid have on them? Did they fade out gradually? How did they survive as long as they did? Alternatively, why did they not survive longer? And what happened to them subsequently?

The answers to these questions could have a bearing on what happened in other areas. Much depends on the date when Teichos Dymaion was finally destroyed and abandoned. It seems possible to place it fairly early, at about the time of the last destruction at Mycenae, before the Dark Ages began, and if that is the case there could be some connexion between the two events. But then one would hardly have expected other Achaean communities to have survived so much longer. In fact, some of the pottery from Teichos Dymaion looks so decadent and chaotic that a later date seems more appropriate. Suppose it did not fall till near the middle of the eleventh century? This would explain reasonably well why no other sites seem to have survived later; links had already been formed with Sub-Mycenaean central Greece, and this sudden disaster will have prompted a movement into that area, especially Attica, and then in time to the west coast of Asia Minor, as Herodotus implies. We could then suppose that the invading body was a substantial one, coming from the other side of the Gulf of Patras, and proceeding on down into the unknown (at least to us) districts of west and south Peloponnese. This sounds a not unattractive solution, but if true it may cast doubt on a very different matter, the establishment of the new Sub-Mycenaean culture in central mainland Greece, which made its first appearance before 1100 B.C. It seems to make the theory of newcomers from this direction rather less plausible, as they would most naturally have to pass through Teichos Dymaion or some other Achaean sites. It is a good example of the difficulties that beset a period such as this, with few sites, insufficiently documented, and the vital evidence of the pottery imprecise.

The groups of Mycenaeans so far discussed consisted either of those who had altogether escaped disaster or of an amalgamation of such with a number of refugees. The third group, centred on Kephallenia and Ithaca, were also a mixture of local and fugitive Mycenaeans, but another element as well is recognisable, of non-Mycenaean origin, and using quite different pottery. In these mixed communities, with the fusion of the civilised and the relatively backward, a rather different attitude was likely, especially as they were situated more on the fringe of the Mycenaean world even than those of Achaea. They seem to have retained Mycenaean cultural characteristics, but not exclusively, and showed themselves quite willing to accept ideas from Epirus and probably beyond, up the Adriatic and across to Italy. They were sea-based, like those of the Aegean, and their interests were no doubt the same, but their outside connexions would be quite different. During the twelfth century until the Dark Ages they continued to keep in touch with adjacent areas of the Mycenaean world, such as Achaea, and Messenia from what slight evidence we have; and there are even echoes of the Close Style of the Argolid. Contacts with north-west Greece may be taken for granted, and generally with maritime areas to the north and west, but the remarkable thing is that they may even have been in touch with the east Mediterranean. If so, they were indeed adventurous, and they will have made full use of the freedom of the seas.

But what happened to them in the early Dark Ages? This is one of the few areas where complete continuity is observable, so there can have been no serious danger, and yet the main cemeteries known to us fell into disuse, as in other parts. All one can say is that this presumably did not have the same significance as elsewhere – unfortunately we have no evidence of burial customs for many centuries to come, but it is known that the type of tomb was not entirely forgotten. Internally, they remained undisturbed, but I think one should picture them as progressively isolated for a while from the Greek mainland, not to mention the Aegean. Once again, the destruction of Teichos Dymaion, if it opened the door for new people moving down the west coast of the Peloponnese, may have had a bearing on this isolation. And yet they were unlikely to remain so for long, as their natural contacts were with the mainland areas to their east.

The north-western Greeks, chiefly those of Epirus, are of importance because they could have been responsible for attacks on the Mycenaean world or for migrations into it. There is no reason why they should not have been related racially to those who lived within the Mycenaean sphere, but their culture was quite different and distinctly backward. These were the people who buried in cist tombs, sometimes – as in Albania – with a surmounting tumulus, who used primitive pottery (the occasional Mycenaean vase, or imitation of such, is to be found, and in fact the influence from the south was by no means negligible), and who regularly went armed, to judge from the small evidence available. So, perhaps a warlike people, and probably a hardy one. Were they the menacing cloud on the horizon of the pleasant and prosperous Mycenaean landscape? One cannot be sure. It is odd to imagine them retreating to their uninviting mountainous area if they took part in what was evidently a notably successful invasion at the end of the thirteenth century, and they showed no signs of belligerence in the first half of the twelfth. At about the end of the twelfth century, so already in the Dark Ages, there is evidence that some of them (their pottery of a more Mycenaean character than is normally found in their own territory) moved into west Thessaly, and one may reasonably speculate as to whether they may not have been responsible for the final destruction of Teichos Dymaion (see above). One is also free to speculate whether groups of them then continued on southwards down the west coast of the Peloponnese, for which there is no archaeological evidence (nor is there for anything else much at this time), or indeed whether others moved eastwards to help in establishing the Sub-Mycenaean culture, but this is a matter of dispute. For the former move there is support from the oral tradition; for the latter there is not. All one can say is that if there were newcomers, this is the sort of area they would have come from, but they could have taken other routes into central Greece.

When we come to consider Thessaly at the outset of the Dark Ages and during their early phase, the initial question to be asked is, who were the Thessalians? And the answer, as has already been seen, is by no means simple. Before 1200 B.C. there were, one supposes, basically two elements, the native Thessalians – a presumably constant element, of whom little is known – and the Mycenaeans, who controlled the coastal area round Iolkos and whose culture was widely though probably superficially diffused throughout much of the central plain of the interior. The disasters further south may not have affected these latter directly, but there can surely be little doubt that the events themselves and their consequences will have done serious indirect damage to security and morale. Perhaps they will have derived some comfort from the partial recovery of certain areas, but it is evident that there appeared some menace which they could not resist unsupported, as the time came – sometime in the twelfth century – when Iolkos fell. Are we here in the presence of some third element, neither native nor Mycenaean? One simply has no means of knowing. It is true that such an element appears in the early Dark Ages, those who came over from the north-west; and later one encounters a fourth in the Macedonian refugees, but these probably did not arrive much earlier than the tenth century. However, the region was distinctly vulnerable from the north, especially where the Haliakmon river, one of the gateways to central Europe, takes a great southern plunge to within a few miles of the Thessalian plain before striking north to empty itself into the sea not far south-west of Salonika. There could indeed have been much unrest and movement in Thessaly in the early Dark Ages, and the term Thessalians could cover a number of very different groups of people. It is even likely enough that many of Mycenaean stock will have remained; there may have been nowhere else much to go at this time – nowhere, that is, where they could find stable communities of their own kind.

Finally, there are the inhabitants of the Argolid and Corinthia, of Boeotia and at least the western part of Attica, those for whom the beginning of the Dark Ages meant an almost total breakaway from Mycenaean civilisation. This is the most difficult group of all to assess, as so much depends on whether they were survivors or a mixture of such and newcomers. I have already discussed this problem at length, and can add nothing: whatever the truth, there seem to be serious objections to both the theories advanced.

The need to solve this problem can be shown by the existence of another one, which it involves. It seems inconceivable that the new culture should have established itself simultaneously in all districts, so from where did it spread? We have to bear in mind the immediately preceding known event, the destruction of Mycenae (and of Argos too, possibly). Was this a spontaneous local affair, in which case the new culture could have arisen out of it, and spread from the Argolid to the other districts? Or was it engineered from outside – which could lead to much the same conclusion if the invaders came across the north Peloponnese or along the Corinthian Gulf, but to a different one if they came through Phocis and Boeotia? Or had the catastrophe nothing at all to do with the changes that took place – in which case the question would remain unanswered?

The community of Ancient Elis, whose fourteen tombs need not cover more than a generation, provides yet another problem. Their culture and customs were precisely the same as those of the regions already mentioned. Do they then represent a westward extension of the central mainland group, or a stage in the progress from west to east across the Peloponnese? Their pottery suggests that the former is right, their archaic weapons lead one to favour the latter. The pottery should be the more decisive, but it is not easy to date, and in any case it is always possible that the earlier stages of this cemetery are missing – and of course no settlement has been identified. The one thing that emerges is that links between west and north-east Peloponnese existed at this time, so the journey across the mountains was made.

The inability to solve these problems certainly imposes severe restrictions on our understanding of the situation. But we do not need to solve them in order to realise how remarkable the changes were, even though not quite so remarkable if they should turn out to have been imposed by newcomers on a dispirited remnant of the old population. They include the adoption of new settlement sites, of new burial customs, and probably of a new type of dress; in general a disregard of the Mycenaean way of life that had predominated for so long, except in the pottery. And all this was achieved while the communities of adjacent districts still clung to the Mycenaean tradition. The quality of the culture that emerged was, it must be admitted, of no great merit, but all the same I believe that these radical changes give a clue to the attitude of the communities concerned. They show a willingness to make a complete breakaway, a realisation that a new start had to be made, and the dynamism to take the first steps. The potential was there, and although there was no realisation of it for perhaps a couple of generations, the later developments need not come as any surprise.

To give a brief summary, the first fifty years of the Dark Ages (c. 1125– c. 1075 B.C.) witnessed the following state of affairs (always bearing in mind that the whole southern part of the Peloponnese remains a virtual blank to us). In central mainland Greece the new Sub-Mycenaean culture constituted a breakaway from its Mycenaean predecessor – this is the most important event, that which I have taken as originating the Dark Ages. In Kephallenia and Ithaca the mixed Mycenaean and native settlements survived undisturbed, and probably became increasingly isolated from the rest of the Greek world. For the purely Mycenaean communities of the central Aegean, however, these years saw the end of their original character and culture, and in many cases may have meant the abandonment of their settlements, due partly to their previous weakening and partly to destructive attacks, either now or before, on those of the east Aegean. The Mycenaeans of Achaea suffered the same fate during this time or shortly afterwards, with the destruction of their coastal fort of Teichos Dymaion probably in some way connected. Unrest in Epirus finds expression in a move to western Thessaly, movements in a southward direction being possible but unverifiable. In Crete, finally, there was evidently further unrest as well, culminating in a move of a group or groups to Cyprus.

The two main phenomena, to my mind, are the breakaway from Mycenaean civilisation in central mainland Greece, and the termination of that civilisation and many of its settlements, without replacement, in the main known areas, especially in the central Aegean where a large unfilled space was thus left. How much movement and unrest there was in the mainland areas of inland character or facing away from the Aegean remains one of the great unsolved problems, but there would seem to be good reason for supposing, especially after the disappearance of the Achaean Mycenaeans, that such areas were backward or isolated, still perhaps the occasion for nervousness to others. But there were not so many others around the Aegean – the coastal dwellers of Thessaly, maybe, the obviously self-sufficient Sub-Mycenaeans, a few islanders in the Cyclades, and the Cretans at a low ebb in their fortunes but the only ones in regular contact with Cyprus.

Altogether it is a strange mixture of an end and a beginning, an empty world and a vulnerable one, still subject to internal movement and influence from outside, especially the north (however debatable some of the manifestations are). Even assuming no further serious disruption, the return to stability would take time, and we need not expect any startling developments for a while.

In spite of this, the concluding years of the early Dark Ages, down to about the middle of the eleventh century, mark a decisive turning point. The area mainly to be affected was central mainland Greece, and what took place was a liberation of energies, on the one hand in art and technology, on the other in an extension into and across the empty spaces of the Aegean. In consequence, the direction of things to come was set, and an Aegean outlook was established, on a firmer and more progressive basis than before, leaving the non-Aegean districts more in the background.

As we have seen, the most compact and self-sufficient group that had emerged was that of the Sub-Mycenaeans, especially the Athenians. But some stimulus was needed. Where was the inspiration to come from? Not from the backward areas to the west and north, nor from anywhere among the 'old' Mycenaeans. The east Mediterranean was the most suitable source, but this was apparently not feasible while its first contacts were with the central Aegean group or with Crete, and thus the elimination of the former was extremely important.

In the event, links with the east Mediterranean, specifically with Cyprus, are clear, visible in the acquaintance with Cypriot pottery, in the appearance of weapons of Cypriot type, and in the introduction of iron. But how were they effected? Was the initiative from the Sub-Mycenaean communities or from Cyprus? I am sure that it came from Cyprus, and also that it was not a matter of casual trading visits. Even if no potters came, there must have been technicians in the new metal, iron – otherwise how could the Athenians and other communities of the central mainland have learnt the processes? I think that here we have an example of the movement of a group from east to west rather than the other way round. What lay behind it we cannot tell, but it was something unforeseeable.

As I have said, the two main developments related to pottery and iron-working. The influence of Cypriot pottery was primarily felt in Athens, and there is no doubt that it had a decisive stimulus on Athenian potters, and that the creation of the Protogeometric style, though essentially local, owed something to it. As to metal-working, the effects were wider, and probably included not only Attica but the Argolid and Euboea as well – it may not be pure chance that the process of silver extraction by cupellation first appears at this time in Argos. On the whole, however, it appears that the Athenians benefited most, and from the later situation that they were best fitted to reap the benefits. Of the other communities, Lefkandi was but newly reoccupied, and apart from this the only significant ones, so far as we know, were those of the Argolid, whose very proximity to one another could be a bar to the unimpeded progress of each. Athens stood by itself, and it is likely that it was at this time the most important town in the Greek world.

The arrival of Cypriotes and what they brought with them will have encouraged the suitably placed communities of the central mainland to become much more maritime in their outlook. This brings us to the other main feature of this short period – the exploitation of the Aegean, as seen in the diffusion of the Sub-Mycenaean culture. One example of it was at Lefkandi, but more important was a thrust eastwards, via Naxos, which terminated in the reoccupation of Miletus on the coast of Asia Minor, in the area which came to be known as Ionia. This seems to involve a further movement of people, in the usual direction, but it did not weaken thereby the district of origin. As people from the central mainland evidently took part, some explanation is needed, and it may be that we have here some evidence of unrest in the areas to west and north. It may be that fugitives had made their way to Athens, and with Athenians set out across the Aegean. There is no archaeological evidence to support this, but the oral tradition gives support, as Herodotus makes mention, among other originating sources, of groups from Phocis, Boeotia, and Achaea.[3]

It is perhaps significant that there is no evidence that the new knowledge of working in iron reached beyond the Sub-Mycenaean districts of the mainland, suggesting that other areas lacked stability, but in the present state of knowledge one cannot speak with certainty – especially, for

[3] The last named area is particularly interesting, as some explanation is needed for the final disappearance of their sites at about this time. Perhaps a mild speculation is permissible. We have seen that the chief reason for believing in their survival to this period is the presence of a few bird vases. This unusual shape seems certain to have reached the Greek mainland with the group of Cypriotes whose effect was so great on the Sub-Mycenaeans. May not some of them, quite possibly of Mycenaean descent, have gone on to visit the remaining Mycenaean communities of Achaea, and persuaded them that it was in their best interests to migrate?

example, of coastal Thessaly, whose inhabitants seem to have had clear links with Euboea very soon after, if not already by this time.[4]

What of the situation in the south Aegean? Surely the communities of the Dodecanese will have been in touch with Cyprus – but we know nothing of them, not even that they existed. The Cretans, on the other hand, were certainly in contact with the east Mediterranean, and it is evident, even though our relative chronology is not too secure, that the knowledge of working in iron reached them at an early stage. There is other slight evidence for contacts with the east, and for that matter this could be the time of a link between the Argolid and central Crete, suggested by bronze pins of a peculiar type (p. 119). In these relationships, however, it looks as though the Cretans were the receivers, without making any attempt to stir outside their own island: they were reverting to their natural insularity.

Inertia in Crete, on the mainland backwardness and flux in the west and north, progress and stability in the centre and an extension eastwards across the Aegean: this is the picture of the last years of the early Dark Ages. The way things were going, we might hope for a major breakthrough in the centre, in the sense of a resumption of normal relations with the east Mediterranean. But this is precisely what did not happen, nor should we really expect it. The previous developments had been due to a move from Cyprus westwards, and there is no sign of any reciprocal move. We should perhaps think of the situation rather as an isolated feeler on the part of a Cypriot group into an area which had undergone considerable change, to people not yet accustomed to using the sea as their highway – a start had been made, admittedly, but only in the sense of migrations. There need be nothing unexpected in the idea of the Athenians, or the Argives, or other communities of the central mainland, taking some time to get used to regular sea voyages, or for that matter to affairs of a commercial nature.

There is a natural tendency to think in terms of Mycenaean times, or of Archaic and Classical Greece, or even of modern conditions, in other words of numerous well-established towns with a high level of civilisation, and organised communications for commerce and other purposes not only within the Aegean but far beyond it as well. In fact, even the progressive settlements of the central mainland will have been few and relatively small, having made their fresh start within the living memory of many of the inhabitants; apart from this, the central and southern Aegean, with the exception of Crete, was probably at its lowest ebb so far as settlements and population were concerned. The groups which had just taken part in movements into and across the Aegean will surely have been extremely small numerically, and when they did settle will have constituted little more than villages, and it was likely to take them a long time before they came to terms with their immediate environment, far less the thought of expanding outside it.

In fact, it does not look as though the initial phase of the later Dark

[4] Is it also significant that among the very few objects of gold of this time and shortly afterwards, known only at Athens, Tiryns, and Lefkandi, some are of undisputed northern origin? At least it is an indication of the complexity of the situation.

Ages (all or part of the second half of the eleventh century)[5] takes us much further forward. Conditions in the central mainland area indicate a gradual and stable progress among individual communities, but no necessary co-ordination or co-operation, nor any one town yet showing signs of dominance, though it is evident that the Athenians made the greatest strides, culturally and probably also in social organisation, and thus had the greatest potential. Elsewhere it is for the most part the same old story. We still know nothing (whatever we may suspect) of what was happening in south and west Peloponnese, the Ionian islanders went their way undisturbed and apparently isolated, there is now no further news from north-west Greece, the Dodecanese remains a blank, and there is nothing new to report from Crete. Nor do we hear of any further groups of people crossing the Aegean eastwards, though it is more than likely that such movements did take place, at least from Attica.

There is, however, one area in which we encounter a new development, though even here we cannot be by any means sure that the situation had not already existed previously. This is the formation of a group with at least common cultural interests, extending from the coast of Thessaly to Euboea and very possibly including the northern Cyclades as well. The prevalence of individual burial, usually associated with cist tombs, is of doubtful significance (see pp. 270 ff.), especially as there is no other conformity in burial customs; the case, as so often, depends mainly on the similarity of the pottery. On the basis of this we can also recognise a curious offshoot or subsidiary of the group in the vases of a tomb at Delphi, very much out of the way for people whose main interests should have been maritime. Its presence may lead one to speculate whether, when some day we get a good sequence from Boeotia, this district may not be found to have been attached, at least at this time, rather to the new group than to Attica. In any case, the formation of this group now, or even earlier, is of considerable interest, as it was the birth of something that was to bear much fruit from the late tenth century onwards.

The tenth century produces evidence of a considerable advance, and the map of the Greek world looks a good deal fuller by the end of it, though it must be borne in mind that many of the sites now appearing for the first time, or reappearing after a long gap, are so ill-known (a single tomb, or a few sherds) that we cannot possibly state with any assurance that they may not have been in existence earlier – and also, of course, there will have been many settlements which still remain to be discovered.

The period is somewhat complex, and for the sake of clarity it will be best to concentrate first on the Aegean – that is to say, its central and southern parts – and in discussing it to separate the main part of the tenth century from its closing years (in so far as this can be done).

In contrast to the preceding phase, some group movements can be

[5] The length of the period is calculated on the time it took the new Athenian Protogeometric style to come to maturity, coupled with its failure to make its mark on the pottery styles of accessible communities. In view of the tremendous later diffusion, proving the obvious attractiveness of the style, I believe the period should be made as short as possible, though one must allow for some conservative resistance and other possibly deterrent factors.

detected during this century, and all seem to precede its final years. Paradoxically, the first one may be earlier and has no direct connexion with the Aegean, but I mention it here because the area affected came into contact with Aegean communities during the tenth century. It involves migrants from Macedonia moving southwards into north-east inland Thessaly, and establishing themselves at Marmariani and no doubt other sites as well, probably in concert with indigenous Thessalians. These are the people distinguished by the use of hand-made pottery and tholos tombs. It is the only movement from outside the Greek world, and may have taken place not long before the beginning of the century.

The other movements were all, so far as one can tell, in an easterly direction across the Aegean. One group settled in Old Smyrna, where it joined the existing native population; here, absence of full publication prevents us from identifying the area of origin (Thessaly or some adjacent district is the most likely), or from giving a more precise date than probably the second half of the century. A similar date is reasonably certain for another group whose cemeteries overlay the Mycenaean settlement of Serraglio on Kos, and it is very possible that these people came from somewhere in the Argolid.[6]

The Athenians were not involved in either of these moves. What then was happening there? It was they who initiated a movement eastwards, before 1050 B.C.; in the tenth century the pottery found would suggest that some of the central Cyclades had been occupied by further groups of them, Paros perhaps already in the late eleventh century. There may also have been a very early foundation on Samos, but in general the material is too scrappy for certainty. All one can add to this is that the literary tradition gives a picture of a number of settlements in the Cyclades and on the coast of Asia Minor, and it is quite likely that settlers were moving across the central Aegean from Attica at intervals throughout the later Dark Ages.

In general, small numbers only were involved in these movements, and it is doubtful whether any new foundation was larger than a village to start with, though in due course the population would grow of itself and also perhaps receive some fresh infusion – but all this would take time. On the other hand, they will have formed compact and independent units, and must have had a primitive political organisation, and the means to repel aggression if the need arose. The underlying causes cannot be established with any certainty by archaeological means: all one can do is to speculate, on the basis of the evidence as a whole; in Thessaly, the migrants very probably left trouble behind them, but elsewhere this is much less likely, at least for the tenth century, though we are still hampered – as will be seen – by our ignorance of the situation during most of this century in many regions to the west, away from the Aegean. We can in any case be reasonably certain that over-population, pure and simple, cannot have been a cause.

If I am right in my opinion that groups left Attica over a fairly long period, it is likely that Athenians provided most of the settlers. This is

[6] There is slight evidence that Rhodes also received settlers from the same area.

hypothetical; on the other hand, there is no doubt that they themselves were culturally outstanding and commercially dominant from the early tenth century until near to its close. For both aspects, culture and trade, the pottery is the more important, the metalwork rather less so, but by no means negligible.

On the cultural side, the style of pottery developed in Athens during the second half of the eleventh century was superior to all other styles current in the Greek world, both technically and artistically; some advance had also been made in the design of both dress pins and fibulae, and for the latter a greater strength was achieved as well, but in the present state of knowledge it would be unwise to claim Athenian superiority over all other metal-workers. Cultural superiority can be established simply by comparing Athenian products with those of other districts, but it is greatly strengthened by the fact that, above all in the pottery, so many other communities were prepared to accept Athenian ideas, and this brings us to the very wide area affected; a brief résumé of the diffusion will make the situation clear.

Wherever one looks, eastwards through the Cyclades to Ionia (i.e., the central portion of the west coast of Asia Minor and the adjacent islands), north to Euboea, Skyros, and Thessaly, south to central Crete and even to Messenia, or west to the old Sub-Mycenaean area of the central mainland and on to Phocis, there is evidence of contact with Athens, either in the guise of Athenian exports or (more significantly) in the adoption of features of the Athenian style by local potters. The presence of the typical Athenian dress pins of iron with bronze globe on all sites in the Argolid and at Theotokou in Thessaly serves to confirm the picture given by the pottery; similar pins have also been found on Kos, where the contact may have been at second-hand through the Argolid, to judge by the style of pottery. At Old Smyrna, too, the pottery indicates that connexions with Athens were of an indirect nature – and yet the only Greek sherd of this period from the nearby island of Lesbos could be an Athenian import. It may be noted, finally, that fibulae of Athenian type are known at Lefkandi, where the presence of a few cremations in the Athenian manner suggests that Athenians themselves may have gone to live there.

These many and varied contacts cover most of the tenth century, and reach a climax about 950 B.C. There are, of course, sizeable regions which show little or no influence from Athens – east and west Crete, Laconia, west Peloponnese as a whole and the Ionian islands, and north-west Greece; even so, the picture of wide communications, with Athens as a focal point, is in startling contrast to the conditions of the eleventh century.

As to the nature of the links, some were no doubt such as would exist between colonists and their city of origin (the central Cyclades and Ionia), but the element of trade must surely come into it as well, and the evidence seems to lead to the conclusion that the Athenians were themselves the traders, covering a very wide area by Dark Age standards.

If this were the case, then it is most likely that the communities with whom the Athenians traded were stable and peaceful, and the adoption or adaptation of elements of the Protogeometric style by local potters strongly supports this conclusion. This being so, will there not have been trading activities or at least contacts in which Athenians were not concerned? There certainly were, and a respectable list can be compiled. The links of affinity noted above between Athens and its offshoots naturally also existed between Kos and the Argolid, and between Old Smyrna and its unknown source. Then a few cross-sections: a vase from Knossos indicates some sort of contact between Crete and the Cyclades; another from Aegina is of Argive origin; a third from Ithaca shows that this island was in touch with Aegean developments; a fourth from Thebes could be from Euboea. Next, we find that the potters of the Dodecanese shared certain motives of decoration with those of the settlements of the west coast of Asia Minor – an interesting link, suggesting friendly relations between communities of different origin. And then there is the northern group as a whole, from coastal Thessaly southwards to Skyros, Euboea, and the north Cyclades, whose interconnexions have already been noted during the preceding phase, now persisting strongly throughout the tenth century. This area I shall discuss more fully at a later point, but one extension outside it may be noted here, a substantial connexion between Iolkos on the coast and Marmariani inland, which resulted in these recently arrived, and obviously peacefully established, settlers adapting the style of the coast to their own pottery.

Trade or contact between the Aegean and the east Mediterranean also deserves mention. During most of the tenth century, such contact seems to have been virtually confined to the Dodecanese and Crete, and for both areas the evidence indicates a flow of trade from the east rather than the other way round – or at least the carriers came from the east. This need not, of course, mean that Crete and the Dodecanese formed some sort of impregnable barrier to entry into the central Aegean, but only that the traders concerned had no desire or incentive to go further. There may also, however, be the factor of a rather closer relationship between Crete and Cyprus, and one wonders whether certain objects, such as the iron pikes, arrived in Crete as purely market commodities.

To sum up, there is plenty of evidence for trade and other connexions between the Aegean communities other than Athens during the greater part of the tenth century, but these were usually localised, and the conclusion that Athens was the dominant cultural and commercial state still stands, though the northern group had a cohesive importance of its own.

The last years of the Dark Ages show a somewhat changed picture from that of the rest of the tenth century, and form an introduction to the situation in the early ninth century.

It is natural to start once more with Athens, the outstanding city of the tenth century both in itself and in the extent of its influence. Towards the end of the century, this influence seems to have been on the wane; the Athenian style of pottery was gradually moving from its previous uniformity through an experimental stage which was to arrive *c.* 900 B.C. at a new style, the Geometric. These developments were no longer reflected as widely as was the Protogeometric style at its zenith; the Argolid was most strongly affected, Corinthia almost as much, probably also Boeotia if we had the evidence, and a few of the central Cyclades; and there is unmistakable evidence at Lefkandi in Euboea and northwards of it. The circle has then contracted, but we must be cautious in our interpretation. It does not necessarily mean, for instance, that the contacts or trading activities of the Athenians were any the less widespread. We have to remember that almost all our evidence is based on the pottery, and we must bear in mind that Athenian Protogeometric pottery owed its importance and influence to the fact that it provided a stimulus to potters of other communities. Once this had happened, there was no particular reason why these non-Athenians should continue to look to Athens for inspiration. It is in any case clear that Athens was once again in touch with the east Mediterranean (mainly Cyprus) by about 900 B.C., and that the following half-century was one of increased prosperity and wealth, based partly on outside contacts.

There is no need, then, to conclude that there was a recession in Athens. It is rather a case of other communities expanding and advancing, thereby being able to threaten the virtual Athenian monopoly. A minor but significant instance of progress in other areas can be seen in the Argolid; here the inhabitants still followed the Athenian ceramic developments very closely, but from the evidence of dress pins and a fibula the signs are that the metalsmiths of this district were equal if not superior to those of Athens by the beginning of the ninth century.

The most important development, however, concerns the northern group. The situation earlier, based inevitably on the pottery, was as follows. The group was already in existence as such in the eleventh century, and could go back to 1050 B.C. or even earlier: the evidence is very slight for the most part, but we can trace it from coastal Thessaly through Euboea to Naxos, and it is therefore likely that Andros, Tenos, and Skyros were also involved. The contacts, then, were by sea, but there is also a curious offshoot at Delphi; the explanation of this is uncertain, but it may be disregarded in this context, as it was an isolated tomb, and there is no later comparable material. During the tenth century the group maintained its uniformity; Skyros can be shown now to belong to it, but we could do with a good deal more evidence from the northern Cyclades. Perhaps at about the middle of the century the whole area succumbed to the influence of the Athenian Protogeometric style, as happened in many other parts of the Aegean. The impact did not, however, destroy the individuality of the group, as the pottery style which emerged, current over the whole area, was in many ways substantially different from that of Athens, and relatively little account was taken of its earliest Geometric developments.

We are now nearing the end of the Dark Ages, and until this time we can do little more than note that the group is a well-defined and fairly long-established one, but with not much evidence that it had made its mark on other districts, except in the case of Marmariani, well inland in Thessaly.

To the closing years of the tenth century, however, the following developments may be attributed. The relationship between coastal and inland
Thessaly to the north became a reciprocal one, and so the outlook of
coastal Thessaly was given a new orientation which may have lessened its
maritime interests. At the same time, certain communities, probably the
island ones, had come into touch with the region of western Macedonia, so
there is an outbreak into an area for long outside the Greek world. And
there is also evidence that contact had been made with the east Mediterranean (most likely Cyprus), this being based not only on the appearance
at Lefkandi of a few objects of gold of presumed eastern origin, probably
to be dated just before 900 B.C., but also on the presence of two vases of the
local Protogeometric style in Cyprus, the only known exports from the
Aegean during the Dark Ages. Such a link with Cyprus would naturally
imply connexions with the south-eastern Aegean, and there may be slight
evidence of such links. These are the positive pointers indicating outside
interests, and it is always possible, with regard to links with the east, that
they may eventually be found to have started slightly earlier.

This tends to show that the group, or at least the southern nucleus of it,
had made some progress in its outside contacts by the end of the Dark Ages,
and was prepared to expand, whether or not in competition with Athens.
The full significance of this progress is not, however, apparent till the next
century, by the end of which there is no doubt that the members of the
group, whether acting in concert or individually, constituted a formidable
commercial power precisely in the areas already mentioned, Macedonia
and the east Mediterranean. But what had not been realised until the
excavations at Lefkandi is how prosperous this particular community was
in the first half of the ninth century. The evidence comes chiefly from the
tombs, and the remarkable fact is that in one cemetery over half contained
one or more objects of gold. One must, furthermore, conclude that the
prosperity resulted chiefly from contacts with the east Mediterranean, for
although some of the artefacts were no doubt produced locally, others –
and not only those of gold – have an eastern origin. In fact, the impression
from the present material is that Lefkandi was wealthier than Athens in
the early ninth century, and such wealth will surely not have come all of a
sudden. It may be added that the end of the tenth century seems to have
been the time when the previous Mycenaean settlement was reoccupied,
and the evidence for the bronze foundry, belonging to the earliest stages of
the new settlement, gives a clue as to the activities of the inhabitants.
Lefkandi was surely one of the most prominent communities of its group,
and one wonders whether it may not have been from this district of Euboea,
of which the fertile Lelantine plain is the main feature, that came the main
direction and organisation of commerce overseas. It may even have been a
matter of political power. Strabo recalls a tradition that the people of
Eretria (a few miles east of Lefkandi) ruled over the inhabitants of Andros,
Tenos, Keos, and other islands; such conditions could apply to the early
ninth century. However that may be, the relevant point is that one can
surely argue, from the situation immediately after the Dark Ages, that

already before their end at least the islands of this group must have been in a position to take advantage of the later developments even if they did not create them themselves. They were well placed geographically in the Aegean, and they were prepared, it would seem, to be more adventurous than the Athenians.

There are, so far as I know, no further significant developments of the late tenth or early ninth centuries among the other communities of the Aegean; it is now possible to take an overall look at this focal area. The contrast between the beginning and end of the later Dark Ages is remarkable. At the middle of the eleventh century we can identify with certainty only two regions that were comparatively stable and undisturbed, the one being Crete, the other the Sub-Mycenaean central mainland. It is probable that some communities north of Attica, in Euboea and on the coast of Thessaly, should be added, but the settlement at Lefkandi seems to have been only very recently re-established, and the situation at Iolkos is not entirely clear. Apart from this, though, there were enormous gaps, in the centre of the Aegean and above all along its eastern coasts – even the Dodecanese may have been severely underpopulated. Intercommunication was negligible, the whole area disjointed. By 900 B.C. all this had changed; not only had the gaps been filled in to a great extent, but we get a balanced picture with all the component parts linked together in one way or another. There is a general air of stability and progress.

On the archaeological side, the one overshadowing factor that promoted the interrelationship of the many communities concerned was the seafaring activity of the Athenians, but this was not the sole factor, as there were a number of minor and independent links based on contiguity or some common interest. There is also another factor which needs stressing, as it undoubtedly led to greater cohesion and solidarity. One of the main features of this period was the movement of groups of people from west to east across the Aegean – and of course it was this which chiefly led to the filling in of the blank spaces mentioned above. In consequence, one naturally expects that between the city of origin on the Greek mainland and the various new settlements in the central and east Aegean there would be many ties of affinity. So one gets a genuine unity between east and west, and fortunately this does not appear to have been seriously threatened by strife between the representatives of the various migrating groups, nor between the cities of origin. It presumably meant that on the whole the communities of the Greek mainland were at least for the time being the stronger and more advanced, and this is borne out by the known facts. Athens remained throughout the most important, and probably the largest, single town. The significance and prosperity of the communities of the northern group have already been sufficiently stressed, and they will have included several towns of individual importance, such as Iolkos in Thessaly, Lefkandi in Euboea, and very likely Grotta on Naxos – it is altogether probable that others will be identified in course of time. And third, there was the Argolid, where the extent of the occupation and cemetery areas shows that at least Argos will have qualified as a town, even though the other three known settlements may not have been bigger than villages.[7] As against these the central and east Aegean has little to show: even Miletus, established in the early eleventh century, may not yet have grown to the stature of the towns of the Greek mainland. However, there is so much that still remains to be uncovered, and few archaeological judgments can be claimed to be final.

In this account of the Aegean, Crete occupies a position all its own, as it had indeed done throughout the Dark Ages and before. It is not that it stood outside the rest of the Greek world; equally with other districts it felt the influence of the Athenian Protogeometric style and absorbed certain features of it; more Athenian vases have been found in Crete than almost anywhere else outside the confines of Attica. It is rather that one looks in vain for any trace of Cretan objects outside the island. It is as though guests were welcome, but no return visits were made. This is perhaps not altogether surprising: Crete is an extremely large island, and entirely self-sufficient; furthermore, the force of tradition was stronger here than anywhere else – in a world of flux, Crete was relatively unchanged. There may, however, be rather more to it than this. It is significant that contacts with the rest of the Aegean were more or less confined to the central region (particularly Knossos, where the communities were clearly prosperous); east Crete had no share in them (nor, so far as we know, did the western regions), and although it was in touch with the centre, its culture and customs were in some respects different. Crete is quite large enough for internal rifts and dissensions, and the unusual number of weapons suggests that these may have existed. In other words, the Cretans may have been too much concerned with their own troubles to take any active outgoing part in the affairs of the rest of the Greek world.

On the whole, one can discuss the affairs of the Aegean without reference to Crete, and from what has been said it will be clear that there was general peace and stability, and that these Aegean communities had flourished during the late Dark Ages. They had indeed prospered to such an extent that they presented, by the end of the tenth century, a definite attraction to the traders of the east Mediterranean, and were now themselves at last ready to break out of their own sphere, whether east to Cyprus and the Levant, or north to Macedonia.

There now remain for general discussion the regions of the Greek world that had either no easy access to the Aegean or no interest in it: most of the Peloponnese (including Laconia, whose coastline faced on to the Aegean, but which does not appear to have profited from this fact), the western islands, the mainland of north-west Greece, Phocis, and the interior of Thessaly. This is a very considerable area, but extremely little is known about most of it – only Ithaca has produced evidence for continuity throughout. Epirus and Acarnania may be left out of the picture altogether: the evidence is slight, and from what is known of them previously they will have been relatively backward. Nor have we much material from the central and western districts of Thessaly, except for the eastern fringe of the great

[7] Argos had probably emerged as the leading community of the Argolid by the end of the eleventh century.

central plains, which may have formed an extension of the culture of the coastal area. The north-eastern inland region, as represented by the community of Marmariani, has already been discussed, both as providing evidence of movement from outside the Greek world, and in its gradually increasing contact with the Aegean at Iolkos.

Phocis is not yet adequately documented (nor is there anything from the districts to its immediate north). Delphi was clearly in touch with the northern (Aegean) group during the eleventh century, and with Athens during the tenth, but the nature or extent of any other contacts is not clear. At Medeon, however, on the Corinthian Gulf, we get a rather different picture, at least for the late tenth century – links not only with Corinth (whose natural tendency would be to look westwards, though at this time her potters were strongly influenced by Athens) but also with Achaea, thus bringing us to the Peloponnese and to a situation of considerable interest, for here we find evidence of a western group covering quite a large area.

The existence of this group as such cannot yet be traced beyond the final years of the Dark Ages. The closest links, in so far as the very small amount of material allows us to judge, were between Achaea, Elis, coastal Aetolia, and Ithaca; the pottery provides the main evidence, but the prevalence of pithos burials (not yet recorded for Ithaca, where no tombs of any sort have been discovered) is an interesting supporting feature, assuming that it has some sort of significance. This type of burial has also been found in Messenia and Triphylia, and in the former district some of the pottery seems to be akin to that of the regions mentioned, so the south-west Peloponnese may belong to the group. Finally,[8] such parallels as can be found between Laconian pottery and any other style belong within the group under discussion – but Laconia is very much a fringe district.

The emergence of this group in an area where evidence for the earlier stages is – except for Ithaca and to a lesser degree Messenia – almost entirely lacking is obviously important, but in what way it should be interpreted one cannot tell. If the pithos burials have any significance, one might very hesitantly suggest some racial affinity, but far more evidence is needed before one can claim that there was even a commonly held burial custom. Apart from that, there is only the pottery. For the group itself, this shows that there must have been fairly frequent intercommunication, as the potters were willing to accept the ideas of whichever was the most advanced district culturally – but which was this? It could have been Ithaca, with its long previous history behind it, but we cannot be sure. It also shows that regions of which we previously knew next to nothing were at least by now fairly stable and peaceful. But perhaps the most interesting feature is the independence of the pottery from that which was generally current in the Aegean at the time; there are a few links – some of the Messenians were familiar with Protogeometric pottery and copied the style; there may be traces of Protogeometric in Ithaca, and there is the imported vase noted earlier; the compass-drawn circles on a vase from Derveni in Achaea proves that there was some contact; but what is surprising is that

---

[8] There is still Arcadia, of course, but so little is known about it that it must be omitted.

there is not very much more of such evidence. One can argue that the local potters were quite well aware of the Aegean developments, and simply chose to ignore them, but the remarkable effect of the Athenian style on all pottery it came into contact with, even the conservative craftsmen of Crete, makes such a theory unlikely.

Nor, one would think, was there any great difficulty in reaching these areas from the Aegean. It may be that journeys by land were arduous, and probably thought to be hazardous when it was a matter of unknown territory, but there was no need to go far by land. The Corinthian Gulf was readily accessible from Attica, even more so from the Argolid. We already find the Corinthians familiar with the latest stages of the Protogeometric style, so why could knowledge of it not have spread from there, or even from Boeotia and Phocis? It has been noted that from the peninsula of Perachora, just north of Corinth, one can on a really clear day see the mountains of Kephallenia, just beyond Ithaca – a long way, indeed, but hardly inaccessible. In default of concrete evidence, it is tempting to suggest that the regions concerned, except of course Ithaca, had been in a rather disturbed state during most of the later Dark Ages, if not before. Suppose there had in fact been southward movements from north-west Greece, starting in the first half of the eleventh century, responsible for the destruction of Teichos Dymaion and for the termination of the Mycenaean settlements in Achaea. One can then quite easily imagine the newcomers making their way further to the south, through Elis into Messenia, with a separate group making for Laconia. It is not likely that they would encounter much resistance, but the whole process could have been spread over a long period, and western and southern Peloponnese could have been in a state of relative flux till the middle of the tenth century. If this were the case, one would not expect much contact with the Aegean communities, and they would have no desire to penetrate to these districts. All this is, however, sheer hypothesis from the archaeological side. Whatever the truth may be, it will have also to explain why, when stability was attained by the end of the tenth century, it was accompanied by sufficient links for one to be able to recognise the distinctive group discussed. In the present state of knowledge, we can say no more than that these districts were not only stable but in certain unaccountable ways separated from those of the Aegean. The Dark Ages may have been darker for some than for others.

When all has been said, one still seems to be so far from understanding, from recapturing the peculiar flavour of the Greek Dark Ages. It is essentially, I think, a time of change and contrast: deterioration is accompanied by rejuvenation, stability goes hand in hand with fluidity, the old world gives way to the new but is reflected in it.

Consider what we can know, or can reasonably surmise, about the communities revealed or half-revealed to us by the all too inadequate evidence. There were not many of them: that we can be sure of. With a few exceptions, they were very small indeed. With hardly any exceptions, their houses must have been exceedingly modest one-room affairs, and the whole effect will have been that of a village, even probably in Athens. There are no traces, except at Iolkos, of any fine stone construction – negative evidence which can with fairness be made use of, since solid foundations resist the passage of time and human destruction: no need to look further than the Mycenaean age to demonstrate this. Sanctuaries there surely were, but these too must have been of a primitive kind, often perhaps simply open-air shrines. Further proof of their insignificance is that the inhabitants obviously had neither the engineering knowledge nor the manpower to fortify their settlements – in certain instances they could possibly have made use of Mycenaean fortifications, but these will by this time have become dilapidated and overgrown. So for defence they will have had to look to the natural strength of some adjoining acropolis, or else take to the hills. All was simple, and indeed rather primitive; they had even lost the art of writing. With no traditions of their own, they clung nostalgically to the spoken and sung tales of a great past, knowing that it was beyond recovery: this is indeed a typical Dark Age characteristic.

All conjures up a picture of a small and depressed population, intent merely on survival. This, however, is very misleading; it may be in part applicable to the early Dark Ages, but no more than that. The conditions may have been those of a village, and yet the atmosphere, the whole outlook, was often more that of a self-sufficient town. Against the obvious stagnation in architecture we can place the high standard of artistic achievement in the pottery – admittedly a great deal was due to the genius who created the Protogeometric style, but other potters had the ability to recognise its worth and to adapt it to their own purposes – and this involved a cultural appreciation in communities as a whole. The metal-workers, too, had their successes, both technical and artistic. There is a feeling of energy and progress. The most important feature, however, is the complexity and range of the outside contacts of these often tiny communities – the Athenians were in a class by themselves, of course, but one is constantly encountering some new link between one part of the Greek world and another – and not only within the Aegean. In other words, people were not content to vegetate, to work out their destiny within sight of their village or small town; they wanted to go beyond, to find out what other communities, near or remote, were doing, to exchange ideas and to trade, in general displaying that quality of adventurous curiosity which is so characteristic of most Greeks of every period.

What must also be realised is that conditions were not always as easy and peaceful as much of the evidence may lead us to believe. Greece was no Paradise, and the weapons eventually buried with their owners were not for ornament. Troubles and disputes could arise at any time, and though presumably they were on a minor scale, the possibility that they could happen only makes the continued progress during the later Dark Ages even more significant.

Furthermore, the communities may often have had to contend with an unsettling hazard either from within their own body or from outside, that is to say the movement of groups of people in search of new homes to settle in. This is one of the constant and characteristic features of the Dark Ages, and the period cannot be understood unless one takes it into account. Most unfortunately, while we can make a reasonable guess at the situation in a settled community, there is hardly a single question that one can and should ask about these movements that can be answered with any certainty.

The earliest ones involve rather fewer problems, as they usually consist of Mycenaeans and Minoans leaving the Aegean in the direction of Cyprus – a continuation of the preceding state of affairs. With these migrants we do not need to concern ourselves, for they pass out of our view, though of course their presence in Cyprus would strengthen the actual or potential westward outlook of that island, and helps to explain such contacts as took place with the Aegean during the Dark Ages. On the other hand, their departure had obvious consequences for Greece, as it meant further de-population, and in particular resulted in the central and south-east Aegean and the adjacent coasts of Asia Minor being left almost uninhabited.[9] And we do not know to what extent some other migrations or invasions may not have occasioned their flight, events which could have a profound influence on the world they left behind.

As to the later movements – and one must remember that there was already a long history, almost a tradition, of restlessness – the problems may best be illustrated by analysing the situation as it affected Athens, together with all the side issues.

Shortly before the middle of the eleventh century there was a new settle-ment at Miletus; from the pottery it would seem that settlers came from within the Sub-Mycenaean area, and the literary tradition gives Athens as the place of origin. From similar evidence we arrive at the conclusion that other groups continued to sail eastwards, settling in the Cyclades or in Ionia, both now and later, probably until the second half of the tenth century. This is straightforward so far, but as soon as we go deeper the problems multiply. First (a relatively minor question), how did the settlers know where to go? May this not have been a case of a few surviving Mycenaeans on at least some of the sites? Secondly, who were the settlers? Many of them, no doubt the major proportion, were Athenians. What circumstances provoked their departure? Is this not evidence of some un-rest in Athens? If so, we know nothing of it, nor did it hinder the com-munity's progress in any way. Why did they go so far afield? Was there not plenty of space in Attica? There may here be an underlying desire for complete independence. Or it may be bound up with another factor altogether: Herodotus, as mentioned earlier (p. 323), stated that not only Athenians, but also people coming from a number of districts to the west of Attica, took part in the trans-Aegean migration. If this is true, and there is no reason to doubt it, quite à few people will have travelled to Athens, and there they will have stayed before going on their way. If the initiative came from them, then many Athenians may have been attracted by the idea of joining in the venture – but why was it to Athens that they came?

[9] Some may, of course, have moved to somewhere else within the Greek world, but of these we know nothing.

How did they travel? Those from Boeotia and Phocis and certain other regions will have journeyed overland; they would have to support themselves on the way – how would their transit be viewed by the people whose lands they passed through? And what caused their original exodus? Disturbed conditions of some kind, but we can say no more.

Besides these, an important part, Herodotus implies, was played by the inhabitants of Achaea, driven out by others. This is the most interesting group of all, for in them we can surely recognise the last remaining substantial body of Mycenaean survivors. The circumstances of their move, and their apparent links with the Athenians – and perhaps even with some Cypriotes – I have discussed earlier (p. 341). One wonders whether it may not have been they who transmitted to Ionia and there perpetuated the traditional lays that formed the basis of the Homeric epic. But how did they get to Athens – by ship? Or did they perhaps go direct to Ionia? Once again one has to ask the question: how did they know where to go?

Finally, who evicted them? Are we to think of aggressors from north-west Greece, crossing the Gulf of Patras and destroying Teichos Dymaion (p. 336)? And did these people, or others of the same origin, then spread not only into Achaea but over the whole of the south and west Peloponnese during the remainder of the eleventh century and some of the tenth, constituting a somewhat isolated and backward block of population, but settling down towards the end of the century, with their racial or tribal affinities visible in the ceramic links? All this shows that a chain reaction may have been involved, and the effects will have been felt in the Aegean as well as in the Peloponnese, to be borne in mind in assessing the atmosphere of the Dark Ages.

So one may conclude, with fact heavily outweighed by hypothesis. But certain basic truths remain. And the most important of these is that in spite of formidable obstacles much had been achieved during the two preceding centuries; not only the Aegean but Greece as a whole was ready to emerge from the long period that was not all dark but is still, for lack of a better phrase, known as the Dark Ages.

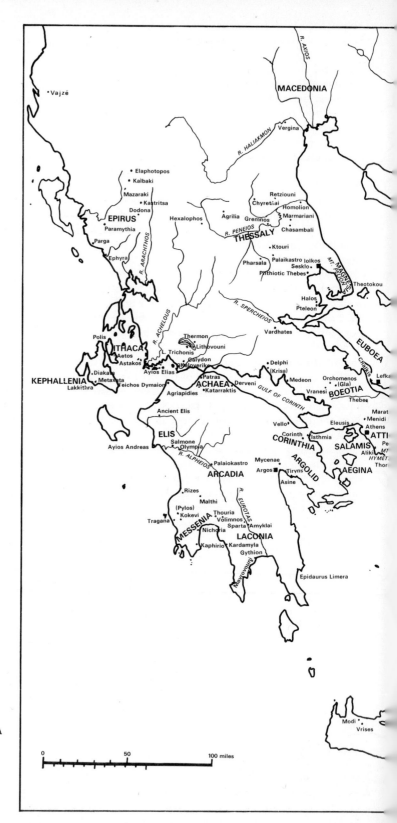

• Vajzë

MACEDONIA

R. AXIOS

R. HALIAKMON

Vergina

• Elaphotopos
• Kalbaki
Mazaraki
• Kastritsa
Dodona

Retziouni
Chyretiai
Homolion
• Marmariani
Chasambali

EPIRUS
Hexalophos
Ágrilia
Gremnos

R. PENEIOS
THESSALY

Paramythia

• Ktouri

Parga

Pharsala
Palaikastro Iolkos
Seskio
Phthiotic Thebes
MT. MAGNESIA

Ephyra

Theotokou

R. ARACHTHOS

Halos
Pteleon

R. SPERCHEIOS

R. ACHELOUS

Thermon
Lithovouni
L. Trichonis
Vardhates

EUBOEA

Polis
ITHACA
Aetos
Astakos
Ayios Elias
Calydon
Rhoverika

Delphi
(Krisa)

Chalkis
Lefka

Medeon

Diakata
Metaxata
Teichos Dymaion
ACHAEA
Patras
Derveni
GULF OF CORINTH

Orchomenos
(Gla)
BOEOTIA

KEPHALLENIA
Lakkithra

Agriapidies
Katarraktis

Vranesi
Thebes

Ancient Elis

Marat
Menidi
Athens
ATTI

Vello
Eleusis

ELIS
Salmone
Olympia

Corinth
CORINTHIA
Isthmia
SALAMIS
Pe
MT
HYMET

Ayios Andreas

R. ALPHEIOS
Palaiokastro
ARCADIA

Mycenae
Argos
Tiryns
Asine
ARGOLID

AEGINA
Thor

Rizes
Malthi

R. EUROTAS

(Pylos)
Kokevi

Thouria
Volimnos
Sparta Amyklai

Tragana
MESSENIA
Nichoria
LACONIA

Kaphirio
Kardamyla
Gythion

Epidaurus Limera

Mavrovouni

Modi
Vrises

0   50   100 miles

N

(Troy)

LESBOS

SKYROS

Phocaea

•Sardis

•Old Smyrna

CHIOS

Clazomenae

Emborio

ANDROS

AEGEAN SEA

Pythagoreion

KEOS

TENOS

SAMOS

MYKONOS

Heraion

•Miletus

RHENEIA DELOS

PAROS NAXOS

Grotta

Cömlekçi

SIPHNOS

Dirmil

Asarlik

Budrum

AMORGOS

KOS Serraglio

IELOS

THERA

Ialysos

Kameiros

RHODES

Lindos

CRETE

Amnisos

Tylissos

Kalochorio

Knossos

Prokastro

Kanli Kastelli

Dreros

Berati

Kourtais

Prinias

Karphi Olous

Kastri

Dictaean Cave

Kritsa

Seteia

Phaestos

Panayia

Mouliana

riadha

Gortyn

Kavousi

Rotasi

Glossary

The following definitions may be helpful in case of difficulty or obscurity.

Amphora   A large jar with two handles placed horizontally or vertically.

Amphoriskos   A small amphora.

Apsidal   A construction, whether a room or a tomb, with the one end semicircular.

Ashlar   Hewn or squared stone used in building.

Bell krater   A high, deep bowl with straight sides gradually flaring outwards to the lip.

Bird vase   A vase which more or less (according to the particular example) resembles a bird.

Catch-plate   That part of a fibula into which the end of the pin fits, as in a safety-pin.

Centaur   A mythical creature, having the head and arms of a man and the body and legs of a horse.

Chamber tomb   A tomb with roughly circular or rectangular chamber, designed for multiple burial.

Cist tomb   A tomb with stone slabs lining the sides as well as covering the top, designed for individual or double burial.

Clay ground   A vase with most of its surface left unpainted.

Compass-drawn   The use of a pair of dividers to produce a decoration of circles or semicircles.

Contracted position   The interment of a corpse with its legs drawn up.

Corbelled roof   Vaulted roof.

Cupellation   A process of obtaining silver from silver-bearing lead.

Dark ground   A vase with most of its surface painted.

Dog tooth   A decorative motive consisting of a series of filled triangles.

Double-axe   A decorative motive of two confronted triangles set horizontally.

Dromos   The passage way leading to a chamber or tholos tomb.

Earth-cut grave   See under *pit grave*.

Fibula   A brooch.

Heroon   A shrine dedicated to a demigod or mortal.

Hour-glass   A decorative motive, two triangles set vertically with their apices meeting.

Hut urn   The term used for a small terracotta model of a round hut with one door. It may have a statuette inside, and presumably had a cult purpose.

Hydria   A jug with one handle from lip to belly, and two horizontal handles on the belly.

Kalathos   A wide-mouthed shallow bowl, normally with flat base and often handleless.

Kantharos   A bowl with two vertical handles from belly to lip.

Krater   A very large bowl with two or four handles.

Kylix   A high-stemmed goblet.

Languettes   A decorative motive consisting of small tongues.

Lekythos   A jug with a narrow neck and one vertical handle.

Megaron   A long rectangular construction with a single door in the narrow end.

Openwork   Cut-out areas (usually triangular) on a vase.

Oxidisation   A natural chemical process leading to the decay of iron.

Pilgrim flask   A vase with a circular body surmounted by a neck and lip, with two vertical handles.

Pit grave   An earth-cut tomb, usually rectangular, which may have covering stone slabs.

Pithos   A large storage jar, which can be used for burial.

Pollen analysis   The reconstruction of the flora of a given era by the examination of the fossil pollen from buried soils.

Pyxis   A small jar, either globular or straight-sided, usually with a lid.

Quillons   The transverse projections of a sword hilt forming a cross with the blade and the barrel at their junction.

Reserved   An area of a vase free of paint in between painted areas.

Rhyton   A funnel-shaped vase used for libations.

Shield-boss   A bronze fitting to the outer face of a shield.

Skyphos   A bowl with two horizontal handles, often with high conical foot.

Spectacle fibula   A brooch consisting of two interconnected spirals of wire mounted on a safety-pin.

Stirrup jar   A closed jar with a false spout on the top supporting two handles (the stirrup) and a real spout on the shoulder.

Tankard   A mug with concave sides and one handle.

Tholos tomb   A beehive-shaped tomb.

Trefoil-lipped oinochoe   A jug with its mouth partially pinched in to facilitate pouring.

Trunnion axe   An axe-like tool with projections on opposite sides of the blade.

Tumulus   A mound.

Urn   In cremations, the receptacle for the ashes of the dead.

Bibliography and Site Index

The detailed bibliography, arranged according to sites and given below, applies primarily to the sites discussed in Parts II and III of this book, and also to those mentioned in the chapter on Sanctuaries and Cult Places that were not dealt with earlier.

For Part I, the summary analysis of the period preceding the Dark Ages, the following suggestions as to general reading may be useful.

P. Ålin   *Das Ende der Mykenischen Fundstätten auf dem Griechischen Festland*, 1962.

R. Carpenter   *Discontinuity in Greek Civilization*, 1968.

V. R. d'A. Desborough   *The Last Mycenaeans and their Successors*, 1964.

M. S. F. Hood   *The Home of the Heroes*, 1967.

R. Hope Simpson   *A Gazetteer and Atlas of Mycenaean Sites*, 1965.

R. W. Hutchinson   *Prehistoric Crete*, 1962.

Sp. Marinatos and M. Hirmer   *Crete and Mycenae*, 1960.

F. Matz   *Crete and Early Greece*, 1962.

G. E. Mylonas   *Mycenae and the Mycenaean Age*, 1966.

J. D. S. Pendlebury   *The Archaeology of Crete*, 1939.

Lord William Taylour   *The Mycenaeans*, 1964.

Mrs E. T. Vermeule   *Greece in the Bronze Age*, 1964.

Part IV is a matter rather of specialist studies, of which there are very few. For the objects of metal found in Athens during the Dark Ages, see H. Müller-Karpe in *JdI* 77 (1962), 59 ff., and more generally for warfare A. M. Snodgrass, *Early Greek Armour and Weapons*, 1964. In the series *Archaeologia Homerica*, Sp. Marinatos, *Kleidung; Haar- und Barttracht* (1967), and M. Andronikos, *Totenkult* (1968), discuss Dark Age as well as Mycenaean developments.

To return to the main bibliography, its purpose is to serve as a site bibliography and site index combined, and to act as a substitute for the relative absence of notes in the text. Division is made by regions, mainly, but not entirely, in accordance with the system adopted in Part III. Under each site I give brief information as to its nature and date. Then I give the main references to the original publication of the material or to significant discussion of it; for the sake of brevity I have not included the names of authors when dealing with articles in periodicals, and for the periodicals themselves only the number of the volume, and not the year, except of course where the periodical is identified by the year alone. At the end of

361

each region or of each aspect of a site, I give the main references to the text of this book, enclosed in square brackets. Some entries will be found to be fuller than others: in this I have been guided by the complexity of the site itself, and occasionally by the desire to mention the more note-worthy objects – there is bound to be inconsistency, but I hope that it will not be excessive. A list of the abbreviations used will be found on pp. 381–2.

ATHENS

(1) Sanctuary material. Very late Protogeometric votive vases. *Pr.* 1958, 8 f.
[278]

(2)*a* Settlement, throughout the Dark Ages. The area is that of the Agora, and the material from pits and wells. This material, to-gether with that of tombs in the area, is soon to be published in full. References to preliminary reports, including the tombs: *Hesp.* 2, 468 ff.; 4, 364; 5, 23 f.; 6, 364 ff.; 7, 325; 18, 275 ff. (earliest Geometric); 21, 108, 279 ff.; 23, 58; 24, 200 f., 217 f.; 25, 48 f.; 35, 82 f. For a probable irrigation system close to Syn-tagma Square, in use *c.* 950–*c.* 750 B.C., see *AE* 1958, 2 ff.

b Tombs (apart from the above). A considerable number, covering the whole period. The main cemetery was that of the Kerameikos, and has been published in *Kerameikos* I (Kraiker and Kübler) and IV (Kübler). Further tombs in this area have been published in *Hesp.* 30, 174 ff. (late Sub-Mycenaean, note the hand-made pyxis and the iron pin with ivory head); *AM* 78, 148 ff. (very late Sub-Mycenaean, note the bird vase and the ring vase); *AM* 81, 4 ff. (note the iron pins, one with ivory head, from a fairly early Proto-geometric grave).
Numerous Sub-Mycenaean and Protogeometric burials have been found in other parts of central Athens; references to these are given by Snodgrass, *Dark Age of Greece*, 202 f. to whose list may now be added *AD* 23, ii, 55 ff., 67, 73 f., and *Athens Annals* 3, 171 ff. for Sub-Mycenaean and Late Protogeometric pit graves south of the Acropolis. Particularly noteworthy are the following: a group of Sub-Mycenaean cist tombs on the Acropolis, Kavva-dias and Kawerau, *Die Ausgrabung der Akropolis*, 77 ff.; a Proto-geometric cremation with sword and spear, adjacent to an ancient road, under the modern Cathedral, *AE* 1953–54, iii, 89 ff.; the Protogeometric tomb with two cups and a toy horse, *AD* 22, ii, 49 and pl. 70 *a–c*; the Sub-Mycenaean tomb with a duck vase, two gold hair spirals, nine bronze rings, and two bronze pins, *AD* 23, ii, 56 and pl. 31 *c*.
A group of tombs in one of the outer suburbs of Athens, Nea Ionia, is also worthy of mention; it is published by Mrs Smithson in *Hesp.* 30, 147 ff. The material belongs to the late tenth century. Discussions of the material will be found in Styrenius's *Sub-*

mycenaean Studies (1967) for the whole period and for all the material (especially useful for the statistics); in Müller-Karpe's long article in *JdI* 77, 59 ff. for the metal objects over the whole period, invaluable for the line drawings not only of the metal objects but for the associated vases as well – note that the weapons with Cypriot links are depicted on fig. 7,4 (spearhead) and fig. 9,4 and 7 (swords); and in my *Protogeometric Pottery*, 1 ff.

[The main page references in my text are as follows.

Early Dark Ages   Early Sub-Mycenaean pottery, 33 ff.; late Sub-Mycenaean pottery and links with Cyprus, 42 ff., 54 f.; description of site (size, settlement, burials, ornaments, weapons), 64 ff.; comparison with other sites, 76 ff.; summary, 340 f.

Late Dark Ages   Chronology, 133 ff.; size of settlement, 135 f.; burials and burial customs, 137 f.; social organization, 138 f.; ornaments, 139 ff.; weapons, armour, tools, 141 f.; handmade ware, 142 ff.; animal figurines, 145; pottery, 145 ff.; summary, 156 ff.; summary of external contacts and influence, 344 f.; lessening influence in late tenth century, 346 f.

General   Undefended, 262; burial customs, 270 f., 274 ff.; diffusion of pottery, 289 f.; social and economic conditions, 292 f.; effects on community of group movements, 354 f.]

ATTICA AND ADJACENT ISLANDS

Aegina   Two child cist tombs; possible cremation; traces of settlement. Late Dark Ages.
W. Kraiker, *Aigina* (1951).
[160]
Aliki   Two vases. Late Dark Ages.
CVA Heidelberg 3, pl. 102,6 and 8.
[159]
Eleusis   Tombs and vases. Late Dark Ages.
AE 1898, 76 ff. *Ker.* i, pls. 42 and 48.
[159]
Hymettus, Mt.   Sanctuary. Late Protogeometric onwards.
AJA 44, 1 ff.
[137, 278]
Kea   (1) Sanctuary at Ayia Irini.
Hesp. 31, 278 ff.; 33, 326 ff.; 35, 367 ff.
[160, 280 f.]
(2) Stray finds.
CVA Heidelberg 3, pls. 100,1 and 2, and 102,4.
[160, n. 1]
Marathon   Tombs. Late Dark Ages.
Pr. 1939, 27 ff.
[159]

Menidi   Adult   inhumation   with   Late   Protogeometric
amphora.
Ker. i, 157, n. 1 and pl. 42.
[159]

Perati   Extensive L.H. III C cemetery, now published in
detail. Sp. Iakovides, *Perati*, vols. I–III (1969–70)
A useful summary in *AD* 19, i, 87 ff. and pls. 85 ff.
[Survival into EDA (arched fibulae), 81 f.; cremations, 77, 80,
268; pit graves, 107; dagger with square shoulders, 74, 308;
ring with double-spiral terminals, 82; iron knife with bronze
rivets, 308.]

Salamis   Large cist-tomb cemetery. Early Dark Ages.
AM 35, 17 ff. Pottery published in greater detail in *Op. Ath.* 4,
103 ff. Finds discussed by Styrenius in *Submycenaean Studies*
(1967).
[Sub-Mycenaean pottery, 33 ff.; burials and non-pottery finds,
67; burials, 76 f.; likelihood of immigrants, 269; organised community, 276; roll-top pins, 297; ring with oval bezel, 304.]

Thorikos   Traces of settlement and silver extraction. End of
Dark Ages.
J. Bingen in *Thorikos* I, 81 ff.; II, 25 ff. (note for the extraction of
silver); III, 34 ff.
[Settlement, 159. Extraction of silver, 159, 314.]

THE ARGOLID AND CORINTHIA

Argos   Settlements and cemeteries. Excavations, which continue, have been conducted by French and Greek archaeolo-
gists. The only full publication is that of the Mycenaean cemetery
by Deshayes, *Argos: les Fouilles de la Deiras* (1966), but there is
also a valuable account of certain of the excavations by Courbin in
Études Archéologiques (1963), 59 ff., which includes a discussion of
the construction for the extraction of silver (pp. 71, 73, 98–100).
The evidence for the settlements, apart from Courbin's article,
will be found chiefly in *Pr.* 1952, 413 ff.; *BCH* 80, 207 ff. and 370;
81, 677 ff.; 83, 762 ff.; and 93, 991 f. (this last of interest as establishing that there was a destruction, apparently of late twelfth-
century date, in this sector).
The references to tombs are too numerous for useful inclusion,
and will be found in many numbers of the *BCH* from 1953 onwards. For recent finds by the Greeks, see particularly *AD* 17,
ii, 55 ff.; 18, ii, 62; and 22, ii, 177 f.
The material is discussed in *Styrenius*, 127 ff. and in *LMTS*, 80 ff.
[Early pottery, 33 ff.; EDA, 72 f.; LDA, 161 f., and generally on
164 ff.]

DODECANESE, WEST COAST OF ASIA MINOR AND ADJACENT ISLANDS

Dirmil   Vaulted tomb, probably cremation. Late Protogeometric.
AJA 67, 357 ff. See Boysal, *op. cit.*, pls. 37 and 38.
[180 ff.]

Emborio   (1) Two L.H. III B cist tombs.
Archaeology in Greece, 1954, 44 and *LMTS*, 159.
[108]
(2) Twelfth-century settlement, destroyed perhaps *c.* 1100 B.C.
LMTS, 159.
[20, 81]

Ialysos   Late Protogeometric tombs.
CR 3, 146 f.; 8, 161 ff.
[177]

Kameiros   (1) Protogeometric sherds from sanctuary area.
CR 6–7, 360 ff.
[178]
(2) Late Protogeometric tombs.
CR 6–7, 119 ff.
[177]

Kos (Serraglio)   Late Protogeometric and Geometric cemeteries, and possible traces of settlement. *Boll. d'Arte* 1950, 320 ff.
Further material mentioned and discussed in *PGP*, 222 ff.
[Burial customs, 172 f.; pottery style and discussion of origin
(Argolid and Cyprus), 173 ff.; other objects (note gold rings,
faience necklaces, and pins of Athenian type), 175 f.]
(Note also Late Mycenaean·settlement and cemeteries; reference
to preliminary publication as above, and add *Ergon* for 1959,
133 f. for settlement, and Morricone's full publication of the
tombs in *Ann.* 27–28 (N.S.), 5 ff.)

Lindos   Traces of settlement in Late Dark Ages.
Lindos I, 57 ff., 126, 233 ff. Discussed in *PGP*, 229 ff.
[178]

Miletus   Settlement. Late Sub-Mycenaean onwards, after
destruction of Mycenaean town *c.* 1100 B.C. *Ist. Mitt.* 7, 102 ff.;
9–10, 1 ff.
[83, 179 f., and 183 for settlers from Athens.]

Old Smyrna   Settlement. Greek intrusion probably from
late tenth century.
BSA 53–4, 10 f., and 35 ff. for the Iron Age fortifications; note
pl. 5 *b* for two Protogeometric vases, and detailed map of site at
the end. *AJA* 66, 369 f. and pl. 96 (Protogeometric krater and
amphora, and the oval house).
Pottery discussed by Coldstream in *GGP*, 338 f.
[183 f.]

Phocaea   Report of Protogeometric pottery from settlement.
AJA 66, 369.
[184]

Samos (Heraion)   Sanctuary. Probable continuity in religious beliefs.
Samos V : Frühe Samische Gefässe (1968): Dark Age sherds.
AM 65, 57 ff.: votive figurines.
[223, 281 f.]

Samos (Pythagoreion)   Settlement or sanctuary. Tenth-century sherds.
Athens Annals 1, 168 f.; *AD* 22, ii, 463, pl. 339 *b*.
[223]

Sardis   Settlement. Sherds of Dark Age type.
BASOR 186, 34 ff.
[184]

Serraglio   See under **Kos**.

EUBOEA AND SKYROS

Chalcis   Cist tombs. Mostly LDA.
Kharistirion eis A.K. Orlandon 2, 248 ff.
[200 f.]

Lefkandi   Excavations 1964–70. The settlement on Xeropolis was occupied, probably, into the early eleventh century, and then again from the late tenth century to the eighth. The cemeteries, which need not have belonged to the known settlement, have a date range from *c.* 1075 B.C. to the second half of the ninth century. The fullest account yet to appear is Popham and Sackett, *Excavations at Lefkandi, Euboea, 1964–66.* See also *BSA* 65, 21 ff. for the centaur, and *Athens Annals* II, 98 ff. for recent discoveries. The present work contains much unpublished material, for permission to mention which I am very much indebted to the excavators and to the Managing Committee of the British School at Athens.

[For the end of the Mycenaean settlement and the Sub-Mycenaean material from the Skoubris cemetery, see pp. 67 f. The main account of the site in the Dark Ages and into the early ninth century is on pp. 188 ff. References to the early pottery will be found on pp. 43 f., and to other aspects in the relevant chapters. For the wealth of Lefkandi in the early ninth century, see p. 348.]

Skyros   Four groups of cist tombs, of the Late Dark Ages and the early ninth century.
(*a*) *BSA* 11, 78 ff. (*b*) *AD* 4, suppl., 41 ff. (*c*) *AA* 1936, 228 ff. (*d*) *BCH* 61, 473. Discussed in *PGP*, 129 f., 163 ff.
[201 f.]

BOEOTIA, PHOCIS AND THE SPERCHEIOS VALLEY

Delphi   Sanctuary, settlement, tombs.
Mycenaean cult objects, *FD* II, v, 13 ff.: V, 14 f.
Settlement as opposed to sanctuary till the late eighth century
B.C., *BCH* 59, 329 ff.; 74, 322 f.; 85, 357 ff.
LDA traces of settlement, *FD* V, 17 and 137; *RA* 12 (1938), 207 ff.
Very late Mycenaean chamber tomb (lekythoi of Sub-Mycenaean
type), *FD* V, 6 ff. Tomb, second half of eleventh century, *BCH*
61, 44 ff.
[Sub-Mycenaean lekythoi, 105; Dark Age tomb and settlement,
203 ff.; question of cult continuity, 279.]
Medeon   Cemeteries and traces of settlement.
AD 19, ii, 223 f.; Vatin, *Médéon de Phocide* (1969).
[105]
Orchomenos   Tombs: LDA and later.
PGP, 198.
[202]
Thebes   (*a*) Tombs. *AD* 3, 25 ff. (cist tombs, discussed in
PGP, 195 f.); *AD* 20, ii, 239 and pl. 283 *a*. (amphora from tomb
of unspecified type).
[69, 203]
(*b*) Spearhead from 'near Thebes'. *LMTS*, 67 and pl. 22 *d*.
[111]
Vardhates   Shaft grave. Thirteenth to twelfth centuries.
BCH 63, 311 f.
[104 f.]
Vranesi   Tumulus mound, with inhumations and cremations.
LDA and later.
Pr. 1904, 39 f.; 1907, 109; *AM* 30, 132 f. Protogeometric vases
published and illustrated in *PGP*, 196 ff. and pl. 17.
[202, 273]

THESSALY

Agrilia   Cist tombs of *c.* 1200 B.C.
Verdhelis, 61 (brief mention). Referred to in *Athens Annals* I,
289 ff.
[98 f., 101 f.]
Chasambali   Cist tomb: possibly earlier than twelfth century. Tholos tomb: *c.* 900 B.C.
Thessalika 4, 35 ff.
[101, n. 13; 102]
Chyretiai   Tholos tombs: LDA or later.
Mentioned in *Pr.* 1914, 168; see *BSA* 31, 12.
[102]
Gremnos   Settlement: possibly continuity. Native ware
predominant. *AA* 1955, 192 ff. Discussed in *LMTS*, 133 f.
[99]

Gritsa   Tholos tombs. Mycenaean burials into L.H. III C; re-use in Dark Ages.
Pr. 1951, 141 ff.; 1952, 164 ff.; 1953, 120 ff. Discussed in *LMTS*, 130 under *Pteleon*.
[101, 207]

Halos   Cist tombs and burial enclosure. Tenth and early ninth centuries.
BSA 18, 1 ff. Discussed in *PGP*, 150 ff.
[207 f., 211]

Hexalophos   Burial tumulus with cist tombs, *c.* 1100 B.C. Link with Epirus.
Athens Annals I, 289 ff.; *AD* 23, ii, 263 ff. Note for dagger, spearhead and ring with double-spiral terminals as well as for vases.
[98, 104]

Homolion   Cave-like graves and tholos tomb, *c.* 900 B.C.; links with Macedonia.
AD 17, ii, 175 f.
[102, 207, 214]

Iolkos   Settlement and tombs.
(1) Settlement. *Pr.* 1960, 49 ff.; 1961, 49 ff.
[Problem of dates of desertion and reoccupation, 100; general account, 208 f.; large community, 215.]
(2) Tombs. (*a*) Child cist-tomb cemetery within settlement area. Protogeometric. References as for the settlement; tomb XII is published in *Pr.* 1960 – vases and fibula with leaf-shaped bow shown on pls. 37 and 38.
  (*b*) Two cist tombs of adults in Nea Ionia suburb, *c.* 900 B.C. *Thessalika* 5, 47 ff.
  (*c*) Tholos tomb at Kapakli; tenth century onwards (for several centuries). *AE* 1914, 141 (brief report). Pottery fully published by Verdhelis in his *Protogeometrikos Rhythmos tis Thessalias* (1958).
[Type of tomb, 102 f.; general account, 210 ff.; pottery detail 215, n. 14; burial customs, 272 f., 277.]

Ktouri   Settlement; possible continuity.
BCH 56, 170 ff.; see *PGP*, 313.
[207]

Marmariani   Tholos tombs, late eleventh to ninth centuries.
BSA 31, 1 ff. Material discussed in *PGP*, 134 ff.
[Absence of continuity from Mycenaean and links with Macedonia in pottery, 102 f.; main account, 213 f.; links with coastal Thessaly, 215; possibly large community, 215.]

Palaiokastro   Two cist tombs. LDA.
BCH 56, 90 ff., especially p. 99. Discussed in *PGP*, 313.
[102, 207]

Pelion, Mt.   Tholos tombs, of uncertain date but post-Mycenaean.
Mentioned in *BSA* 31, 12 (Argelaste, Meleai, Lestiane).
[102]
Pharsala   Tomb. Late use, preserving earlier Mycenaean burial.
Pr. 1953, 127 ff.
[101]
Phthiotic Thebes   Low-footed skyphos with concentric circles.
PGP, 153.
[207]
Retziouni   Two cist tombs, probably of the eleventh century.
Brief account in *Verdhelis*, 52 f. and pl. 3, 9.
[102]
Sesklo   Tholos tombs of post-Mycenaean date.
Mentioned in *BSA* 31, 12. *Ergon* for 1965, 8 for one of probable tenth-century date.
[102 and n. 14]
Theotokou   Three cist tombs: one each for the eleventh, tenth, and ninth centuries.
Wace and Thompson in *Prehistoric Thessaly*, 209 ff. Discussed in *PGP*, 148 ff.
(*a*) EDA tomb.
[79, 102, 208 (Note lekythos and iron ring.)]
(*b*) LDA tomb.
[208 (Note iron pins with bronze globe.)]

MACEDONIA

Vergina   Extensive tumulus cemetery.
The two main publications are those of Petsas in *AD* 17, i, 218 ff., and Andronikos, *Vergina* I (1969). The 'experimental' pithos is also published separately by Petsas in *Essays in Memory of Karl Lehmann*, 255 ff.
[217 ff.]

THE CYCLADES

Amorgos   Two Protogeometric vases.
PGP, 214.
[223]
Andros   (*a*) Protogeometric amphora.
Ker. I, 118 and pl. 44. *CVA* Heidelberg 3, 33 and pl. 100, 3 and 4.
[185]
(*b*) Cist tombs, of late tenth and ninth centuries.
PGP, 128 f.; 161 ff. and pl. 16.
[186]

Delos   Traces of settlement, possibly evidence for continuity of worship from Mycenaean times onwards.
The argument for continuous cult practice is set out by Gallet de Santerre, *Délos Primitive et Archaique* (1958), and summarised in *LMTS*, 44 ff. See also *BCH* 35, 355 ff.
[223, 279]
There were also tombs, but for their contents, see under Rheneia, to which island they were transferred in antiquity.

Melos   Two stray Protogeometric vases.
Tiryns I, 154, fig. 18 (skyphos). *ÖJh* 39, 53 ff. (amphora).
[222]

Naxos (Grotta and vicinity)   Settlement and tombs.
The various stages of the settlement seem to show continuous use from Mycenaean to Geometric; preliminary reports have appeared in *Praktika* for 1949, 1950, 1951, 1963, 1965, and 1967. For burials, there are chamber tombs, discussed reasonably fully in *Praktika* for 1958, 1959, 1960 (see pl. 275 *a* for a bird vase), and *Ergon* for 1969. Following these, there are pit graves, reported in *Pr.* 1960, 258 ff.
The material is discussed in *LMTS*, 149 ff.
[82 f., 221 f.]

Paros   Traces of settlement, tenth century onwards.
AM 42, 73 ff.
[222]

Rheneia   (*a*) Tomb group, late tenth century. *GGP*, 149.
(*b*)   Tomb material, transferred from *Delos*; tenth century onwards. *AD* 15, 181 ff.; *Délos* vols. XV and XVII.
[223]

Siphnos   Settlement, late tenth century onwards.
BSA 44, 40 f. Only a very few sherds attributable to the LDA.
[222]

Tenos   Group of vases, probably from one tomb. Late tenth century. *GGP*, 149
[186]
For early ninth-century tombs, see *PGP*, 158 ff.
[186]

CRETE

Amnisos   Settlement, probably continuous.
AA 1935, 245.
[233]

Ayia Triadha   Sanctuaries.
Ann. 3–5 (N.S.), 9 ff. See also Borda in *Arte Cretese-Micenea nel Museo Pigorini di Roma* (1946).
[112, n. 1, 285 f.]

Berati   Tombs.
Pr. 1953, 292 ff.
[235 (instances of cremation).]

Dictaean Cave   Sanctuary.
Boardman, *The Cretan Collection in Oxford,* 1 ff.
[128, 284, 286]

Dreros   (1) Sub-Minoan tomb.
Van Effenterre, *Nécropoles du Mirabello,* 17 f.
[117]
(2) Late sanctuary of type recalling Sub-Minoan.
Hutchinson, *Prehistoric Crete,* 332.
[285]

Gortyn   (1) Settlement and possible cult evidence.
Rizza and Santa Maria Scrinari, *Il Santuario sull' Acropoli di Gortina,* I.
[113, 116 (note fibulae), 225, 286 (later votive animals).]
(2) Tholos tomb of late tenth and ninth centuries.
Pr. 1966, 189 ff.
[226, 231, 233 (note for weapons and tools).]

Kalochorio Pedhiadhos   Settlement and cult evidence.
KChr. 1951, 98 ff.; 1958, 214 (head of goddess figurine).
[234, 285]

Kanli Kastelli   Tenth-century tomb with imported Athenian skyphos.
PGP, 259.
[234]

Karphi   Settlement, sanctuary, tombs: *c.* 1150–*c.* 1050 B.C. or later.
Two main publications. (1) *BSA* 38, 57 ff. The account of the investigations as a whole, listing all the finds, includes illustrations of the objects other than pottery. (2) *BSA* 55, 1 ff. A detailed analysis of the pottery.
[Nature and extent of site, 120 f.; pottery, 121 ff.; length of occupation, 123, 125; cult objects (note goddesses), 125; weapons and tools, 126; ornaments (note fibulae and pins), 126 f.; evidence for animals and cultivation, 127; reasons for existence of settlement, 128 f.; non-Minoan type of house, 129. For the pottery, see also 58 ff., and for the pins, 297.]

Kastri   Settlement, apparently confined to the twelfth century.
BSA 60, 248 ff.
[58, 61, 113 f.]

Kavousi   Tombs.
AJA 5, 125 ff. See also *Ann.* 10–12, 562 ff., 582 ff.
[117, 235 f., 286 (for later votive animals).]

Knossos   For the whole area, see *Archaeological Survey of the Knossos Area* (1957), which lists all the known sites.

There is no doubt that there was a settlement just west of the Palace area, from Late Minoan onwards, but the material remains unpublished: see *JHS* 56, 150; 57, 137 f. There must also have been other areas of settlement, linked with the cemeteries, but of these nothing is yet known. The main evidence comes from the Spring Chamber sanctuary, and the tombs, as listed below.

(1) *Spring Chamber*; attached to the Caravanserai, just south of the Palace. Sub-Minoan. *P. of M.* ii, 123 ff.

Discussed in *PGP*, 236 ff.

[59, 62, 116, 125, 284]

(2) (*a*) *Ayios Ioannis*. Chamber tombs, Sub-Minoan onwards.
  BSA, 55, 128 ff. (note instances of inhumation and cremation in one tomb, and the two silver rings).
  BSA 63, 205 ff. (Sub-Minoan tomb, note two dress pins, one with ivory head).
  (*b*) *Fortetsa*. Chamber tombs. Protogeometric onwards.
  Brock, *Fortetsa* (1957). Most of the material, including small finds and weapons, comes from tombs VI, pp. 11–15, and XI, pp. 18–22.
  (*c*) *Gypsades*. Late Minoan chamber tombs, also used in Sub-Minoan times.
  BSA 53–4, 194 ff., tombs VI, VIa and VII (note iron knife with bronze rivets, p. 234; dress pins, pp. 236 f.)
  (*d*) *Kephala* area   (i) Tholos tomb re-used in L.M. III C and Sub-Minoan times. *BSA* 51, 74 ff.; 62, 257 ff. (the late pottery).
                (ii) Chamber tombs on the ridge. Protogeometric onwards. *BSA* 6, 82 ff.; 29, 224 ff.
  (*e*) *Teke*. Sub-Minoan tomb.
  Brock, *Fortetsa*, 8 ff. (tomb Π).
[Sub-Minoan pottery, 58 ff. Sub-Minoan tombs, 115 f.; Protogeometric tombs and finds, 225 ff.]

Kourtais   Tholos tombs. Late Dark Ages onwards.
AJA 5, 290 ff., 306 ff.
[234]

Kritsa   Two Protogeometric tholos tombs.
KChr. 1953, 485; *BCH* 78, 155.
[235 f.]

Modi   Tombs. Possibly as early as the late tenth century.
KChr. 1953, 485 f. Further details in *LMTS*, 267 f. (note weapons and fibulae).
[234 f.]

Mouliana   Two tombs, of which tomb B is twelfth century, but tomb A may go on into the Dark Ages, and is reported to have contained both inhumation and cremation.
AE 1904, 21 ff. Discussed in *PGP*, 269 f. and *LMTS*, 188.
[306 (shield-bosses).]
Olous   Tombs. Inhumation and cremation. Material difficult to date.
Van Effenterre, *Nécropoles du Mirabello*, 7 ff. Discussed in *LMTS*, 188 f.
[235, n. 8 (omitted from discussion).]
Pachlitsani Agriadha (near Kavousi).   Sanctuary, used from twelfth or eleventh century onwards.
KChr. 1956, 7 ff. Mentioned by Hutchinson, *Prehistoric Crete*, 323 f.
[285 (for continuity of type of shrine).]
Panayia   Tholos tombs. Eleventh or tenth century.
AJA 5, 283 ff. *Ann.* 10–12, 389 ff. Note iron weapons.
[116 f.]
Patso   Cave sanctuary.
Boardman, *The Cretan Collection in Oxford*, 76 ff.
[284, 286]
Petrokephali (near Phaestos).   Tomb. Probably late tenth century.
Ann. 29–30 (N.S.), 181 ff. (note the small hand-made vase with incised decoration, p. 207, fig. 50).
[226, 231 f., 234]
Phaestos   Cult objects, settlement, tombs.
(1) Cult objects. *MA* 12, 118, 122 ff. *Ann.* 25–26 (N.S.), 7 ff.
[112, 285 f.]
(2) Settlement (early twelfth century onwards). *Ann.* 19–20 (N.S.), 255 ff. Stray sherds of the twelfth century illustrated in Borda's *Arte Cretese-Micenea*.
[112 f., 116, 225 f.]
(3) Tombs. (*a*) *Liliana*. Twelfth century, continuing into eleventh. *MA* 14, 627 ff. Borda, *Arte Cretese-Micenea*, pls. 33 and 34. Discussed by Furumark in *OA* 3, 230.
[60 f., 116, 226 (cremation).]
   (*b*) *Phaestos hill*. Sub-Minoan. *Boll. d'Arte* 1955, 159 (note two arched fibulae).
   [59, 116]
   (*c*) *Mulino*. Protogeometric tomb. *Ann.* 19–20 (N.S.), 355 ff. (note violin-bow fibula and iron weapons, p. 357, fig. 215).
   [225, 231 f.]
Prinias   Sanctuary evidence and tombs.
For sanctuary evidence, *AM* 26, 247 ff., *Ann.* 1, 71 and see *KChr.* 1958, 181 ff. (Goddess with raised arms, snake-tubes, sherds.)

For seventh-century sanctuary recalling Late Minoan shrines, see Hutchinson, *Prehistoric Crete*, 333.

[234, 285]

For tombs, *AJA* 1, 252, figs. 1 and 2 (Protogeometric krater). Further tombs have now been discovered; see Rizza in *Cronache di Archeologia* 8, 7 ff.

[234]

Rotasi   Protogeometric tholos tombs.

KChr. 1954, 516; *BCH* 79, 304; 80, 343.

[234]

Seteia district   Cemeteries. Dark Ages and later.

For references, see *LMTS*, 268.

[117, 235]

Tylissos   Tomb. Tenth century.

AM 56, 112 ff.

[233]

Vrises   Traces of very late Minoan, or Sub-Minoan, settlement, and tombs.

BSA 60, 106.

[236, n. 10]

Vrokastro   Settlement and tombs. Twelfth century onwards.

Hall, *Excavations in Eastern Crete, Vrokastro* (1914).

Discussed in *PGP*, 262 ff. and *LMTS*, 185 ff.

[117 (general description), 235 (inhumation and cremation), 236 (non-pottery finds, including tripod stand), 286 (later votive animals), 302 ff. (fibula, rings), 308 (knife).]

SOUTH AND WEST PELOPONNESE

Achaea   Except for *Teichos Dymaion, Derveni*, and *Agriapidies*, I deal with the sites as a whole. They are, almost without exception, Mycenaean chamber-tomb cemeteries of the twelfth century, some continuing into the eleventh century. There has not yet been a full publication. Reports will be found in *AD* 9 and in *Praktika* for 1925 and the years following until the war, since when further finds continue to be made, mentioned in the relevant *Chronique des Fouilles* of *BCH*. There are also two extremely useful summaries, those of Mrs Vermeule in *AJA* 64, 1 ff., and Prof. Åström in *Op. Ath.* 5, 89 ff. (both have maps). Note particularly the details of the material from *Klauss (Koukoura)* in *AJA* 64, and the report of *Kangadhi* in *BCH* 79, 252, the two sites which produced duck vases.

[My main account, 91 ff.; general remarks, 335 f., 355.]

Agriapidies   Cist tombs, probably covered by a mound. Date unknown (hand-made vases).

Pr. 1930, 85 and 87, fig. 10; *Op. Ath.* 5, 101.

[92, 274, n. 6]

Amyklai   Sanctuary deposit. Continuous worship from Mycenaean times.
AE 1892, 1 ff.; *JdI* 33, 107 ff.; *AM* 52, 1 ff. (the most detailed). Discussed in *PGP*, 283 ff., and *LMTS*, 88 f.
[83 f., 240 ff., 280]

Ancient Elis   Fourteen pit graves, early eleventh century.
ÖJh 46, Beiblatt, 33 ff. *Ergon* for 1963, 117 ff.; *AD* 19, ii, 181. Discussed in *Styrenius*, 139 ff.
[Pottery, 33 ff.; tombs and contents (note for weapons, fibulae, pins and amber), 74; problem of interpretation, 339.]

Ayios Andreas   Harbour site. Continuity possible, but not established.
AE 1957, 31 ff.; *AJA* 65, 224.
[250]

Derveni   Pithos burial; early ninth century?
BCH 76, 222; *AJA* 64, 16 f. and pl. 5 (fullest account). Vases discussed in *GGP*, 221 ff.
[248 f.]

Kaphirio   Settlement: possible continuity.
BCH 84, 700; *AJA* 65, 248 and 258, n. 16. Sherds mentioned in *GGP*, 222.
[252]

Kardamyla   Traces of settlement, date uncertain.
AD 20, ii, 208 and pl. 222 *b*.
[84, 254]

Kokevi   Protogeometric tholos tomb.
AJA 63, 127. Full publication shortly.
[251 f.]

Malthi   Settlement, probably continuous.
Valmin, *Swedish Messenia Expedition.* Discussed briefly in *LMTS*, 94.
[84, 251 (kylix stems, objects of iron).]

Mavrovouni   Probable tomb group.
BSA 56, 115, fig. 2 (two vases, part of iron weapon).
[241]

Nichoria   (*a*) Settlement and cemetery, including cist tombs and pithos burials. Continuity possible.
AJA 65, 248 f.; *BCH* 84, 700; 85, 697.
[85, 252 f.]
(*b*) Protogeometric tholos tomb: inhumations and later (ninth century?) cremations.
Athens Annals I, 205 ff.
[253]

'North Peloponnese'   Contents of a tomb, type unknown, *c.* 900 B.C.
CVA Mainz I, 12 ff.; pl. 3 and figs. 1–10.
[250]

Olympia   Settlement. Continuity suggested, not established.
BCH 84, 720; 85, 722. *BSA* 44, 311 (ribbed kylix stems).
Evidence for sanctuary use as early as the Dark Ages – see
Olympische Forschungen III, 166 ff. (tripod cauldrons) – not
certain.
[84, 281]

Palaiokastro   Chamber-tomb cemetery, no full publication
yet.
BCH 80, 522 ff. and fig. 18 (L.H. III C stirrup jar).
[84]

Palaiopyrgo   See under **Salmone**.

Rizes   Pithos burial. Tenth century?
Pr. 1965, 111 f. and pl. 121 (wheel-made cups, hand-made jugs).
[251]

Salmone (Palaiopyrgo)   Pithos burial, *c.* 900 B.C. or later.
AJA 65, 226. Vases discussed in *GGP*, 221 f.
[250]

Sparta   Settlement and sanctuaries. A little material may be as
early as the tenth century.
BSA 28, 49 ff. (settlement on acropolis); *Artemis Orthia*, 58 (fig.
32); *BSA* 13, 142 ff. (Chalkioikos); *BSA* 12, 288 ff. (Heroon).
Discussed in *PGP*, 289 f., and unpublished sherds illustrated on
pl. 38.
[241 f., 278]

Teichos Dymaion   Settlement and fort. Date of final
destruction uncertain, probably between *c.* 1125 and *c.* 1075 B.C.
Pr. 1962, 127 ff.; 1963, 93 ff.; 1964, 60 ff.; 1965, 121 ff. (the best
illustrated). *AD* 18, ii, 111 ff.
[Reoccupied after destruction *c.* 1200 B.C., 87; final destruction and
related pottery, including kylikes, 94; significance of date of final
destruction for movements of people, 110, 336.]

Thouria   (*a*) Traces of settlement, tenth century at earliest.
BSA 52, 245.
(*b*) Tomb of tenth century.
AD 20, ii, 207 and pl. 215 (vases).
[254]

Tragana   Mycenaean tholos tomb, re-used in Dark Ages.
AE 1914, 99 ff. Discussed in *PGP*, 281 ff. and in *LMTS*, 95.
[Earlier material, 83 ff.; later material, 251.]

Volimnos   Traces of settlement, tenth century onwards.
Surface sherds.
AJA 65, 255.
[254]

NORTH-WEST GREECE AND THE IONIAN ISLANDS

Ayios Elias   Tholos tombs still in use in twelfth century.
Pr. 1963, 203 ff.
[95]
Calydon   Pithos burial of *c.* 900 B.C. or perhaps later.
AD 17, ii, 183.
[247]
Dodona   Settlement.
AE 1956, 140, fig. 9, 15 for dagger. *PPS* for 1967, 31 f. for sherd
of *c.* 1200 B.C. and possible kylix stems.
[97]
Elaphotopos   Four cist tombs. Probably late thirteenth and
early twelfth centuries.
AE 1969, 179 ff. Note ring with double-spiral terminals, pl. 24 *a*.
[97]
Ephyra   Dagger.
AD 18, ii, 153 and pl. 187 *e*.
[97]
Ithaca   There are two relevant sites, Polis and Aetos.
(*a*) *Polis.* Cave sanctuary, not certainly used as such in the Dark
Ages.
BSA 35, 45 ff.; 39, 1 ff. (note pls. 6 and 8–10 for kylikes and cups);
44, 307 ff. Discussed in *PGP*, 272 ff. and in *LMTS*, 108 ff.
(*b*) *Aetos.* Settlement, and sanctuary perhaps already used as such
in the Dark Ages.
BSA 33, 22 ff.; 48, 255 ff. Discussed in *PGP* and *LMTS* as above;
note *PGP*, pl. 37, no. 84 for the fragments of the imported Protogeometric lekythos.
Note also a sword with down-turned quillons, which may have
come from Ithaca, *AJA* 67, 152 and pl. 26, 49.
[Continuity from Mycenaean times through the Dark Ages, 88,
243; bronze pin, 88; sword, 88; fibulae, 245; analysis of pottery,
245 f.; imported Protogeometric vase, 246, n. 5; links with nearby
areas, 247 ff.]
Kalbaki   Four cist tombs. Late thirteenth century?
AE 1956, 114 ff. Discussed in *PPS* for 1965, 222 (pl. 33 *c* for short
sword and spearhead).
[97]
Kaloyeriko (Pylene)   Pithos burials; *c.* 900 B.C. or perhaps
later.
AD 22, ii, 320 and pl. 228 *e* for krater.
[247]
Kastritsa   Cist tomb with stirrup jar of *c.* 1200 B.C., and a
dagger without context.
PPS for 1967, 30 ff.
[97]

Kephallenia   Several cemeteries, of which the most important are:
(*a*) *Diakata. AD* 5, 92 ff. (for the dress pins, see p. 117).
(*b*) *Lakkithra. AE* 1932, 17 ff.
(*c*) *Metaxata. AE* 1933, 73 ff.
All twelfth century, and could continue into the eleventh.
[Links with Ithaca, 88; pottery (note kylikes and hand-made ware), 89 f.; fibulae, amber, weapons, 90; links with Ancient Elis, 91; pins from Diakata and their context, 91.]
Lithovouni   Sword and spearhead from chamber tomb.
AD 18, ii, 147 and pl. 186 *a. AD* 22, ii, 318.
[95]
Mazaraki   Cist tomb, probably late thirteenth century.
AE 1969, 191 ff. (stirrup jar and weapons).
[97]
Paramythia   Cist tomb, probably late thirteenth century.
AD 20, ii, 349 f.; see *PPS* for 1967, pl. 1, nos. 5 and 6 for dagger and spearhead.
[97]
Parga   Tholos tomb, thirteenth century.
Pr. 1960, 123 ff.
[97]
Thermon   Settlement.
AD 1, 225 ff. and supplement, 46 f.; 2, 179 ff. See Hope Simpson, *Gazetteer and Atlas of Mycenaean Sites*, 91 f. for L.H. III C pottery. See also *BSA* 32, 239.
[86, 95]
Vajzë   Tumulus with cist tombs.
Hammond, *Epirus*, 228 ff. and 338 (spearhead).
[97]
(Other tumulus sites in Albania are recorded by Hammond.)

CYPRUS

(There is no discussion of individual sites, but the bibliography is included as possibly of interest.)

Amathus   Probable tomb group of period *c.* 950–*c.* 850 B.C.
JHS 77, 212 ff.: two Late Protogeometric vases of possible Euboean origin.
[196]
Enkomi   Settlement, sanctuaries, tombs.
Schaeffer, *Enkomi-Alasia* I (1952). Dikaios, *Enkomi* I–III (1969 and 1971): note pl. 220,8 for the bronze pin with ivory head. Murray, Smith, and Walters, *Excavations in Cyprus*, 53 for tomb with iron pin with ivory head. Summaries of recent excavations in *BCH* 83 ff. *CRAI* 1963, 155 ff. for sanctuary.
[56]

Idalion   Tomb.
Karageorghis, *Nouveaux Documents* (1965), 185 ff.
[52, 56]
Kition   Settlement. Excavations in progress.
Reports in *BCH* 84 ff.
[56]
Kouklia (Old Paphos)   Settlement and tombs. Material as
yet not fully published, with the exception of one extremely
important early eleventh-century tomb, *Report of the Department
of Antiquities, Cyprus,* 1967, 1 ff.
[Most of the L.C. III B shapes discussed on pp. 51 ff. represented
in this tomb.]
Kourion   Settlement and tombs.
AJA 41, 56 ff. (tombs); 42, 261 ff. (settlement).
[56]
Lapithos   Eleventh-century tomb.
OA 3, 76 ff.
[56]
Salamis   Eleventh-century tomb.
M. Yon, *Salamine de Chypre* II (1971).
[56]

Abbreviations

GENERAL

EDA	Early Dark Ages
LDA	Late Dark Ages
L.C.	Late Cypriot
L.H.	Late Helladic
L.M.	Late Minoan
Sub-Min.	Sub-Minoan
Sub-Myc.	Sub-Mycenaean
PG	Protogeometric (hence EPG, MPG, LPG: Early, Middle, Late PG)
G	Geometric
CG	Cypro-Geometric

PUBLICATIONS

Borda	M. Borda, *Arte Cretese-micenea nel Museo Pigorini di Roma* (1946)
Corinth	*American School of Classical Studies: Excavations at Corinth* (1932 onwards)
CR	*Clara Rhodos* (1928–41)
CVA	*Corpus Vasorum Antiquorum* (1922 onwards)
FD	*Fouilles de Delphes: École française d'Athènes* (1902 onwards)
GGP	J. N. Coldstream, *Greek Geometric Pottery* (1968)
Ker.	*Kerameikos: Ergebnisse der Ausgrabungen* (1939 onwards)
LMTS	V. R. d'A. Desborough, *The Last Mycenaeans and their Successors* (1964)
P. of M.	Sir Arthur Evans, *The Palace of Minos at Knossos* (1921–36)
PGP	V. R. d'A. Desborough, *Protogeometric Pottery* (1952)
SCE	*The Swedish Cyprus Expedition* (1934 onwards)
Styrenius	C.-G. Styrenius, *Submycenaean Studies* (1967)
Tiryns	*Tiryns: Ergebnisse der Ausgrabungen* (1912–38)
Verdhelis	N. M. Verdhelis, *O Protogeometrikos Rhythmos tis Thessalias* (1958)

PERIODICALS

AA	*Archäologischer Anzeiger: Beiblatt zum Jahrbuch des deutschen archäologischen Instituts*
AD	*Archaiologikon Deltion*
AE	*Archaiologike Ephemeris*
AJA	*American Journal of Archaeology*
AM	*Mitteilungen des deutschen archäologischen Instituts; athenische Abteilung*
Ann.	*Annuario della scuola italiana di Atene e delle missioni italiane in oriente*
AR	*Archaeological Reports*
Athens Annals	*Athens Annals of Archaeology*
BASOR	*Bulletin of the American Schools of Oriental Research*
BCH	*Bulletin de Correspondance Hellénique*
Boll. d'Arte	*Bollettino d'Arte del Ministero della pubblica Istruzione*
BSA	*Annual of the British School at Athens*
CRAI	*Académie des inscriptions et belles-lettres. Comptes rendus des séances*
Ergon	*Ergon tis Arkhaiologikes Etaireias*
Hesp.	*Hesperia: Journal of the American School of Classical Studies at Athens*
Ist. Mitt.	*Istanbuler Mitteilungen*
JdI	*Jahrbuch des deutschen archäologischen Instituts*
JHS	*Journal of Hellenic Studies*
KChr.	*Kretika Chronika*
MA	*Monumenti antichi pubblicati a cura . . . dei Lincei*
OA	*Acta Instituti Romani Regni Sueciae: Opuscula Archaeologica*
Op. Ath.	*Acta Instituti Atheniensis Regni Sueciae: Opuscula Atheniensia*
ÖJh	*Jahreshefte des Österreichischen archäologischen Instituts*
Pr.	*Praktika tis Arkhaiologikes Etaireias*
PPS	*Proceedings of the Prehistoric Society*
RA	*Revue Archéologique*
RDAC	*Report of the Department of Antiquities, Cyprus*

General Index

Printed in Great Britain
by
Jarrold & Sons Limited,
Norwich